NICHOLSON

MINI ATLAS LONDON

Nicholson
An Imprint of HarperCollins*Publishers*

First published 1992
Second edition 1993
Third edition 1995

Generated from the Bartholomew London Digital Database

London Underground Map by permission of
London Regional Transport
LRT Registered User Number 95/1496

Printed by Bartholomew, The Edinburgh Press Limited

Bartholomew, HarperCollins Publishers
Unit 4, Manchester Park
Tewkesbury Road
Cheltenham, Glos.
GL51 9EJ

ISBN 0 7028 2786 X
GM 7579 ANB

MINI ATLAS LONDON

CONTENTS

Key to Map Pages 4-5
Key to Map Symbols 6-7
Map Pages 8-42
Central London Maps 43-44
Index to Street Names 45-91

Nicholson

An Imprint of HarperCollins*Publishers*

KEY TO MAP PAGES

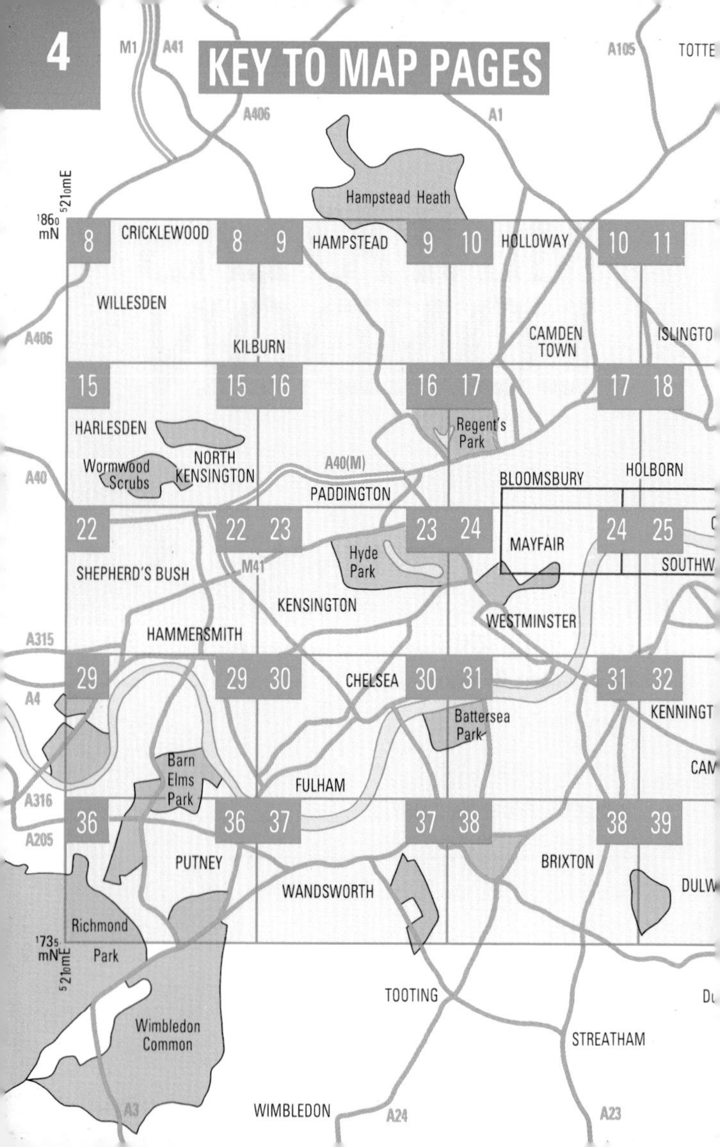

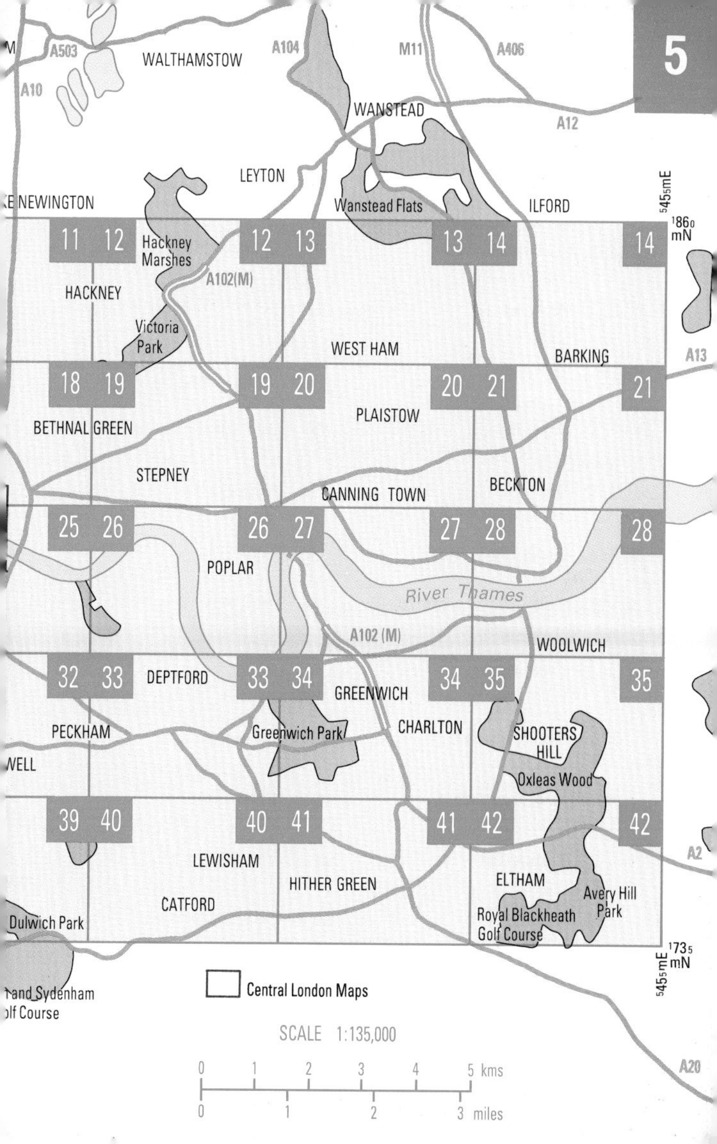
A503
A10
WALTHAMSTOW
A104
M11
A406
WANSTEAD
A12
LEYTON
NEWINGTON
Wanstead Flats
ILFORD
545₅mE
186₀ mN
11 12
Hackney Marshes
12 13
13 14
14
A102(M)
HACKNEY
Victoria Park
WEST HAM
BARKING
A13
18 19
19 20
20 21
21
BETHNAL GREEN
PLAISTOW
STEPNEY
CANNING TOWN
BECKTON
25 26
26 27
27 28
28
POPLAR
River Thames
A102 (M)
WOOLWICH
32 33
DEPTFORD
33 34
GREENWICH
34 35
35
PECKHAM
Greenwich Park
CHARLTON
SHOOTERS HILL
WELL
Oxleas Wood
39 40
40 41
41 42
42
A2
LEWISHAM
HITHER GREEN
ELTHAM
CATFORD
Avery Hill Park
Dulwich Park
Royal Blackheath Golf Course
173₅ mN
545₅mE
and Sydenham
olf Course
Central London Maps
SCALE 1:135,000
0 1 2 3 4 5 kms
0 1 2 3 miles
A20

KEY TO MAP SYMBOLS

M41	Motorway
Dual A4	Primary Route
Dual A40	'A' Road
B504	'B' Road
	Other Road
	Toll
	Street Market
	Pedestrian Street
	Cycle Path
	Track/Footpath
	One Way Street
P	Pedestrian Ferry
V	Vehicle Ferry
	Borough Boundary
	Postal District Boundary

	Main British Rail Station
	Other British Rail Station
	London Underground Station
	Docklands Light Railway Station
	Bus/Coach Station
H	Heliport
P	Car Park
i	Tourist Information Centre
WC	Public Toilet
USA	Embassy
Pol	Police Station
Fire Sta	Fire Station
PO	Post Office
Lib	Library
	Youth Hostel

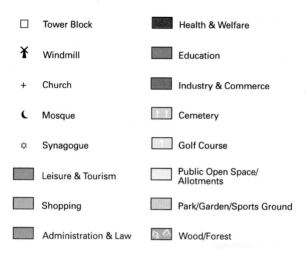

□	Tower Block		Health & Welfare
	Windmill		Education
+	Church		Industry & Commerce
	Mosque		Cemetery
✡	Synagogue		Golf Course
	Leisure & Tourism		Public Open Space/ Allotments
	Shopping		Park/Garden/Sports Ground
	Administration & Law		Wood/Forest

The reference grid on this atlas coincides with the Ordnance Survey National Grid System.

A 3 Grid Reference

25 Page Continuation Number

Main London Maps

Scale 1:20,000 (3.17 inches to 1 mile)

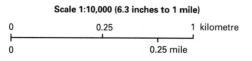

0 0.25 0.50 0.75 1 kilometre

0 0.25 0.5 mile

Central London Maps

Scale 1:10,000 (6.3 inches to 1 mile)

0 0.25 1 kilometre

0 0.25 mile

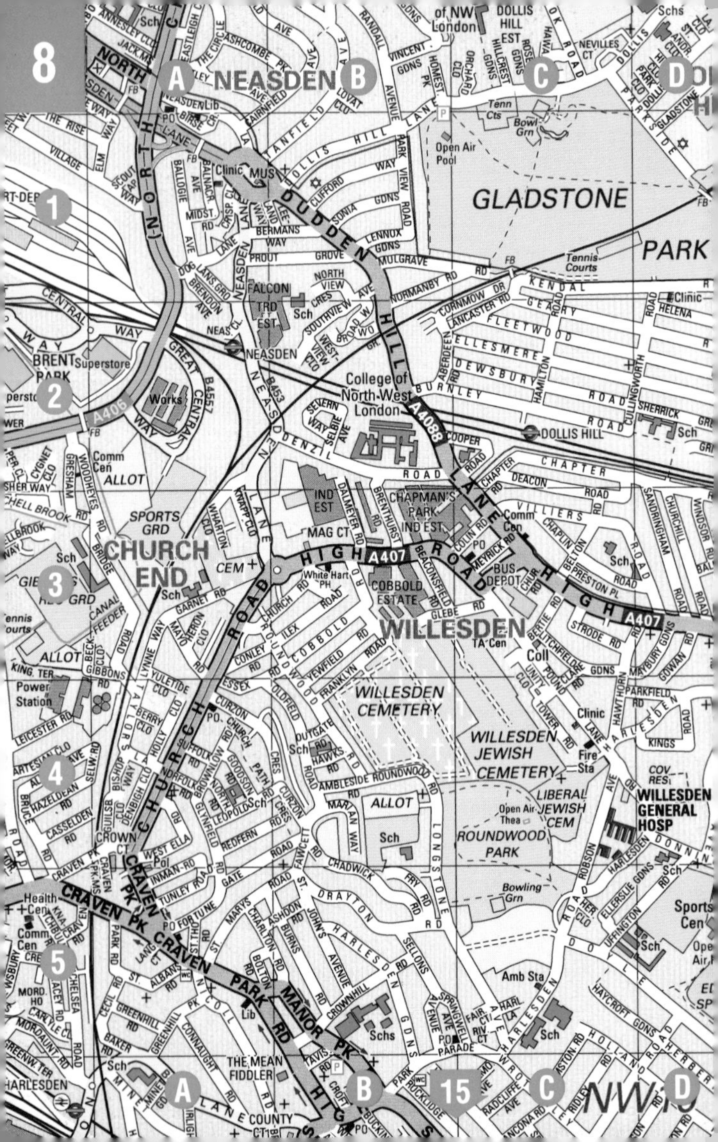
A
B
C
D
1
2
3
4
5
NEASDEN
GLADSTONE
PARK
CHURCH
END
WILLESDEN
NW10
15
College of North West London
WILLESDEN CEMETERY
WILLESDEN JEWISH CEMETERY
LIBERAL JEWISH CEM
ROUNDWOOD PARK
WILLESDEN GENERAL HOSP
COBBOLD ESTATE
CHAPMAN'S PARK IND EST
FALCON TRD EST
BRENT PARK
Superstore
Works
SPORTS GRD
ALLOT
CEM
Power Station
Health Cen
Comm Cen
Sports Cen
Open Air Pool
Open Air Thea
Tennis Courts
Bowling Grn
Bowl Grn
Tenn Cts
THE MEAN FIDDLER
White Hart PH
BUS DEPOT
TA Cen
Amb Sta
Fire Sta
Clinic
Lib
Sch
Schs
Coll
DOLLIS HILL EST
NEASDEN
DOLLIS HILL
HARLESDEN
A406
A4088
A407
B4557
B453
NORTH CIRCULAR
DUDDEN HILL LANE
HIGH ROAD
CHURCH ROAD
CRAVEN PK
CRAVEN PARK RD
MANOR PK RD
GREAT CENTRAL WAY
CENTRAL WAY
NEASDEN LANE
DENZIL ROAD
KENDAL
GEARY
FLEETWOOD
ELLESMERE
DEWSBURY
BURNLEY ROAD
CHAPTER
DEACON ROAD
VILLIERS
HARLESDEN
DOYLE
HARLESDEN RD
LONGSTONE
DRAYTON
ROUNDWOOD
HAWTHORN
SANDRINGHAM
CHURCHILL
WINDSOR
CRICKLEWOOD
GLADSTONE
MULGRAVE
NORMANBY RD
CORNMOW DR
LANCASTER RD
CULLINGWORTH
HELENA
SHERRICK
GARNET RD
CONLEY RD
ILEX
COBBOLD
YEWFIELD
FRANKLYN
OLDFIELD
ESSEX
CURZON
SUFFOLK
NORFOLK
BROWNLOW
GOODSON
LEOPOLD
REDFERN
WEST ELLA
INMAN RD
TUNLEY ROAD
FORTUNE GATE
ST. MARYS
CHARLTON RD
BOLTON RD
ASHDON
BURNS
JOHN'S AVENUE
CROWNHILL
SELLONS
SPRINGWELL AVE
PARADE
GREENHILL
CONNAUGHT
BAKER
MORDAUNT RD
CARLYLE CL
CHELSEA
CECIL RD
ST. ALBANS
PARK RD
CRAVEN PK MS
LYNNE WAY
YULETIDE
TAYLORS LA
BISHOP WAY
DENBIGH CLO
HOLLY CLO
BERRY CLO
LEICESTER RD
HAZELDEAN RD
CASSELDEN RD
BRUCE ROAD
GRESHAM
WOODHEYES RD
GIBBONS RD
KING TER
BRIDGE ROAD
WHARTON CLO
KNAPP CLO
DALMEYER RD
BRENTHURST
BEACONSFIELD
MEYRICK RD
COLIN RD
GLEBE RD
BERTIE RD
LITCHFIELD GDNS
STRODE RD
PRESTON PL
BELTON
MAYBURY GDNS
GOWAN RD
PARKFIELD RD
KINGS
TOWER RD
UNITY CLO
POUND
CLARE RD
ROBSON AVE
ELLERSLIE GDNS
UFFINGTON RD
HAYCROFT GDNS
HOLLAND ROAD
HERBERT
RIDLEY
RADCLIFFE AVE
COUNTY CT
BUCKINGHAM
RUCKLIDGE
TAVISTOCK RD
CROFT
SEVERN WAY
SELBIE AVE
SOUTHVIEW
BROADWAY
NORTH VIEW
PROUT GROVE
BERMANS WAY
SONIA GDNS
LENNOX GDNS
CLIFFORD WAY
PARK VIEW ROAD
DOLLIS HILL LANE
TANFIELD
LOVAT CLO
CAIRNFIELD AVE
ASHCOMBE PK
THE CIRCLE
EASTLEIGH
ANNESLEY CLO
VINCENT GDNS
RANDALL AVE
HOMESTEAD PK
ORCHARD CLO
HILLCREST GDNS
ROSE GDNS
NEVILLES CT
PARKSIDE
THE RISE
VILLAGE
SCOUT WAY
BALLOGIE AVE
BRENDON AVE
DOG LANE
MUS
Clinic
FB
PO
P

8
CRICKLEWOOD
NW2
BRONDESBURY
WILLESDEN GREEN
BRONDESBURY PARK
NW6
WILLESDEN LANE CEMETERY
QUEEN'S PARK
STADIUM
BARNET
CAMDEN
BRENT
CRICKLEWOOD BROADWAY
A5
SHOOT UP HILL
CHICHELE ROAD
A407
WALM LANE
WILLESDEN LANE
A4003
CRICKLEWOOD LANE
A407
ANSON ROAD
MELROSE AVENUE
OLIVE ROAD
MORA ROAD
ST. GABRIEL'S ROAD
TEIGNMOUTH RD
DARTMOUTH ROAD
CHATSWORTH ROAD
CHAMBERLAYNE ROAD
SIDMOUTH ROAD
BRONDESBURY PARK
BRONDESBURY ROAD
CHRISTCHURCH AVE
SALUSBURY ROAD
KINGSWOOD AVE
WILLESDEN GREEN
KILBURN
SUMMIT CT
WINDMILL CT
WATLING GDNS
MINSTER ROAD
FORDWYCH ROAD
EXETER ROAD
MAPESBURY ROAD
ST. PAUL'S AVENUE
STATION PAR
WILLESDEN LIB CEN
Superstore
ANSON HALL
Tennis Cts
Bowling Grn
Pav
Sch
Lib
PO
Coll
Works
GARAGE
Pumping Sta
ALLOT
D
E
F
G
1
2
3
4
5
9
15

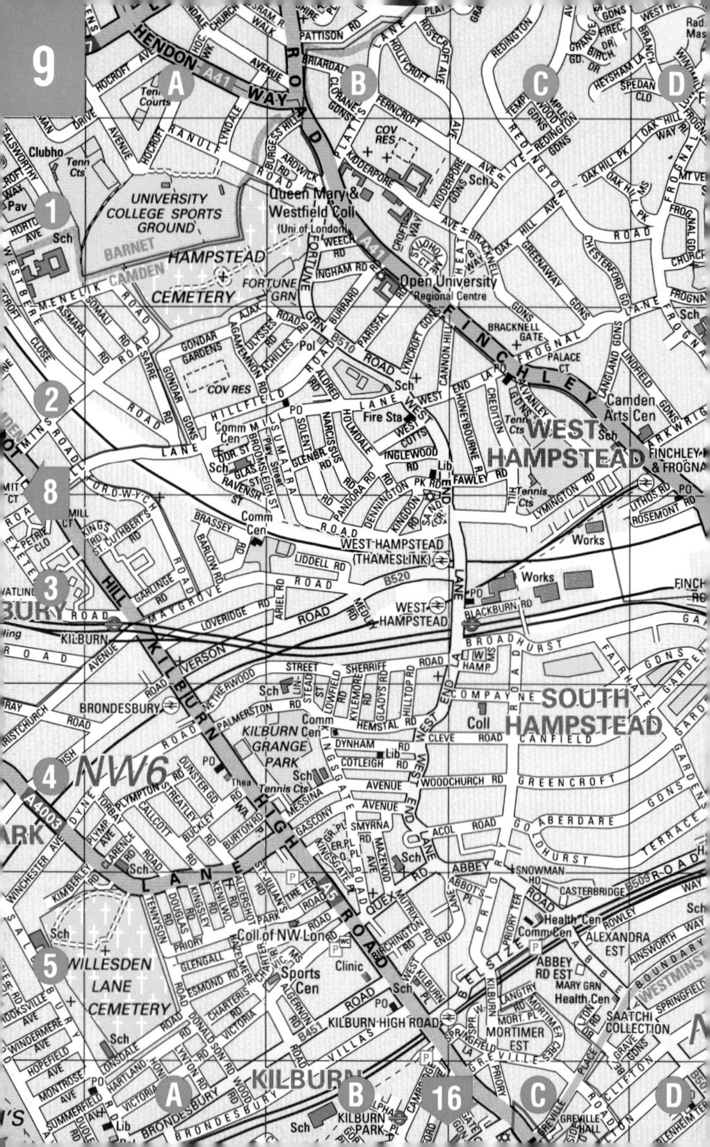
A
B
C
D
1
2
3
4
5
8
16
HENDON WAY
A41
FINCHLEY ROAD
UNIVERSITY COLLEGE SPORTS GROUND
BARNET
CAMDEN
HAMPSTEAD CEMETERY
Queen Mary & Westfield Coll
(Uni of London)
Open University
Regional Centre
FORTUNE GRN
GONDAR GARDENS
COV RES
WEST HAMPSTEAD
Camden Arts Cen
FINCHLEY & FROGNAL
WEST HAMPSTEAD (THAMESLINK)
WEST HAMPSTEAD
KILBURN
BRONDESBURY
SOUTH HAMPSTEAD
NW6
KILBURN GRANGE PARK
KILBURN HIGH ROAD
A5
A4003
B510
B520
B509
B451
WILLESDEN LANE CEMETERY
Coll of NW Lond
Sports Cen
Clinic
ALEXANDRA EST
ABBEY RD EST
MORTIMER EST
SAATCHI COLLECTION
MARY GRN Health Cen
Health Cen
Comm Cen
Fire Sta
Works
KILBURN PARK
GREVILLE HALL
WESTMINSTER
HILLFIELD
MILL LANE
WEST END LANE
ABBEY ROAD
BELSIZE ROAD
PRIORY ROAD
KILBURN HIGH ROAD
WILLESDEN LANE
SALUSBURY ROAD
BRONDESBURY VILLAS
SHOOT UP HILL
FORTUNE GREEN ROAD
REDINGTON ROAD
FROGNAL LANE
WEST HEATH ROAD
BROADHURST GDNS
GOLDHURST TERRACE
ABERDARE GDNS
GREENCROFT GDNS
CANFIELD GDNS
COMPAYNE GDNS
CLEVE ROAD
ACOL ROAD
QUEX ROAD
MESSINA AVENUE
KINGSGATE ROAD
IVERSON ROAD
MAYGROVE ROAD
LOVERIDGE RD
SUMATRA ROAD
PANDORA RD
HONEYBOURNE RD
CREDITON HILL
FAWLEY RD
LYMINGTON RD
BLACKBURN RD
NETHERWOOD
PALMERSTON RD
CHRISTCHURCH AVENUE
BRONDESBURY ROAD

HAMPSTEAD
HAMPSTEAD PONDS
Parliament Hill
THE PRYORS
Preacher's Hill
RUNNING TRACK
Pav
Lido
HAMPSTEAD HEATH
KEATS HO
ROYAL FREE HOSPITAL
Sports Cen
GOSPEL OAK EST
LISMORE CIRCUS
TOWN HALL
Post House Hotel
Old Town Hall Theatre
BELSIZE PARK
ST. DOMINIC'S PRIORY
MAITLAND PARK EST
FREUD MUSEUM
TAVISTOCK CEN
NW3
BELSIZE PARK
SWISS COTTAGE
Sports Cen
Regents Park Marriott
PRIMROSE HILL
PRIMROSE HILL
St. John's Wood Barracks
LONDON ZOO
Main Gate
HAMPSTEAD HIGH ST
ROSSLYN HILL
HAVERSTOCK HILL
FINCHLEY RD
AVENUE RD
ADELAIDE ROAD
PRINCE ALBERT ROAD
A502
A41
A5205
B518
B509
B511
B517
B525
D
E
F
G
1
2
3
4
5
10
16

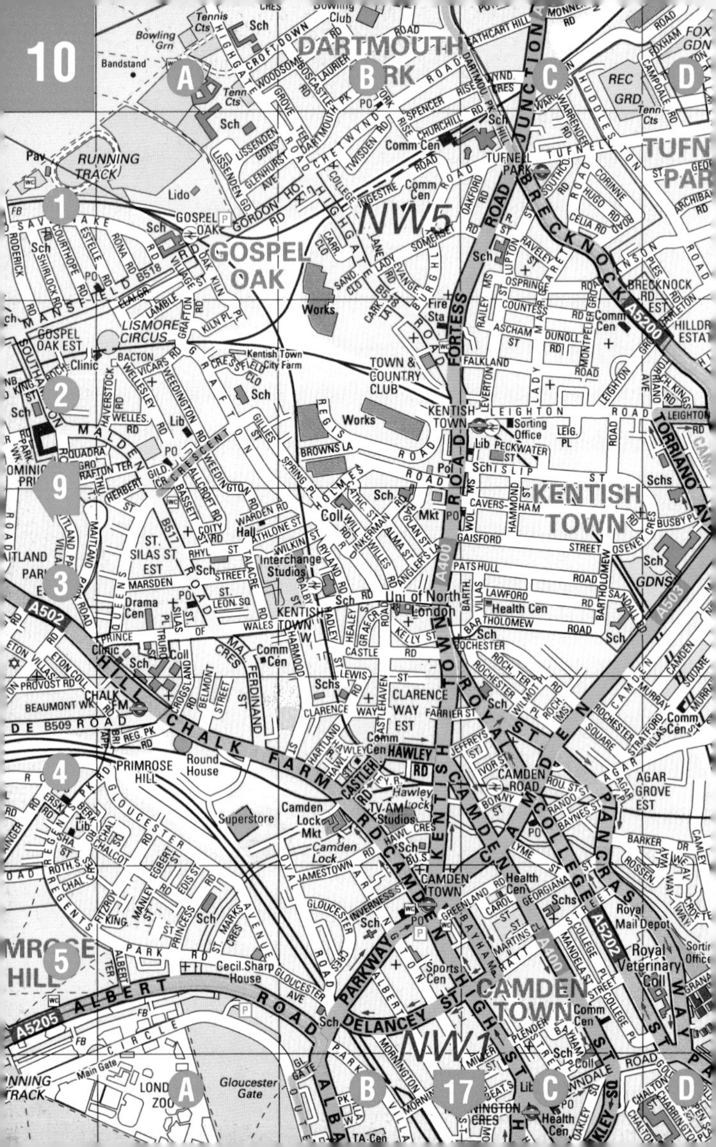
DARTMOUTH PARK
GOSPEL OAK
NW5
KENTISH TOWN
CAMDEN TOWN
NW1
TUFNELL PARK
LISMORE CIRCUS
RUNNING TRACK
Lido
Bandstand
Bowling Grn
Tennis Cts
HIGHGATE RD
CROFTDOWN RD
WOODSOME RD
BOSCASTLE RD
LAURIER RD
GROVE TER
DARTMOUTH PK RD
CHETWYND RD
SPENCER RISE
CHURCHILL RD
TWISDEN RD
Comm Cen
LISSENDEN GDNS
GLENHURST AVE
GORDON HO RD
COLLEGE LA
INGESTRE RD
OAKFORD RD
JUNCTION ROAD
TUFNELL PARK
BRECKNOCK RD
A5200
BRECKNOCK RD EST
HILLDROP ESTATE
FORTESS RD
FALKLAND RD
LEIGHTON RD
TORRIANO AV
KENTISH TOWN
Sorting Office
PECKWATER ST
ISLIP ST
CAVERSHAM RD
GAISFORD ST
PATSHULL RD
LAWFORD RD
BARTHOLOMEW RD
Health Cen
A503
CAMDEN SQUARE
AGAR GROVE EST
MANSFIELD RD
B518
GOSPEL OAK EST
SOUTHAMPTON RD
MALDEN RD
QUADRANT GRO
GRAFTON TER
HERBERT ST
MAITLAND PARK
A502
PRINCE OF WALES RD
ST. SILAS ST EST
Kentish Town City Farm
TOWN & COUNTRY CLUB
Works
REGIS RD
BROWNS LA
Interchange Studios
Coll
Uni of North London
KENTISH TOWN RD
A400
ROYAL COLLEGE ST
CAMDEN RD
CHALK FARM
CHALK FARM RD
ADELAIDE RD
B509
PRIMROSE HILL
Round House
Superstore
Camden Lock Mkt
TV-AM Studios
Hawley Lock
CLARENCE WAY EST
HAWLEY RD
PARKWAY
DELANCEY ST
GLOUCESTER AVE
REGENTS PARK RD
ALBERT RD
A5205
Cecil Sharp House
ST. PANCRAS WAY
A5202
Royal Mail Depot
Royal Veterinary Coll
CAMDEN ST
MORNINGTON CRES
LONDON ZOO
Main Gate
Gloucester Gate
PRIMROSE HILL
17
9

D
E
F
G
1
2
3
4
5
11
17
GILLESPIE CONSERVATION PARK
ARSENAL FC
HIGHBURY
HORNSEY ROAD
A503
SEVEN
HOLLOWAY ROAD
TOLLINGTON
Sports Cen
Shop Cen
Uni of N Lon
St George's Theatre
HOLBROOKE CT
TA Cen
PARKHURST RD
CAMDEN RD
North London College
H. M. PRISON HOLLOWAY
HOLLOWAY
Comm Cen
HARVIST ESTATE
A103
Works
Sorting Office
QUEENSLAND RD
DRAYTON PARK
HOLLOWAY ROAD
Uni of North London
LOWER HOLLOWAY
HILLMARTON ROAD
CALEDONIAN ROAD
N7
BR. DEPOT
PARADISE PARK
Freightliners City Farm
CALEDONIAN ROAD
Uni North London
James Leicester Hall
Health Cen
Clock Tower
CALEDONIAN PARK
Clubhouse
Tennis Courts
MARKET ROAD
SPORTS GRD
PENTONVILLE PRISON
A5203
BARNSBURY
CALEDONIAN ROAD & BARNSBURY
HIGHBURY & ISLINGTON
YORK WAY
A5200
UPPER STREET
A1
KING'S CROSS
PANCRAS HOSP & HOSP FOR TROPICAL DISEASES
DEPOT
London Wildlife Trust
CAMLEY STREET NATURAL PARK
Gas Works
Swimming Pool
BARNARD PARK
ISLINGTON
N1
ROYAL MAIL
BUS DES. CEN
COPENHAGEN ST
B514
B515
Clinic
WHARFDALE RD
PRIORY GREEN
RICHMOND AVENUE

A
B
C
D
1
2
3
4
5
10
18
HIGHBURY
N5
HIGHBURY ARSENAL FC
University of North London
HIGHBURY GROVE
HIGHBURY PARK
HIGHBURY FIELDS
HIGHBURY & ISLINGTON
HIGHBURY EST
CANONBURY
DRAYTON PARK
HOLLOWAY ROAD
ST. PAUL'S ROAD
A1199
A1201
A105
A104
A1200
A1
B104
B102
BALLS POND ROAD
NEWINGTON GREEN
GREEN LANES
ESSEX ROAD
NEW NORTH ROAD
UPPER STREET
ISLINGTON GREEN
SOUTHGATE ROAD
ALBION ROAD
MILDMAY PARK
MILDMAY GROVE
MARQUESS EST
DE BEAUVOIR EST
ROSEMARY GDNS
COLVILLE EST
HOXTON
SHOREDITCH PARK
REGENT'S CANAL
THE SUTTON EST
TOWN HALL
ROYAL MAIL
BARNSBURY
ISLINGTON
Swimming Pool
Comm Cen
Health Cen
Sports Cen
Swim Pool

11
12
18
D
E
F
G
1
2
3
4
5
SHACKLEWELL
HACKNEY
DALSTON
HAGGERSTON
E8
HACKNEY DOWNS
SPORTS GRD
LONDON FIELDS
Tenn Cts
DALSTON REC GRD
HAGGERSTON PARK
A10
A104
A1207
A107
A106
B108
B127
STOKE NEWINGTON ROAD
KINGSLAND HIGH ST
KINGSLAND ROAD
STOKE NEWINGTON HIGH ST
MANSE RD
REVERI. RD
AMHURST ROAD
SYDNER ROAD
FOULDEN RD
FARLEIGH ROAD
SHACKLEWELL RD
SOMERFORD GRO
BEATTY ROAD
WALFORD ROAD
BRIGHTON ROAD
PALATINE ROAD
PRINCE GEORGE ROAD
BELGRADE ROAD
PRINCESS MAY RD
BARRETTS GROVE
DOWNS ROAD
DOWNS PARK RD
AMHURST PASSAGE
CECILIA RD
ANDRE STREET
RODNEY ROAD
PEMBURY RD
CRICKET. RD
QUEENSDOWN ROAD
CLARENCE ROAD
LOWER CLAPTON ROAD
CLAPTON WAY
NIGHTINGALE EST
HEYWORTH RD
TIGER WAY
KENNINGHALL RD
RECTORY RD
EVERING RD
SHELLNESS RD
HINDREY RD
TOLSFORD RD
DALSTON LA
DALSTON LANE
AMHURST RD
HACKNEY DOWNS
HACKNEY CENTRAL
GRAHAM RD
DALSTON
MONTAGUE ROAD
CRESCENT
COLVESTONE CRES
SANDRINGHAM RD
RIDLEY ROAD
Shopping Cen
NAVARINO RD
GREENWOOD RD
WILTON WAY
RICHMOND ROAD
FOREST ROAD
MAPLEDENE ROAD
LAVENDER GROVE
MIDDLETON ROAD
ALBION DRIVE
SHRUBLAND ROAD
QUEENSBRIDGE RD
LANSDOWNE DRIVE
LONDON FIELDS W. SIDE
MARE ST
TOWN HALL
MUS
Amb Sta
PARAGON ROAD
WELL ST
LONDON FLDS
BLACKSTONE EST
FIELDS EST
Hackney Coll
Hospice
HAGGERSTON RD
DUNSTON ROAD
REGENTS ROW
WHISTON ROAD
Swimming Pool
Health Centre
Fire Sta
CULT. HERITG. MUS
Gas Works
CAMBRIDGE HEATH
WATERLOO EST
NORTHIAM
VYNER STREET
BROADWAY MKT
Sports Cen
Clinic
Health Centre
Comm Cen

HACKNEY
CLAPTON PARK
LOWER CLAPTON
HOMERTON
MABLEY GREEN
SOUTH HACKNEY
VICTORIA PARK
WELL STREET COMMON
E9
HOMERTON HOSPITAL
HACKNEY HOSP
HACKNEY CENTRAL
HOMERTON HIGH ST
LOWER CLAPTON RD
WICK RD
CASSLAND ROAD
VICTORIA PARK ROAD
MARE ST
WELL STREET
GROVE ROAD
RIVER LEE NAVIGATION
A102
A106
A107
B113
A
B
C
D
1
2
3
4
5
11
19

D
E
F
G
1
2
3
4
5
13
19
ALLOT
A106
New Spitalfields Market
SHERRIN ROAD
Works
Bowl Grn
ETON MANOR SPORTS GRD
Eastway Sports Centre
RIVER LEE or LEA
Pav
EASTWAY
RUCKHOLT ROAD
TEMPLE MILL LANE
QUARTER MILE LANE
B112
WICK FIELD
EASTWAY CYCLE CIRCUIT
TWEEDALE CT
CLAYS LANE
TRAFFORD CLOSE
CLAYS LA CLO
CONTAINER TERMINAL
WALTHAM FOREST
NEWHAM
EASTWAY COMMERCIAL CENTRE
WATERDEN ROAD
ALLOTMENTS
HACKNEY WICK
HACKNEY STADIUM
ARENA FIELD
Cold Stores
TROWBRIDGE EST
Sch
LEABANK SQ
BERKSHIRE RD
TROWBRI.RD
ELSTEAD ST
INTERNATIONAL FREIGHT TERMINAL
STRATFORD
STRATFORD RD
CARPENTERS ROAD
A115
WHITE POST LA
ROTHBURY ROAD
BOW IND EST
MARSHGATE LANE
WATERWORKS RIVER
E15
Sports Cen
BUS STA
GREAT EASTERN
STATION ST
DENNISON PT
KENNAR RD
GIBBINS RD
DORAN WK
ROSHER CLO
JUPP ROAD
WILMER LEA CLO
Comm Cen
Uni. of E. London
WARTON RD
ROWSE CL
BIGGERST. RD
Sch
PO
EAST CROSS ROUTE
WANSBECK ROAD
WYKE ROAD
ROACH ROAD
BEACHY ROAD
STOUR ROAD
SMEED ROAD
MONIER ROAD
DACE ROAD
WICK LANE
LEE NAVIGATION
Northern Outfall Sewer
RIVER LEE or LEA
CITY MILL RIVER
KNOBS HILL RD
MARSHGATE LANE
PUDDING MILL LANE
RIVER BLAKER RD
BRIDGWATER RD
Works
A11
UNION ST
LIVINGSTONE RD
Gas Works
ABBEY RD
BISSON RD
ABB.CLO
CLAY RD
Power Sta
CROWO CLO
ICELAND RD
AUTUMN ST
DYE HO LA
MAVE LANE
ATLEY RD
A102(M)
BLACKWALL
TREDEGAR RD
FAIRFIELD
BLONDIN ST
PARNELL RD
USHER RD
OLD FORD RD
CANDY
ELTON HO
RUST. ST.
WAVERTON HO
Fire Sta
B142
LEYTON HIGH ROAD
A112
MAJOR RD
LEYTON ROAD
HENRIETTA ST
NUTFIELD RD
ETCHING RD
CRANB. RD
GORDON RD
WESTDOWN ROAD
DRAPERS FIELD REC GRD
FRITH ROAD
MILLAIS ROAD
LESLIE
DOWNSELL
STEWART
DRAPERS
CROWNFIELD
COLEGRAVE
CHANDOS
ELLINGHAM ROAD
LEYTON
ALEXA.RD
DUNEDIN
ADELAIDE
RUCKHOLT CL
Depot

A
B
C
D
RC CEMETERY
SOUTH BIRBECK RD
BIRBECK ROAD
HOLLOWAY RD
DENM. ST
Lib
Sports Cen
Sch
CLO
CALDERON
FRITH ROAD
MILLAIS ROAD
LESLIE ROAD
LANGTHORNE HOSP
LANGTHORNE ROAD
BRIERLEY RD
TOR. RD
Schs
ELLINGHAM ROAD
HALL ROAD
ASHDOWN EST
HIGH ROAD
NAPIER RD
ELSHAM RD
WORSLEY ROAD
RANELAGH ROAD
STEELE ROAD
BELTON RD
EVE RD
CANN HALL ROAD
KINGS RD
CHEN RD
WRAGBY RD
CHICHESTER RD
ROAD
HAMPTON ROAD
RAMSAY ROAD
CANN ROAD
TRUMPINGTON ROAD
THORPE ROAD
HUDDLESTONE RD
PEVENSEY RD
VANSITTART RD
SHERIDAN RD
WINCHELSEA RD
BROXB. RD
HESKETH RD
DAM RD
PO
Schs
JEWISH CEM
WEST HAM CEMETERY
BLENHEIM RD
NUTFIELD RD
ETCHING. RD
CRANB. RD
GORDON RD
1
DOWNSELL ROAD
STEWART ROAD
AMETH. RD
MORRIS RD
CROWNFIELD RD
Pav
DRAPERS FIELD REC GRD
A112
DRAPERS ROAD
CROWNFIELD ROAD
DUNMOW RD
ASHLIN RD
BURGESS RD
GILB. ST
BORTHWICK RD
ARUNDEL CLO
ARGYLE RD
DEV. CLO
CRUIKSHANK RD
TREVELYAN RD
GOUGH RD
HEYWORTH RD
CEMETERY RD
CORMORANT RD
TOWER HAMLETS ROAD
WELLINGTON ROAD
ODESSA RD
WOOD. GD.
LEONARD RD
DEAN ST
CLA. ERIC GDNS
MACD.
PO
COLEGRAVE ROAD
Comm Cen
PINE AV
WIN. RD
JANSON ROAD
BUCK. RD
IDMISTON RD
ST JAMES' RD
MAGPIE CLO
MILL LANE
CHANDOS ROAD
BRYD.
NEW. HU. RD
BOND ST
GURNEY ROAD
Sch
HAT-FIELD
ASH ROAD
ALF. RD
MAJOR RD
HENRIETTA
LEYTON ROAD
2
OBHAM RD
A112
A11
ROAD
PO
BUXTON ROAD
ALB. SQ
ALBERT SQUARE
CARR. CLO
CHATSW. RD
GLO. RD
Sch
FB
FOREST GATE
HENNIKER ROAD
Comm Cen
HENNIKER PT
Sch
BOW. ST
MARY. PK
MARYL. SQUARE
THORO GDNS
WAR. CLO
ASHTON R.
COM. RD
MARYLAND ROAD
ST. PAULS RD
WADDINGTON
FAL STORE
MARYLAND STREET
FRANCIS ST
LEYTONSTONE ROAD
MARYLAND PK
Sch
FOREST ROAD
EARLHAM GROVE
Sch
NORWICH RD
THORN GROVE
LEYTON
12
ALMA ST
WHLWK
DAVID ST
WEL.
DORSET PL
WADDINGTON ST
WADDINGTON ST
MARYLAND
KEOGH RD
LOUISE ROAD
MCGRATH RD
CARNARVON ROAD
DORMER CLO
Sports Cen
ATHERTON ROAD
CLOVA ROAD
ATHERTON MEWS
ROAD
Sch
CROSBY RD
MARGERY
Depot
WINDMILL LANE
ARTS CEN
MANBEY PK RD
MANBEY GROVE
MANBEY ST
CEDARS
WATER LANE
B164
TOR. SQ
TOR. RD
GREEN PT
HAME RD
STRATFORD
3
INTERNATIONAL TERMINAL
A112 RD
ANGEL LA
THE GROVE
GROVE CRES RD
OXFORD RD
OXF.
A11
PO
PARK
GROVE GDNS
THE GREEN
Lib
Sch
Uni of E. London
MUS
WOLFFE GDNS
Fire Sta
A118
TOWN. CT
VAUGHAN RD
DYSON RD
ELM RD
KNOX
WARWICK
BOLTON ROAD
ELEANOR RD
STORK ROAD
YORK ROAD
SALISBURY
STRATFORD
STRATFORD
GREAT EASTERN RD
SALWAY RD
MAG CT
LITCHFIELD AVE
DEANERY ROAD
ROMFORD ROAD
COUNTY CT
TAVISTOCK RD
MAITLAND RD
HOLLAND RD
FAIRLAND RD
FARADAY RD
MATH. PK AVE
REGINALD RD
Theatre Royal
Shopping Centre
BUS STA
SUB
BROADWAY
TRA
TENNYSON ROAD
VERNON ROAD
GLENAVON RD
MAUDEN RD
WO. RD
WHI. RD
SHIRL
VICARAGE
VICARAGE RD
Sch PARK
Pav
15
STATION ST
OLD TH CONF CEN
PO
VICTORIA STREET
ELLIOT CLO
ALDWORTH RD
FARINGFORD ROAD
WELFARE RD
HAY CL
PO
VINE RD
HARTLAND RD
SKELL RD
DEVENAY RD
HAM
WEST HAM PARK
Bandstand
Spo... n
4
FB
DENNISON PT
KENNAR RD
ROSHER CLO
JUPP ROAD
GIBBINS RD
DORAN WK
WEST HAM LANE
MAG CT
CHANDLER CH. SQ
BRIDGE
BRYANT ST
WIDDIN ST
ST PITCH
FORD ST
WEST HAM LA REC GRD
Pav
Coll
BYFORD CL
GOVIER CL
HURRY CLO
ED. TEMME AVE
EVESHAM ROAD
MEESON RD
AMITY RD
MOR. RD
WEST HAM
TA Cen
WILMER LEA CLO
Comm Cen
Uni of E. London
JUPP ROAD W
Schs
PAUL STREET
Tenn Cts
Bowl Grn
DENSHAM RD
B165
PO
PORTWAY
Sch
ROAD
BURFORD ROAD
WHARF RD
CAM. RD
SH. RD
MARRIOTT RD
BARNBY ST
ARTHINGWORTH ST
ROKEBY
HOTHAM ST
SANDAL ST
Health Cen
CHURCH ST
NEW PLAISTOW ROAD
CHURCH
MA. CT
MARCUS ST
GILD.
DIRLETON RD
RICHFORD RD
LUDDINGTON RD
HARBERSON RD
PARK RD
WEST RD
Sch
EAST RD
PARK ROAD
BIGGERST
FB
Sch
PO
5
A11
WISE RD
KERRISON RD
CHANNELSEA RD
Mkt
ASLA. RD
SKIERS STREET
MORTHAM ST
HUBB. ST
ABBEY RD
TURLE C.
EAST BOU RD
JOHN ST
PLAISTOW GR
ADA GD.
GEERE RD
CAISTOR RD
STRATFORD RD
REDRIFFE RD
MAUD ROAD
MA. GDNS
ALETTA GROVE
BROOKS RD
UNION ST
LIVINGSTONE RD
ST. A RD
Works
A112
PLAISTOW ROAD
A1011 ROAD
STEPHEN'S RD
CHA RD
RANE
BAKERS ROW
MITRE RD
Gas Works
A
B
20
C
D
ABBEY LANE
BISSON RD
LEGGA
ABB. CLO
CLAY RD
GAY RD
ABBEY RD
CANNING
POND RD
RICH. RD
NAKE RD
Sch
PIER RD
Sch
MEATH RD
HARCOURT RD
HOLBROOK RD
Coll
WIL RD
MORLEY ROAD
STREET
PO
PLAISTOW
Comm Cen
ROAD

D
E
F
G
1
2
3
4
5
14
20
REDBRIDGE
NEWHAM
MANOR PARK CEMETERY
Crematorium
WOODGRANGE PARK CEM
PLASHET CEMETERY
PLASHET PARK
PRIORY PARK
OLD EAST HAM MEML HOSP
UPTON
UPTON PARK
E7
E13
WANSTEAD PARK
WOODGRANGE PARK
MANOR PARK STATION
UPTON PARK
PLAISTOW
WEST HAM UTD FC
BUS GAR
CEARNS HO
JAMES SINCLAIR PT
Sorting Office
Comm Cen
Sch
Schs
Lib
PO
Coll
Clinic
Health Cen
Mkt
Tenn Cts
Bowl Grn
ZOO
A118
A117
A114
A124
B109
B167
B165
CAPEL ROAD
ALDERSBROOK
FOREST DRIVE
FOREST VIEW ROAD
CARLYLE RD
WOODFORD ROAD
WOODGRANGE ROAD
FOREST ROAD
BECTIVE RD
CHESTNUT AVE
STRACEY RD
GODWIN ROAD
AVENUE ROAD
CRANMER ROAD
LATIMER ROAD
LORNE ROAD
TYLNEY ROAD
RIDLEY ROAD
BALMORAL ROAD
THE CHASE
WHITTA ROAD
GLADDING RD
DURHAM ROAD
CUMBERLAND RD
WENTWORTH RD
ALBANY RD
CARLTON RD
MANOR PK RD
CLARENCE ROAD
SEBERT ROAD
HAMPTON ROAD
OSBORNE ROAD
CLAREMONT ROAD
WINDSOR ROAD
RICHMOND ROAD
ROMFORD ROAD
HIGH STREET NORTH
SALISBURY RD
SNOWSHILL RD
ROSEDALE ROAD
BIRCHDALE ROAD
NIGEL ROAD
SHREWSBURY ROAD
SHERRARD ROAD
HALLEY ROAD
MONEGA ROAD
STRONE ROAD
COLSTON RD
CLIFTON RD
BATH RD
LINCOLN ROAD
SHELLEY AVE
BYRON AVE
WORDSWORTH AVE
TENNYSON AVE
WOODHOUSE GROVE
GROVE
UPTON LANE
NURSERY LANE
SYLVAN RD
VALE ROAD
PALMERSTON ROAD
WESTBURY ROAD
GLENPARKE ROAD
WHYTEVILLE ROAD
STUDLEY ROAD
KITCHENER ROAD
GROSVENOR ROAD
CHESHUNT RD
CHAUCER ROAD
GOWER ROAD
DUNBAR RD
SKELTON RD
WYATT ROAD
FINDEN RD
RATCLIFF RD
SANDRINGHAM ROAD
HENDERSON ROAD
GREEN STREET
KATHERINE ROAD
SOUTH ESK ROAD
BRISTOL ROAD
STAFFORD ROAD
DERBY ROAD
RUTLAND ROAD
CHESTER ROAD
MARLBOROUGH RD
ROTHSAY RD
JEPHSON RD
LANSDOWN RD
WOODSTOCK RD
PRESTBURY RD
CROMWELL RD
SHAFTESBURY ROAD
LENS RD
DORSET ROAD
ST. GEORGES ROAD
ST. GEORGES SQ
ST. GEORGES AVE
BEAUCHAMP RD
WOLSELEY ROAD
BELTON RD
ISMAILIA RD
OAKDALE RD
FERNDALE RD
ELMHURST ROAD
UPTON PARK ROAD
STUKELEY ROAD
ST. ANTONY'S ROAD
BOLEYN ROAD
NEVILLE ROAD
PLASHET ROAD
KINGSLEY RD
LANCASTER RD
UPTON AVE
DORIS RD
STOPFORD ROAD
CECIL ROAD
DACRE ROAD
SELWYN ROAD
CLAUDE ROAD
GWENDOLINE AVENUE
LAWRENCE RD
DONALD ROAD
CHURSTON AVENUE
LUCAS AVE
THORNGROVE ROAD
PENGE ROAD
RAYMOND ROAD
HAROLD ROAD
QUEENS ROAD
ROCHESTER AVE
WAGHORN RD
ORWELL ROAD
KIRTON RD
WALTON RD
FAWN RD
CREDON RD
SELSDON ROAD
KINGS ROAD
TUDOR ROAD
REDCLYFFE ROAD
WILLIAM MORLEY CLO
PRIORY ROAD
CLEVES ROAD
BOLEYN RD
PARR ROAD
ARRAGON ROAD
WAKEFIELD STREET
ABBOTS ROAD
ST. BERNARD'S ROAD
FRIARS ROAD
GROSVENOR RD
SPENCER RD
EVERSLEIGH RD
VICTORIA AVE
GRANGEWOOD STREET
ELIZABETH ROAD
ST. STEPHENS ROAD
WATER RD
WALPOLE RD
WHITFIELD RD
WYNDHAM RD
WORTLEY RD
FRY RD
MILTON AVENUE
HEIGHAM ROAD
LAWRENCE ROAD
OUTRAM ROAD
MALVERN ROAD
TEMPLE ROAD
AINTREE AVE
HARTLEY AVE
KIMBERLEY
LADYSMITH
MAFEKING
GILLETT AVE
BARKING ROAD
TERRACE ROAD
WEST ROAD
PLAISTOW ROAD
NORTHERN ROAD
ST. MARYS ROAD
MAY RD
CASTLE ST
EDITH RD
HILDA RD
CRESCENT ROAD

A
B
C
D
1
2
3
4
5
13
21
E12
MANOR PARK
ROMFORD ROAD
A118
A116
A117
A406
A124
B165
B109
ALDERSBROOK ROAD
FOREST VIEW ROAD
CARLYLE RD
MANOR PARK
Sorting Office
Three Rabbits PH
STATION RD
WOODGRANGE PARK
WOODGRANGE PARK CEM
PLASHET CEMETERY
PLASHET PARK
OLD EAST HAM MEML HOSP
ZOO
Tenn Cts
Bowl Grn
LITTLE ILFORD PARK
STEWART RAINBIRD HO
JOHN CORNWALL VC HO
ALFRED PRIOR HO
JACK CORNWELL ST
SOUTH WOODFORD TO BARKING RELIEF ROAD
RIVER RODING
BARRINGTON PLAYING FIELDS
BARRINGTON RD
CHESTERFORD ROAD
HATHAWAY CRESCENT
SHAKESPEARE CRES
DEPOT
STEVENAGE ROAD
SPORTS GRD
Gasholder
Pav
WATSON AVE
BARKING ROAD REC GRD
BARKING ROAD
HIGH STREET NORTH
EAST HAM
TOWN HALL
TH annexe
Shopping Cen
Coll
Lib
PO
Sch
Schs
Comm Cen
Health Cen
Works
Superstore
PLAYING FIELD
CHURCH RD
RECTORY RD
SHERIDAN ROAD
MORRIS AVE
ESSEX RD
WARWICK RD
BERKELEY RD
STANLEY RD
COLERIDGE AVE
RUSKIN AVE
GOLDSMITH AVE
ROSEBERY AVENUE
BROWNING RD
SHELLEY AVE
BYRON AVE
KENSINGTON AVE
WORDSWORTH AVE
GLADSTONE AVENUE
TENNYSON AVE
EAST AVE
SIBLEY GROVE
GROVE
MILTON AVENUE
HEIGHAM ROAD
LAWRENCE ROAD
BENDISH RD
OUTRAM ROAD
MALVERN ROAD
STAMFORD ROAD
OAKFIELD ROAD
HARROW RD
HOLME ROAD
MYRTLE RD
ST. JOHNS RD
SKEFFINGTON RD
KEMPTON ROAD
THORPE RD
LLOYD RD
LATHOM ROAD
CLEMENTS ROAD
CAULFIELD ROAD
CALEDON ROAD
HOLLAND ROAD
BURGES ROAD
ALTMORE AVENUE
KEPPEL ROAD
SOUTHEND ROAD
NORTHFIELD RD
ASHFORD RD
LEIGH ROAD
WALL END ROAD
LANGDON RD
NELSON ST
SUSSEX ROAD
DUKES CT
HERTFORD ROAD
FIRST AVENUE
SECOND AVENUE
THIRD AVENUE
FOURTH AVENUE
FIFTH AVE
SIXTH AVE
SEVENTH AVE
EIGHTH AVE
LITTLE ILFORD LANE
SHERINGHAM AVENUE
DERSINGHAM AVENUE
GRANTHAM ROAD
WALTON ROAD
WARRIOR SQ
BRANCASTER RD
TREVELYAN AVE
HARCOURT AVENUE
VERNON AV
SCHOOL RD
WOLSEY RD
LAWRENCE AVENUE
PARKHURST ROAD
ALVERS RD
GAINSBORO RD
LANDSEER AVENUE
DORE AVENUE
MILLAIS AVE
REYNOLDS AVE
LEIGHTON AV
ELSENHAM RD
ST. WINEFRIDE'S RD
ST. MARY'S APP
SALISBURY RD
HERBERT ROAD
MEANLEY RD
NINE ACRES CLO
SNOWSHILL RD
LINCOLN RD
WOODHOUSE GROVE
EVERSLEIGH RD
SPENCER RD
ST. BERNARD'S ROAD
ARRAGON RD
WAKEFIELD ST
ABBOTS ROAD
AINTREE AVE
HARTLEY AVE
CAMPBELL AVE
WINTER AVE
BARTLE AVENUE
NAVARRE RD
HENRY RD
ST BARTHOLOMEW'S RD
KIMBERLEY
LADYSMITH
GILLETT AVENUE
MARKET ST
WELLINGTON RD
NAPIER
RANELAGH ROAD
BEDFORD ROAD
NORFOLK ROAD
CALVERTON RD
ST. OLAVES ROAD
MIERS CLO
STREATFIELD AVE
LATIMER AVE
REDBRIDGE
BARKING

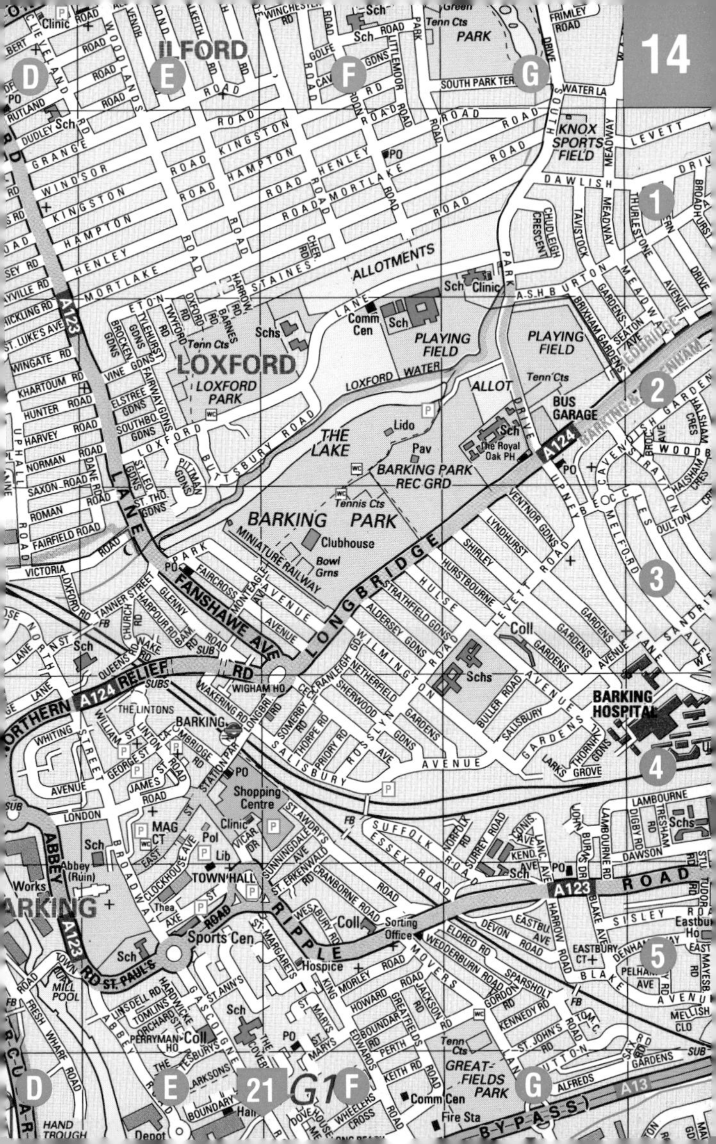
ILFORD
LOXFORD
LOXFORD PARK
BARKING PARK
THE LAKE
BARKING PARK REC GRD
ALLOTMENTS
PLAYING FIELD
KNOX SPORTS FIELD
BUS GARAGE
BARKING HOSPITAL
The Royal Oak PH
Lido
Pav
Clubhouse
Bowl Grns
Tennis Cts
MINIATURE RAILWAY
LOXFORD WATER
Comm Cen
Shopping Centre
TOWN HALL
Abbey (Ruin)
Sports Cen
Sorting Office
Hospice
GREATFIELDS PARK
BARKING
ARKING
A123
A124
A13
LONGBRIDGE
FANSHAWE AVE
NORTHERN RELIEF RD
RIPPLE ROAD
ABBEY
BY-PASS
UPHALL
STAINES
MORTLAKE
HENLEY
HAMPTON
KINGSTON
WINDSOR
GRANGE
DUDLEY
RUTLAND
VICTORIA
FAIRFIELD ROAD
ROMAN
SAXON ROAD
NORMAN
HARVEY
HUNTER ROAD
KHARTOUM RD
WINGATE RD
ST. LUKE'S AVE
DAWLISH
ASHBURTON
LEVETT
SOUTH PARK TER
WATER LA
MEADWAY
THURLESTONE
TAVISTOCK
CHUDLEIGH CRESCENT
VENTNOR GDNS
LYNDHURST
SHIRLEY
HURSTBOURNE
STRATHFIELD GDNS
ALDERSEY GDNS
WILMINGTON
NETHERFIELD
SHERWOOD
SALISBURY AVENUE
SUFFOLK
ESSEX ROAD
STATION PAR
MAG CT
LONDON
THE LINTONS
WHITING AVENUE
ST. PAUL'S RD
TOWN QUAY
MILL POOL
FRESH WHARF ROAD
HAND TROUGH
Depot
BROADWAY
CLOCKHOUSE AVE
WESTBURY RD
ST. MARGARETS
EASTBURY CT
DENHAM
PELHAM AVE
MELLISH CLO
LAMBOURNE
DAWSON
TUDOR
SISLEY
D
E
F
G
1
2
3
4
5
21
G1

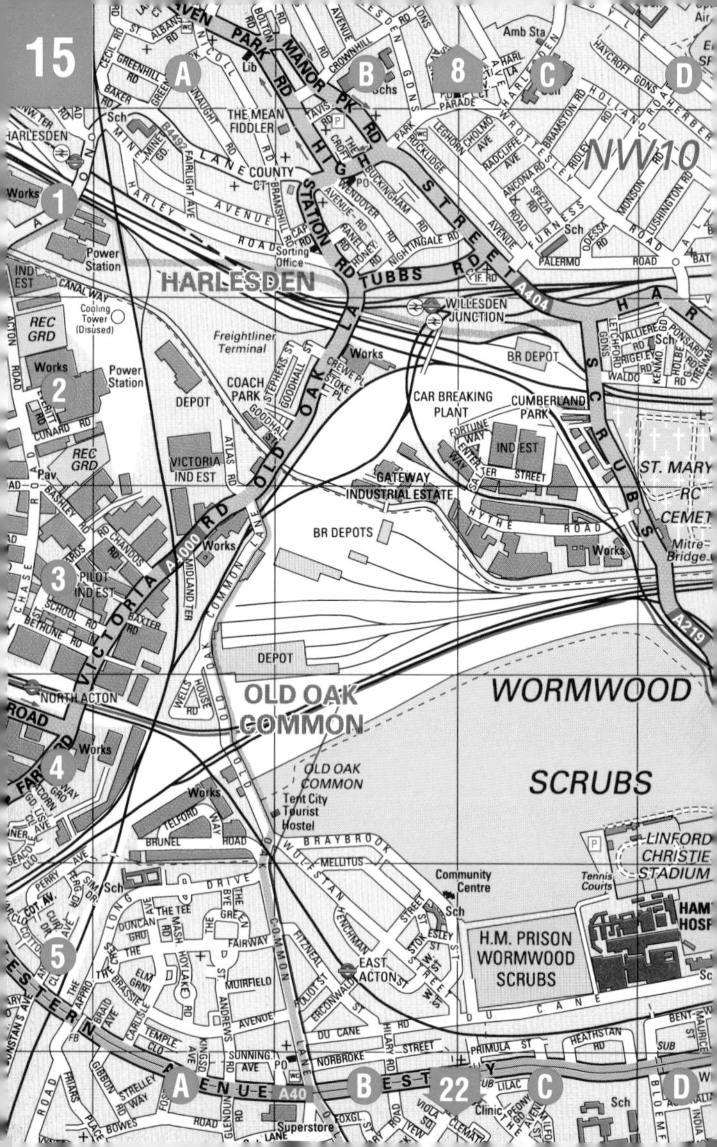
NW10
HARLESDEN
WILLESDEN JUNCTION
OLD OAK COMMON
WORMWOOD SCRUBS
H.M. PRISON WORMWOOD SCRUBS
LINFORD CHRISTIE STADIUM
ST. MARY RC CEMET
NORTH ACTON
EAST ACTON
THE MEAN FIDDLER
GATEWAY INDUSTRIAL ESTATE
VICTORIA IND EST
PILOT IND EST
CAR BREAKING PLANT
CUMBERLAND PARK
Freightliner Terminal
COACH PARK
BR DEPOTS
BR DEPOT
DEPOT
Power Station
Cooling Tower (Disused)
REC GRD
Tent City Tourist Hostel
Community Centre
Tennis Courts
Sorting Office
Superstore
Clinic
Mitre Bridge
HIGH STREET
MANOR PK RD
STATION RD
TUBBS RD
OLD OAK LA
OLD OAK COMMON LANE
VICTORIA RD
HYTHE ROAD
SCRUBS LA
HARLESDEN RD
DU CANE RD
WESTERN AVENUE
BRAYBROOK ST
WULFSTAN ST
HARLEY AVENUE
CRAVEN PARK RD
LEGHORN RD
WROTTESLEY RD
FURNESS RD
PALERMO ROAD
A404
A4000
A219
A40
B4492
A B C D
1 2 3 4 5
8
22

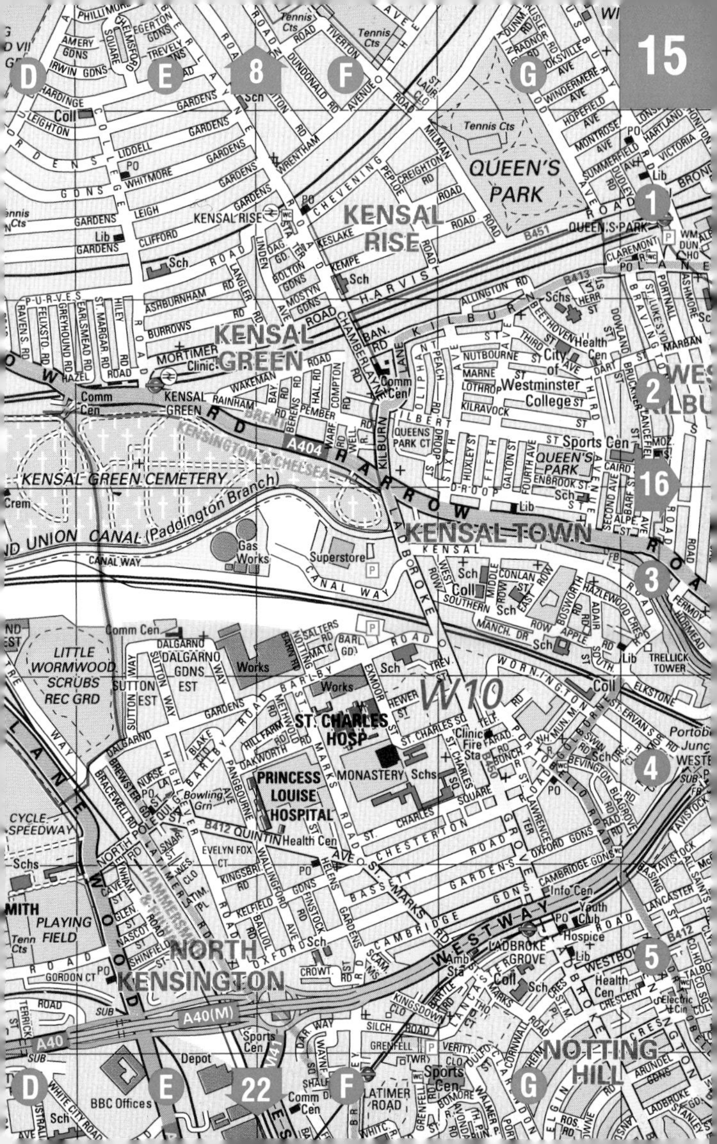
8
D
E
F
G
KENSAL RISE
KENSAL GREEN
QUEEN'S PARK
KENSAL GREEN CEMETERY
GRAND UNION CANAL (Paddington Branch)
KENSAL TOWN
W10
ST. CHARLES HOSP
PRINCESS LOUISE HOSPITAL
MONASTERY
LITTLE WORMWOOD SCRUBS REC GRD
CYCLE SPEEDWAY
PLAYING FIELD
NORTH KENSINGTON
NOTTING HILL
City of Westminster College
Gas Works
Superstore
Works
TRELLICK TOWER
BBC Offices
Depot
LATIMER ROAD
LADBROKE GROVE
WESTWAY
A40(M)
A40
A404
B451
B413
B412
B450
M41
HARROW ROAD
KILBURN LANE
LADBROKE GROVE
CHAMBERLAYNE ROAD
WOOD LANE
PORTOBELLO ROAD
CANAL WAY
HARVIST ROAD
KENSAL RISE
KENSAL GREEN
QUEEN'S PARK
1
2
3
4
5
16
22

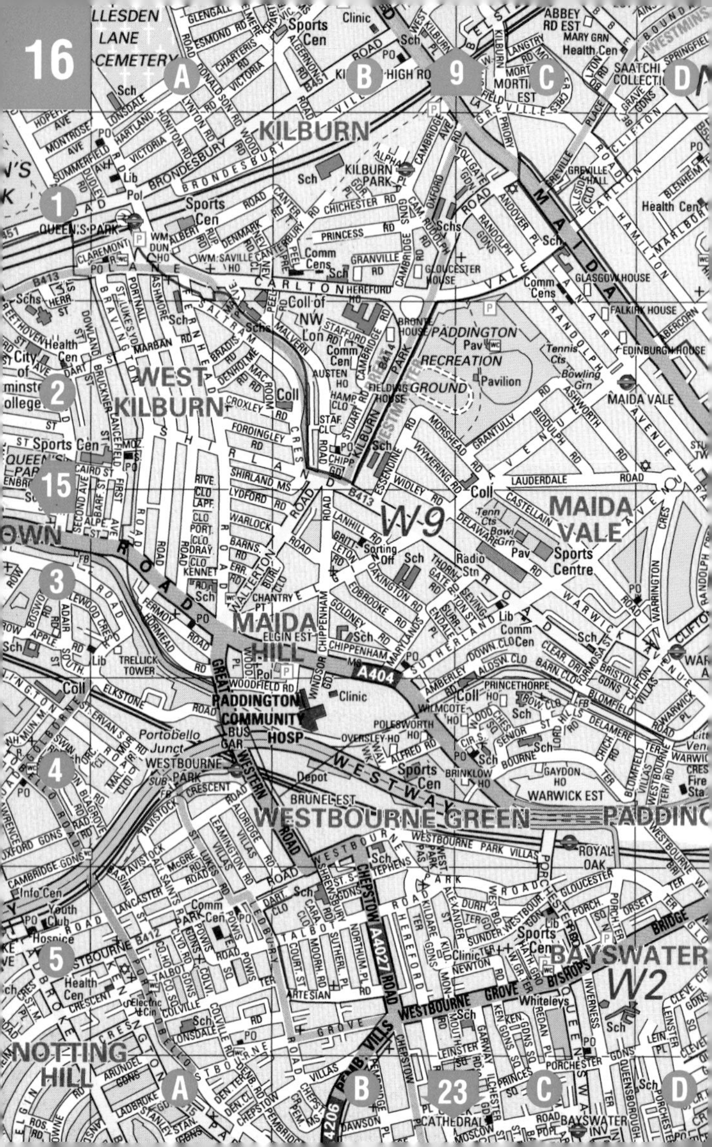
WILLESDEN LANE CEMETERY
A
B
9
C
D
KILBURN
KILBURN HIGH RD
ABBEY RD EST
MARY GRN Health Cen
SAATCHI COLLECTION
MORTIMER EST
KILBURN PARK
BRONDESBURY RD
QUEEN'S PARK
Sports Cen
CHICHESTER RD
PRINCESS RD
GRANVILLE RD
CARLTON VALE
GLOUCESTER HOUSE
GLASGOW HOUSE
FALKIRK HOUSE
EDINBURGH HOUSE
HEREFORD HO
Coll of NW Lon
PADDINGTON RECREATION GROUND
Pavilion
MAIDA VALE
1
2
3
4
5
WEST KILBURN
City of Westminster College
SALTRAM CRES
SHIRLAND ROAD
15
HARROW ROAD
W9
LAUDERDALE ROAD
MAIDA VALE
Sports Centre
Radio Stn
MAIDA HILL
ELGIN EST
CHIPPENHAM
SUTHERLAND AVENUE
A404
TRELLICK TOWER
ELKSTONE ROAD
GREAT PADDINGTON COMMUNITY HOSP
Clinic
Portobello Junct
WESTBOURNE PARK
WESTWAY
BRUNEL EST
WESTBOURNE GREEN
WARWICK EST
PADDINGTON
ROYAL OAK
WESTBOURNE PARK VILLAS
GLOUCESTER TER
BISHOPS BRIDGE
BAYSWATER
W2
CHEPSTOW A4027 ROAD
WESTBOURNE GROVE
Whiteleys
PORCHESTER GDNS
QUEENSWAY
NOTTING HILL
LEDBURY RD
PORTOBELLO RD
KENSINGTON PARK RD
LADBROKE GDNS
PEMB. VILLS
A4206
A
B
23
C
D
CATHEDRAL
BAYSWATER

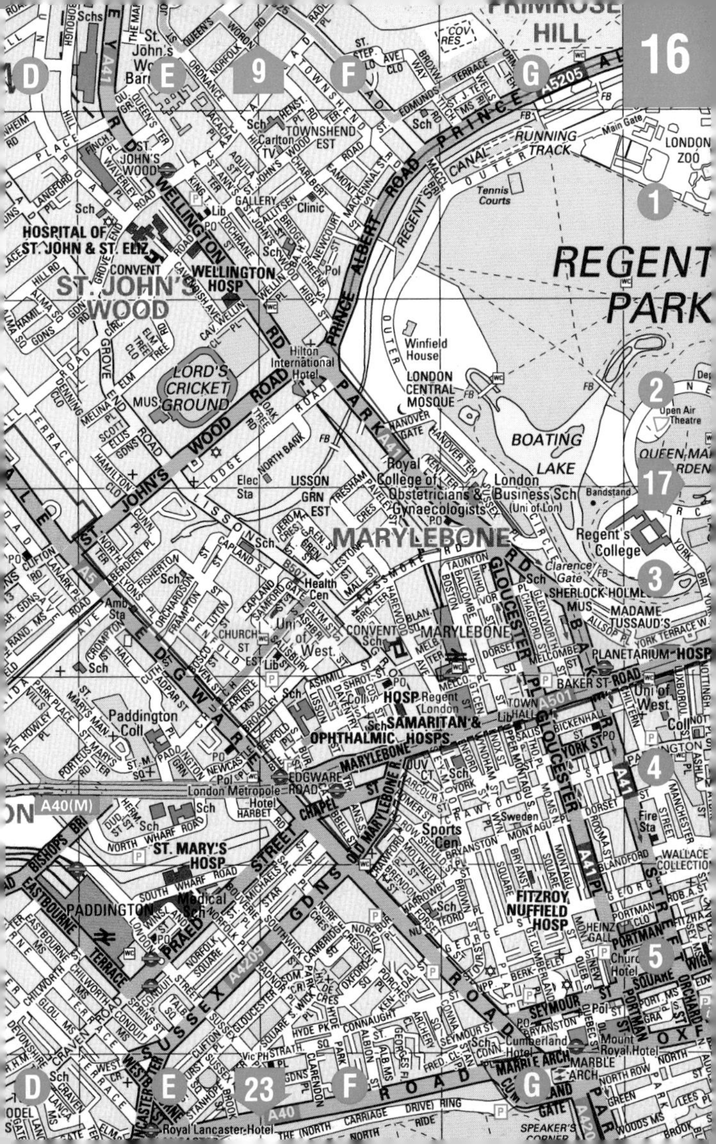
PRIMROSE HILL
REGENT'S PARK
LONDON ZOO
Main Gate
RUNNING TRACK
Tennis Courts
OUTER CIRCLE
PRINCE ALBERT ROAD
A5205
ST. JOHN'S WOOD
ST. JOHN'S WOOD ROAD
WELLINGTON ROAD
WELLINGTON HOSP
HOSPITAL OF ST. JOHN & ST. ELIZ
LORD'S CRICKET GROUND
MUS
Hilton International Hotel
PARK ROAD
A41
Winfield House
LONDON CENTRAL MOSQUE
HANOVER GATE
BOATING LAKE
Open Air Theatre
QUEEN MARY'S GARDENS
Bandstand
London Business Sch (Uni of Lon)
Royal College of Obstetricians & Gynaecologists
Regent's College
Clarence Gate
SHERLOCK HOLMES MUS
MADAME TUSSAUD'S
PLANETARIUM
BAKER ST
MARYLEBONE
LISSON GRN EST
Uni of West.
SAMARITAN & OPHTHALMIC HOSPS
MARYLEBONE ROAD
A501
EDGWARE ROAD
A5
Paddington Coll
London Metropole Hotel
A40(M)
ST. MARY'S HOSP
Medical Sch
PADDINGTON
PRAED ST
SUSSEX GDNS
A4209
FITZROY NUFFIELD HOSP
WALLACE COLLECTION
Cumberland Hotel
Mount Royal Hotel
MARBLE ARCH
BAYSWATER ROAD
A40
Royal Lancaster Hotel
SPEAKER'S CORNER
D
E
F
G
9
23
17
1
2
3
4
5

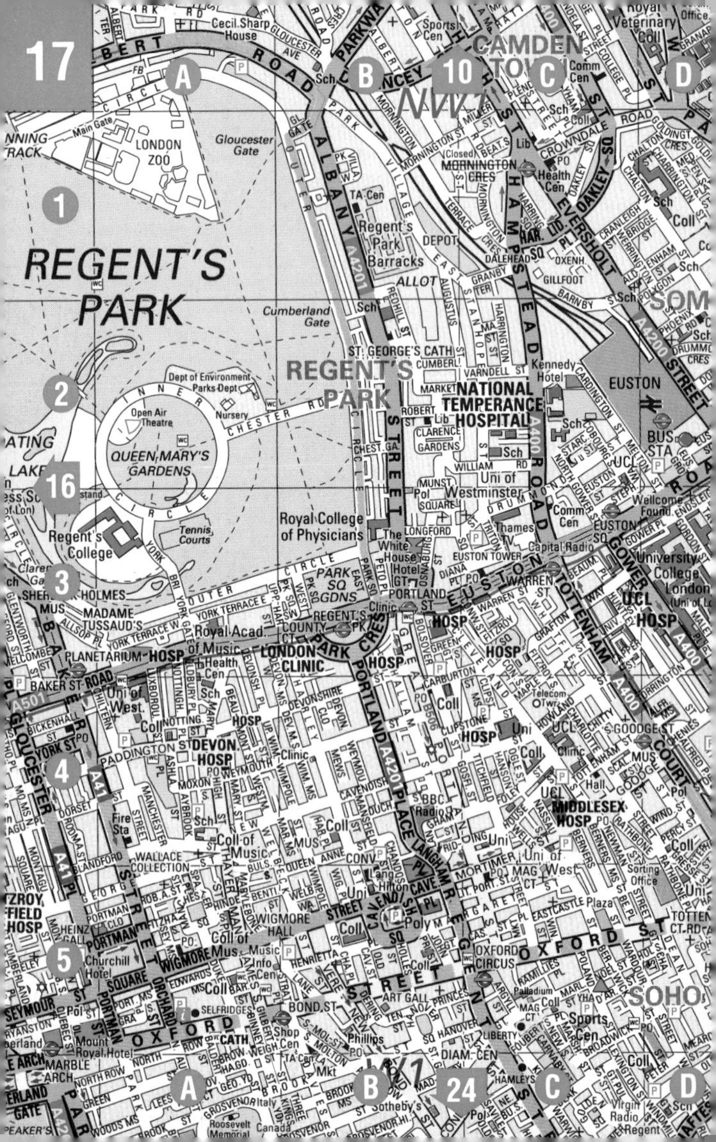

REGENT'S PARK
LONDON ZOO
Main Gate
Cecil Sharp House
Gloucester Gate
Cumberland Gate
CAMDEN TOWN
NW1
10
16
24
W1
A
B
C
D
1
2
3
4
5
Regent's Park Barracks
ST. GEORGE'S CATH
REGENT'S PARK
NATIONAL TEMPERANCE HOSPITAL
Dept of Environment Parks Dept
Nursery
Open Air Theatre
QUEEN MARY'S GARDENS
INNER CIRCLE
CHESTER RD
Tennis Courts
Regent's College
Royal College of Physicians
The White House Hotel
SHERLOCK HOLMES
MADAME TUSSAUD'S
PLANETARIUM
Royal Acad. of Music
LONDON CLINIC
EUSTON
BUS STA
EUSTON SQ
EUSTON TOWER
Uni of Westminster
Thames TV
Capital Radio
Kennedy Hotel
University College London
UCL HOSP
MIDDLESEX HOSP
Telecom Twr
BBC Radio
WALLACE COLLECTION
Coll of Music
WIGMORE HALL
Langham Hilton
OXFORD CIRCUS
OXFORD ST
SELFRIDGES
BOND ST
Churchill Hotel
Mount Royal Hotel
MARBLE ARCH
Palladium
HAMLEYS
Sotheby's
Roosevelt Memorial
Phillips
SOHO
Virgin Radio
MORNINGTON CRES
HAMPSTEAD ROAD
EVERSHOLT ST
TOTTENHAM COURT RD
GOWER ST
PORTLAND PLACE
BAKER ST
GLOUCESTER PL
MARYLEBONE
PORTMAN SQ
CAVENDISH SQ
REGENT ST
GREAT PORTLAND ST
ALBANY ST
PARKWAY
A4201
A400
A501
A41
A4200

17
D
E
10
F
G
1
2
3
4
5
18
24
ISLINGTON
PENTONVILLE
ST PANCRAS
BLOOMSBURY
HOLBORN
WC1
KING'S CROSS
ST. PANCRAS
NEW BRITISH LIB (Opening 1995)
CAMLEY ST NATURAL PARK
London Wildlife Trust
Gas Works
City Ballet
CALEDONIAN ROAD
PENTONVILLE RD
A501
A5200
A5202
A401
A201
A40
B502
B514
KING'S CROSS RD
GRAY'S INN ROAD
GRAY'S INN RD
FARRINGDON ROAD
ROSEBERY AVE
CLERKENWELL ROAD
THEOBALD'S ROAD
SOUTHAMPTON ROW
HIGH HOLBORN
HOLBORN
KINGSWAY
ALDWYCH
STRAND
FLEET ST
EMBANKMENT
NEW OXFORD ST
CHARING CROSS
ST. GILES HIGH ST
BLOOMSBURY WAY
RUSSELL SQUARE
WOBURN PL
UPPER ST
GOSWELL
CITY RD
ST. JOHN ST
THAMESLINK
EASTMAN DENTAL HOSP
Mount Pleasant Post Office
Thames Water Authority
Sadler's Wells Theatre
The Angel Centre
ANGEL
Royal Scot Hotel
Vernon Square Cen
T. CORAM FOUND.
CORAM'S FIELDS
HOSPS
Royal Nat Hotel
University of London
BRITISH MUSEUM & BRITISH LIB
St. Giles Hotel
Freemasons' Hall
LINCOLN'S INN FIELDS
Lincoln's Inn
ROYAL COURTS OF JUSTICE
PUBLIC RECORD OFF
PATENT OFF
Silver Vaults
GRAY'S INN GDNS
Gray's Inn
City Lit. Inst
Prince Henry's Room
Temple Bar
ROYAL OPERA HO
COVENT GDN
Covent Gdn Mkt
Theatre Royal
BBC
Strand Palace
SOMERSET
King's Coll
TEMPLE
CHARTERHOUSE
Smithfield Cen Mkt
FARRINGDON
Shopping Centre
Sports Cen
Health Cen
TOWN HALL
Comm Cen
Uni
Coll
Sch
Lib
Mus
Hosp
PO
Pol
Fire Sta

HOXTON
SHOREDITCH PARK
FINSBURY
CLERKENWELL
EC1
ST. LUKE'S
EC2
EC4
ANGEL
The Angel Centre
Thames Water Authority
Sadlers Wells Theatre
City Uni
St. MARK'S HOSP
MOORFIELDS EYE HOSP
KING SQ GDNS
BUNHILL FLDS
BURIAL GRD
Barracks
Whitbread Brewery
St. Bartholomew's Med Coll
Charterhouse
BARBICAN
BARBICAN ARTS & CONF CEN
MUSEUM OF LONDON
Smithfield Central Mkts
ST. BART'S HOSP
Royal Mail
CENT CRIM CT (Old Bailey)
ST. PAUL'S CATH
Chapter Ho
The Guildhall
Bank of Eng
Stock Exch
Royal Exch
Lloyds
Nat West Twr
City of London Club
MONUMENT
The Monument
BLACKFRIARS
TELECOM TECH. SHOW.
CITY THAMESLINK
FARRINGDON
MOORGATE
BANK
LIVERPOOL ST
BROADGATE
Mirror Group
City Lit. Inst
Prince Henry's Room
REGENT'S CANAL
CITY ROAD BASIN
WENLOCK BASIN
CITY ROAD
OLD STREET
GOSWELL ROAD
UPPER STREET
NEW NORTH ROAD
EAST ROAD
ALDERSGATE ST
LONDON WALL
HOLBORN VIADUCT
NEWGATE ST
CHEAPSIDE
CANNON ST
QUEEN VICTORIA ST
A1
A1200
A501
A5201
A1211
A201
A40
A10
B144
B502
B100
B101
11
25

HAGGERSTON
HAGGERSTON PARK
BETHNAL GREEN
SHOREDITCH
WHITECHAPEL
E2
11
19
25
D
E
F
G
1
2
3
4
5
KINGSLAND
HACKNEY ROAD
A1208
A1209
BETHNAL GREEN ROAD
CAMBRIDGE HEATH ROAD
A107
A10
A1202
COMMERCIAL STREET
WHITECHAPEL ROAD
MILE END ROAD
A11
COMMERCIAL ROAD
A13
A106
REGENTS ROW
MARE ST
QUEEN ELIZ. HOSP
ROYAL LONDON HOSP TRUST
MILDMAY MISS. HOSP
Old Spitalfields Mkt
WEAVERS FLDS
JEWISH BURIAL GRD
Gas Works
COLUMBIA ROAD
MINORIES
MANSELL
LEMAN
ALDGATE
ALDGATE BUS STA
TOWER GTWY
ROYAL MINT ST
CABLE ST
Toynbee Hall
SHADWELL
MUS OF CHILDHOOD
Haggerston City Farm
Uni of Greenwich
HOUNDSDITCH
MIDDLESEX STREET

PARK
A
B
C
D
12
26
18
1
2
3
4
5
St. Agnes Gate
Gore Gate
DEER PARK
Skew Bridge
Crown Gate West
Gate East
Three Colt Bri
HARTFORD
GROVE
GORE
MORPETH
ROAD
WADESON
WATERLOO EST
Health Centre
SEWARDSTONE ROAD
CAMBRIDGE HEATH
BISHOPS
LONDON CHEST HOSP
PARK VIEW EST
The Royal Cricketer's PH
OLD
ROYAL VICTOR P.
CHISENHALE ROAD
ZEALAND ROAD
ELLESMERE ROAD
DRIFFIELD ROAD
HEWLETT RD
DALING WAY
ROMAN
Lib
PO
Sch
TOWN HALL
Sports Cen
MUS OF CHILDHOOD
CYPRUS STREET
CRANBROOK EST
MACE STREET
ROYS ST
BONNER ST
B118
B119
B127
PALMERS RD
REGENT'S
ALLOT
MEATH GARDENS
HAVERFIELD RD
CORDOVA RD
ARBERY ROAD
STRAHAN RD
ANTILL
Fire Sta
LAMONT
ROMAN
E2
BETHNAL GREEN
BETHNAL GRN GDNS
CORNWALL AVE
GLOBE
SCEPTRE ROAD
DIGBY
KNOTTISFORD
BULLARDS PL
WARLEY ST
BANCROFT
PORTELET ROAD
GRANTLEY
BRADWELL ST
MILE END
LONDON HOSPITAL (Mile End)
Queen Mary College (Uni of Lon)
CANAL
ROAD
MORGAN
RHONDDA
ABERAVON RD
TREDEGAR
SQUARE
MILE END
BURDETT
ROAD
A107
CAMBRIDGE
HEATH
CUDWORTH
BUCKHURST STREET
COLLINGWOOD STREET
HEADLAM ST
CEPHAS
CLEVELAND WAY
WICKFORD ST
MALCOLM RD
COLEBERT
FOX
AVENUE
ALDERNEY ROAD
MILE END PL
STEPNEY GRN
OCEAN EST
Amb Sta
TOBY
SOLEBAY
EMMOTT
HARFORD
COMMODORE
Tenn Crts
ERNEST
DUCKETT
REC GRD
ESSIAN ST
Gas Works
Comm Centre
END
PARK
MIDLOTHIAN RD
MILE END STAD
MUS
Pav
Clinic
LONDON INDEP HOSP
BEAUMONT
SHANDY
TRAF. GDNS
MILE
A11
ASSEMBLY PAS
HANNIBAL
STEPNEY
CRESS
TINSLEY
B121
REDMAN'S
ADELINA GRO
LINDLEY ST
SMITHY STREET
CLICHY EST
STEPNEY
STEPNEY GREEN
JONSON
B140
RD
HALLEY ST
LIMEHOUSE
RHODESWELL
ST. PAUL'S
BEN
Comm Cen
STEPNEY WAY
Stepping Stones Farm
BROMLEY
BELGRAVE ST
REC GRD
MAROON
FLDS EST
BLOUNT
NEWARK ST
CLARK ST
SIDNEY
JUBILEE
MUSBURY ST
JAMAICA
AYLWARD
WALTER TER
LATHAM HO
MATLOCK
REPTON
CHUDLEIGH ST
AVIS SQ
CORNWOOD DR
E1
COMMERCIAL
Coll
ROAD
WHITE HORSE
SALMON
LANE
YORKSHIRE RD
ANGLIA HO
FLAMBORO
A13
LIMEHOUSE
ROAD
CONV
LIMEHOUSE BASIN
LIMEHOUS
Health Cen
DAY HOSP
TARLING STREET
TARLING ST EST
GELSTON PT
SHADWELL
Fire Sta
Comm.Cem
MARTINEAU
CABLE
B126
STREET
GLAMIS PLACE
ELF ROW
HIGHWAY
THE
A1203
JARDINE RD
Ratcliffe
BRANCH
NORTHEY
DEVONPORT
CARROL

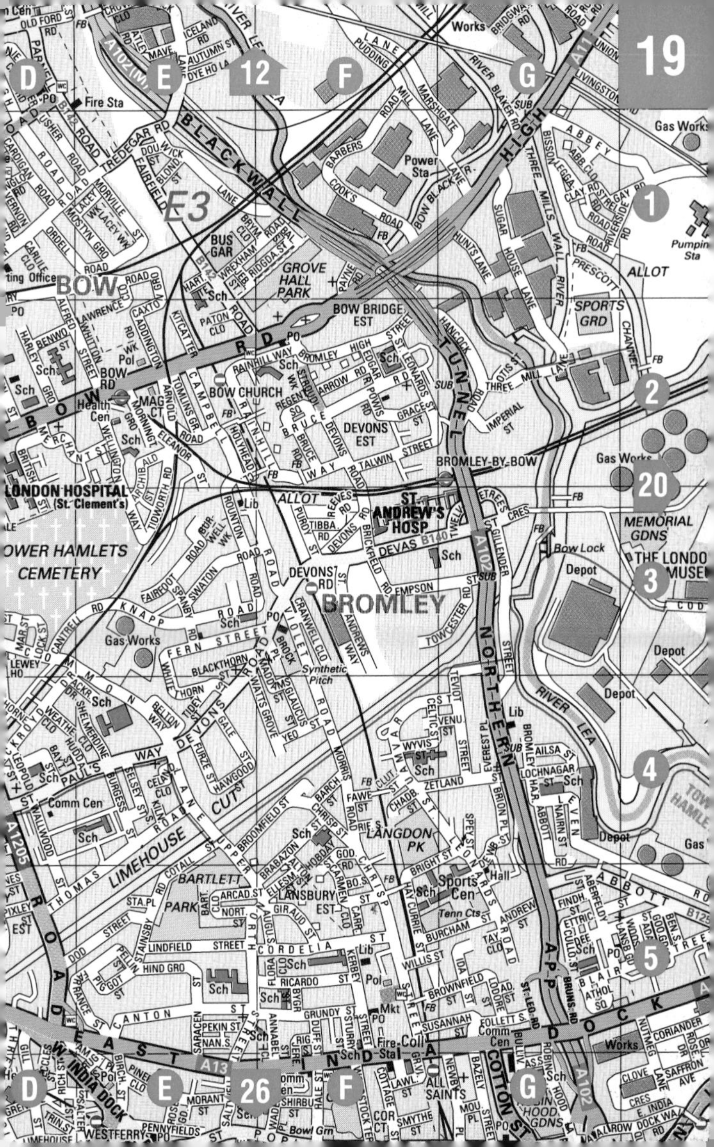

12
20
26
D
E
F
G
1
2
3
4
5
E3
BOW
BROMLEY
BLACKWALL
TUNNEL
NORTHERN
APP
HIGH
EAST INDIA DOCK RD
LIMEHOUSE CUT
BOW RD
DEVONS RD
DEVONS WAY
A102(M)
A102
A11
A13
A1205
B140
B142
GROVE HALL PARK
BOW BRIDGE EST
BOW CHURCH
DEVONS EST
BROMLEY-BY-BOW
ST. ANDREW'S HOSP
LONDON HOSPITAL (St. Clement's)
TOWER HAMLETS CEMETERY
BARTLETT PARK
LANSBURY EST
LANGDON PK
ALL SAINTS
ROBIN HOOD GDNS
MEMORIAL GDNS
THE LONDON MUSEUM
RIVER LEA
Bow Lock
Power Sta
Gas Works
Depot
Works
Pumping Sta
SPORTS GRD
ALLOT
BUS GAR
Fire Sta
Health Cen
Sports Cen
Tenn Cts
Synthetic Pitch
Comm Cen
Mkt
Fire Coll
Bowl Grn
THREE MILL LANE
SUGAR HOUSE LANE
THREE MILLS WALL RIVER
PRESCOTT CHANNEL
MARSHGATE LANE
PUDDING MILL LANE
COOK'S ROAD
BARBERS ROAD
HUNTS LANE
ABBEY RD
RIVERSIDE RD
IMPERIAL ST
HANCOCK ROAD
ST. LEONARDS ST
TALWIN STREET
REGENT SQ
BRUCE ROAD
RAINHILL WAY
CAMPBELL ROAD
KNAPP ROAD
FERN STREET
DEVAS ST
EMPSON ST
TOWCESTER RD
GILLENDER ST
VIOLET ROAD
CRANWELL CLO
ANDREWS WAY
BROMLEY HIGH ST
DEVONS RD
ZETLAND
CHRISP ST
CORDELIA ST
RICARDO ST
CANTON ST
LINDFIELD STREET
DOD STREET
THOMAS ST
ABBOTT RD
BRUNSWICK RD
BRUNS. RD
COTTON ST
WESTFERRY RD
PENNYFIELDS
WEST INDIA DOCK RD
LIMEHOUSE
DOCK
NORTH ST
SUSANNAH ST
BROWNFIELD ST
WILLIS ST
BURCHAM ST
ANDREW ST
WYVIS ST
LOCHNAGAR ST
AILSA ST
ABBOTT RD
FINDH. ST
ABERFELDY ST
BLAIR ST
ATHOL SQ
NUTMEG
CORIANDER
SAFFRON AVE
CLOVE CRES
TREDEGAR RD
FAIRFIELD
MORVILLE ST
LACEY WK
OLD FORD RD
TIDWORTH RD
WELLINGTON WAY
MERCHANT ST
BRITISH ST
ELEANOR ST
MORNING LA
ARNOLD RD
BLACKTHORN ST
WHITE HORN ST
BELTON WAY
FURZE ST
HAWGOOD ST
GALE ST
MORRIS ROAD
BROOMFIELD ST
UPPER NORTH ST
PAUL'S WAY
BURGESS ST
SELSEY ST
WALLWOOD ST

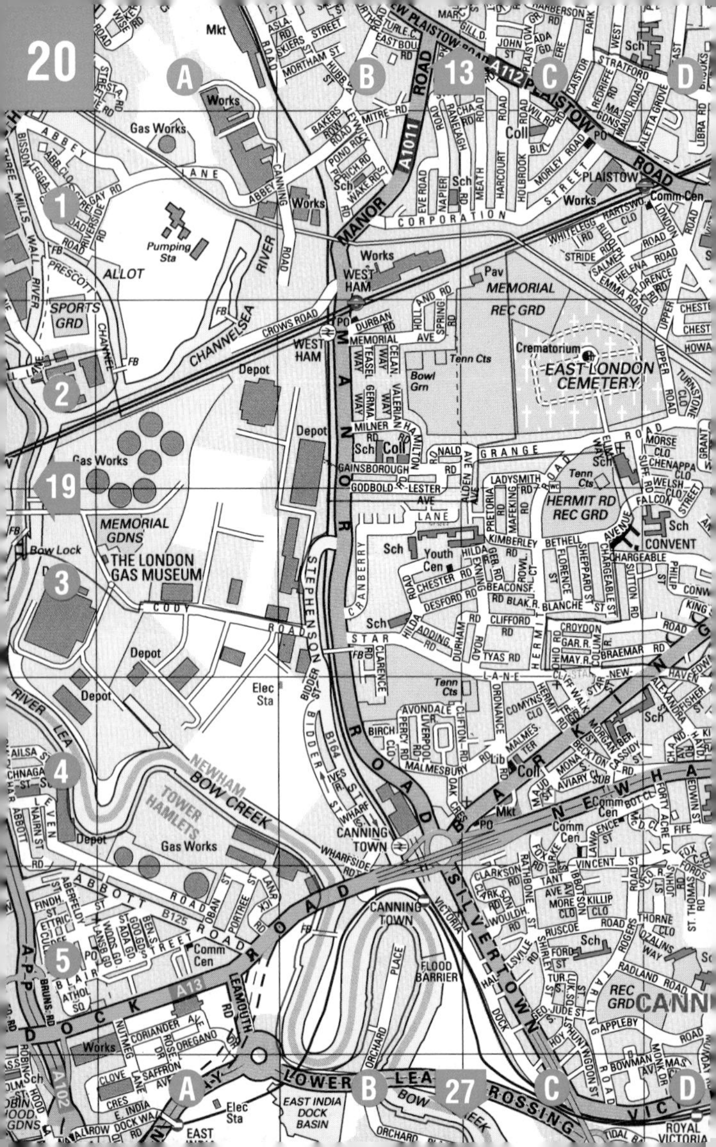
A
B
C
D
13
19
27
1
2
3
4
5
Mkt
Works
Gas Works
ABBEY LANE
Pumping Sta
ALLOT
SPORTS GRD
PRESCOTT
CHANNELSEA RIVER
CHANNELSEA
CROWS ROAD
MANOR ROAD
A1011
NEW PLAISTOW ROAD
PLAISTOW ROAD
A112
PLAISTOW
CORPORATION STREET
WEST HAM
MEMORIAL REC GRD
Crematorium
EAST LONDON CEMETERY
Tenn Cts
Bowl Grn
Pav
Depot
MEMORIAL GDNS
THE LONDON GAS MUSEUM
Bow Lock
CODY ROAD
STEPHENSON ST
GRANGE ROAD
HERMIT RD REC GRD
CONVENT
Youth Cen
STAR LANE
NEW BARN STREET
Elec Sta
RIVER LEA
NEWHAM
TOWER HAMLETS
BOW CREEK
ABBOTT ROAD
B125
B164
CANNING TOWN
BARKING ROAD
NEWHAM WAY
SILVERTOWN WAY
VICTORIA DOCK ROAD
FLOOD BARRIER
EAST INDIA DOCK ROAD
A13
A102
LOWER LEA CROSSING
EAST INDIA DOCK BASIN
ROYAL VICTORIA
REC GRD
CANN
Sch
Coll
Lib
Comm Cen
PO
FB

UPTON PARK
PRIORY PARK
E13
PLAISTOW
PLAISTOW HOSP
WEST HAM UTD FC
BALAAM ST REC GRD
NEWHAM GENERAL HOSPITAL
TERENCE MCMILLAN STADIUM
PLAYING FIELDS
NORTH BECKTON DISTRICT PARK
EAST HAM IND PK
CANNING TOWN REC GRD
CUSTOM HOUSE
KING GEORGE V PARK
Newham City Farm
ALLOTMENTS
ALLOT
TOWN
ROYAL ALBERT
CUSTOM HOUSE
PRINCE REGENT LANE
BARKING ROAD
A124
A112
A13
A1020
B167
NEWHAM WAY
PRINCE REGENT LANE
GREENGATE STREET
BOUNDARY ROAD
TOLLGATE ROAD
HUMBERSTONE ROAD
LONSDALE
HOLBORN
CHADWIN ROAD
ROYAL ROAD
BECKTON ROAD
KING GEORGE AVE
CENTRAL PARK ROAD
DOCK ROAD
D
E
F
G
1
2
3
4
5
13
21
27

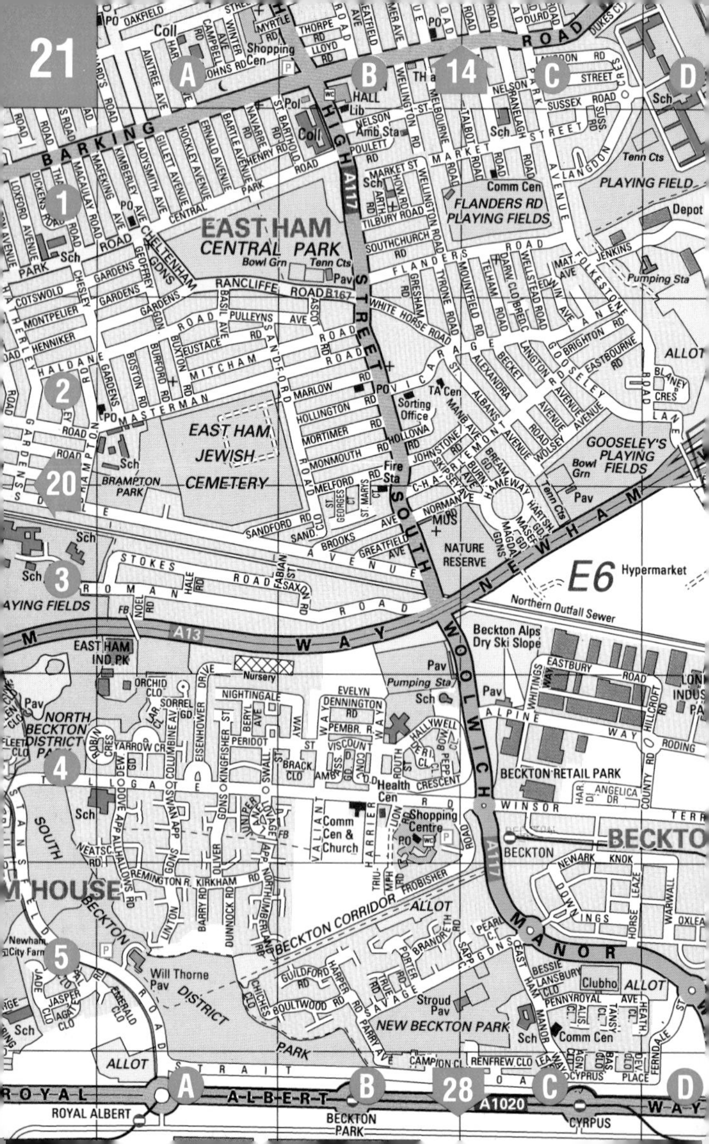

21
14
20
28
A
B
C
D
1
2
3
4
5
EAST HAM CENTRAL PARK
Bowl Grn
Tenn Cts
Pav
EAST HAM JEWISH CEMETERY
FLANDERS RD PLAYING FIELDS
Comm Cen
PLAYING FIELD
Tenn Cts
Depot
Pumping Sta
ALLOT
GOOSELEY'S PLAYING FIELDS
Bowl Grn
Tenn Cts
Pav
BRAMPTON PARK
NATURE RESERVE
MUS
E6
Hypermarket
Northern Outfall Sewer
Beckton Alps Dry Ski Slope
BECKTON RETAIL PARK
BECKTON
NORTH BECKTON DISTRICT PARK
EAST HAM IND PK
Nursery
Pumping Sta
Health Cen
Comm Cen & Church
Shopping Centre
Will Thorne Pav
BECKTON DISTRICT PARK
NEW BECKTON PARK
Stroud Pav
Clubho
Comm Cen
Newham City Farm
ALLOT
BARKING ROAD
HIGH STREET SOUTH
A117
A13
NEWHAM WAY
WOOLWICH MANOR WAY
ROYAL ALBERT WAY
A1020
BECKTON CORRIDOR
ROYAL ALBERT
BECKTON PARK
CYPRUS
Shopping Cen
TH
HALL
Lib
Coll
Amb Sta
Sorting Office
TA Cen
Fire Sta
Sch
PO
Pol
MARKET STREET
CENTRAL PARK ROAD
RANCLIFFE ROAD B167
WHITE HORSE ROAD
FLANDERS ROAD
POVICARAGE LANE
MASTERMAN ROAD
STOKES ROAD
ROMAN ROAD
TOLLGATE ROAD
WINSOR TERR
ALPINE WAY
EASTBURY ROAD
FOLKESTONE ROAD
LANGDON CRES
GOOSELEY LANE
HAMEWAY
SANDFORD RD
BROOKS AVE
GREATFIELD AVE

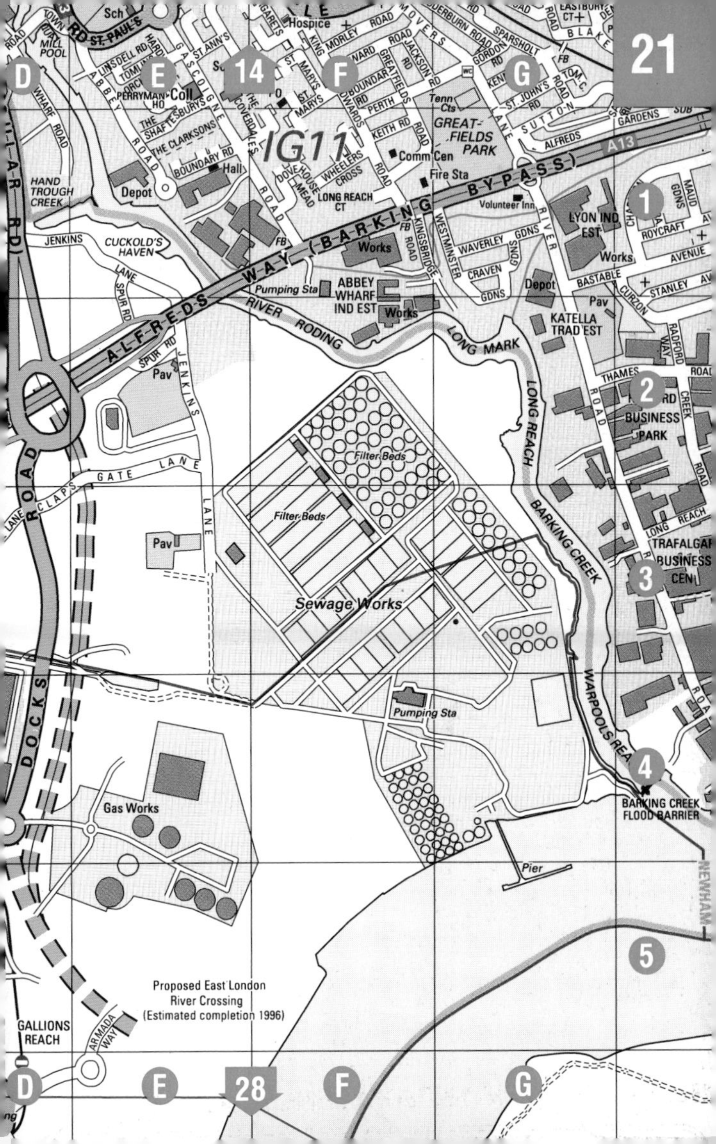
14
IG11
ALFREDS WAY (BARKING BYPASS)
A13
RIVER RODING
LONG MARK
LONG REACH
BARKING CREEK
WARPOOLS REACH
Sewage Works
Filter Beds
Gas Works
Pumping Sta
Pier
HAND TROUGH CREEK
CUCKOLD'S HAVEN
ABBEY WHARF IND EST
LYON IND EST
KATELLA TRAD EST
THAMES BUSINESS PARK
TRAFALGAR BUSINESS CEN
BARKING CREEK FLOOD BARRIER
GREATFIELDS PARK
NEWHAM
Proposed East London River Crossing (Estimated completion 1996)
GALLIONS REACH
DOCKS ROAD
CLAPS GATE LANE
JENKINS LANE
28

WORMWOOD SCRUBS
EAST ACTON
15
A
B
C
D
1
2
3
4
5
AVENUE
A40
WESTWAY
EAST ACTON
BROMYARD AVE SPORTS GRD
SPORTS GRD
ACTON PARK
GOVT BLDGS
WORMHOLT PARK
CLEVERLY ESTATE
W12
THE VALE
A4020
UXBRIDGE
ACTON PARK IND EST
ALLIED IND EST
Sewage Works
WENDELL PARK
BEDFORD PARK
Tennis Courts
Starch Green
GOLDHAWK
RAVENSCOURT PARK
ROYAL MASONIC HOSP
QUEEN CHARLOTTE'S HOSP
ACTON GREEN COMN
TURNHAM GREEN
STAMFORD BROOK
BUS DEPOT
CHISWICK COMN
A315
KING
CHISWICK HIGH RD
W4
CONVENT
29
A
B
C
D

NORTH KENSINGTON
NOTTING HILL
W11
SHEPHERD'S BUSH
W14
W6
HOLLAND PARK
HAMMERSMITH
15
23
29
D
E
F
G
1
2
3
4
5
A40(M)
A40
M41
A402
A219
A3220
A315
A4
BBC Offices
BBC TV Centre
WHITE CITY
Warehouse
Works
Depot
LRT DEPOT
WEST CROSS ROUTE
HAMMERSMITH PARK
LATIMER ROAD
Sports Cen
Comm Cen
AVONDALE PARK
HENRY DICKENS COURT
Indoor Tennis Club
SHEPHERD'S BUSH COMMON
SHEPHERD'S BUSH GRN
Shopping Cen
Hammersmith West London College
GOLDHAWK ROAD
HOLLAND ROAD
HOLLAND PARK AVENUE
KENSINGTON (OLYMPIA)
OLYMPIA
Post Office Savings Bank
BROOK GREEN
Queen's Head PH
LE PALAIS
CONVENT
Hammersmith & West London College
Novotel
HAMMERSMITH APOLLO
The Ark
LYRIC
BARONS COURT
TALGARTH ROAD
HAMMERSMITH ROAD
KING ST
WEST KENSINGTON
NORTH END HOUSE
Hilton Int
ICE HOUSE
LADBROKE GROVE

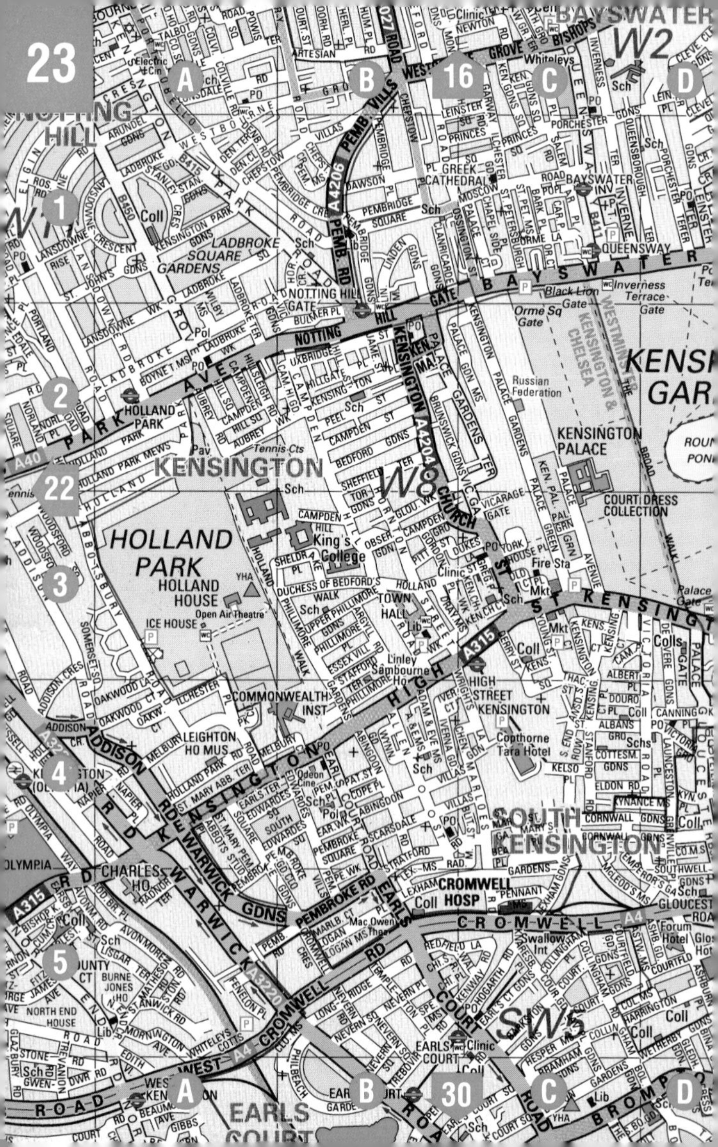

BAYSWATER
W2
NOTTING HILL
W11
KENSINGTON
W8
HOLLAND PARK
HOLLAND HOUSE
Open Air Theatre
ICE HOUSE
YHA
COMMONWEALTH INST
LEIGHTON HO MUS
KENSINGTON PALACE
COURT DRESS COLLECTION
KENSINGTON GAR
ROUND POND
Russian Federation
Black Lion Gate
Orme Sq Gate
Inverness Terrace Gate
Palace Gate
KENSINGTON & CHELSEA
WESTMINSTER
King's College
TOWN HALL
Linley Sambourne Ho
HIGH STREET KENSINGTON
Copthorne Tara Hotel
SOUTH KENSINGTON
CROMWELL HOSP
Swallow Int
Forum Hotel
SW5
EARLS COURT
WEST KENSINGTON
OLYMPIA
KENSINGTON (OLYMPIA)
NORTH END HOUSE
BURNE JONES HO
GREEK CATHEDRAL
BAYSWATER ROAD
NOTTING HILL GATE
HOLLAND PARK AVE
KENSINGTON HIGH ST
KENSINGTON CHURCH ST
CROMWELL ROAD
WARWICK RD
WARWICK GDNS
PEMBROKE RD
EARLS COURT RD
WEST CROMWELL RD
LADBROKE SQUARE GARDENS
LADBROKE GROVE
PEMBRIDGE VILLAS
QUEENSWAY
KENSINGTON PARK RD
CAMPDEN HILL
Tennis Cts
A40
A315
A4
A4204
A4206
A3220
B450
B415
B411
A
B
C
D
1
2
3
4
5
16
22
30

16
24
30
D
E
F
G
1
2
3
4
5
HYDE PARK
THE SERPENTINE
THE LONG WATER
BIRD SANCTUARY
Pol
COV RES
SPEAKER'S CORNER
MARBLE ARCH
Cumberland Hotel
CUMBERLAND GATE
Grosvenor House Hotel
Dorchester Hotel
Fountain
Bandstand
NORTH ROW
PARK LANE
A4202
A40
BAYSWATER ROAD
SUSSEX GARDENS
A4209
WESTBOURNE TER
LANCASTER TER
Royal Lancaster Hotel
LANCASTER GATE
Lancaster Gate
Victoria Gate
Marlborough Gate
The Fountains
BUDGE'S WALK
Monument
Peter Pan
Physical Energy Statue
LANCASTER WALK
SERPENTINE GALLERY
THE (NORTH CARRIAGE DRIVE) RING
NORTH RIDE
THE (WEST CARRIAGE DRIVE) RING
SERPENTINE ROAD
Pier
The Lido
Clubhouse
Weir
ROTTEN ROW
FLOWER WALK
Albert Memorial
Alexandra Gate
Bowling Grn
Tennis Cts
Coalbrookdale Gate
Prince of Wales Gate
Rutland Gate
NEW RIDE
Edinburgh Gate
Albert Gate
SOUTH CARRIAGE DRIVE
Barracks
HYDE PARK CORNER
WELLINGTON
KENSINGTON GORE
KNIGHTSBRIDGE
SW7
Royal Coll of Art
ROYAL ALBERT HALL
Roy. Geog. Soc.
EXHIBITION ROAD
PRINCE CONSORT ROAD
Royal College of Music
Imperial College
Queen's Tower
Lib
IMPERIAL COLLEGE RD
Goethe Institut
SCIENCE MUS
NAT. HISTORY MUS
GEOL. MUS
VICTORIA & ALBERT MUSEUM
BADEN-POWELL HO
CROMWELL ROAD
BROMPTON ROAD
BROMPTON
HARRODS
Fire Sta
SLOANE STREET
A3216
A4
BEAUCHAMP PL
ENNISMORE GDNS
RUTLAND GATE
MONTPELIER SQ
TREVOR SQ
LOWNDES SQUARE
CADOGAN PL
CHESHAM ST
Portugal
Denmark
Tenn Cts
SOUTH KENSINGTON
THURLOE SQ
ISMAILI CEN
PELHAM
SW3
SLOANE AVENUE
DRAYCOTT AV
WALTON ST
FULHAM ROAD
A3218
A3217
KING'S ROAD
SLOANE SQ
Duke of York's Headquarters
LOWER SLOANE ST
PIMLICO
ROYAL MARSDEN HOSP
ROYAL BROMPTON HOSP
SUTTON EST
Shopping Cen
SYDNEY ST
ONSLOW SQ
ONSLOW GDNS
CRANLEY GDNS

A
B
17
C
D
1
2
3
4
5
23
31
OXFORD CIRCUS
OXFORD
SOHO
WIGMORE ST
SELFRIDGES
BOND ST
Palladium
Sports Cen
MARBLE ARCH
W1
Sotheby's
HAMLEYS
Roosevelt Memorial
Canada
USA
Italy
Virgin Radio
Regent Palace Hotel
Trocadero
Grosvenor House Hotel
MAYFAIR
ROYAL ACAD. OF ARTS
PICCADILLY CIRCUS
N'Ireland Tourist Info Board
Dorchester Hotel
PARK LANE
A4202
Fountain
Bandstand
War Memorial
Achilles Statue
Hotel Inter-Continental
WELLINGTON MUS
Hilton Hotel
Japan
GREEN PARK
Christie's
ST. JAMES'S
MARLBOROUGH HOUSE
St. James's Palace
Clarence Ho
Lancaster House
Queen Victoria Memorial
ST. JAMES PARK
Albert Gate
HYDE PARK CORNER
Wellington Arch
CONSTITUTION HILL
BUCKINGHAM PALACE GARDENS
BUCKINGHAM PALACE
QUEEN'S GALLERY
THE ROYAL MEWS
GUARDS MUS
Wellington Barracks
HOME OFF
ST. JAMES PARK
CAXTON HALL
CITY HALL
KNIGHTSBRIDGE
Minema Cinema
BELGRAVE SQUARE
Portugal
Germany
Spain
Belgium
BELGRAVIA
WESTMINSTER
WESTMINSTER CATH
Victoria Palace Thea
Apollo Victoria Thea
BUS STA
VICTORIA
SW1
NEW RHS HALL
OLD RHS HALL
VICTORIA COACH STA
SLOANE SQ
Duke of York's Headquarters
GORDON HOSP
PIMLICO
Chelsea
A3216
A3217
A302
A3213
A4201
A4

D
E
17
F
G
STRAND
WC2
CHARING CROSS
Cleopatra's Needle
Charing Cross Pier
EMBANKMENT
Festival Pier
QUEEN ELIZABETH HALL
ROYAL FESTIVAL HALL
HUNGERFORD BRI
VICTORIA EMBANKMENT
HQS WELLINGTON
HMS PRESIDENT
The London Television Centre
National Theatre
MOMI
HAYWARD GALLERY
Oxo Tower
STAMFORD ST
Nautical Sch
WATERLOO
WATERLOO INTERNATIONAL
WATERLOO EAST
The Young Vic Theatre
Old Vic Theatre
BLACKFRIARS BRI
BLACKFRIARS ROAD
ROYAL COURTS OF JUSTICE
The Temple
Temple Bar
King's Coll
SOMERSET HO
Savoy Hotel
Strand Palace Hotel
ROYAL OPERA HO
Covent Gdn Mkt
LEICESTER SQ
NAT. GALL
PORT. GALL
TRAFALGAR SQ
Nelson's Col
ADMIRALTY ARCH
Horse Guards Parade
Guards Memorial
Banqueting House
PS. TATTERSHALL CASTLE
WHITEHALL
MOD
CABINET OFF
DOWNING ST
FOREIGN OFFICE
HM TREASURY
Cenotaph
Westminster Pier
WESTMINSTER
WESTMINSTER BRIDGE
A302
Old County Hall
Big Ben
HOUSES OF PARLIAMENT
FLORENCE NIGHTINGALE MUS
ST. THOMAS' HOSPITAL
A3036
Victoria Tower
Burghers of Calais Mon
ABBEY
Jewel Twr
St. Thomas' Medical School
LAMBETH PALACE GDNS
Lambeth Palace
Lambeth Pier
LAMBETH BRI
MILLBANK
THAMES HOUSE
MILLBANK TOWER
TATE GALLERY
Millbank Barracks
LAMBETH
LAMBETH NORTH
ST. GEORGE'S CATH
GER. MARY HARMSWORTH PARK
IMPERIAL WAR MUS
SPORTS GRD
KENNINGTON ROAD
SE11
A3204
Nat. Army & Air Force Inst. Depot
A201
A301
B300
PEABODY SQ
Day Hosp
Health Cen
25
1
2
3
4
5
31

A
B
C
D
18
EC4
ST. PAUL'S
Chapter Ho
ST. PAUL'S CATH
CHEAPSIDE
LOTHBURY
Bank of Eng
Stock Exch
City of London Club
THREADNEEDLE STREET
Royal Exch
CORNHILL
BANK
POULTRY
GRACECHURCH ST
A10
FENCHURCH
NEW BRI ST
LUDGATE HILL
Coll of Arms
QUEEN VICTORIA
MANSION HO
TELECOM. TECH. SHOW
Pool
Sal. Army HO
UPPER THAMES
CANNON ST
London Stone
MONUMENT
The Monument
BLACKFRIARS
Pier
HMS PRESIDENT
RIVER
THAMES
CITY
SOUTHWARK
Southwark Bridge Steps
Swan Lane Pier
LONDON BRI
KING WILL ST
Offices
Custom
1
2
3
4
5
Oxo Tower
BANKSIDE GALL
Shakespeare Globe Thea
Power Sta (Disused)
SHAKESPEARE GLOBE MUS
SCHOONER KATHLEEN & MAY
LONDON BRIDGE HOSP
City Pier
Hay's Galleria
Express Newspapers
SOUTHWARK
SOUTHWARK BRI
SOUTHWARK ST
ST. CHRISTOPHER HOUSE
CLINK MUS
CATH
LONDON BRIDGE
TOOLEY ST
BLACKFRIARS BRI
BLACKFRIARS ROAD
A201
A3200
Sports Cen
Coll
BRIT. LIB
UNION STREET
B300
24
The Young Vic
NELSON SQ
COPPERFIELD
Fire Sta & Mus
A300
BORROUGH HIGH ST
A3
GUY'S HOSPITAL
ST. THOMAS ST
SNOWSFIELDS
MARSHALSEA RD
THE BOROUGH
BOROUGH
LONG LANE
A2198
Sorting Office
A2
KIPLING EST
LEATHERMARKET STREET
Leather Mkt
TABARD GDN EST
TABARD GARDENS
GREAT DOVER STREET
PEABODY SQ
BOROUGH ROAD
ST. GEORGES CIR.
LONDON ROAD
BOROUGH HIGH ST
Uni
HOSP
INN. LON CROWN CT
NEWINGTON CAUSEWAY
NEWINGTON
ROCKINGHAM EST
Health Cen
BRIDGE RD
CATH
ST GEORGES ROAD
IMPERIAL WAR MUS
Coronet Centre
ELEPHANT & CASTLE
NEW KENT ROAD
A201
Bricklayer's Arms
COUNTY STREET
Shop Cen
NEWINGTON BUTTS
WALWORTH ROAD
SE17
KENNINGTON LANE
A3204
Nat. Army & Air Force Inst. Depot
KENNINGTON
32
WALWORTH
BROWNING EST
ALBERTA EST
TAPLOW

18
26
32
D
E
F
G
1
2
3
4
5
ALDGATE
TOWER HILL
THE TOWER
Tower Pier
HMS BELFAST
TOWER BRIDGE MUS & EXHIBITIONS
Tower Thistle Hotel
St. Katharine's Pier
World Trade Cen
ST. KATHARINE'S DOCK
PRESCOT ST
CABLE
B126
ROYAL MINT ST
ROYAL MINT CT
EAST SMITHFIELD
A1203
THE HIGHWAY
SHADWELL
Uni of Greenwich
CHAPMAN ST
Swimming Pool
News International
Tobacco Dock
WAPPING
Sports Cen
Wapping Dock Stairs
Wapping Old Stairs
Wapping New Stairs
THE UPPER POOL
LOWER POOL
DESIGN MUSEUM
TEA & COFFEE MUS
George's Stairs
Mill Stairs
East Lane Stairs
Cherry Garden Pier
Fountain Stairs
King's Stairs
Princes Stairs
KING'S STAIRS GDNS
A200
TOWER BRIDGE ROAD
A100
A2207
JAMAICA ROAD
DICKENS EST
ST. SAVIOUR'S EST
NECKINGER EST
BERMONDSEY
BERMONDSEY SPA
ABBEY STREET
GRANGE ROAD
TOWN HALL
VAUBAN EST
EVELINE LOWE EST
KIRBY EST
CHAUCER DAY HOSPITAL
SE16
Works
SOUTHWARK PARK ROAD
A2206
RAYMOUTH RD
A2208
MANOR EST
TRADING EST
RENNIE EST
LORRY PARK
Offices
STEVENSON CRES
SOUTH BERMONDSEY

A
B
C
D
19
COMMERCIAL
CABLE STREET
B126
SHADWELL
MARTINEAU EST
THE HIGHWAY
A1203
HORSEFERRY RD
NARROW ST
LIMEHOUSE
LIMEHOUSE BASIN
BRANCH RD
ROTHERHITHE TUNNEL APP
DAY HOSP
Health Cen
Fire Sta
Comm Cem
GLAMIS PLACE
JARDINE RD
Stone Stairs
Ratcliffe Cross Stairs
Pier
The Grapes PH
KING EDWARD MEML PARK
TOWER HAMLETS
SOUTHWARK
SHADWELL BASIN
NEWLANDS QUAY
SHADWELL
WAPPING WALL
Prospect of Whitby PH
New Crane Stairs
WAPPING
Wapping Dock Stairs
ROTHERHITHE TUNNEL
Lavender Wharf
Limehouse Hole Stairs
Sunderland Wharf
ROTHERHITHE
HERITAGE MUS
SPORTS GRD
SALTER ROAD
B205
Fisher Athletic FC
SMITH CLOSE
SURREY WATER
ECOLOGICAL PARK
STAVE HILL
RUSSIA DOCK WOODLAND
Surrey Docks Farm
ROTHERHITHE
Health Cen
BRUNEL ROAD
ALBION EST
QUEBEC WAY
CANADA EST
CANADA WATER
Mail Newspapers Printing Wks
CANADA YARD SOUTH
REDRIFF ROAD
REDRIFF EST
NORWAY DOCK
FINLAND QUAY
GREENLAND DOCK
SOUTH DOCK
KING'S Stairs
Princes Stairs
POOL
25
1
2
3
4
5
KIRBY EST
CHAUCER DAY HOSPITAL
LOWER ROAD
A200
Sports Cen
SE16
Surrey Quays Shopping Centre
SURREY QUAYS
SOUTHWARK PARK
Lido
GALLERY
HAWKSTONE ROAD
PLOUGH WAY
Sports Centre
EVELYN STREET
RAYMOUTH RD
NEW ROAD
A2208
TRADING EST
RENNIE EST
BERMONDSEY
BESTWOOD STREET
CROFTERS COURT
Youth Cen
DEPTFORD
33

D
E
19
F
G
EAST INDIA DOCK RD
A13
A102
WEST INDIA DOCK RD
WESTFERRY
LIMEHOUSE CAUSEWAY
POPLAR HIGH STREET
B123
ASPEN WAY
E14
POPLAR
WEST INDIA QUAY
Billingsgate Mkt
NORTH SECTION
WEST
CABOT NORTH COLONNADE
SOUTH COLONNADE
CANARY WHARF
CHURCHILL PLACE
CART. CIR.
BLACKWALL BASIN
POPLAR DOCK
MIDDLE SECTION
INDIA
HERON QUAYS
ISLE
Britannia Grand Hotel
MAIN SECTION
DOCKS
Cannon Workshops
Westferry Circus
Pier
West India Dock Pier
Shopping Centre
SOUTH QUAY
MERIDIAN GATE
WALL
MARSH
WESTFERRY ROAD
PRESTONS ROAD
MANCHESTER RD
A1206
BLACKWALL TUNNEL
27
Pumping Sta
Delta Wharf
LONDON ARENA
OF
CUBITT TOWN
CROSSHARBOUR
MILLHARBOUR
LIMEHARBOUR
Printing Works
Swim Pool
Docklands Sailing Centre
MILLWALL OUTER DOCK
MILLWALL
Superstore
MUDCHUTE
Mudchute Farm
PARK
DOGS
ALLOT
SPINDRIFT AVENUE
EAST FERRY ROAD
MUDCHUTE
MILLWALL PARK
TOWER HAMLETS
LEWISHAM
Landing Stage
33
ISLAND GARDENS
SAUNDERS NESS RD
Sports Cen
Fire Sta
1
2
3
4
5

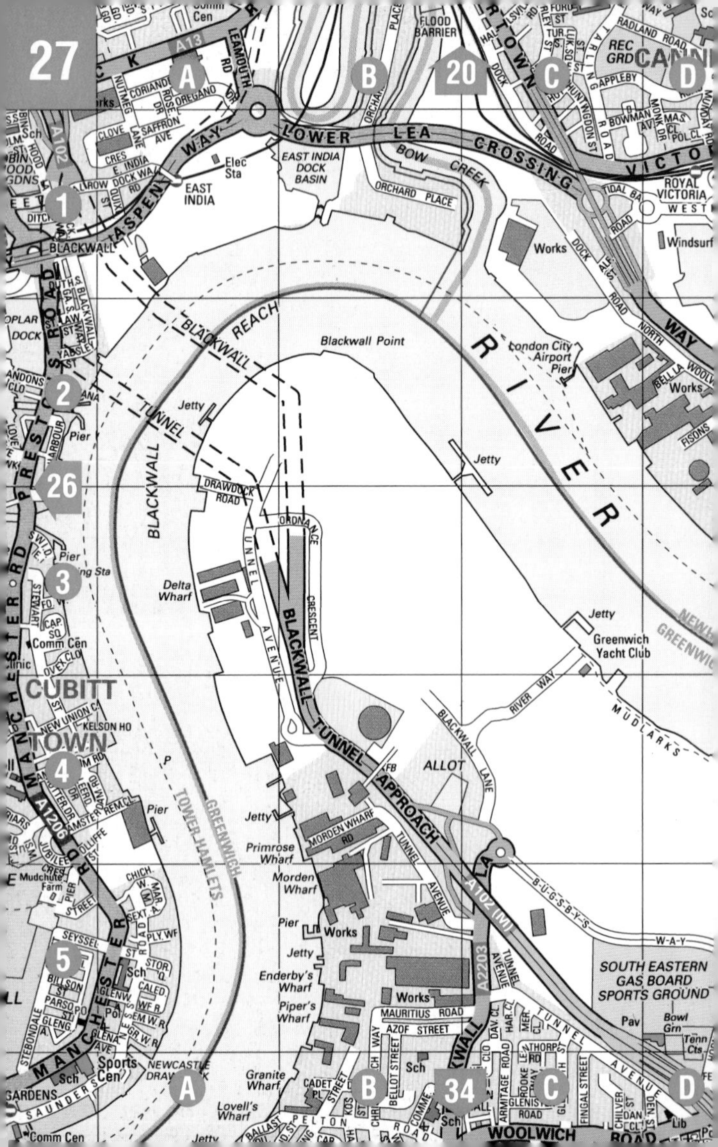
A
B
C
D
1
2
3
4
5
20
26
34
FLOOD BARRIER
LOWER LEA CROSSING
EAST INDIA DOCK BASIN
EAST INDIA
Elec Sta
BOW CREEK
ORCHARD PLACE
ASPEN WAY
BLACKWALL
LEAMOUTH RD
CORIANDER
OREGANO
NUTMEG
ROSEMARY DR
SAFFRON AVE
CLOVE CRES
E. INDIA DOCK RD
A13
A102
ROYAL VICTORIA
RADLAND ROAD
REC GRD
APPLEBY
BOWMAN AV
MONK DR
TIDAL BASIN ROAD
Windsurf
Works
DOCK ROAD
NORTH WOOLWICH ROAD
London City Airport Pier
RIVER
BLACKWALL REACH
BLACKWALL TUNNEL
Blackwall Point
Jetty
DRAWDOCK ROAD
ORDNANCE CRESCENT
TUNNEL AVENUE
BLACKWALL TUNNEL APPROACH
Delta Wharf
Greenwich Yacht Club
RIVER WAY
MUDLARKS
BLACKWALL LANE
ALLOT
FB
BUGSBYS WAY
A102 (M)
A2203
MORDEN WHARF RD
Primrose Wharf
Morden Wharf
Pier
Enderby's Wharf
Piper's Wharf
Granite Wharf
Lovell's Wharf
MAURITIUS ROAD
AZOF STREET
BELLOT STREET
Sch
CADET PL
PELTON ROAD
WOOLWICH ROAD
ARMITAGE ROAD
FINGAL STREET
GLENISTER ROAD
TUNNEL AVENUE
SOUTH EASTERN GAS BOARD SPORTS GROUND
Pav
Bowl Grn
Tenn Cts
Lib
PRESTONS ROAD
POPLAR DOCK
Pier
CUBITT TOWN
Comm Cen
KELSON HO
NEW UNION CL
MANCHESTER RD
MANCHESTER
A1206
Mudchute Farm
PIER STREET
SEYSSEL ST
BILLSON ST
Sch
Sports Cen
NEWCASTLE DRAW DOCK
SAUNDERS
GARDENS
Comm Cen
TOWER HAMLETS
GREENWICH

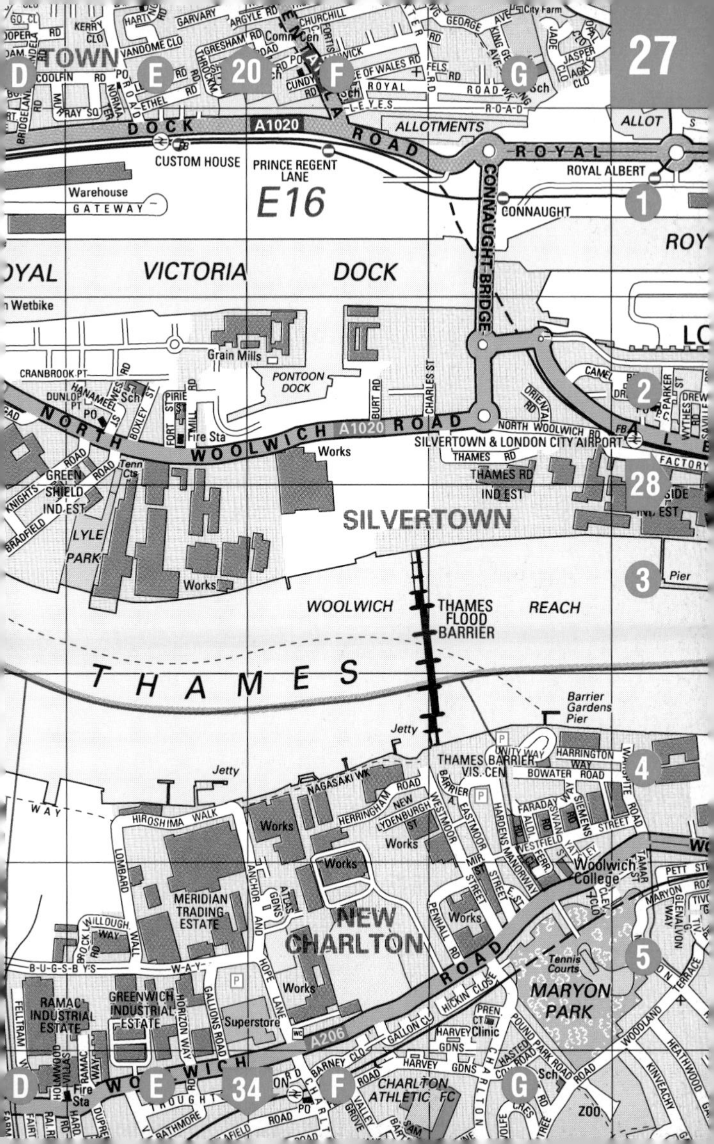

D
E
20
F
G
TOWN
KERRY CLO
GARVARY RD
ARGYLE RD
CHURCHILL
GEORGE AVE
City Farm
VANDOME CLO
GRESHAM RD
Comm Cen
JADE CLO
JASPER
AGATE CLO
COOLFIN RD
MURRAY SQ
ETHEL RD
CUNDY RD
PRINCE OF WALES RD
FELS RD
ROYAL ROAD
ROAD WK
L-E-Y-E-S
R-O-A-D
Sch
DOCK
A1020
ROAD
ALLOTMENTS
ALLOT
R-O-Y-A-L
CUSTOM HOUSE
PRINCE REGENT LANE
ROYAL ALBERT
Warehouse
GATEWAY
E16
CONNAUGHT
CONNAUGHT BRIDGE
1
ROYAL
VICTORIA
DOCK
Wetbike
Grain Mills
PONTOON DOCK
CRANBROOK PT
HANAMEEL ST
DUNLOP PT
PO
Sch
BOXLEY ST
PIRIE ST
MILL RD
FORT ST
BURT RD
CHARLES ST
Fire Sta
CAMEL
ORIENTAL RD
PARKER ST
WYTHES
DREW
2
NORTH WOOLWICH ROAD
A1020
NORTH WOOLWICH RD
SILVERTOWN & LONDON CITY AIRPORT
THAMES RD
THAMES RD IND EST
FACTORY
28
Works
GREEN SHIELD IND EST
Tenn Cts
KNIGHTS ROAD
BRADFIELD
LYLE PARK
SILVERTOWN
3
Pier
Works
WOOLWICH
REACH
THAMES FLOOD BARRIER
THAMES
Barrier Gardens Pier
Jetty
UNITY WAY
HARRINGTON WAY
THAMES BARRIER VIS. CEN
BOWATER ROAD
4
NAGASAKI WK
HERRINGHAM ROAD
NEW LYDENBURGH ST
BARRIER
WESTMOOR
EASTMOOR
HARDENS MANORWAY
FARADAY WAY
SIEMENS RD
STREET
WESTFIELD
WOOLWICH ROAD
WAY
HIROSHIMA WALK
Works
LOMBARD WALL
MERIDIAN TRADING ESTATE
ANCHOR AND HOPE LANE
ATLAS GDNS
NEW CHARLTON
MIR ST
PENHALL RD
Woolwich College
TAMAR ST
PETT ST
MARYON
GLENALVON WAY
5
Tennis Courts
MARYON PARK
TERRACE
WILLOUGHBY WAY
B-U-G-S-B-Y-S
W-A-Y
RAMAC INDUSTRIAL ESTATE
GREENWICH INDUSTRIAL ESTATE
HORIZON WAY
GALLIONS ROAD
Superstore
A206
HICKIN CLOSE
GALLON CL
PREN. CT
Clinic
HARVEY GDNS
POUND PARK ROAD
WOODLAND
HEATHWOOD
KINVEACHY
FELLTRAM
HOLMWOOD VILLAS
RAMAC WAY
Fire Sta
D
E
34
F
G
BARNEY CLO
CHARLTON ATHLETIC FC
HARVEY GDNS
VALLEY GROVE
Sch
ZOO
WOOLWICH
TROUGHTON
BATHMORE
ROAD
PO
CHARLTON

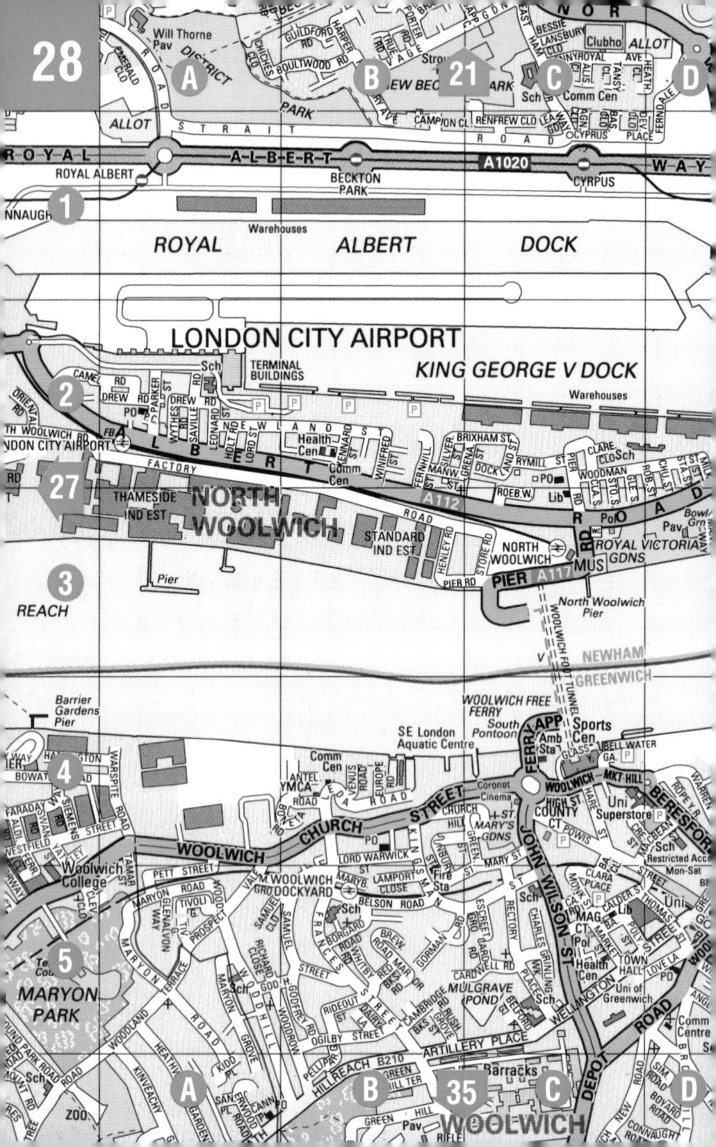
Will Thorne Pav
DISTRICT
PARK
ALLOT
GUILDFORD RD
HARPER
PORTER
BOULTWOOD RD
Strou
21
NEW BEC
ARK
Sch
Comm Cen
Clubho
ALLOT
BESSIE LANSBURY CLO
ROYAL AVE
TANSY CL
HEATH CL
FERNDALE
CAMPION CL
RENFREW CLO
CYPRUS
PLACE
STRAIT ROAD
ROYAL ALBERT WAY
A1020
ROYAL ALBERT
BECKTON PARK
CYPRUS
Warehouses
ROYAL ALBERT DOCK
LONDON CITY AIRPORT
KING GEORGE V DOCK
TERMINAL BUILDINGS
Warehouses
Sch
CAMEL RD
DREW RD
PARKER ST
WYTHES RD
SAVILLE RD
LEONARD ST
HOLT RD
LORD ST
NEWLAND ST
Health Cen
KENNARD ST
WINIFRED ST
Comm Cen
FERNHILL ST
MANW. ST
SILVER.
GRENA.
BRIXHAM ST
DOCKLAND ST
RYMILL ST
PIER RD
CLARE. CLO
Sch
WOODMAN
PO
Lib
ROEB.W.
ALBERT ROAD
A112
ORIENTAL RD
LONDON CITY AIRPORT
FACTORY ROAD
27
THAMESIDE IND EST
NORTH WOOLWICH
STANDARD IND EST
HENLEY RD
STORE RD
NORTH WOOLWICH
MUS
ROYAL VICTORIA GDNS
Bowl Grn
Pav
Pier
PIER RD
PIER A117
North Woolwich Pier
REACH
NEWHAM
GREENWICH
WOOLWICH FOOT TUNNEL
WOOLWICH FREE FERRY
South Pontoon
Barrier Gardens Pier
SE London Aquatic Centre
FERRY APP
Amb Sta
Sports Cen
BELL WATER GA
Comm Cen
YMCA
ANTEL. RD
VENUS RD
EUROPE RD
LEDA ROAD
BONETA RD
HARRINGTON WAY
BOWATER RD
WARSPITE ROAD
FARADAY WAY
SIEMENS RD
STREET
WESTFIELD ST
WOOLWICH CHURCH STREET
Coronet Cinema
CHURCH HILL
ST. MARY'S GDNS
WOOLWICH HIGH ST.
COUNTY CT
MKT HILL
Uni
Superstore
BERESFORD
POWIS ST
HARE ST
Sch
Restricted Access Mon-Sat
PO
LORD WARWICK ST
KINGSMAN ST
MARY ST
JOHN WILSON ST
Woolwich College
TAMAR ST
PETT STREET
MARYON ROAD
TIVOLI G.
PROSPECT
VALE
M. WOOLWICH DOCKYARD
LAMPORT CLOSE
BELSON ROAD
Fire Sta
Sch
RECTORY
CHARLES GRINLING WK
CLARA PLACE
CALDER ST
THOMAS ST
MAG CT
Lib
Pol
MARKET
POLYTECHNIC STREET
Health Cen
TOWN HALL
LOVE LA
Uni of Greenwich
WELLINGTON
MARYON PARK
MARYON TERRACE
SAMUEL CLO
SAMUEL ST
FRANCES ST
BORGARD ROAD
BREW. ROAD
GORMAN RD
ESCREET GRO
CARDWELL RD
MULGRAVE POND
BELFORD GR.
Sch
DEPOT ROAD
Comm Centre
GROVE
WOODHILL
RICHARD CLOSE
GODFREY RD
WOODROW
RIDEOUT ST
DAIRY LA
OGILBY STREET
CAMBRIDGE BKS RD
RUSH GROVE ST
ARTILLERY PLACE
Barracks
HILLREACH B210
GREEN HILL TER
35
WOOLWICH
GREEN HILL
Pav
RIFLE
WOODLAND TERRACE
HEATHWOOD
KINVEACHY
KIDD PL
SANDERWOOD PL
ROAD
NEW ROAD
CONNAUGHT
BOYARD ROAD
SIM. ROAD
Sch
POUND PARK ROAD
MOUNT RD
ZOO
A
B
C
D
1
2
3
4
5

Proposed East London River Crossing
21
D
E
F
G
1
2
3
4
5
GALLIONS REACH
ARMADA WAY
GALLIONS ROAD
ALBERT BASIN
Pier
Pier
Gallions Point
GALLIONS REACH
SE28
WAREPOINT DRIVE
MERBURY RD
BATTERY ROAD
GOLDFINCH RD
A2016
WESTERN WAY
HM PRISON BELMARSH
Works
NUTHATCH GARDENS
HARR.
CAMELOT CL
TEMPLE CL
PIER WAY
CARROL PLACE
WHINCHAT ROAD
WIG. PATH
WREN PATH
AVOCET MS
GOLDFINCH ROAD
THAMESMEAD WEST
GOOSANDER WAY
BROADWATER GREEN
Sch
Tenn Cts
BROADWATER
PETTMAN CRES
KELLNER WAY
BOUGHTON RD
Southern Outfall Sewer
HADDEN ROAD
GRIFFIN MANOR WAY
Works
TOM CRIBB ROAD
BUS GARAGE
NATHAN WAY
NORTH ROAD
PLUMSTEAD ROAD
A206
Woolwich Coll of Furth. Ed.
Mkt
Coll
JESSUP CLO
MAXEY ROAD
VILLAS ROAD
POLTHORNE GRO
LENTON ST
PLUMSTEAD
PARRY PL
SPRAY STREET
BURRAGE GRO
WALKER CLO
WOOLWICH ARSENAL
WALMER TERRACE
MARMADON ROAD
REIDHAVEN RD
HART ROAD
GAVIN ST
HEVER
GUNN. ST
HARTVILLE ROAD
PLUMSTEAD HIGH ST
BURRAGE ROAD
RICHMOND PLACE
INVERMORE PLACE
ARTHUR GROVE
TROY CT
RUDD CLOSE
DAWSON CLOSE
GLYNDON ROAD
SOUTHPORT ROAD
Schs
STREET
RISE
STREET
ROAD
EARL
ELMLEY
KENTMER RD
BARTH RD
BANNOCKBURN RD
BENARES
CERES
Sch
Fire Sta
MINERAL STREET
HECTOR
BEB. RD
GALLOSS ROAD
Sch
TEWSON ROAD
CONWAY ROAD
COXWELL RD
INGLEDEW RD
LIFFLER ROAD
MIRIAM ROAD
ORISSA RD
Sch
SANDBACH PLACE
Comm Cen
RAGLAN ROAD
CLAYMILL HOUSE
HUDSON PLACE
35
Schs
BREWERY ROAD
PO
MAJENDIE ROAD
STRANDFIELD CLO
DRAWELL CLO
Health Centre
Pol
Lib
MUS
Sports Cen
ESPERANZA ST
KASHGAR
PLACE
PLUMSTEAD

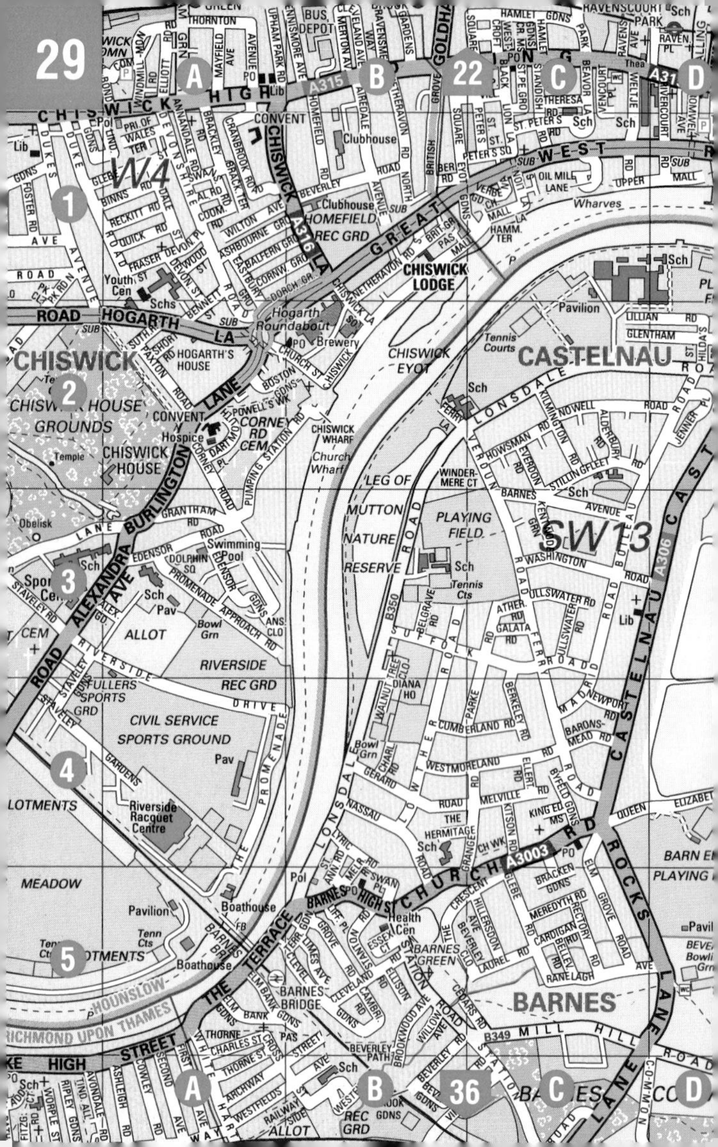
29
22
36
A
B
C
D
1
2
3
4
5
W4
SW13
CHISWICK
CASTELNAU
BARNES
CHISWICK HIGH RD
A315
A316
A306
A3003
A31
B350
B349
GREAT WEST RD
HOGARTH LA
Hogarth Roundabout
BURLINGTON LANE
ALEXANDRA AVE
CHISWICK HOUSE GROUNDS
CHISWICK HOUSE
Temple
Obelisk
HOGARTH'S HOUSE
Brewery
CHISWICK LODGE
CHISWICK EYOT
CORNEY RD CEM
CHISWICK WHARF
Church Wharf
HOMEFIELD REC GRD
Clubhouse
CONVENT
Hospice
Youth Cen
Schs
Sch
Swimming Pool
Bowl Grn
ALLOT
RIVERSIDE REC GRD
RIVERSIDE DRIVE
FULLERS SPORTS GRD
CIVIL SERVICE SPORTS GROUND
Pav
Riverside Racquet Centre
MEADOW
Pavilion
Tenn Cts
Boathouse
LEG OF MUTTON NATURE RESERVE
PLAYING FIELD
Tennis Courts
LONSDALE RD
CASTELNAU
ROCKS LANE
CHURCH RD
BARNES HIGH ST
THE TERRACE
BARNES BRIDGE
BARNES GREEN
Health Cen
MILL HILL RD
HOUNSLOW
RICHMOND UPON THAMES
HIGH STREET
Wharves
OIL MILL LANE
UPPER MALL
HAMM. TER
RAVENSCOURT PARK
BUS DEPOT
STATION RD

D
E
22
F
G
1
2
30
3
4
5
36
HAMMERSMITH
HAMMERSMITH CEMETERY
THE QUEEN'S CLUB
Holborn Coll
CHARING CROSS HOSP
FRANK BANFIELD PARK
RIVERSIDE STUDIOS
Works
Warehouse
Filter Beds
Wharves
RICHMOND UPON THAMES
HAMMERSMITH & FULHAM
Blakes Wharves
Eternit Wharf
Stevenage Wharves
Sports Cen
QUEEN ELIZABETH WALK
Pavilions
Tennis Cts
Boathouse
BARN ELMS SCHOOLS SPORTS CENTRE
PUTNEY
Bowling Green
PUTNEY HOSP
PUTNEY CEM
LOWER
FULHAM
FULHAM CEM
LILLIE RD REC GRD
ROBERT OWEN HO
FULHAM FOOTBALL CLUB
ALLOTMENTS
Fulham Palace
FULHAM PALACE GDNS
BISHOP'S PARK
Open Air Theatre
Bowl Grns
MUS
RIVER
PUTNEY BRIDGE
HURLINGHAM COURT
ARTHUR HENDERSON HO
NORMAND PARK
HAMMERSMITH FLYOVER
TALGARTH ROAD
HAMMERSMITH BRI. RD
FULHAM PALACE ROAD
LILLIE ROAD
DAWES RD
FULHAM RD
FULHAM HIGH ST
NEW KING'S RD
HAMMERSMITH RD
BARONS COURT
WEST KENSINGTON
A4
A219
A3218
B306
Novotel
LYRIC ART GALL
Shopping Cen
Fire Sta
HAMMERSMITH APOLLO
The Ark
CONVENT
Hammersmith & West London College
NORTH END HOUSE
London Globe PH
Offices
Clinic
Comm Cen
Sch
PO
Lib
BARN ELMS WATER WORKS (DISUSED)

EARLS COURT
EARLS COURT EXHIBITION CENTRE
WEST BROMPTON
BROMPTON CEMETERY
KENSINGTON & CHELSEA
STAMFORD BRIDGE CHELSEA FC
SAMUEL LEWIS TRUST DWS
FULHAM BROADWAY
WALHAM GREEN
EEL BROOK COMMON
PARSONS GREEN
SANDS END
SW6
SOUTH PARK
HURLINGHAM PARK
HURLINGHAM CLUB GDNS
PUTNEY BRIDGE
Gas Works
CROMWELL ROAD
WEST CROMWELL ROAD
OLD BROMPTON ROAD
REDCLIFFE GARDENS
FINBOROUGH ROAD
LILLIE ROAD
NORTH END ROAD
FULHAM ROAD
FUL. BROADWAY
MUNSTER ROAD
DAWES ROAD
KINGS ROAD
NEW KINGS ROAD
WANDSWORTH BRIDGE ROAD
FULHAM HIGH ST
HURLINGHAM ROAD
A4
A3220
A3218
A3219
A304
A308
A217
23
29
37
A
B
C
D
1
2
3
4
5

SW3
23
ROYAL MARSDEN HOSP
ROYAL BROMPTON HOSP
Duke of York's Headquarters
FULHAM ROAD
KING'S ROAD
King's College
TOWN HALL
Sports Cen
Clinic
Shopping Cen
BURTON'S CT
ROYAL HOSP MUS
ROYAL HOSPITAL CHELSEA
NAT ARMY MUS
CHELSEA PHYSIC GDN
Carlyle's House
Cheyne Cen
CHELSEA
Old Man Theatre
BURIAL GRD
CHEYNE WALK
CHELSEA EMBANKMENT
CHELSEA REACH
Cadogan Pier
Peace Pagoda
31
WATERSIDE POINT
Festival Pleasure Gardens
FOUNTAIN LAKE
ZOO
BATTERSEA PARK
REC GRD
Bowling Grn
ALBERT BRIDGE
BATTERSEA BRIDGE
BATTERSEA BRIDGE ROAD
WORLD'S END EST
CREMORNE RD
Chelsea Wharf
Chelsea Creek
Go-Karting
DOCK
SOMERSET EST
SURREY LANE EST
PRINCE OF WALES DRIVE
Chelsea Harbour
Bascule Bri
Wharves
Royal Acad. of Dancing
Regent Wharf
BATTERSEA REACH
Lensbury Wharf
Shell Wharf
LONDON WESTLAND HELIPORT
Sch
Coll
Health Cen
Bridge La Thea
CASTLEMAINE TOWER
Comm Cen
Sports Cen
PARK ROAD
SHEEPCOTE LANE
LATCHMERE ROAD
BATTERSEA PARK ROAD
FALCON ROAD
FALCON PARK
OPEN SPACE
SW11
Warehouse
Lib
Fire Sta
37
D
E
F
G
1
2
3
4
5

VICTORIA COACH STA
BELGRAVE RD
GORDON HOSP
PIMLICO
PIMLICO RD
CHELSEA BRIDGE ROAD
Chelsea Barracks
ROYAL HOSP MUS
RANELAGH GARDENS
ROYAL HOSPITAL CHELSEA
NAT ARMY MUS
LISTER HOSP
EBURY BRIDGE EST
CHURCHILL GARDENS ESTATE
DOLPHIN SQUARE
GROSVENOR ROAD
A3212
EMBANKMENT
RIVER THAMES
KENSINGTON & CHELSEA
WANDSWORTH
CHELSEA REACH
CHELSEA BRI
GROSVENOR BRIDGE
Works
Jetty
Battersea Power Station (Disused)
NINE ELMS LANE
A3205
New Covent Garden Sorting Office
New Covent Garden Market
CARRIAGE DRIVE NORTH
Festival Pleasure Gardens
ZOO
Tenn Cts
RUNNING TRACK
CARRIAGE DRIVE EAST
BATTERSEA PARK
Bowling Grn
BOATING LAKE
REC GRD
SOUTH DRIVE
QUEENSTOWN RD
A3216
The Observer
Gas Works
Battersea Dogs Home
BATTERSEA PARK ROAD
PRINCE OF WALES DR
BATTERSEA PARK
SAVONA EST
SW8
PATMORE EST
Vauxhall LORRY PARK
Battersea City Farm
Westmin Coll
QUEENSTOWN RD (BATTERSEA)
BR DEPOT
BATTERSEA
HEATHBROOK PARK
WANDSWORTH ROAD
SW11
24
30
38
A B C D
1 2 3 4 5

24
32
38
D
E
F
G
1
2
3
4
5
SE11
SW9
MILLBANK TOWER
TATE GALLERY
Millbank Barracks
VAUXHALL BRI RD
VAUXHALL
VAUXHALL Mkt
ALBERT EMB
SPRING GDNS
KENNINGTON LA
HARLEYFORD RD
KENNINGTON OVAL
THE OVAL SURREY CC GRD
KENNINGTON
KENNINGTON RD
KENNINGTON PARK
KENNINGTON PARK PL
CAMBERWELL NEW RD
Nat. Army & Air Force Inst. Depot
COUNTY CT
CLEAVER SQUARE
Gas Works
VAUXHALL PARK
Oval House Theatre
FENTIMAN ROAD
CLAPHAM ROAD
A3
A23
A203
A3204
B301
OVAL
Lido
REC GRD
Tennis Courts
PARRY ST
SOUTH LAMBETH RD
SOUTH LAMBETH
Superstore
Health Cen
Comm Cen
Sports Cen
Vauxhall College
LANSDOWNE WAY
BUS GARAGE
STUDLEY ESTATE
LARKHALL PARK
STOCKWELL
STOCKWELL RD
STOCKWELL GDNS EST
STOCKWELL PK EST
STOCKWELL PARK CRES
SLADE GDNS
MOSTYN GDNS
MURSELL EST
Warehouse
MYATT'S FIELDS SOUTH EST
VASSALL RD
LOUGHBOROUGH RD
BRIXTON RD
Sorting Office
CONF CEN
YMCA
Activity Cen
CLAPHAM RD EST
Clinic

SE17
25
A
B
C
D
1
2
3
4
5
WALWORTH
KENNINGTON
KENNINGTON PARK
31
CAMBERWELL
SE5
39
Nat. Army & Air Force Inst. Depot
GUINNESS TRUST BLDGS
ALBERTA EST
BROWNING EST
Walworth City Farm
TA Cen
Sch
Lib
Health Cen
Coll
Pol
PO
Depot
TAPLOW
ELIZ. EST
WYNDHAM EST
ELMINGTON EST
RUST SQUARE
BRANDON EST
Tennis Courts
MYATT'S FIELDS
Tenn Cts
MOSTYN GDNS
MYATT'S FIELDS SOUTH EST
CRAWFORD EST
Sports Centre
Sports Cen
CATHEDRAL
BUS GAR
THE MAUDSLEY HOSPITAL
KING'S COLLEGE HOSPITAL
DENMARK HILL
Salvation Army College
RUSKIN PARK HO
RUSKIN
LOUGHBOROUGH JUNCTION
Comm Cen
Clinic
Hall
A3204
A3
A215
A202
A2217
B214
KENNINGTON PARK ROAD
NEWINGTON BUTTS
WALWORTH ROAD
CAMBERWELL ROAD
CAMBERWELL NEW ROAD
CAMBERWELL CHURCH ST
DENMARK HILL
COLDHARBOUR LANE
CHAMPION PK
CHAMPION GROVE
ALBANY ROAD
WYNDHAM ROAD
BETHWIN ROAD
RUSKIN STREET
CHURCH STREET
EAST STREET
PENTON PLACE
MANOR PLACE
OCCUPATION RD
PORTLAND STREET
THURLOW STREET
WELLS WAY
MEDLAR ST
CAMBERWELL STATION RD
DENMARK ROAD
CAMBERWELL GROVE
LOVE WK
DE CRESPIGNY PARK
LOUGHBOROUGH ROAD
AKERMAN ROAD
ELAM ST
FLAXMAN ROAD

D
E
F
G
25
33
39
1
2
3
4
5
PECKHAM
SE15
NORTH PECKHAM EST
KENT ROAD
A2
ROTHERHITHE
OLD KENT ROAD
PECKHAM HIGH ST
QUEENS ROAD
QUEENS ROAD PECKHAM
PECKHAM RYE
RYE LANE
A2215
A2214
EVELINA
A202
B203
B204
B215
B216
GESS PARK
REC GRD
ROSEMARY GDNS
WARWICK GDNS
COSSALL PARK
PATERSON PARK
MANOR EST
TRADING EST
RENNIE EST
TUSTIN EST
FRIARY EST
LEDBURY EST
MAWBEY EST
SUMNER EST
PELICAN EST
CAMDEN EST
SCEAUX EST
GLOS. GRO EST
SOUTH BERMON
South Eastern Gas Works
Civic Centre
Lib
Sch
Coll
Fire Sta
Clinic
Health Centre
Sports Cen
BUS GARAGE
The Aylesham Shop Cen
Mkt
Comm Cen
MUS
PO
Pol
FB
Offices
LORRY PARK
THORBURN SQUARE
LONGFIELD EST
BALACLAVA RD
FORTA
STRATHN.
SIMMS
EMERALDA RD
BEATRICE RD
CAMILLA
ANCHOR
ROSEBERRY
GALLEYWALL ROAD
ALMOND ROAD
BUSHW. DRIVE
CADET DRIVE
WELSFORD ST
OXLEY CLOSE
ABERCORN WAY
ROLLS ROAD
JAMES'S
ROSSETTI RD
STEVENSON CRES
SHEPHARD
DR. STUBBS
CATLIN STREET
EGAN WAY
ILDERTON
BRAMCOTE GROVE
CREDON RD
DELAFORD RD
CRANSWICK RD
VERNEY
VARCOE RD
GER. CL
RECORD ST
PENARTH ST
HATCHAM ROAD
MANOR GROVE
DEVONSHIRE GROVE
DEVON ST
SYLVAN GROVE
HILLBECK
DROVER LA
GERVASE ST
LEO ST
DROVE
CLIFTON
CULMORE ROAD
STUDHOLME ST
SPRINGALL ST
KINGS GRO
ASTBURY RD
COLLS RD
CAYTON GRO
YORK GROVE
DUNDAS RD
ANSDELL RD
BRABOURN GRO
KIMBERLEY
HOWBURY RD
BARSET
NUNHEAD GRN
MADRON ST
MINA ROAD
SMYRKS ROAD
SHORTS
EARL RD
HUMPHREY ST
ROWCROSS STREET
COOPERS
MAWBEY PL
AVON SQ
MARLBOROUGH GROVE
LOVEGROVE STREET
OSSORY ROAD
MALT ST
OLMAR STREET
GLENGALL
GLEN TER
NILE TER
OAKLEY PL
TRAFALGAR AVE
COBOURG ROAD
CALMINGTON ROAD
LONCROFT ROAD
WAITE ST
CANAL GROVE
SANDGATE ST
HYNDMAN STREET
RUBY ST
MURDOCK
PENCRAIG WAY
ETHNARD RD
GREEN HUNDRED RD
FRENSHAM STREET
PARK ROAD
FRIARY
BIANCA RD
LATONA RD
UNWIN CLO
REDDINS RD
HAYMERLE RD
BIRD IN BUSH ROAD
LYMPSTONE GARDENS
LEDBURY ST
CAROLINE GDNS
CARDINE MEWS
NAYLOR
ASYLUM
COMMERCIAL WAY
FURLEY RD
LEONTINE CLO
HOLBECK ROW
ELCOT AVE
NUTCROFT RD
FENHAM ROAD
PENNETHORNE RD
KINCAID RD
GELDART RD
GOLDSMITH ROAD
WENTWORTH CRES
CLONEVILLE CLO
BULLER CLO
HAS. C
BONAR RD
HILL STREET
PECKHAM
SUMMER RD
SUMNER ROAD
WILLOWBROOK RD
BOATWALK
COLEGROVE ROAD
PENN RD
DAVEY ST
SALDER CLO
CATOR ST
GEORGES WAY
BIBURY CLO
LONGHOPE CLO
DANIEL GDNS
BLAKES ROAD
PENTRIDGE ST
DIAMOND ST
PECKHAM GROVE
EAST SURREY GRO
ROSEMARY RD
JOWETT STREET
NUTT ST
MARCH. CL
REDBRI. GDNS
EXETER
PITT ST
SCEAUX GDNS
LISFORD STREET
STANTON
MELON RD
SIDMOUTH ROAD
HOLLYDENE
CARLTON GROVE
MONTPELIER ROAD
MARMONT ROAD
STAFFORDSHIRE ST
MEETING
HOUSE
COLMORE MEWS
WOODS ROAD
BURCHELL RD
CONSORT ROAD
CLAYTON RD
McK.R.
HANOVER PK
CERISE ROAD
RAUL RD
CICELY RD
MONC. ST
HARDERS RD
GORDON ROAD
KIRKWOOD ROAD
LUGARD RD
CAULFIELD RD
FIRBANK
STANBURY RD
HOLLYDALE ROAD
CHATHAM
WROXTON ROAD
CREWYS RD
BRAYARDS ROAD
BLACKPOOL RD
BOURNEMOUTH RD
ALMOND CLO
BIRCH CLO
COPELAND ROAD
GODMAN RD
STURDY RD
ELLERY ST
HEATON ROAD
WIVEN
PHILIP
SCYLLA
OPHIR TER
SHORE ROAD
ELM GROVE
HOLLY GROVE
BLENHEIM GROVE
CHOUMERT ROAD
CHO. SQ
ALPHA ST
CHADWICK ROAD
LINWOOD CLOSE
PARK
AZENBY RD
CROFTON
BUSHEY HILL ROAD
TALFOURD PL
DENMAN ROAD
GRUMMANT ROAD
LYNDHURST SQ
LYN. SQ
HIGH-
BELLENDEN ROAD
SHENLEY RD
LINNELL RD
OSWYTH RD
GAIRLOCH RD
LYNDHURST
WARWICK GDNS
IVANHOE RD
MALFORT RD
AVONDALE RISE
HOWDEN
REEDHAM ST
COSTA ST
WINGFIELD ST
WAGHORN ST
BELLENDEN
S. LON. ART GALL
ART GALL

A
B
C
D
1
2
3
4
5
26
32
40
ABBEY RD
ROAD
MILLENDER
W. Health Cen
ST. HELENA ROAD
OLDFIELD
BUSH RD
CHILTON
CROFT ST
CROFTERS COURT
CARTERET WAY
Clinic
WINDLASS PLACE
SAPPHIRE ROAD
AVENUE
EVELYN
JODA ST
DANSEN TOWER
A2208
NEW
JARROW ROAD
EUGENIA ROAD
GOLDS GDNS
ALPINE RD
CRANE MEAD
RECULVER ROAD
SKETCHLEY GDNS
STREET
SOUTH BERMONDSEY
TRUNDLEYS ROAD
JOHN SILKIN LA
OXESTALLS ROAD
Youth Cen
BOWDITCH
B206
HITHE
PO
Sch
ILDERTON
BRAMCOTE
AB ROAD
ABLETT STREET
GROVE
ROAD
VARCOE ROAD
GER. CL
ZAMPA ROAD
STOCKHOLM ROAD
BOLINA RD
Sports Cen
SENEGAL FIELDS
MILLWALL F.C.
ALLOA RD
CROOKE RD
HICKS ST
SCAWEN ROAD
DEPTFORD PARK
GRINSTEAD ROAD
APPROACH
BLACKHORSE ROAD
CANAL
GOSTERWOOD STREET
ALVERTON ST
Fire Sta
Coll
DRAGOON ROAD
B207
SURREY CANAL ROAD
LANDMANN WAY
RECORD ST
PENARTH ST
ROLLINS STREET
ORMSIDE STREET
HATCHAM ROAD
SHARRATT ST
LOVELINCH ST
South Eastern Gas Works
MANOR GROVE
TUSTIN EST
HORNSHAY STREET
MYERS LA
MERCURY WAY
BRIDGE HOUSE MEADOWS
JUNO WAY
Depot
SAMUEL CLO
COLD BLOW LANE
FOLKESTONE GDNS
ETTA STREET
CHILDERS STREET
ROLT STREET
MILTON COURT
CHUBWORTHY STREET
WOODPECKER
ALVERSTON
DORKING
DEVON ST
DEVONSHIRE GROVE
SYLVAN GROVE
HILLBECK CLOSE
PATTERDALE RD
A2
HUNSDON
WATER LA
FARROW LA
PUMP LA
EDRIC ROAD
MONSON ROAD
CAMPLIN
ROBERT LOWE CLO
SANFORD STREET
NYNEHEAD ST
VANSITTART
BOWERMAN
EDWARD
PAGNELL STREET
ARKLOW RD
AMERSHAM
ASYLUM
GERVASE ST
LEO STREET
DROVERS PL
WAGNER ST
WARDALLS GROVE
AVONLEY
BARLBOROUGH STREET
WRIGGLE ST
REASTON ST
LEYLANG ROAD
VENTNOR ROAD
BROCKLEHURST ST
SOUTHERNGATE WAY
CHILDERIC ROAD
ANGUS ST
FORDHAM PARK
NEW CROSS ROAD
Amb Sta
CLIFTON CRES
CULMORE ROAD
CHESTER WAY
ECKINGTON GDNS
HAT CLO
CASELLA RD
EGMONT ST
SE14
GOODWOOD ROAD
ACHILLES ST
CLIFTON RI
BATAVIA RD
Goldsmiths Gall
STUDHOLME ST
SPRINGALL ST
LANE
KINGS GRO
CLIFTON WAY
LODER STREET
B2207
KENDER STREET
LUBBOCK ST
FAIRLIE ST
BRIANT ST
Lib
BILLING ST
HATCHAM PARK RD
NETTLETON ROAD
HARTS LANE
NEW CROSS GATE
5
GROVE
MONTPELIER ROAD
KINGS GROVE
QUEENS ROAD PECKHAM
ASTBURY RD
COLLS RD
DAYTON GR
ASTBURY RD
HATCHAM GDNS
POMEROY STREET
BESSON ST
PO
ST JAMES'S
DIXON ROAD
DONATTS RD
LEWISHAM
Fire Sta
NEW CROSS GATE
TROUTBECK ROAD
Sch
Goldsmiths College (Univ. of London)
A202
ROAD
BURCHELL RD
WALK
LAUSANNE RD
WILD GOOSE DRIVE
SWALLOW CLO
DENNETTS ROAD
WALLER ROAD
ERLANGER ROAD
PEPYS ROAD
MUSGROVE ROAD
BUS GARAGE
OMMANEY ROAD
NEW CROSS
COSSALL
BIDWELL ST
STANBURY ROAD
HOLLYDALE ROAD
ST. MARY'S RD
Coll
RUTTS TER
SHERWIN RD
WALSHAM RD
ARBUTHNOT ROAD
JERNINGHAM ROAD
SANDBOURNE RD
BARRIEDALE
Comm Cen
ALLOT
KIRKWOOD
LUGARD
CAULFIELD RD
FIRBANK RD
CHATHAM
ROAD
BELFORT RD
GAUTREY ROAD
DUNDAS RD
ANSDELL ROAD
ST. MARY'S ROAD
MONA ROAD
ARBUTHNOT ROAD
BOUSFIELD ROAD
TELEGRAPH HILL PARK
VULCAN ROAD
RESERVOIR RD
VESTA ROAD
LANVANOR ROAD
WROXTON ROAD
BRABOURN GRO
GELLATLY ROAD
SELDEN ROAD
GIBBON ROAD
KITTO ROAD
WALLBUTTON ROAD
SPRULES ROAD
ENDWELL ROAD
MILLMARK GROVE
SHARDELOES ROAD
MALPAS
HOLLYDALE ROAD
EVELINA ROAD
NUNHEAD
KIMBERLEY
B2142
DRAKEFELL ROAD
TELEGRAPH HILL PARK
PENDRELL ROAD
ELLERY ST
AVENUE
OAKDALE RD
Lib
A2214
HOWBURY RD
BUCHAN RD
BARSET
SALTER
ST. ASAPH ROAD
ASPINALL
SEYMOUR GDNS
ENDWELL RD
BROCKLEY
UPPER BROCKLEY
CRANFIELD

MUDCHUTE
MILLWALL PARK
Comm Cen
WESTFERRY ROAD
MANCHESTER
ISLAND GARDENS
SAUNDERS NESS
Sports Cen
Sch
Fire Sta
Pier
Landing Stage
Palmer's Wharf
Payne's Wharf
Borthwick Wharf
DEPTFORD
ROYAL NAVAL YARD
TOWER HAMLETS
GREENWICH
GREENWICH REACH
GREENWICH FOOT TUNNEL
Comm Cen
Clubhouse
Trafalgar Rowing Centre
Royal Naval College
The Trident Hall Theatre
Greenwich Pier
GIPSY MOTH IV
CUTTY SARK
Power Station (Disused)
HOSP
ROMNEY ROAD
QUEEN'S HOUSE
SE8
Uni of Greenwich
CREEK ROAD
A200
Clinic
DEPTFORD CHURCH STREET
A2209
DEPTFORD CREEK
CREEKSIDE
NORMAN ROAD
B208
DEPTFORD
Albany Empire Theatre
Sports Cen
Lib
GREENWICH HIGH ROAD
A206
GREENWICH SOUTH ST
GREENWICH Comm Cen
FAN MUS
Clinic
Pol
Circus Gate
CROOMS HILL
B209
LEWISHAM
A2
DEPT. BRO. RD
DEPTFORD BRIDGE
BLACKHEATH RD
BLACKHEATH HILL
Coll
Water Works
BROOKMILL ROAD
RAVENSBOURNE
LEWISHAM ROAD
A2211
TA Centre
FRIENDLY GDNS
ST JOHN'S
ST. JOHN'S
Wickham Bldg
Lewisham Coll
Breakspears Bldg
A20
LOAMPIT HILL
LOAMPIT VALE
THURSTON RD
A2210
RIVER
LEWISHAM
GRANVILLE
D
E
F
G
26
34
40
1
2
3
4
5

27
33
41
A
B
C
D
1
2
3
4
5
SOUTH EASTERN GAS BOARD SPORTS GROUND
Pav
Jetty
Enderby's Wharf
Piper's Wharf
Works
MAURITIUS
AZOF STREET
A2203
TUNNEL AVENUE
Sports Cen
NEWCASTLE DRAW DOCK
GARDENS
SAUNDERS
Granite Wharf
Lovell's Wharf
CADET PL
CHRISTCHURCH WAY
BELLOT STREET
Sch
BLACKWALL
MINI TOWN HALL
ARMITAGE ROAD
GLENISTER ROAD
GLENFORTH ST
FINGAL STREET
CHILVER ST
PELTON ROAD
WOOLWICH ROAD
Lib
TRINITY HOSP
Comm Cen
GREENWICH DISTRICT HOSP
CHEVENING ROAD
EAST GREENWICH PLEASAUNCE
REACH
Trafalgar Rowing Centre
Royal Naval College
Power Station
TRAFALGAR ROAD
WOODLAND GROVE
EARLSWOOD ST
TYLER ST
CALVERT RD
ANNANDALE ROAD
Health Centre
ANNANDALE RD
GREENWICH FOOT TUNNEL
Pier
The Trident Hall Theatre
OLD WOOLWICH ROAD
TUSKAR ST
WOODLANDS PK RD
LEMMON RD
VANBRUGH HILL
DINSDALE RD
HUMBER ROAD
PEACHUM ROAD
HOSP
KING WILLIAM WALK
A206
ROMNEY ROAD
PARK ROW
MAZE HILL
VISTA
Sports Cen
RESTELL CLOSE
NORFOLK HOUSE
JENNER HOUSE
LISTER HOUSE
ROAD
ULUNDI RD
FOYLE ROAD
COLERAINE ROAD
WEBB RD
(Mkt)
QUEEN'S HOUSE
NATIONAL MARITIME MUS
CROSS AVE
HILL
One Tree Hill
WESTCOMBE PARK
HARDY ROAD
BEACONSFIELD ROAD
WOOD. LOCAL CEN
Comm Cen
GREENWICH
SE10
Greenwich Theatre
GREENWICH PARK
LOVERS WK
HIGH RD
VANBRUGH FIELDS
MYCENAE RD
Clinic
Circus Gate
THE AVENUE
CROOMS HILL
FLAMSTEED HOUSE (Old Royal Observatory)
BLACKHEATH AVENUE
GREAT CROSS AVE
BOWER AVENUE
WYCHERLEY CLOSE
COMBE AV.
VANBRUGH PARK
FERNDALE CT
PARKSIDE
VANBRUGH PARK
ROYAL HILL
GEORGE STREET
Croom's Hill Gate
The Gardens
THE WILDERNESS DEER PARK
B210
CHARLTON WAY
HEATHWAY
ST JOHN'S PARK
LUTON PL
B209
HYDE VALE
COV RES
Tenn Cts
RANGER'S HOUSE
CHESTERFIELD WALK
GENERAL WOLFE ROAD
PRINCE CHARLES ROAD
MAZE HILL
VANBRUGH TER
LANGTON WAY
DIAMOND TER
WESTGROVE LA
CADE ROAD
Blackheath Gate
SHOOTER'S HILL ROAD
A2
ROYAL PAR
WEST GROVE
DARTMOUTH ROW
DARTMOUTH HILL
DUKE HUMPHREY ROAD
BLACKHEATH
LONG POND ROAD
PRINCE OF WALES RD
B212
ST. GERMANS PLACE
DARTMOUTH GROVE
WHITFIELD ROAD
TYLER RD
TA Centre
HARE AND BILLET ROAD
GOFFERS ROAD
TALBOT PLACE
BLACKHEATH VALE
MORDEN LA
MACAULEY
PROSPECT VALE
SOUTH ROW
THE PARAGON
ORCHARD DRIVE
THE ORCHARD
ALL SAINTS DRIVE
PARAGON PL
RYCULFF SQUARE
POND ROAD
FULTHORP RD
MONTPELIER ROW
Clarendon Hotel
MOUNTS POND ROAD
ABERDEEN TER.
ELIOT VALE
ELIOT PLACE
TRANQUIL VALE
GROTES PLACE
PAGODA GDNS
HEATH LANE
WEMYSS RD
PRINCES RISE
ELIOT HILL
ELIOT PARK
OAKCROFT ROAD
BAIZDON ROAD
CAMDEN ROW
SOUTH ROW
COLLINS ST
BLACKHEATH GROVE
BLACKHEATH
PO
BLACKHEATH VILLAGE
BENNETT PARK
LEWISHAM
LEWIS GROVE
WALERAND ROAD
ELIOT PK
ST. JOSEPH'S VALE
GRANVILLE PARK
HURREN CLOSE
CORNER GREEN
BLACKHEATH PK
CRESSINGHAM RD
BOYNE RD
BLACKHEATH CONCERT HALLS

CHARLTON
BUGSBY'S WAY
RAMAC INDUSTRIAL ESTATE
GREENWICH INDUSTRIAL ESTATE
HORIZON WAY
GALLIONS ROAD
HOPE LANE
Works
27
WOOLWICH ROAD
A206
MARYON PARK
Tennis Courts
HICKIN CLOSE
GALLON CL
BARNEY CLO
PREN CT
Clinic
HARVEY GDNS
HASTED ROAD
CHARLTON ATHLETIC FC
VALLEY GROVE
FLOYD ROAD
CHARLTON
TROUGHTON
RATHMORE
DELAFIELD ROAD
SUNDORNE ROAD
Fire Sta
FAIRTHORN RD
GURDON ROAD
Warehouses
DUPREE RD
VICTORIA
FOSS ROAD
BERN. ASH. DR
CALY. RD
INVERINE ROAD
SWALLOWFIELD ROAD
PRIOLO ROAD
VALIANT HOUSE
SAM BARTRAM CLO
LANSDOWNE MEWS
WOLFE CRES
THORNTREE
COXMOUNT RD
ZOO
MARYON WILSON PARK
KINVEACHY
GARDENS
McCALL CRES
1
WESTCOMBE PARK
Works
BRAMSHOT
WELLINGTON GDNS
NADINE ST
GOLL TER
ELLISCOMBE ROAD
CHURCH LANE
THE HEIGHTS
LANSDOWNE LANE
ST. PAUL'S CL
Health Cen
CHARLTON LANE
BEACHAM CLOSE
GUILD ROAD
ST. ALFEGE ROAD
MACARTHUR TER
CHARLTON
SANDTOFT RD
AVENUE
WYNDCLIFF ROAD
THE BIRCHES
TALLIS GROVE
EVERSLEY ROAD
HIGHCOMBE
BRAMHOPE LANE
ELLIS MS
MASCALLS RD
FLETCHING RD
FAIRFIELD
THE VILLAGE
CHARLTON PARK ROAD
MULBERRY CLOSE
Pav
2
SE7
SPRINGFIELD GROVE
COPSE CLO
ST. JOSEPH'S CT
EASTCOMBE AVENUE
HOPEDALE RD
MAYHILL RD
SHERINGTON RD
A102(M)
SIEBERT ROAD
INVICTA ROAD
WESTCOMBE HILL
Community Centre
CHARLTON PARK
HORNFAIR ROAD
CHARLTON ROAD
B210
Tennis Cts
RECTORY FIELD
RECTORY FIELD CRESCENT
FAIRLAWN
THE AVENUE
SHIRLEY HO. DR
MARLBOROUGH LANE
CANBERRA ROAD
SUTLEJ ROAD
INDUS ROAD
MONTCALM ROAD
KASHMIR RD
MERIDIAN RD
35
INIGO JONES ROAD
FURZEFIELD
HASSEN RD
COUTH. RD
CRAIG
LYVEDEN RD
BANCHORY RD
LIZBAN STREET
SUNF. PL
BOWAT. PL
REYNOLDS PL
NIGERIA ROAD
ST. MAR. C.
GREENBAY ROAD
PRINCE HENRY ROAD
3
SPORTS GROUND
DORN. CL
OLD DOVER ROAD
THE GLADE
CHARLTON DENE
INDUS RD
GRENADA RD
KENYA ROAD
Bowl Grn
Tennis Cts
PARK
Lib
Clinic
SUN LA
ALLOT
RUSS. CL
SHOOTER'S HILL
A207
ARNOLD HOUSE HOSP
CHI. CLO
STANE WAY
PAL WAY
GUNNER
ABERFORD GDNS
MASTER
TELSON AVENUE
ROAD
ROCHESTER WAY
EASTBROOK ROAD
HARVEY
MERRIMAN ROAD
WEYMAN ROAD
FARJEON ROAD
Pav
SPORTS GROUND
MELTHORPE GDNS
ZANGWILL
THELMA GARDENS
Amb Sta
4
ROSSE MS
ANNESL RD
GROVE CT
KIDBROOKE GARDENS
WESTBROOK ROAD
KIDBROOKE PARK CLOSE
BEGBIE ROAD
HARRADEN RD
SPORTS GROUND
WRICKLEMARSH ROAD
HOLBURNE ROAD
CORELLI
KIDBROOKE
WRICKLE. ROAD
A2213
HOLBURNE CLOSE
HARGOOD ROAD
ALLOT
FAIRFAX GDNS
HOLBURNE GDNS
DURSLEY GDNS
WHETSTONE ROAD
DURSLEY CLO
WOOLACOMBE
Morden College
ROCHESTER WAY RELIEF RD
BROOKELSA
DEIME CRES
BALCHEN ROAD
KELLAWAY
DURSLEY
PLAYING FIELDS
THE PLANTATION
GROVE
PARK
SWEYN PL
SUS. RD
PO
KIDBROOKE
Clubho
SPORTS GROUND
5
Tenn Cts
KIDBROOKE WAY
SPORTS GROUNDS
BROAD WALK
Pav
SPORTS GROUNDS
Tennis Cts
LANGBROOK ROAD
CROSSBROOK
KELBROOK RD
FLINTMILL CRESCENT
PADDO. CLOSE
Depot
Sch
41
A2
ROCHESTER
POLEB. RD
HALSBROOK ROAD
HIGHBROOK
SLADEBROOK ROAD
SHIREBROOK ROAD
SEDGEBROOK ROAD
BOURNBROOK ROAD
CARNBROOK
MINI TOWN HALL
PHINEAS
D
E
F
G

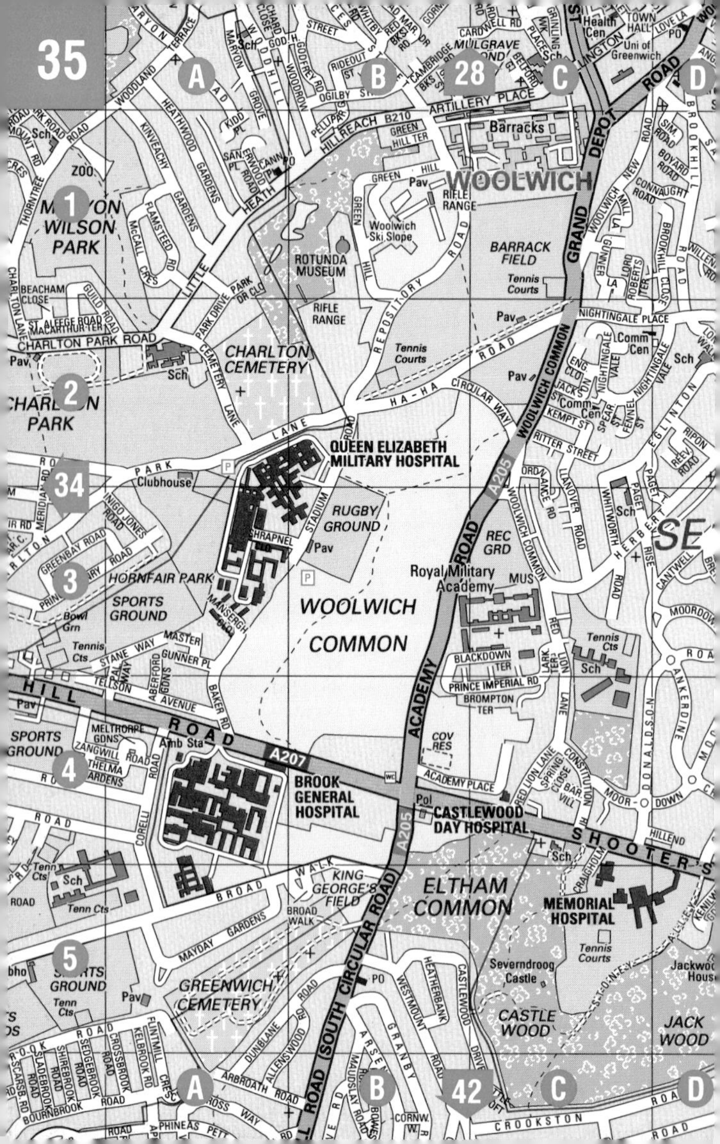
A
B
28
C
D
WOOLWICH
Barracks
ARTILLERY PLACE
MARYON WILSON PARK
ZOO
CHARLTON PARK
CHARLTON PARK ROAD
CHARLTON CEMETERY
ROTUNDA MUSEUM
Woolwich Ski Slope
RIFLE RANGE
BARRACK FIELD
Tennis Courts
NIGHTINGALE PLACE
HA-HA ROAD
CIRCULAR WAY
GRAND DEPOT ROAD
WOOLWICH COMMON
QUEEN ELIZABETH MILITARY HOSPITAL
RUGBY GROUND
STADIUM
SHRAPNEL CLO
34
Clubhouse
HORNFAIR PARK
SPORTS GROUND
WOOLWICH COMMON
REC GRD
Royal Military Academy
MUS
BLACKDOWN TER
PRINCE IMPERIAL RD
BROMPTON TER
ACADEMY ROAD
A205
SHOOTERS HILL ROAD
A207
BROOK GENERAL HOSPITAL
CASTLEWOOD DAY HOSPITAL
ACADEMY PLACE
COV RES
ELTHAM COMMON
KING GEORGE'S FIELD
MEMORIAL HOSPITAL
Severndroog Castle
CASTLE WOOD
JACK WOOD
GREENWICH CEMETERY
SOUTH CIRCULAR ROAD
MAYDAY GARDENS
BROAD WALK
SPORTS GROUND
Amb Sta
42
CROOKSTON ROAD
BOURNBROOK ROAD
ARBROATH ROAD
SE
1
2
3
4
5

28
42
D
E
F
G
1
2
3
4
5
PLUMSTEAD
PLUMSTEAD COMMON
WINN'S COMMON
SHREWSBURY PARK
SHOOTER'S HILL GOLF COURSE
SHOOTER'S HILL
OXLEAS WOOD
OXLEAS MEADOW
CLOTHWORKERS WOOD
EAGLESFIELD REC GRD
PLAYING FIELD
SHOULDER OF MUTTON GREEN
WOOLWICH CEM
WALMER
BURRAGE ROAD
ARTHUR GROVE
RICHMOND PLACE
INVERMORE
DAWSON CLOSE
SANDBACH PLACE
RAGLAN ROAD
CLAYMILL HOUSE
HUDSON PLACE
CONGLETON GROVE
COUPLAND PLACE
Greenwich Young Peoples Theatre
Comm Cen
Sch
Schs
PO
Fire Sta
Health Centre
Sports Cen
Lib
Clinic
Tenn Cts
Bowl Grn
ST. MARGARET'S GROVE
VICARAGE PK
BLENDON TERRACE
ST. JOHNS TER
WERNBROOK ST
WAVERLEY ROAD
WAVERLEY CRES
DURHAM RISE
BRAMBLEBURY RD
BURWASH RD
HEAVITREE ROAD
MANTHORP RD
BREWERY ROAD
MAJENDIE ROAD
GRIFFIN ROAD
ANCONA ROAD
CONGO RD
LEGHORN RD
TUSCAN RD
PIEDMONT ROAD
HEARD ROAD
CONWAY ROAD
COXWELL RD
INGLEDEW RD
LIFFLER ROAD
MIRIAM ROAD
ORISSA RD
CHESTNUT RISE
PARKDALE ROAD
ROYDENE ROAD
SLADEDALE ROAD
LAKEDALE ROAD
TORMOUNT ROAD
WARWICK TER
MILL ROAD
OLD MILL ROAD
TEWSON ROAD
PLUMSTEAD HIGH STREET
STRANDFIELD CLO
DRAWELL CLO
VIEWLAND ROAD
HEATH VILL
WINN COMMON ROAD
KINGS HIGHWAY
BLEAK HILL
Pav
HEATHFIELD ROAD
BASSANT ROAD
REVELL RISE
GILBOURNE RD
KINGSDALE
CAMDALE ROAD
THE SLADE
RAVINE GROVE
SUTCLIFFE ROAD
FLAXTON ROAD
MALTON STREET
SWINGATE LANE
MELLING STREET
KIRKHAM STREET
MOUNT CLO
TIMBERCROFT LANE
ALBAT ST
PEGWELL ST
LUCKN ST
CARDIFF ST
ALABAMA STREET
IRWIN AVENUE
THORNHILL AVENUE
EASTVIEW AVE
ANCASTER RD
DUNCROFT
HIGHMEAD
EDISON GROVE
COMBE SIDE
ERINDALE TER
ERINDALE
MACOMA ROAD
MACOMA TER
TUAM ROAD
CHELSWORTH DRIVE
CHERITON DR
ST. MERRYN CLOSE
CLOTHWORKERS ROAD
HATTON CLOSE
DOTHILL RD
GARLAND RD
LANDSTEAD ROAD
RAYMERE GARDENS
DOR GRD
WARLAND ROAD
WELTON ROAD
VOCE ROAD
HIGH GROVE
FLAXT RD
ALLOT
JAGO CLOSE
ENNIS ROAD
ADMASTON ROAD
UPTON RD
OLVE RD
HINSTOCK RD
ROWTON ROAD
WREKIN RD
NITHDALE ROAD
DALLIN ROAD
PLUM LANE
GENESTA ROAD
VAMBERY ROAD
ISLA RD
KIRK LANE
VERNHAM ROAD
WROTTESLEY ROAD
BARNFIELD RD
BLOOMFIELD ROAD
CAMROSE ROW
THE OAKS
COMMON ROAD
MAYPLACE LANE
BRINKLOW CRES
ASHRIDGE CRESCENT
MEREWORTH DRIVE
BUSHMOOR CRES
KINLET ROAD
EAGLESFIELD RD
FOXCROFT ROAD
Tennis Courts
Clubhouse
Woodlands Farm
Nursery
GREENWICH
BEXLEY
A207
SHOOTERS HILL
We Anchor In Hope PH
ROKESBY CLO
HILL VIEW DRIVE
SANDRINGHAM DR
MARINA DRIVE
PETER'S CLO
WICKHAM STREET
WICKHAM
EXETER
HONITON ROAD
TIDFORD
LYN ROAD
BALTIMORE PLACE
BELLEGROVE CLO
BELLEGROVE
MONTROSE CLOSE
FALCONWOOD AVENUE
SUNDRIDGE AVE
BELMONT AVE
SHERWOOD
EASTCOTE ROAD
OXLEAS CLOSE
ASHMORE
WOODS LANE
DRYDEN
KEATS RD
MILTON RD
EDISON
WORDSWORTH RD
TENNYSON
SHELLEY DR
BROWNING CLO
BLAKE CLO
CHAUCER
BURNS CLOSE
BLENHEIM DRIVE
WYCLIFFE CLO

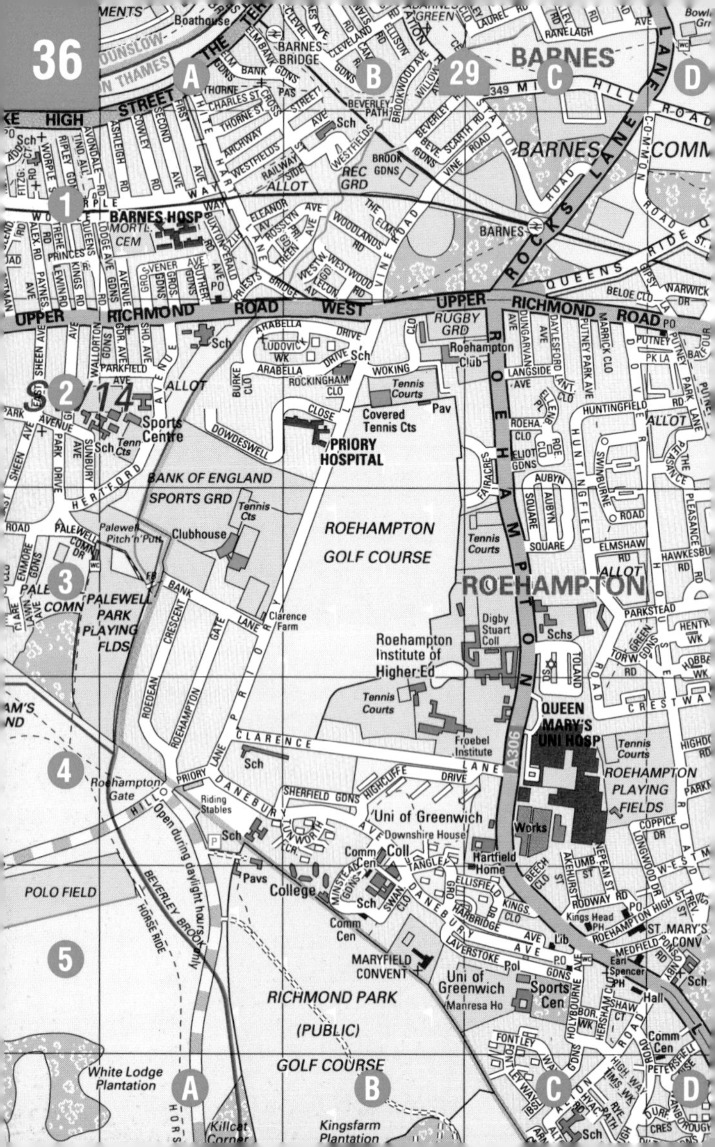

BARNES
BARNES BRIDGE
Boathouse
HIGH STREET
BARNES HOSP
MORTL CEM
UPPER RICHMOND ROAD WEST
UPPER RICHMOND ROAD
BARNES COMMON
ROCKS LANE
BARNES
REC GRD
ALLOT
RUGBY GRD
Roehampton Club
PRIORY HOSPITAL
Sports Centre
BANK OF ENGLAND SPORTS GRD
Clubhouse
Palewell Pitch'n'Putt
PALEWELL COMN
PALEWELL PARK PLAYING FLDS
ROEHAMPTON GOLF COURSE
Covered Tennis Cts
Tennis Courts
ROEHAMPTON
ROEHAMPTON LANE
Digby Stuart Coll
Roehampton Institute of Higher Ed
QUEEN MARY'S UNI HOSP
Froebel Institute
ROEHAMPTON PLAYING FIELDS
CLARENCE LANE
PRIORY LANE
BANK LANE
Clarence Farm
Roehampton Gate
Riding Stables
Open during daylight hours only
BEVERLEY BROOK
HORSE RIDE
POLO FIELD
Uni of Greenwich
Downshire House
Hartfield Home
Works
College
MARYFIELD CONVENT
Uni of Greenwich Manresa Ho
Sports Cen
RICHMOND PARK (PUBLIC) GOLF COURSE
White Lodge Plantation
Killcat Corner
Kingsfarm Plantation
ROEHAMPTON HIGH ST
Kings Head PH
Earl Spencer PH
ST. MARY'S CONV
A306
29
A B C D
1 2 3 4 5

PUTNEY
Bowling Green
PUTNEY HO
29
Tenn Cts
RIVER
BISHOP'S PARK
Air Theatre
ALLOTMENTS
MUS
Fulham Palace
FULHAM PALACE GDNS
FULHAM HIGH ST
CHURCH GA
PUTNEY BRIDGE
PRIOR BANK GDNS
RANELAGH GDNS
HURLINGHAM
SWAN DOCK
Putney Pier
THAMES
Wharves
LOWER RICHMOND ROAD
B306
COMMON
LOWER COMMON SOUTH
EGLISTON MS
FELSHAM ROAD
EMBANKMENT
HOTHAM
ERPINGHAM
LANDFORD RD
CLARENDON DRIVE
LACY ROAD
Sports Cen
Hall
SOUTH CIRCULAR ROAD
A205
PUTNEY HIGH STREET
Jubilee Ho
Shopping Cen
PUTNEY
A3
WANDSWORTH
Clinic
MUS
Lib
DISRAELI ROAD
PUTNEY
Coll
UPPER RICHMOND ROAD
37
COUNTY CT
OAKHILL
EAST PUTNEY
HOWARDS LANE
Pol
YWCA
Sorting Office
NURSERY CLO
ST. JOHN'S AVENUE
PUTNEY
Health Cen
CAMBALT ROAD
CHERRY DR
South Thames Coll
CARLTON
Schs
SW15
CHARTFIELD AVE
AVENUE
WHITNELL WAY
A219
WESTLEIGH AVENUE
LYTTON
RADCLIFFE SQ
CORTIS ROAD
TILDESLEY ROAD
HAYWARD GDNS
Clinic
Sch
Tennis Cts
MANOR FIELDS
HEATH RISE
PUTNEY HILL
Green Man PH
HEATH
PUTNEY HEATH
PUTNEY HEATH LA
GROVE
ROYAL HOSPITAL
WEST HILL
Whitelands Training College
ROYAL ORCHARD CLO
LINSTEAD WAY
TELEGRAPH
WILDCROFT
COV RES
TIBBET'S RIDE
TIBBET'S CORNER
Telegraph Inn PH
Tibbet's Corner
ROAD
HIGHLANDS HEATH
PORTSMOUTH
Comm Cen
KEEVIL DRIVE
PRINCES WAY
GIROWOOD ROAD
SKEENA HILL
Sch
WHITLOCK
EDGECOMBE HO
SOUTHMEAD
DRIVE
SOUTHFIELDS
WINDLESHAM
SCIO POND
KING'S MERE
D
E
F
G
1
2
3
4
5

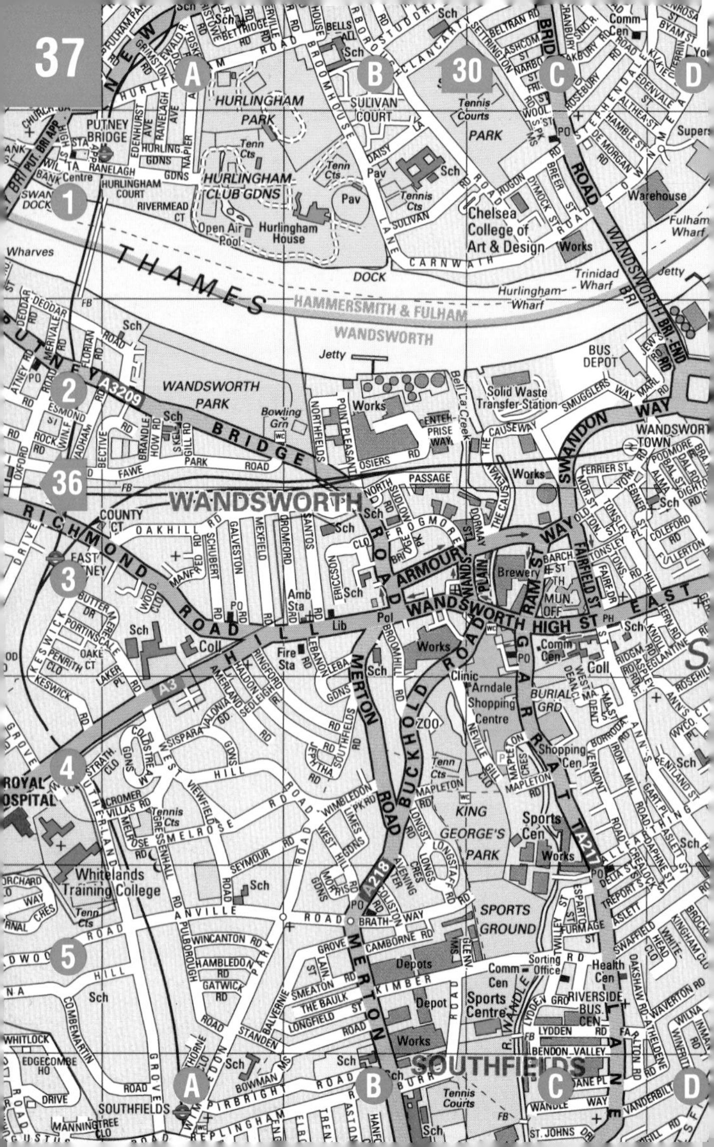

A
B
30
C
D
1
2
3
4
5
36
THAMES
HAMMERSMITH & FULHAM
WANDSWORTH
HURLINGHAM PARK
HURLINGHAM CLUB GDNS
Hurlingham House
Open Air Pool
PUTNEY BRIDGE
SULIVAN COURT
Chelsea College of Art & Design
Tennis Courts
PARK
DOCK
CARNWATH
Trinidad Wharf
Hurlingham Wharf
Fulham Wharf
Wharves
Jetty
WANDSWORTH PARK
BUS DEPOT
Solid Waste Transfer Station
SWANDON WAY
WANDSWORTH TOWN
WANDSWORTH BRI
WANDSWORTH BRI. END
PUTNEY BRIDGE ROAD
A3209
RICHMOND ROAD
WEST HILL
A3
OAKHILL RD
ARMOURY WAY
WANDSWORTH HIGH ST
EAST HILL
RAM ST
FAIRFIELD ST
Brewery
GARRATT LANE
A217
MERTON ROAD
A218
BUCKHOLD ROAD
KING GEORGE'S PARK
Arndale Shopping Centre
BURIAL GRD
Shopping Cen
Sports Cen
SPORTS GROUND
ROYAL HOSPITAL
Whitelands Training College
ANVILLE ROAD
WIMBLEDON PARK ROAD
REPLINGHAM ROAD
PIRBRIGHT ROAD
SOUTHFIELDS
Depots
Depot
Works
Sports Centre
RIVERSIDE BUS CEN
LYDDEN RD
BENDON VALLEY
WANDLE WAY
Health Cen
Comm Cen
Sorting Office

30
38
D
E
F
G
1
2
3
4
5
SW11
SW17
Lensbury Wharf
Shell Wharf
LONDON WESTLAND HELIPORT
YORK GDNS
Warehouse
Superstore
Comm Cen
WINSTANLEY EST
Clinic
Sports Cen
Sch
CLAPHAM JUNCTION
Shopping Cen
Buses and taxis only
TA Centre
CLAPHAM JUNCTION EST
Amb Sta
OPEN SPACE
FALCON PARK
Fire Sta
Com Cem
Lib
Libs
PO
Pol
MAG CT
Battersea Arts Centre
A3205
A3207
A3036
A3220
A3
B229
A214
B234
FALCON ROAD
LAVENDER HILL
ST. JOHN'S HILL
BATTERSEA RISE
CLAPHAM COMMON
CLAPHAM COMMON WEST SIDE
ELSPETH RD
WANDS. COMMON NORTH SIDE
ST. JOHN'S HEALTH CARE UNIT
ST. MARY'S CEM
SPENCER PARK
PLAYING FIELDS
Pav
WANDSWORTH COMMON
BOLINGBROKE HOSP
Health Cen
Mkt
FITZHUGH GROVE EST
Tenn Cts
Bowl Grn
Neals Nurseries
H.M. PRISON WANDSWORTH
Tennis Cts
Clubhouse
Crem
WANDSWORTH CEMETERY
Bowling Grn
THE AVENUE
WANDSWORTH COMMON
FB
TRINITY ROAD
WANDSWORTH COMMON WEST SIDE
HEATHFIELD ROAD
WINDMILL ROAD
SPENCER ROAD
BOLINGBROKE GROVE
NORTHCOTE ROAD
BELLEVUE ROAD
NIGHTINGALE LANE
BALHAM
EARLSFIELD

CLAPHAM COMMON
CLAPHAM
SW12
BALHAM
WANDSWORTH ROAD
CLAPHAM COMMON NORTH SIDE
LONG ROAD
CLAPHAM COMMON SOUTH SIDE
CLAPHAM COMMON WEST SIDE
THE AVENUE
CEDARS ROAD
A3216
QUEENSTOWN
WANDSWORTH
LAVENDER HILL
A3036
A3
A205
B303
B237
CAVENDISH ROAD
POYNDERS RD
BALHAM HILL
CLAPHAM SOUTH
CLAPHAM COMMON
TRINITY HOSPICE
S. Bank Uni
Battersea Arts Centre
MACAULAY SQUARE
COCK POND
LONG POND
MOUNT POND
EAGLE POND
Bandstand
REC GRD
King's College
WINDMILL DRIVE
NIGHTINGALE LANE
LA RETRAITE CONVENT
OAKLANDS EST
NOTRE DAME EST
WEIR EST
Go-Karting
PARK
SW
31
37
A
B
C
D
1
2
3
4
5

STOCKWELL
CLAPHAM RD EST
CLAPHAM NORTH
SOUTH WESTERN HOSP
STOCKWELL PK EST
MYATT'S FIELDS SOUTH EST
ANGELL PARK
BRIXTON ACADEMY
LOUGHB EST
Brixton College
SANDMERE ROAD
FERNDALE
BRIXTON
ATLANTIC
ELECTRIC AVE
COLDHARBOUR LANE
MOORLANDS EST
TOWN HALL
THE FRIDGE
Superstore
ACRE LANE
BRIXTON
ELLERSLIE SQ IND EST
BRIXTON WATER LANE
EFFRA ROAD
MORVAL RD
DULWICH ROAD
SW2
TULSE HILL ESTATE
H.M. PRISON BRIXTON
Ashby Windmill
BRIXTON HILL
LYHAM ROAD
STREATHAM PL
STREATHAM HILL
CHRISTCHURCH
BROCKWELL PARK
Lido
Bowling Green
Tennis Courts
GUINNESS TRUST EST
31
39
D
E
F
G
1
2
3
4
5

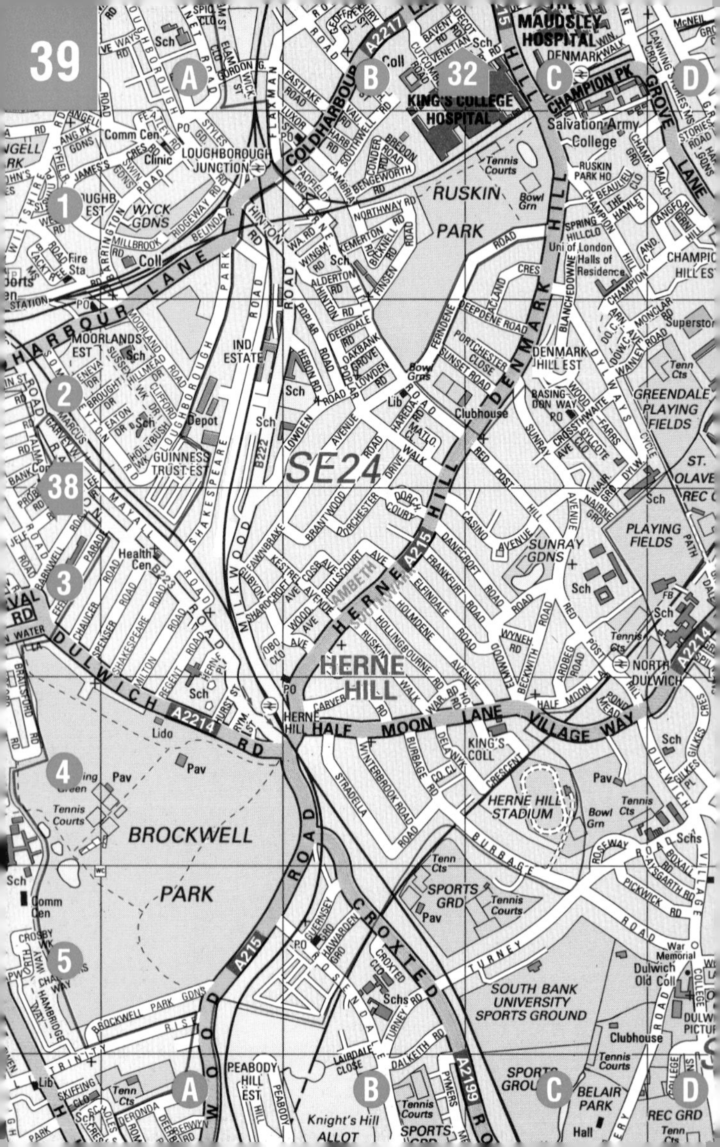
32
38
A
B
C
D
1
2
3
4
5
MAUDSLEY HOSPITAL
KING'S COLLEGE HOSPITAL
DENMARK WALK
CHAMPION PK
Salvation Army College
GROVE LANE
COLDHARBOUR
A2217
LOUGHBOROUGH JUNCTION
Comm Cen
Clinic
WYCK GDNS
LOUGHBOROUGH EST
MILLBROOK RD
BELINDA R.
RIDGEWAY RD
Coll
Fire Sta
COLDHARBOUR LANE
STATION
MOORLANDS EST
Sch
FLAXMAN
EASTLAKE ROAD
LUXOR ST
SOUTHWELL RD
CONDER RD
BREDON ROAD
BENGEWORTH RD
CAMBRIA
PADFIELD RD
NORTHWAY RD
KEMERTON RD
BICKNELL RD
FINSEN
ALDERTON RD
HINTON RD
RUSKIN PARK
Tennis Courts
Bowl Grn
RUSKIN PARK HO
CHAMPION HILL
SPRING HILL CLO
Uni of London Halls of Residence
CHAMPION HILL EST
LANGFORD GRN
BLANCHEDOWNE
DENMARK HILL
DENMARK HILL EST
DEEPDENE ROAD
FERNDENE
ACLAND CRES
PORTCHESTER CLOSE
SUNSET ROAD
Clubhouse
BASINGDON WAY
CROSSTHWAITE AVE
GYLCOTE CLO
FARRS
DYLWAYS
WANLEY ROAD
MONCLAR RD
Superstore
GREENDALE PLAYING FIELDS
ST. OLAVE'S REC GRD
PLAYING FIELDS
IND ESTATE
Depot
GUINNESS TRUST EST
LOUGHBOROUGH ROAD
SHAKESPEARE ROAD
POPLAR ROAD
HERON RD
DEERDALE RD
OAKBANK GROVE
LOWDEN RD
LOWDEN ROAD
Lib
Bowl Grns
HAREDALE RD
MATLOCK CL
SE24
B222
MILKWOOD ROAD
BRANTWOOD ROAD
DORCHESTER DRIVE
DORCHESTER COURT
CASINO AVENUE
DANECROFT ROAD
FRANKFURT ROAD
ELFINDALE ROAD
HOLMDENE AVENUE
HOLLINGBOURNE ROAD
RUSKIN WALK
RED POST HILL
SUNRAY AVE
SUNRAY GDNS
ELMWOOD ROAD
WYNEHAM RD
BECKWITH RD
ARDBEG ROAD
HALF MOON LA
NORTH DULWICH
A2214
A215
HERNE HILL
LAMBETH
SOUTHWARK
FAWNBRAKE
KESTREL AVE
ROLLSCOURT AVE
SHARDCROFT AVE
GUBYON AVE
WOOD AVE
CARVER RD
HALF MOON LANE
VILLAGE WAY
KING'S COLL
HERNE HILL STADIUM
WINTERBROOK ROAD
STRADELLA ROAD
BURBAGE ROAD
DELAWYK CRES
CROXTED ROAD
Health Cen
MAYALL ROAD
B223
CHAUCER ROAD
SPENSER ROAD
MILTON ROAD
REGENT ROAD
SHAKESPEARE ROAD
RAILTON ROAD
HURST ST
DULWICH RD
Lido
Pav
Tennis Courts
BROCKWELL PARK
Comm Cen
CROSBY WK
HAMBRIDGE WAY
BROCKWELL PARK GDNS
TRINITY RISE
DULWICH WOOD ROAD
A215
GUERNSEY GRO
HAWARDEN GRO
ROSENDALE ROAD
CROXTED CLO
Schs
TURNEY RD
DALKEITH RD
LAIRDALE CLOSE
PEABODY HILL EST
PEABODY HILL
Knight's Hill ALLOT
Tennis Courts
SPORTS GRD
PYMERS
A2199
TURNEY ROAD
SOUTH BANK UNIVERSITY SPORTS GROUND
Clubhouse
Tennis Courts
SPORTS GROUND
BELAIR PARK
Hall
REC GRD
ROSEWAY
BURBAGE ROAD
BOXALL RD
AYSGARTH RD
PICKWICK RD
War Memorial
Dulwich Old Coll
DULWICH VILLAGE
GILKES CRES
Lib
SKIFFING CLO
DERONDA RD
Tenn Cts

32
40
21
D
E
F
G
1
2
3
4
5
SE22
EAST DULWICH
PECKHAM RYE COMMON
PECKHAM RYE PARK
CAMBERWELL OLD CEMETERY
DULWICH PARK
DAWSON HEIGHTS EST
NUNHEAD
DULWICH HOSPITAL
GROVE VALE
EAST DULWICH ROAD
NUNHEAD LANE
DULWICH GROVE
LORDSHIP LANE
PECKHAM RYE
RYE LANE
DULWICH COMMON
COURT LANE
GOOSE GREEN
UNDERHILL ROAD
FOREST HILL ROAD
WOOD VALE
OVERHILL ROAD
LANGTON RISE
HONOR OAK PARK
BELLENDEN ROAD
CHOUMERT ROAD
DOG KENNEL HILL
MELBOURNE GROVE
CRYSTAL PALACE ROAD
UPLAND ROAD
BARRY ROAD
FRIERN ROAD
DUNSTANS ROAD
STRAKER'S ROAD
Bowling Green
PLAYING FIELDS
Tennis Courts
Sports Cen
Health Cen
Comm Cen
Lib
Sch
Coll
Clinic
PO
Pol
A2216
A2215
A2214
A205
B219

A
B
C
D
1
2
3
4
5
33
39
NUNHEAD
BROCKLEY
HONOR OAK
SE23
EVELINA ROAD
2214
NUNHEAD
NUNHEAD GROVE
WAVERLEY PARK
NUNHEAD CEMETERY
PLAYING FIELDS
Tennis Courts
TELEGRAPH HILL PARK
B2142 DRAKEFELL ROAD
PENDRELL ROAD
VESTA ROAD
WALLBUTTON ROAD
ENDWELL ROAD
MILLMARK GROVE
ST. ASAPH ROAD
SEYMOUR GDNS
BROCKLEY ROAD
B218
HAREFIELD RD
FOXBERRY RD
ARABIN ROAD
BRAXFIELD ROAD
COMERFORD ROAD
WHITBREAD ROAD
DALRYMPLE RD
BEECROFT RD
MERRITT
DARFIELD
CROFTON PARK
Lib
SOUTHWARK
HAINFORD CL
BILLINGFORD CL
FRENDSBURY RD
ST. NORBERT ROAD
CHELWOOD WALK
Health Cen
TURNHAM ROAD
CROFTON GATE WAY
Community Centre
BROCKLEY WAY
BROCKLEY MEWS
HOLDENBY ROAD
HAZELDON ROAD
EDDYSTONE RD
Brockley Jack PH
BARTRAM ROAD
SEVENOAKS
BEARSTEAD RISE
GUY'S UMDS ATHLETIC GROUND
CRESCENT
HONOR OAK PARK
COURTRAI ROAD
HOLMESLEY RD
KILGOUR ROAD
MACLEAN ROAD
PARBURY ROAD
TATNELL ROAD
RISELDINE ROAD
STONDON PARK
STILLNESS
BLYTHE HILL FIELDS
COMM CEN
DUNCOMBE HILL
BROCKLEY HILL PARK
LOWTHER HILL
OWENS WAY
BLYTHE CLOSE
FIRS CLOSE
GROVE CLO
Fire Sta
Health Centre
STANSTEAD ROAD
A205
RYE HILL EST
ALLOTMENTS
LIMESFORD ROAD
HARLESCOTT ROAD
LANBURY ROAD
BELLWOOD ROAD
ALDERSFORD CLOSE
MERTINS RD
STUART RD
CHELTENHAM ROAD
Pumping Station
AQUARIUS GOLF COURSE
COV RES
Clubhouse
HOMESTALL ROAD
PEckham RYE
REC GRD
PLAYING FIELDS
COLYTON
SCUTARI
MUNDANIA
THERAPIA
MARMORA
CAMBERWELL NEW CEMETERY
ONE TREE HILL
HONOR OAK SPORTS GROUND
Crem
Pav
Tennis Courts
ALLOT
BRENCHLEY GDNS
KELVINGTON RD
ATHENLAY
GARDENS
CAMBERWELL OLD CEMETERY
VALE
WOOD
HONOR OAK ROAD
B238
Nursery
WALTERS WAY
COACH HO MS
HENGRAVE RD
BOWMANS LEA
DUNOON
GREYSTEAD ROAD
NETHERBY ROAD
CANONBIE ROAD
FAIRLIE GARDENS
BOVENEY
GARTHORNE ROAD NATURE RESERVE
WHATMAN
EBSWORTH ST
BOVILL RD
HERSCHELL RD
EWART ROAD
TYSON ROAD
TEWKESBURY AVE
WESTWOOD PARK
RINGMORE RISE
HORNIMAN
ROCOMBE CRES
THE HERMITAGE
BENSON ROAD
CLEEVE HI
STANSTEAD RD
GABRIEL STREET
GRIERSON RD
BALLINA ST
LESSING ST
WYLEU ROAD

33
41
D
E
F
G
1
2
3
4
5
Lewisham CoH
Brookspears
A20
LOAMPIT HILL
LOAMPIT VALE
LEWISHAM
GRANVILLE
CRESSINGHAM RD
BOYNE ROAD
BELMONT
LEE BRIDGE
MARISCHAL RD
QUAGGY
SE13
LEWISHAM
Lewisham Centre
Sports Cen
Bowl. Alley
MOLESWORTH ST
LEWIS HIGH ST
ALBION WAY
BONFIELD ROAD
LIMES GROVE
SLAITHWAITE ROAD
CLARENDON RISE
Lib
Council Depot
HILLY FIELDS
Tennis Courts
Bowling Green
HILLY FIELDS CRES
TRESSILLIAN
CRESCENT WAY
BROOKBANK ROAD
ELLERDALE STREET
VICARS HILL
ERMINE RD
EMBLETON ROAD
ALGERNON ROAD
MARSALA ROAD
VEDA ROAD
ALGIERS ROAD
GREATFIELD CLOSE
ADELAIDE AVENUE
B236
LADYWELL CEMETERY
War Memorial
LADYWELL ROAD
GILLIAN ST
MERCY TER
Comm Cen
CORONATION CT
Sports Cen
LADYWELL
LEWISHAM HOSPITAL
A21
LEWISHAM HIGH ST
Fire Sta
COURTHILL ROAD
LONGBRIDGE WAY
ROMBOROUGH GDNS
LEGGE ST
ROMBOROUGH WAY
GUYSCLIFF ROAD
LEWISHAM PARK
THORNFORD RD
HARVARD ROAD
HITHER GREEN
ENNERSDALE
MOUNTSFIELD COURT
THEODORE ROAD
LADYWELL
CHUDLEIGH ROAD
Water Twr (Dis)
FOXBOROUGH GARDENS
RUSHEY MEAD
Ladywell Centre
MALYONS ROAD
Tenn Cts
ALBACORE CRES
Health Centre
MOUNT PLEASANT ROAD
FELDAY ROAD
GEORGE LANE
LARA CLOSE
The George Inn
CATFORD GREYHOUND STADIUM
MEDUSA ROAD
HAWSTEAD ROAD
DAVENPORT ROAD
ROSENTHAL ROAD
PATROL PLACE
SE6
EARLEY
WILDFELL ROAD
HONLEY ROAD
RUSHEY GREEN
MOUNTSFIELD PARK REC GRD
HITHER GREEN HOSPITAL
Bowling Green
STAINTON ROAD
LADYWELL FIELDS
Bowl Grn
RINGSTEAD ROAD
MELBOURNE MEWS
CARSWELL ROAD
REDFERN ROAD
BROWNHILL ROAD A205 (SOUTH
LEWISHAM TOWN HALL
Lewisham Theatre
PLASSY RD
BOURNVILLE ROAD
WESTDOWN RD
CATFORD BRIDGE
CATFORD ROAD
CATFORD
PLAYING FIELDS
Pav
SOUTH CIRCULAR ROAD
ELMER ROAD
ENGLEHEART ROAD
SPORTSBANK ST
SHORNDEAN ST
ARNGASK
FORDEL
GLENFARG
SANDHURST
KILLEARN
SANGLEY
Cannon Cinema
BROMLEY RD
CULVERLEY ROAD
PRIVATE BANKS SPORTS GROUND
Clubho
CANADIAN
Comm Cen

A
B
C
D
34
40
1
2
3
4
5
SE13
LEE
HITHER GREEN
HIGH ROAD
LEE HIGH ROAD
LEE BRIDGE
A20
A205
A2212
B212
B220
SOUTH CIRCULAR ROAD
BURNT ASH ROAD
BURNT ASH HILL
ST. MILDREDS ROAD
BLACKHEATH
BLACKHEATH HOSPITAL
BLACKHEATH CONCERT HALLS
LEE TERRACE
BELMONT HILL
BELMONT PARK
BELMONT GROVE
LEWISHAM HIGH ST
GRANVILLE
CRESSINGHAM RD
BOYNE ROAD
CATERHAM RD
MARISCHAL RD
BLESSINGTON ROAD
MERCATOR RD
QUAGGY
GILMORE ROAD
CLARENDON RISE
ALBION WAY
BONFIELD ROAD
LIMES GROVE
SLAITHWAITE ROAD
MORLEY RD
CLIPPER WAY
COLLEGE PK CLO
HOLLYHILL
DERMODY GDNS
COURTHILL ROAD
CAMPSHILL RD
MONUMENT GDNS
THORNFORD RD
HARVARD ROAD
MOUNTSFIELD COURT
MOUNTSFIELD PARK
REC GRD
Bowling Green
HITHER GREEN HOSPITAL
HITHER GREEN LANE
SPRINGBANK ROAD
WELLMEADOW ROAD
DUNCRIEVIE RD
NIGHTINGALE GROVE
MANOR PARK
MANOR HOUSE GARDENS
MANOR LANE
OLD ROAD
WEARDALE RD
LEAHURST ROAD
STAPLEHURST RD
FERNBROOK ROAD
EFFINGHAM ROAD
HANDEN ROAD
MICHELDEVER ROAD
SOUTHBROOK ROAD
CHILTONIAN IND. ESTATE
HOLME LACEY ROAD
DALLINGER ROAD
NEWSTEAD ROAD
MILBOROUGH CRESCENT
BR DEPOT
ALLOT
RAYFORD AVENUE
LINCHMERE RD
WAITE DAVIES ROAD
SUMMERFIELD ST
BONVER ROAD
NORTHBROOK PARK
ARNGASK ROAD
FORDEL ROAD
GLENFARG ROAD
SANDHURST
KILLEARN ROAD
ELMER ROAD
TORRIDON ROAD
ARDGOWAN ROAD
MINARD ROAD
BROADFIELD ROAD
VERDANT LANE
FURTHER GREEN ROAD
CUMBERLAND PL
SOUTH PARK
SPORTS GROUND
Old Tiger's Head PH
MANOR WAY
PRIORY PARK
THE PRIORY
LEYLAND
Clarendon Hotel
Amb Sta
Comm Cem
Comm Cen
Health Cen
Sch
Lib
PO
Coll
Pol
Fire Sta
Bowl. Alley
Sorting Office

41
34
42
D
E
F
G
1
2
3
4
5
KIDBROOKE
ELTHAM
ROCHESTER WAY
A2
A20
A210
A213
KIDBROOKE PARK ROAD
SIDCUP ROAD
WESTHORNE AVENUE
ELTHAM ROAD
ELTHAM HILL
ELTHAM PALACE ROAD
SUTCLIFFE PARK
REC GRD
Bowl Grn
Tenn Cts
Clubhouse
Amb Sta
Yorkshire Grey PH
WEIGALL ROAD
SPORTS GROUND
LYME FARM ROAD
TUDWAY ROAD
Sports Cen
Health Cen
Coll
Comm Cen
Lib
Sch
Depot
SPORTS GROUNDS
MINI TOWN HALL
NELSON MANDELA ROAD
LANGBROOK ROAD
BOURNBROOK ROAD
WENDOVER
WINCHCOMB GARDENS
ROCHESTER WAY
UNIVERS OF GREEN SPORTS GR
OLD COLFEIAN'S SPORTS GROUND
MIDDLE PARK FIELD
MIDDLE PARK AVENUE
CIVIL SERVICE SPORTS GROUND
SPORTS GROUNDS
ALLOT
QUAGGY RIVER
Dutch House PH
MOTTINGHAM LANE
SIBTHORPE ROAD
GAVESTONE RD
GAVESTONE CRESCENT
HORSA ROAD
ALNWICK
KING JOHN PLAYING FIELDS
QUEENSCROFT
KINGSGROUND
GLASBROOK ROAD
GREGORY CRESCENT
JOAN CRESCENT
CHURCHBURY RD
CAMPFIELD RD
WINN ROAD
CORONA ROAD
12

GREENWICH CEMETERY
Pav
A
B
C
D
35
41
1
2
3
4
5
Severndroog Castle
Tennis Courts
CASTLE WOOD
JACKWOOD
Jackwood House
MAYDAY
CROSSBROOK ROAD
KELBROOK RD
FLINTMILL CRESCENT
SLADEBROOK ROAD
HIREBROOK ROAD
EDGEBROOK ROAD
SCARSB. RD
BOURNBROOK ROAD
DUNBLANE RD
ALLENSWOOD RD
ROAD
ARBROATH ROAD
ROSS WAY
PHINEAS PETT ROAD
APPLETON RD
WHINYATES ROAD
DOWNMAN RD
WENDOVER
WINCHCOMB GARDENS
DICKSON RD
SANDBY GRN
COBBETT RD
SHO. W.
Sch
WELL HALL ROAD (SOUTH CIRCULAR)
PO
HEATHERBANK
WESTMOUNT ROAD
CASTLE DRIVE
GRANBY ROAD
ARSENAL RD
MAUDSLAY ROAD
MARTIN BOWES ROAD
CONGREVE RD
LOVELACE
CORNW. RD
SHRA. RD
BROME RD
GRN
GAR. CLO
LITTLE CROFT
CROOKSTON ROAD
DAIRSIE ROAD
GLENESK ROAD
FB
ROCHESTER WAY
A2
WAY
BRISET
LYNSTED GDNS
BRENLEY GDNS
NESBIT RD
KINGSHOLM GDNS
RANCLIFFE GARDENS
AVENUE A205
ELMB. GD
RIC. P.
KIDBROOKE LANE
Pav
UNIVERSITY OF GREENWICH SPORTS GROUND
SUB Bowl Grn
MOAT
WELL HALL PLEASANCE
Coronet Cinema
WELL HALL RD
CONGREVE RD
PRINCE RUPERT RD
ADMIRAL SEYMOUR ROAD
MOIRA ROAD
Comm Cen
GRANGEHILL ROAD
DUMBRECK ROAD
ELIBANK ROAD
EARLSHALL ROAD
GREENVALE ROAD
CRAIGTON ROAD
DUNVEGAN ROAD
WESTMOUNT ROAD
ELTHAM PARK GDNS
BERRYHILL
BERRYHILL GDNS
RELIEF ROAD
ELTHAM
WAY
PINNELL RD
CATHERINE GARDENS
HORSFELD GDNS
FOXHOLE RD
Hall
Clinic
Sch
BASKET GDNS
TATTERSALL CLOSE
MILNE GDNS
FROISSART ROAD
BLOXAM GDNS
KEYNSHAM GDNS
KEYNSHAM ROAD
JOHN ROAD
LILBURNE RD
PRINCE JOHN ROAD
VANDYKE CROSS
YOLANDE GDNS
CARNECKE GDNS
SHERARD ROAD
EVEREST ROAD
SPENCER GDNS
LASSA RD
Coll
A208
BUS STA
STRONGBOW CRES
STRONGBOW ROAD
ARCHERY
BALCASKIE RD
BEECHILL RD
GLENHOUSE RD
GLENLEA
GLENLYON RD
GLENSHIEL ROAD
CONV OF MERCY
McAULEY CLOSE
SE9
GLENURE ROAD
ELDERSLIE ROAD
GREENHOLM ROAD
ELSTOW CLOSE
GOUROCK ROAD
BLUNTS RD
FRIARS MEWS
DOBELL ROAD
ORANGERY LANE
ST. JOHN'S CEMETERY
SOWERBY CLO
Pol
P
Sch
COV RES
PO
ELTHAM HILL
QUEENSCROFT
Comm Cen
Swim Pool
ELTHAM HIGH ST
Lib
Fire Sta
Sports Cen
TOWN HALL
WYTHENS WK
SOUTHEND CRES
Sch
Clubhouse
QUEENSCROFT REC GROUND
BEECH CT
CEDAR CT
KINGS
WYTHFIELD
ORCHARD ROAD
CHAUNDRYE CLOSE
COURT YARD
TILT YARD APPROACH
COURT ROAD
PO
Sorting Off
WENSLEY CLOSE
Superstore
ELTHAM & MOTTINGHAM HOSPITAL
WOODING CLO
NORTH PARK
GREENACRES
Sch
FOOTSCRAY ROAD
Clinic
ANDREWS PLACE
ELTHAM
ROAD
ALLOT
GLASBROOK ROAD
CUFF CRES
KINGSGROUND
KING JOHN'S WALK
ELTHAM PALACE
LANGLEY COURT
LADYSMITH ROAD
HALONS RD
Bowling Green
Superstore
SPORTS GRD
Clubhouse
Coll
ROYAL BLACKHEATH GOLF COURSE
INCA DR
Tenn Cts
Clubhouse
Tenn Cts
SPORTS GRD
A211
CLARE CORNER
KING JOHN PLAYING FIELDS
VISTA
CRESCENT
JOAN CRESCENT
Comm Cen
Sch
WOODMERE
TARNWOOD
MIDDLE PARK AVENUE
ALLOT
A20
MOTTINGHAM
A208
SANCTUARY
SPORT.

35
A207
We Anchor In Hope PH
SANDRINGHAM DR
SHOULDER OF MUTTON GREEN
OXLEAS WOOD
OXLEAS MEADOW
OXLEAS CLOSE
FALCONWOOD AVENUE
EASTCOTE ROAD
SUNDRIDGE AVE
BELMONT AVE
SHERWOOD RD
GROVE
ASHMORE
MONTROSE CLOSE
A2
A209
WELLING WAY
SOUTH AVE
YORKLAND AVENUE
WESTWOOD
DA16
FALCONWOOD
SPORTS GROUND
SHEPHERDLEAS WOOD
ROCHESTER WAY
FALCONWOOD FIELD
MONTROSE
NORTHUMBERLAND
WESTMORELAND AVENUE
CUMBERLAND AVENUE
CORNWALL AVENUE
ALLOT
Elec Sta
FALCONWOOD
MILL CRESCENT
LINGFIELD
BRAYWOOD ROAD
WINCROFTS DRIVE
Schs
ELTHAM PARK NORTH
CAMBRIDGE
DORSET AVENUE
FB
ROAD
THE SUTHERLAND
BUCKINGHAM GREEN
Comm Cen
Clin
FALCONWOOD PARADE
PO
HOOK LANE
ELTHAM CEMETERY
EAST
Crematorium
ELTHAM PARK SOUTH
RIEFIELD ROAD
COLEPITS WOOD ROAD
LANE
PIT
ELTHAM WARREN GOLF COURSE
Sch
ORCHARD RISE
RIDGEWAY WEST
FAIROAK DRIVE
CROWN WOODS WAY
RENNETS WOOD ROAD
RENNETS CLOSE
BOUNDARY ROAD
GORDON RD
CHESTER RD
RIDGEWAY EAST
ORCHARD RISE EAST
LEECHCROFT AVE
GRAVEL
Clubhouse
Environment Study Centre
Tennis Courts
PLAYING FIELD
A210
BLACKFEN ROAD
The Jolly Fenman PH
LEMONWELL CT
PACKMORES RD
BLAIR CLOSE
ALEXANDER CLOSE
MONTGOMERY CL
WAV DR
FEN
QUEENSWOOD ROAD
ALLOT
Nursery
University of Greenwich Avery Hill Campus
Pavs
AVERY HILL
AVERY HILL ROAD
RESTONS CRESCENT
ANSTRIDGE ROAD
ALDERWOOD
RAINHAM CL
PARISH GATE DR
RIDER CLO
RAEBURN
RONALDSTONE ROAD
DA15
ALLOT
PARISH WOOD
HOLBEACH GDNS
CLOVERDALE GDNS
GROVE
Sch
LYDD CT
PERPINS ROAD
LINSTEAD CT
WAY LINK
Comm Cen
AVERY HILL PARK
BERWICK CRESCENT
CAITHNESS GDNS
LANE
SPORTS GRDS
University of Greenwich Halls of Residence
RESTONS CRESCENT
RADFIELD WAY
NORFOLK CRESCENT
BLAC
CAMBRIDGE MISSION SPORTS GROUND
Tenn Cts
B2214
SPRING
GREENHITHE CLOSE
ROSEBERY AVENUE
HARBOROUGH AVE
OAKLANDS
BEVERLEY AVENUE
CHARLTON ATHLETIC FC TRAIN. GROUND
Sports Cen
Bowling Green
Clubhouse
CROYDE CLOSE
HAM RD
SOUTHSPRING
HAMBLEDO RD
DAYS LANE
CORBYLANDS ROAD
ANNANDALE
RIVER SHUTTLE
OVERMEAD
HALFWAY STREET
FOREST WAY
ARLINGTON CLOSE
STREAM
SHUTTLE CLO
SPORTS GROUNDS
THE FOOTWAY
Pav
Pavs
SPORTS GROUND
MERRILEES ROAD
WOODBINE
WOODLANDS AVENUE
SPARROWS LANE
MILLWALL TRAINING GRD
Works
TIVERTON
ALV GDNS
HILL
SIDEWOOD
CAMBRIA CLOSE
ROAD
RD

MIDDLESEX HOSP
UNI OF WEST
MORTIMER
Langham Hilton
GT. PORTLAND ST
All Saints
Welsh Baptist
EASTCASTLE
BERNERS
NEWMAN
RATHBONE PLACE
Birkbeck College
TOTTENHAM COURT ROAD
Centre-point
NEW OXFORD
DOMINION
BEDFORD SQUARE
BLOOMSBURY
MUSEUM AND BRITISH LIBRARY
Bedford Corner
SCH OF ARCHIT
YMCA
GT. RUSSELL ST
ST. GILES HIGH ST
OXFORD ST
A40
OXFORD CIRCUS
LITTLEWOODS
M & S
French Protestant
SOHO SQUARE
St. Patrick (RC)
Hostel
PHOENIX ART COLL
Salvation Army
DICKINS & JONES
PALLADIUM
LIBERTY
GT. MARLBOROUGH ST
COLL OF MUSIC
Marshall St Leisure Cen
BROADWICK
WARDOUR
BERWICK
DEAN
FRITH
GREEK
CHARING CROSS ROAD
PRINCE EDWARD
OLD COMPTON
SOHO
St. Anne
SHAFTESBURY
CURZON
Fire Sta
HANOVER ST
DIAM. CEN
St. George
CONDUIT ST
REGENT STREET
CARNABY
KINGLY
HAMLEYS
Westminster Coll
ASTRAL
Prim. Sch
QUEEN'S
GIELGUD
APOLLO
LYRIC
GERRARD ST
EMPIRE
LEICESTER
HIPPODROME
B406
Westbury
A4201
Our Lady (RC)
Virgin Radio
GOLDEN SQUARE
Regent Pal
PICCADILLY
METRO
Trocadero Cen
ODEON
GLASSHOUSE STREET
Evangelical Cen
VIGO ST
AQUA SCUTUM
CEN AT THE CIRCUS
EROS
PICCADILLY CIR.
HAYMARKET
NATIONAL GALLERY
BRUTON LANE
FARADAY MUS
MUS OF MANKIND
ROYAL ACAD OF ARTS
SACKVILLE ST
LILLYWHITES
Le Meridien
SIMPSON
A4
FORT & MASON
St. James
JERMYN
PLAZA
BRIT. TRAV CEN
NEW ZEALAND & TONGA
TRAFALGAR
PALL MALL E
COCKSPUR
Canada Ho
Nelson's Column
UGANDA
Charles I Statue
Holiday Inn
Forte Crest
ST. JAMES'S SQUARE
CRAFTS COUNCIL GALL
PAP NEW GUINEA
WATERLOO
WAR.HO.ST
SPRING GARDENS
ADMIRALTY ARCH
MALL GALLERIES
STRATTON ST
The Ritz
ARLING. ST
ST. JAMES'S ST
CHRISTIE'S
KING
PALL MALL
A4
WATERLOO GDNS
CARLTON HOUSE TER
ICA
GREEN PARK
Stafford
Dukes
CHANCELLORS DEPT
SUDAN
ST. JAMES'S
MARLBOROUGH HOUSE
Chapel Royal
OLD ADMIRALTY BLDGS
WHITEHALL
PARLIAMENTARY COUNSEL OFFICE
QUEEN'S WALK
Bandstand
CLEVELAND ROW
MALL
HORSE GUARDS RD
Guards Memorial
ARMY HQ
CABINET OFFICE
St. James's Palace
LANCASTER HOUSE
ST. JAMES'S
Duck Island
FOREIGN OFFICE
A B C D E
1 2 3 4 5 6
17
24

HOLBORN
LINCOLN'S INN FIELDS
HIGH HOLBORN
BLOOMSBURY WAY
NEW OXFORD ST
KINGSWAY
CHANCERY LANE
FETTER LANE
PUBLIC RECORD OFFICE
ROYAL COLL OF SURGEONS
LAND REGISTRY OFFICE
ROYAL COURTS OF JUSTICE
PUBLIC TRUSTEE OFFICE
CAREY STREET
STRAND
ALDWYCH
St. Clement Danes
UNI OF LON Sch of Econ
BBC
INDIA
AUSTRALIA
Prince Henry's Room
MIDDLE TEMPLE LANE
Middle Temple
TEMPLE
VICTORIA EMBANKMENT
HQS WELLINGTON Master Mariners'
SOMERSET HOUSE
UNI OF LON King's Coll
COURTAULD INST. GALLERIES
DRURY LANE
GT. QUEEN STREET
LONG ACRE
COVENT GDN
The Market
ROYAL OPERA HOUSE
BOW ST
WELLINGTON ST
TAVISTOCK ST
SOUTHAMPTON ST
SAVOY PLACE
WC2
STRAND
CHARING CROSS
EMBANKMENT
Charing Cross Pier
Cleopatra's Needle
HUNGERFORD BRI
WATERLOO BRI
A3211
NATIONAL THEATRE
NAT FILM
London Weekend Television Centre
QUEEN ELIZABETH HALL AND PURCELL ROOM
ROYAL FESTIVAL HALL
HAYWARD GALLERY
UNI OF LONDON KING'S COLL
MOMI
UPPER GROUND
STAMFORD ST
A301
Shell Centre
CON.HALL APP
HOME OFFICE
St. John the Evangelist
TENISON WAY
WATERLOO EAST
WATERLOO
WATERLOO INTERNATIONAL
THE YOUNG VIC
JUBILEE GDNS
1 BOYCE ST
2 WHICHCOTE ST
3 BUCKLEY ST
4 MEPHAM ST
PS TATTERSHALL CASTLE
MIN.OF AG FISH & FOOD
Royal Horseguards
MINISTRY OF DEFENCE
WHITEHALL
HORSE GUARDS AVE
The Cenotaph
NORTHUMBERLAND AVE
B308
A4
B400
B401
B402
17
24
44
E F G H J
1 2 3 4 5 6

A
B
C
D
E
18
1
2
3
4
5
6
43
25
HOLBORN CIRCUS
HOLBORN A40
VIADUCT
B500
FARRINGDON ST
FARRINGDON ROAD
NEW FETTER LANE
FETTER LANE A4
ST. ANDR. ST
SHOE LA
SHOE LANE
ST. BRIDE ST
St. Sepulchre
SNOW HILL
GILTSPUR ST
KING EDWARD ST
ALDERSGATE
ST. MARTIN'S LE GRAND
ST. BARTHOLOMEW'S HOSPITAL
LITTLE BRITAIN
MONTAGUE ST
CHIEF OFFICE
POSTAL MUS
CENTRAL CRIMINAL COURT (Old Bailey)
NEWGATE ST
OLD BAILEY
WARWICK LA
PATERNOSTER SQ
ST. PAUL'S
St. Vedast
CHEAPSIDE
NEW CHANGE
ST. PAUL'S CATHEDRAL
ST. PAUL'S CHURCHYARD
Choir School
WATLING
CANNON ST
Goldsmiths' Hall
St. Botolph
ANGEL ST
FOSTER LANE
GUTTER LANE
GRESHAM ST
NOBLE ST
Pewterers' Hall
Ironmongers' Hall
Barbers' Hall
PUBLIC RECORD OFFICE
CHANCERY LANE
St. Dunstan
FLEET STREET
LUDGATE CIRCUS
LUDGATE HILL
CITY THAMESLINK
STONE CUTTER ST
CARTOONIST PH
GUNPOW SQ
CITY LIT INST
DR. JOHNSONS HO
St. Martin
Stationers' Hall
Cutlers' Hall
St. Bride
CRYPT MUS
NEW BR ST
BRIDE LANE
BRIDEWELL PLACE
DORSET RISE
WHITEFRIARS ST
BOUVERIE ST
TUDOR STREET
MIDDLE TEMPLE LANE
CROWN OFFICE ROW
KINGS BENCH WALK
Inner Temple
TEMPLE AVENUE
TALLIS ST
CARMELITE ST
J. CARPENTER ST
EC4
BLACK FRIARS LA
CARTER LANE
Apoth. Hall
PLAYH. YARD
IRELAND YARD
ST. ANDREW HILL
GODLIMAN ST
Coll of Arms
KNIGHTRIDER ST
QUEEN VICTORIA STREET
St. Andrew
STORY OF TELECOMMUN
MERMAID THEATRE
St. Benet
BAYNARD
SALVATION ARMY INT. HQ
City of Lon Sch
Swim Pool
DISTAFF
LAMB. HILL
Painters Hall
BREAD ST
FRIDAY ST
UPPER THAMES ST
WHITE LION
BLACKFRIARS
EMBANKMENT
HMS PRESIDENT
Pier
RIVER THAMES
Southwark Bridge
KING'S REACH
BLACKFRIARS BRIDGE
A201
HM CUSTOMS & EXCISE
UPPER GROUND
RENNIE ST
Express Newspapers
BANKSIDE GALL
RIVERSIDE WALK
SHAKESPEARE GLOBE THEATRE
BANKSIDE
Power Station (Disused)
HOLLAND STREET
HOPTON ST
HOPTON GDNS
PARK STREET
SHAKESPEARE GLOBE MUS
NEW GLOBE WK
BEAR GDNS
ROSE ALL
SUMNER STREET
ZOAR STREET
GREAT GUILDFORD ST
STAMFORD STREET A3200
KING'S REACH TWR
DUCHY
BROADWALL
HATFIELDS
PARIS GARDEN
LONDON NAUTICAL SCH
Christ Church
BURRELL ST
ST. CHRISTOPHER HOUSE
SOUTHWARK ST
A3200
SOUTHWARK BRIDGE ROAD
A300
INLAND REVENUE
Colombo Street Sports & Community Centre
COLOMBO ST
MEYMOTT ST
CHANCEL ST
BEAR LANE
PRICE'S ST
SUFFOLK ST
LAVINGTON STREET
HOME OFFICE
EWER ST
THEED ST
ROUPELL STREET
WATERLOO EAST
JOAN STREET
SCORE. ST
SOUTHWARK
B300
UNION STREET
Most Precious Blood
British Library (India Office & Records)
ISA. ST
WOOTTON ST
GREET ST
THE CUT
THE YOUNG VIC
SOUTHWARK COLLEGE
COPPERFIELD STREET
LOMAN STREET
SAWYER STREET
Fire Sta & London Fire Brigade Mus
PARK ST
St. Andrew with St. Thomas
SURREY ROW
POCOCK ST
WEBBER ST
MITRE ROAD
CORNWALL RD
WATERLOO RD
MARSHALSEA RD
KEPPEL ROW

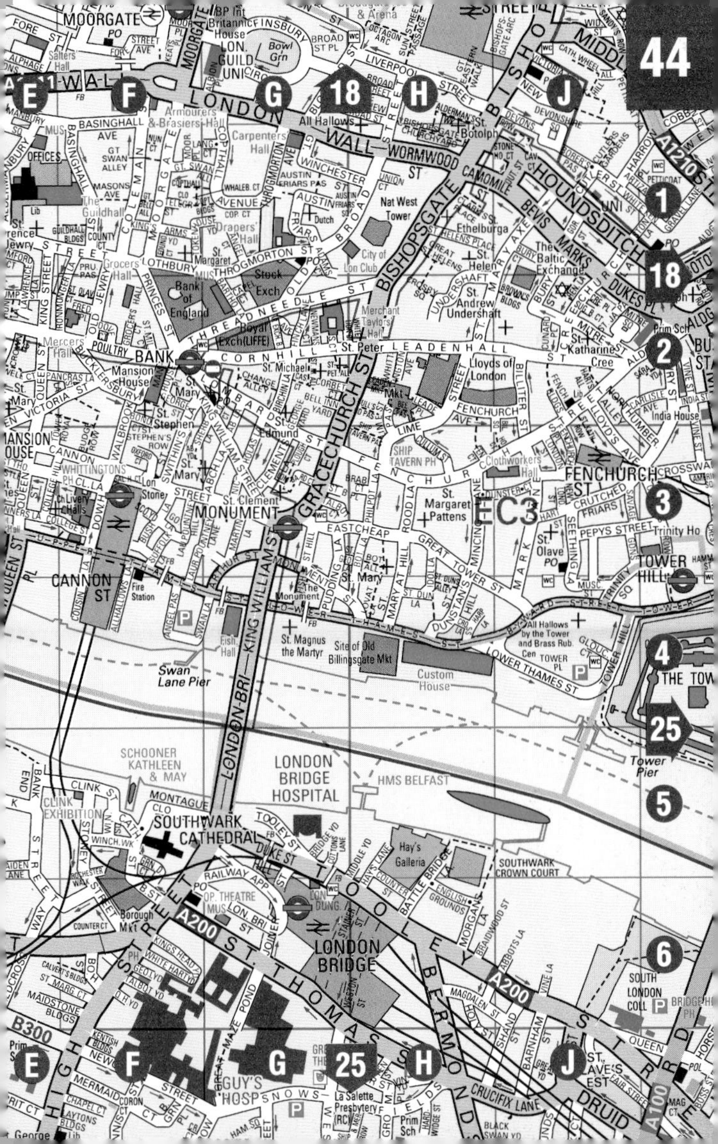

MOORGATE
LONDON WALL
WORMWOOD ST
BISHOPSGATE
HOUNDSDITCH
BEVIS MARKS
DUKES PL
The Guildhall
Drapers' Hall
Stock Exch
Bank of England
THREADNEEDLE ST
CORNHILL
LEADENHALL
Lloyds of London
Nat West Tower
City of Lon Club
The Baltic Exchange
St. Andrew Undershaft
St. Katharine Cree
Merchant Taylors' Hall
Royal Exch (LIFFE)
BANK
Mansion House
POULTRY
KING WILLIAM STREET
GRACECHURCH ST
FENCHURCH ST
FENCHURCH ST
Clothworkers Hall
St. Margaret Pattens
EC3
MONUMENT
EASTCHEAP
GREAT TOWER ST
CANNON ST
UPPER THAMES ST
LOWER THAMES ST
Fire Station
Fish. Hall
St. Magnus the Martyr
Site of Old Billingsgate Mkt
Custom House
All Hallows by the Tower and Brass Rub. Cen
TOWER HILL
Trinity Ho
THE TOWER
Tower Pier
Swan Lane Pier
LONDON BRIDGE
SCHOONER KATHLEEN & MAY
LONDON BRIDGE HOSPITAL
HMS BELFAST
CLINK EXHIBITION
SOUTHWARK CATHEDRAL
Hay's Galleria
SOUTHWARK CROWN COURT
TOOLEY ST
Borough Mkt
OP. THEATRE MUS
LONDON BRIDGE
A200
ST. THOMAS ST
BERMONDSEY ST
CRUCIFIX LANE
GUY'S HOSP
La Salette Presbytery (RC)
SOUTH LONDON COLL
DRUID ST
B300
A100
A1210
E F G H J
1 2 3 4 5 6
18
25

INDEX TO STREETS

General Abbreviations

All	Alley	Cov	Covered	Ho	House	Res	Reservoir
Allot	Allotments	Crem	Crematorium	Hosp	Hospital	Ri	Rise
Amb	Ambulance	Cres	Crescent	Ind	Industrial	S	South
App	Approach	Ct	Court	Junct	Junction	Sch	School
Arc	Arcade	Ctyd	Courtyard	La	Lane	Shop	Shopping
Ave	Avenue	Dep	Depot	Lo	Lodge	Sq	Square
Bdy	Broadway	Dr	Drive	Lwr	Lower	St	Street, Saint
Bks	Barracks	Dws	Dwellings	Mag	Magistrates	Sta	Station
Bldgs	Buildings	E	East	Mans	Mansions	Sub	Subway
Boul	Boulevard	Elec	Electricity	Meml	Memorial	Swim	Swimming
Bowl	Bowling	Embk	Embankment	Mkt	Market	TA	Territorial Army
Bri	Bridge	Est	Estate	Mkts	Markets	Tenn	Tennis
Cath	Cathedral	Ex	Exchange	Ms	Mews	Ter	Terrace
Cem	Cemetery	FB	Footbridge	Mt	Mount	Thea	Theatre
Cen	Central, Centre	Fld	Field	Mus	Museum	Trd	Trading
Cft	Croft	Flds	Fields	N	North	Twr	Tower
Ch	Church	Fm	Farm	Off	Office	Und	Underpass
Chyd	Churchyard	Gall	Gallery	PH	Public House	Vill	Villas
Cin	Cinema	Gar	Garage	Par	Parade	Vw	View
Circ	Circus	Gdn	Garden	Pas	Passage	W	West
Clo	Close	Gdns	Gardens	Pk	Park	WC	Toilet
Coll	College	Govt	Government	Pl	Place	Wd	Wood
Comm	Community	Gra	Grange	Pow	Power	Wds	Woods
Conv	Convent	Grd	Ground	Prec	Precinct	Wf	Wharf
Cor	Corner	Grds	Grounds	Pt	Point	Wk	Walk
Coron	Coroners	Grn	Green	Rd	Road	Wks	Works
Cotts	Cottages	Gro	Grove	Rec	Recreation	Yd	Yard

Abbreviations of District Names

Bark.	Barking	Ilf.	Ilford	Sid.	Sidcup	Well.	Welling

NOTES

The figures and letters following a street name indicate the Postal District page and map square where the name can be found

Street names shown in **bold type** indicate streets which appear in the enlarged Central London pages 43-44

Abbeville Rd. SW4 38 C4
Abbey Gdns. NW8 16 D1
Abbey Gdns. W6 29 G2
Abbey La. E15 19 G1
Abbey Orchard St. SW1 24 D4
Abbey Rd. E15 20 A1
Abbey Rd. NW6 9 C4
Abbey Rd. NW8 9 C5
Abbey Rd., Bark. 14 D4
Abbey Rd. Est. NW8 9 C5
Abbey St. E13 20 D3
Abbey St. SE1 25 E4
Abbey Wf. Ind. Est., Bark. 21 F1
Abbeyfield Rd. SE16 26 A5
Abbot St. E8 11 E3
Abbots La. SE1 44 J6
Abbot's Pl. NW6 9 C5
Abbot's Rd. E6 13 G5
Abbotsbury Clo. E15 19 G1
Abbotsbury Ms. SE15 40 A1
Abbotsbury Rd. W14 22 G3
Abbotstone Rd. SW15 36 E1
Abbotswell Rd. SE4 40 D3
Abbott Rd. E14 19 G5
Abchurch La. EC4 44 G3
Abchurch Yd. EC4 44 F3
Abdale Rd. W12 22 D2
Aberavon Rd. E3 19 C2
Abercorn Clo. NW8 16 D2
Abercorn Pl. NW8 16 D2
Abercorn Way SE1 32 F1
Abercrombie St. SW11 30 F5
Aberdare Gdns. NW6 9 C4
Aberdeen La. N5 11 B2
Aberdeen Pk. N5 11 B2
Aberdeen Pk. Ms. N5 11 B1
Aberdeen Pl. NW8 16 E3
Aberdeen Rd. N5 11 B1
Aberdeen Rd. NW10 8 B2
Aberdeen Ter. SE3 34 A5
Aberdour St. SE1 25 D5
Aberfeldy St. E14 19 G5
Aberford Gdns. SE18 35 A4
Abergeldie Rd. SE12 41 E4
Abernethy Rd. SE13 41 B2
Abersham Rd. E8 11 E2
Abery St. SE18 28 G5
Abingdon Rd. W8 23 B4
Abingdon St. SW1 24 E4
Abingdon Vill. W8 23 B4
Abinger Gro. SE8 33 D2
Abinger Rd. W4 22 A4
Ablett St. SE16 33 A1
Acacia Pl. NW8 16 E1
Acacia Rd. NW8 16 E1
Academy Pl. SE18 35 B4
Academy Rd. SE18 35 B4
Acanthus Dr. SE1 32 F1
Acanthus Rd. SW11 38 A1
Acfold Rd. SW6 30 C4
Achilles Clo. SE1 32 F1
Achilles Rd. NW6 9 B2
Achilles St. SE14 33 C3
Ackmar Rd. SW6 30 B4
Ackroyd Dr. E3 19 D4
Ackroyd Rd. SE23 40 B5
Acland Cres. SE5 39 C2
Acland Rd. NW2 8 D3
Acol Rd. NW6 9 B4
Acorn Wk. SE16 26 C2
Acre La. SW2 38 E2
Acris St. SW18 37 D3
Acton Ms. E8 11 E5
Acton St. WC1 17 F2
Ada Gdns. E14 20 A5
Ada Gdns. E15 13 C5
Ada Pl. E2 11 F5
Ada Rd. SE5 32 D3
Ada St. E8 11 G5
Adair Rd. W10 15 G3
Adam & Eve Ct. W1 43 B1
Adam & Eve Ms. W8 23 B4
Adam St. WC2 43 F4
Adam Wk. SW6 29 E3
Adams Ct. EC2 44 G1
Adams Row W1 24 A1
Adamson Rd. E16 20 D5
Adamson Rd. NW3 9 E4
Adderley St. E14 19 G5
Addington Rd. E3 19 E2
Addington Rd. E16 20 B3
Addington Sq. SE5 32 C2
Addison Ave. W11 22 G2
Addison Bri. Pl. W14 23 A5
Addison Cres. W14 22 G4
Addison Gdns. W14 22 F4
Addison Gro. W4 22 A4
Addison Pl. W11 22 G2
Addison Rd. W14 22 G4
Addle Hill EC4 44 C2
Adelaide Ave. SE4 40 D2
Adelaide Gro. W12 22 C2
Adelaide Rd. NW3 9 E4
Adelaide St. WC2 43 E4
Adelina Gro. E1 19 A4
Adeline Pl. WC1 17 D4
Adelphi Ter. WC2 43 F4
Aden Gro. N16 11 C1
Aden Ter. N16 11 C1
Adeney Clo. W6 29 F2
Adenmore Rd. SE6 40 E5
Adie Rd. W6 22 E4
Adine Rd. E13 20 E3
Adler St. E1 18 F5
Adley St. E5 12 C1
Admaston Rd. SE18 35 E2
Admiral Pl. SE16 26 C2
Admiral Seymour Rd. SE9 42 B2
Admiral Sq. SW10 30 D4
Admiral St. SE8 33 E4
Admirals Way E14 26 E3
Adolphus St. SE8 33 D3
Adpar St. W2 16 E4
Adrian Ms. SW10 30 C2
Adys Rd. SE15 39 E1
Afghan Rd. SW11 30 F5
Agamemnon Rd. NW6 9 A2
Agar Gro. NW1 10 C4
Agar Gro. Est. NW1 10 C4
Agar Pl. NW1 10 C4
Agar St. WC2 43 E4
Agate Clo. E16 20 G5
Agate Rd. W6 22 E4
Agave Rd. NW2 8 E1
Agdon St. EC1 18 A3
Agincourt Rd. NW3 9 G1
Agnes Ave., Ilf. 14 D1
Agnes Clo. E6 28 C1
Agnes Rd. W3 22 B2
Agnes St. E14 19 D5
Agnew Rd. SE23 40 B5
Ailsa St. E14 19 G4
Ainger Rd. NW3 9 G4
Ainsley St. E2 18 G2
Ainsworth Rd. E9 12 A4
Ainsworth Way NW8 9 D5
Aintree Ave. E6 14 A5
Aintree St. SW6 29 G3
Air St. W1 43 B4
Airdrie Clo. N1 10 F4
Airedale Ave. W4 22 B5
Airedale Rd. SW12 37 G5
Aisgill Ave. W14 30 A1

Aislibie Rd. SE12 41 B2
Ajax Rd. NW6 9 A2
Akehurst St. SW15 36 C4
Akenside Rd. NW3 9 E2
Akerman Rd. SW9 32 A5
Alabama St. SE18 35 F3
Alanthus Clo. SE12 41 C3
Alaska St. SE1 43 J6
Albacore Cres. SE13 40 F4
Albany, The W1 43 A4
Albany Ctyd. W1 43 B4
Albany Rd. E12 13 G1
Albany Rd. SE5 32 C2
Albany St. NW1 17 B1
Albatross St. SE18 35 G3
Albemarle St. W1 24 B1
Albert Ave. SW8 31 F3
Albert Bri. SW3 30 F2
Albert Bri. SW11 30 F3
Albert Bri. Rd. SW11 30 F3
Albert Ct. SW7 23 E3
Albert Embk. SE1 31 E1
Albert Gdns. E1 19 B5
Albert Pl. W8 23 C3
Albert Rd. E16 28 A2
Albert Rd. NW6 16 A1
Albert Sq. E15 13 B2
Albert Sq. SW8 31 F3
Albert St. NW1 10 B5
Albert Ter. NW1 10 A5
Alberta Est. SE17 32 A1
Alberta St. SE17 32 A1
Albion Ave. SW8 31 D5
Albion Dr. E8 11 E4
Albion Est. SE16 26 A3
Albion Gdns. W6 22 D5
Albion Gro. N16 11 D1
Albion Ms. N1 10 G4
Albion Ms. W2 16 F5
Albion Pl. EC1 18 A4
Albion Rd. N16 11 C1
Albion Sq. E8 11 E4
Albion St. SE16 26 A3
Albion St. W2 16 F5
Albion Ter. E8 11 E4
Albion Way SE13 40 G2
Albrighton Rd. SE22 39 D1
Albury St. SE8 33 E2
Albyn Rd. SE8 33 E4
Aldbourne Rd. W12 22 B2
Aldbridge St. SE17 32 D1
Aldebert Ter. SW8 31 E3
Aldeburgh St. SE10 34 D1
Alden Ave. E15 20 C3
Aldenham St. NW1 17 C1
Aldensley Rd. W6 22 D4
Alder Clo. SE15 32 E2
Alderbrook Rd. SW12 38 B4
Alderbury Rd. SW13 29 C2
Aldermanbury EC2 44 E1
Alderney Rd. E1 19 B3
Alderney St. SW1 24 B5
Aldersey Gdns., Bark. 14 F3
Aldersford Clo. SE4 40 B3
Aldersgate St. EC1 18 B4
Aldershot Rd. NW6 9 A5
Alderton Rd. SE24 39 B1
Alderville Rd. SW6 30 A5
Alderwood Rd. SE9 42 F4
Aldford St. W1 24 A2
Aldgate High St. EC3 18 E5
Aldine St. W12 22 E2
Aldington Rd. SE18 27 G4
Aldred Rd. NW6 9 B2
Aldridge Rd. Vill. W11 16 A4
Aldsworth Clo. W9 16 C3
Aldworth Gro. SE13 40 G4
Aldworth Rd. E15 13 B4
Aldwych WC2 43 G3
Alexander Ave. NW10 8 D4
Alexander Clo., Sid. 42 G4
Alexander Pl. SW7 23 F5
Alexander Sq. SW3 23 F5
Alexander St. W2 16 B5
Alexandra Ave. SW11 31 A4
Alexandra Cotts. SE14 33 D4
Alexandra Est. NW8 9 C5
Alexandra Gdns. W4 29 A3
Alexandra Pl. NW8 9 D5
Alexandra Rd. E6 21 C2
Alexandra Rd. NW8 9 D4
Alexandra St. E16 20 D4
Alexandra St. SE14 33 C3
Alexis St. SE16 25 F5
Alfearn Rd. E5 12 A1
Alford Rd. SW8 31 D4
Alfred Ms. W1 17 D4
Alfred Pl. WC1 17 D4
Alfred Prior Ho. E12 14 C1
Alfred Rd. E15 13 C2
Alfred Rd. W2 16 B4
Alfred St. E3 19 D2
Alfred St. E16 27 C1
Alfreda St. SW11 31 B4
Alfreds Gdns., Bark. 21 G1
Alfreds Way, Bark. 21 E2
Alfriston Rd. SW11 37 G3
Algernon Rd. NW6 9 B5
Algernon Rd. SE13 40 F1
Algiers Rd. SE13 40 E2
Alice Gilliatt Ct. W14 30 A1
Alice St. SE1 25 D4
Alie St. E1 18 E5
Alison Clo. E6 21 C5
Aliwal Rd. SW11 37 F2
Alkerden Rd. W4 29 A1
All Saints Dr. SE3 34 B5
All Saints Rd. W11 16 A5
All Saints St. N1 17 F1
All Souls Ave. NW10 15 D1
Allard Gdns. SW4 38 D3
Allardyce St. SW4 38 F2
Allcroft Rd. NW5 10 A2
Allen Edwards Dr. SW8 31 E4
Allen Rd. E3 19 D1
Allen Rd. N16 11 D1
Allen St. W8 23 B4
Allensbury Pl. NW1 10 D4
Allenswood Rd. SE9 42 A1
Allestree Rd. SW6 29 G3
Allfarthing La. SW18 37 C4
Allgood St. E2 18 E1
Allhallows La. EC4 44 F4
Allhallows Rd. E6 21 A4
Alliance Rd. E13 20 F3
Allied Ind. Est. W3 22 A3
Allingham St. N1 18 B1
Allington Rd. W10 15 G1
Allington St. SW1 24 B4
Allitsen Rd. NW8 16 F1
Allnutt Way SW4 38 D3
Alloa Rd. SE8 33 C1
Alloway Rd. E3 19 C2
Allsop Pl. NW1 16 G3
Alma Gro. SE1 25 E5
Alma Rd. SW18 37 D2
Alma Sq. NW8 16 D2
Alma St. E15 13 A3
Alma St. NW5 10 B3
Alma Ter. SW18 37 E5
Almack Rd. E5 12 A1
Almeida St. N1 11 A4
Almeric Rd. SW11 37 G2
Almond Clo. SE15 32 F5
Almond Rd. SE16 25 G5
Almorah Rd. N1 11 C4
Alnwick Rd. E16 20 F5
Alnwick Rd. SE12 41 E5
Alperton St. W10 15 G3
Alpha Gro. E14 26 E3
Alpha Pl. NW6 16 B1
Alpha Pl. SW3 30 F2
Alpha Rd. SE14 33 D4
Alpha St. SE15 32 F5
Alpine Rd. SE16 26 A5
Alpine Way E6 21 C4
Alscot Rd. SE1 25 E5
Alscot Way SE1 25 E5
Altenburg Gdns. SW11 37 G2
Althea St. SW6 30 C5
Altmore Ave. E6 14 B4
Alton St. E14 19 F4
Alvanley Gdns. NW6 9 C2
Alverstone Rd. E12 14 C1
Alverstone Rd. NW2 8 E4
Alverton St. SE8 33 D1
Alvey St. SE17 32 D1
Alvington Cres. E8 11 E2
Alwold Cres. SE12 41 E4
Alwyne Pl. N1 11 B3
Alwyne Rd. N1 11 B4
Alwyne Sq. N1 11 B3
Alwyne Vill. N1 11 A4
Ambassador Gdns. E6 21 B4
Ambassador's Ct. SW1 43 B6
Ambergate St. SE17 32 A1
Amberley Rd. W9 16 B4
Ambleside Rd. NW10 8 B4
Ambrosden Ave. SW1 24 C4
Ambrose St. SE16 25 G5
Amelia St. SE17 32 A1
Amen Cor. EC4 44 C2
Amen Ct. EC4 44 C1
America St. SE1 44 D6
Amerland Rd. SW18 37 A3
Amersham Gro. SE14 33 D3
Amersham Rd. SE14 33 D4
Amersham Vale SE14 33 D3
Amery Gdns. NW10 8 D5
Amethyst Rd. E15 13 A1
Amhurst Pas. E8 11 F2
Amhurst Rd. E8 11 G2
Amhurst Rd. N16 11 E1
Amhurst Ter. E8 11 F1
Amiel St. E1 19 A3
Amies St. SW11 37 G1
Amity Rd. E15 13 C5
Amner Rd. SW11 38 A4
Amor Rd. W6 22 E4
Amott Rd. SE15 39 F1
Amoy Pl. E14 19 E5
Ampton Pl. WC1 17 F2
Ampton St. WC1 17 F2
Amsterdam Rd. E14 26 G4
Amwell St. EC1 17 G2
Amyruth Rd. SE4 40 E3
Ancaster St. SE18 35 G3
Anchor & Hope La. SE7 27 F5
Anchor St. SE16 25 G5
Ancill Clo. W6 29 G2
Ancona Rd. NW10 15 C1
Ancona Rd. SE18 35 F1
Andalus Rd. SW9 38 E1
Anderson Rd. E9 12 B3
Anderson St. SW3 30 G1
Anderton Clo. SE5 39 C1
Andover Pl. NW6 16 C1
Andre St. E8 11 F2
Andrew Borde St. WC2 43 D1
Andrew St. E14 19 G5
Andrews Crosse WC2 43 J2
Andrews Pl. SE9 42 D4
Andrew's Rd. E8 11 G5
Anerley St. SW11 30 G5
Angel Ct. EC2 44 G1
Angel Ct. SW1 43 B6
Angel La. E15 13 A3
Angel Ms. N1 17 G1
Angel Pas. EC4 44 F4
Angel St. EC1 44 D1
Angel Wk. W6 29 E1
Angelica Dr. E6 21 C4
Angell Pk. Gdns. SW9 38 G1
Angell Rd. SW9 38 G1
Angerstein La. SE3 34 C4
Angler's La. NW5 10 B3
Anglesea Ave. SE18 28 D5
Anglesea Rd. SE18 28 D5
Anglia Ho. E14 19 C5
Anglo Rd. E3 19 D1
Angrave Ct. E8 11 E5
Angus Rd. E13 20 F2
Angus St. SE14 33 C3
Anhalt Rd. SW11 30 F3
Ankerdine Cres. SE18 35 D4
Anley Rd. W14 22 F3
Ann La. SW10 30 E3
Ann St. SE18 35 E1
Anna Clo. E8 11 E5
Annabel Clo. E14 19 F5
Annandale Rd. SE10 34 C1
Annandale Rd. W4 29 A1
Annandale Rd., Sid. 42 G5
Anne St. E13 20 D3
Annesley Rd. SE3 34 E4
Annie Besant Clo. E3 12 D5
Annis Rd. E9 12 C3
Ansdell Rd. SE15 33 A5
Ansdell St. W8 23 C4
Anselm Rd. SW6 30 B2
Ansleigh Pl. W11 22 F1
Anson Rd. N7 10 C1
Anson Rd. NW2 8 D2
Anstey Rd. SE15 39 F1
Anstice Clo. W4 29 A3
Anstridge Rd. SE9 42 F4
Antelope Rd. SE18 28 B4
Antill Rd. E3 19 C2
Antill Ter. E1 19 B5
Anton St. E8 11 F2
Antrim Gro. NW3 9 G3
Antrim Rd. NW3 9 G3
Apothecary St. EC4 44 B2
Appach Rd. SW2 38 G3
Apple Tree Yd. SW1 43 B5
Appleby Rd. E8 11 F4
Appleby Rd. E16 20 C5
Appleby St. E2 18 E1
Appleford Rd. W10 15 G3
Applegarth Rd. W14 22 F4
Appleton Rd. SE9 42 A1
Appold St. EC2 18 D4
Approach Rd. E2 19 A1
April St. E8 11 E1
Aquila St. NW8 16 E1
Aquinas St. SE1 44 A6
Arabella Dr. SW15 36 A2
Arabin Rd. SE4 40 C2
Arbery Rd. E3 19 C2
Arbour Sq. E1 19 B5
Arbroath Rd. SE9 42 A1
Arbuthnot Rd. SE14 33 B5
Arbutus St. E8 11 E5
Arcadia St. E14 19 E5
Arch St. SE1 25 B4
Archangel St. SE16 26 B3
Archbishops Pl. SW2 38 F4
Archdale Rd. SE22 39 E3
Archel Rd. W14 30 A2
Archer St. W1 43 C3

Archery Clo. W2	16	F5
Archery Rd. SE9	42	B3
Arches, The WC2	**43**	**F5**
Archibald Ms. W1	24	A1
Archibald Rd. N7	10	D1
Archibald St. E3	19	E3
Archway St. SW13	36	A1
Arcola St. E8	11	E2
Ardbeg Rd. SE24	39	C3
Arden Cres. E14	26	E5
Arden Est. N1	18	D1
Ardgowan Rd. SE6	41	B5
Ardilaun Rd. N5	11	B1
Ardleigh Rd. N1	11	D3
Ardmere Rd. SE13	41	A4
Ardwick Rd. NW2	9	B1
Argon Ms. SW6	30	B3
Argyle Pl. W6	22	D5
Argyle Rd. E1	19	B3
Argyle Rd. E15	13	B2
Argyle Rd. E16	20	E5
Argyle Sq. WC1	17	E2
Argyle St. WC1	17	E2
Argyll Rd. W8	23	B3
Argyll St. W1	**43**	**A2**
Arica Rd. SE4	40	C2
Ariel Rd. NW6	9	B3
Ariel Way W12	22	E2
Aristotle Rd. SW4	38	D1
Arklow Rd. SE14	33	D2
Arkwright Rd. NW3	9	D2
Arlesford Rd. SW9	38	E1
Arlingford Rd. SW2	38	G3
Arlington Ave. N1	11	B5
Arlington Clo., Sid.	42	G5
Arlington Lo. SW2	38	F2
Arlington Rd. NW1	10	B5
Arlington Sq. N1	11	B5
Arlington St. SW1	**43**	**A5**
Arlington Way EC1	17	G2
Armada St. SE8	33	E2
Armada Way E6	28	E1
Armadale Rd. SW6	30	B3
Armagh Rd. E3	12	D5
Arminger Rd. W12	22	D2
Armitage Rd. SE10	34	C1
Armoury Rd. SE13	33	F5
Armoury Way SW18	37	B3
Armstrong Rd. SW7	23	E4
Armstrong Rd. W3	22	B2
Arnal Cres. SW18	36	G5
Arndale Cen., The SW18	37	C4
Arne St. WC2	**43**	**F2**
Arne Wk. SE3	41	C2
Arngask Rd. SE6	41	A5
Arnold Circ. E2	18	E2
Arnold Est. SE1	25	E3
Arnold Rd. E3	19	E2
Arnould Ave. SE5	39	C2
Arnside St. SE17	32	B2
Arodene Rd. SW2	38	F4
Arragon Rd. E6	13	G5
Arran Wk. N1	11	B4
Arrow Rd. E3	19	F2
Arsenal Rd. SE9	35	B5
Artesian Rd. W2	16	B5
Arthingworth St. E15	13	B5
Arthur Gro. SE18	28	E5
Arthur Henderson Ho. SW6	30	A5
Arthur Rd. E6	21	B1
Arthur Rd. N7	10	F1
Arthur St. EC4	**44**	**G3**
Arthurdon Rd. SE4	40	E3
Artichoke Pl. SE5	32	C4
Artillery La. E1	18	D4
Artillery Pl. SE18	28	B5
Artillery Row SW1	24	D4
Artizan St. E1	**44**	**J1**
Arundel Clo. E15	13	B1
Arundel Gdns. W11	23	A1
Arundel Great Ct. WC2	**43**	**H3**
Arundel Gro. N16	11	D2
Arundel Pl. N1	10	G3
Arundel Sq. N7	10	G3
Arundel St. WC2	**43**	**H3**
Arundel Ter. SW13	29	D2
Arvon Rd. N5	10	G2
Ascalon St. SW8	31	C3
Ascham St. NW5	10	C2
Ascot Rd. E6	21	B2
Ash Gro. E8	11	G5
Ash Gro. NW2	8	F1
Ash Rd. E15	13	B2
Ashbourne Gro. SE22	39	E3
Ashbourne Gro. W4	29	A1
Ashbridge St. NW8	16	F3
Ashburn Gdns. SW7	23	D5
Ashburn Pl. SW7	23	D5
Ashburnham Gro. SE10	33	F3
Ashburnham Pl. SE10	33	F3
Ashburnham Retreat SE10	33	F3
Ashburnham Rd. NW10	15	E2
Ashburnham Rd. SW10	30	D3
Ashburton Ave., Ilf.	14	G1
Ashburton Gro. N7	10	G1
Ashburton Rd. E16	20	D5
Ashbury Rd. SW11	37	G1
Ashby Gro. N1	11	B4
Ashby Ms. SE4	33	D5
Ashby Rd. SE4	33	D5
Ashchurch Gro. W12	22	C4
Ashchurch Pk. Vill. W12	22	C4
Ashchurch Ter. W12	22	C4
Ashcombe St. SW6	30	C5
Ashcroft Rd. E3	19	C2
Ashdon Rd. NW10	8	B5
Ashenden Rd. E5	12	C2
Asher Way E1	25	F2
Ashfield Rd. W3	22	B2
Ashfield St. E1	18	G4
Ashford Rd. E6	14	C3
Ashford Rd. NW2	8	F1
Ashington Rd. SW6	30	A5
Ashland Pl. W1	17	A4
Ashleigh Rd. SW14	36	A1
Ashley Cres. SW11	38	A1
Ashley Pl. SW1	24	C4
Ashley Rd. E7	13	F4
Ashlin Rd. E15	13	A1
Ashlone Rd. SW15	36	E1
Ashmead Rd. SE8	33	E5
Ashmere Gro. SW2	38	E2
Ashmill St. NW1	16	F4
Ashmole Pl. SW8	31	F2
Ashmole St. SW8	31	F2
Ashmore Gro., Well.	42	F1
Ashmore Rd. W9	16	A1
Ashness Rd. SW11	37	G3
Ashridge Cres. SE18	35	E3
Ashton Rd. E15	13	A2
Ashton St. E14	26	G1
Ashwin St. E8	11	E3
Ashworth Rd. W9	16	C2
Askew Cres. W12	22	B3
Askew Rd. W12	22	B2
Askham Ct. W12	22	C2
Askham Rd. W12	22	C2
Asland Rd. E15	13	A5
Aslett St. SW18	37	C5
Asmara Rd. NW2	8	G2
Aspen Gdns. W6	29	D1
Aspen Way E14	27	A1
Aspenlea Rd. W6	29	F2
Aspern Rd. NW3	9	F2
Aspinall Rd. SE4	40	B1
Aspinden Rd. SE16	25	G5
Aspley Rd. SW18	37	C3
Assembly Pas. E1	19	A4
Astbury Rd. SE15	33	A4
Aste St. E14	26	G3
Astell St. SW3	30	F1
Astle St. SW11	31	A5
Astley Ave. NW2	8	E2
Aston St. E14	19	C5
Astoria Wk. SW9	38	G1
Astrop Ms. W6	22	E4
Astrop Ter. W6	22	E3
Astwood Ms. SW7	23	C5
Asylum Rd. SE15	32	G3
Atalanta St. SW6	29	F4
Atheldene Rd. SW18	37	D5
Athelstane Gro. E3	19	D1
Athenlay Rd. SE15	40	B3
Atherden Rd. E5	12	A1
Atherfold Rd. SW9	38	E1
Atherstone Ms. SW7	23	D5
Atherton Ms. E7	13	C3
Atherton Rd. E7	13	C3
Atherton Rd. SW13	29	C3
Atherton St. SW11	30	F5
Athlone Rd. SW2	38	F5
Athlone St. NW5	10	A3
Athol Sq. E14	19	G5
Atkins Rd. SW12	38	D5
Atkinson Rd. E16	20	F4
Atlantic Rd. SW9	38	G2
Atlas Gdns. SE7	27	F5
Atlas Ms. N7	10	F3
Atlas Rd. E13	20	D1
Atlas Rd. NW10	15	A2
Atley Rd. E3	12	E5
Atney Rd. SW15	36	G2
Atterbury St. SW1	24	E5
Atwood Rd. W6	22	D5
Aubert Pk. N5	10	G1
Aubert Rd. N5	11	A1
Aubrey Rd. W8	23	A2
Aubrey Wk. W8	23	A2
Aubyn Sq. SW15	36	C2
Auckland Rd. SW11	37	F2
Audley Clo. SW11	38	A1
Audrey St. E2	18	F1
Augurs La. E13	20	E2
Augusta St. E14	19	F5
Augustine Rd. W14	22	F4
Augustus St. NW1	17	B1
Auriga Ms. N16	11	C2
Auriol Rd. W14	22	G5
Austen Ho. NW6	16	B2
Austin Clo. SE23	40	D5
Austin Friars EC2	**44**	**G1**
Austin Friars Pas. EC2	**44**	**G1**
Austin Friars Sq. EC2	**44**	**G1**
Austin Rd. SW11	31	A4
Austin St. E2	18	E2
Austral St. SE11	25	A5
Australia Rd. W12	22	D1
Autumn St. E3	12	E5
Avalon Rd. SW6	30	C4
Ave Maria La. EC4	**44**	**C2**
Aveline St. SE11	31	G1
Avening Ter. SW18	37	B4
Avenons Rd. E13	20	D3
Avenue, The NW6	8	F5
Avenue, The SE7	34	F3
Avenue, The SE10	34	A3
Avenue, The SW4	38	A3
Avenue, The SW18	37	F5
Avenue, The W4	22	A4
Avenue Clo. NW8	9	F5
Avenue Gdns. SW14	36	A1
Avenue Rd. E7	13	E1
Avenue Rd. NW3	9	E4
Avenue Rd. NW8	9	E4
Avenue Rd. NW10	15	B1
Averill St. W6	29	F2
Avery Hill Rd. SE9	42	F4
Avery Row W1	24	B1
Aviary Clo. E16	20	C4
Avignon Rd. SE4	40	B1
Avis Sq. E1	19	B5
Avocet Ms. SE28	28	F4
Avon Rd. SE4	40	E1
Avondale Pk. Gdns. W11	22	G1
Avondale Pk. Rd. W11	22	G1
Avondale Ri. SE15	39	E1
Avondale Rd. E16	20	B4
Avondale Sq. SE1	32	F1
Avonley Rd. SE14	33	A3
Avonmore Rd. W14	22	G5
Avonmouth St. SE1	25	B4
Axe St., Bark.	14	E5
Aybrook St. W1	17	A4
Aycliffe Rd. W12	22	B2
Aylesbury Rd. SE17	32	C1
Aylesbury St. EC1	18	A3
Aylesford St. SW1	31	D1
Aylestone Ave. NW6	8	F4
Aylmer Rd. W12	22	B3
Aylward St. E1	19	A5
Aylwyn Est. SE1	25	D4
Aynhoe Rd. W14	22	F5
Ayres Clo. E13	20	D2
Ayres St. SE1	25	B3
Aysgarth Rd. SE21	39	D4
Aytoun Pl. SW9	31	F5
Aytoun Rd. SW9	31	F5
Azenby Rd. SE15	32	E5
Azof St. SE10	27	B5

B

Baalbec Rd. N5	11	A2
Babmaes St. SW1	**43**	**C5**
Baches St. N1	18	C2
Back Ch. La. E1	25	F1
Back Hill EC1	17	G3
Bacon Gro. SE1	25	E4
Bacon St. E1	18	E3
Bacon St. E2	18	E3
Bacton NW5	10	A2
Baden Rd., Ilf.	14	D2
Badminton Rd. SW12	38	A4
Badsworth Rd. SE5	32	B4
Bagley's La. SW6	30	C4
Bagshot St. SE17	32	D1
Bainbridge St. WC1	**43**	**D1**
Baizdon Rd. SE3	34	B5
Baker Rd. NW10	8	A5
Baker Rd. SE18	35	A4
Baker St. NW1	16	G3
Baker St. W1	16	G4
Bakers Row E15	20	B1
Baker's Row EC1	17	G3
Balaam St. E13	20	D3
Balaclava Rd. SE1	25	E5
Balcaskie Rd. SE9	42	B3
Balchen Rd. SE3	34	G5
Balchier Rd. SE22	39	G4
Balcombe St. NW1	16	G3
Balcorne St. E9	12	A4
Balderton St. W1	17	A5
Baldock St. E3	19	F1
Baldwin Cres. SE5	32	B4
Baldwin Ter. N1	18	B1
Baldwin's Gdns. EC1	17	G4
Balfe St. N1	17	E1

Balfern Gro. W4 29 A1
Balfern St. SW11 30 F5
Balfour Pl. SW15 36 D2
Balfour Rd. N5 11 B1
Balfour St. SE17 25 C5
Balham Gro. SW12 38 A5
Balham Hill SW12 38 B5
Balham New Rd. SW12 38 B5
Ballance Rd. E9 12 B3
Ballantine St. SW18 37 D2
Ballast Quay SE10 34 A1
Ballater Rd. SW2 38 E2
Ballina St. SE23 40 B5
Ballingdon Rd. SW11 38 A4
Balliol Rd. W10 15 F5
Ballogie Ave. NW10 8 A1
Balls Pond Rd. N1 11 C3
Balmer Rd. E3 19 D1
Balmes Rd. N1 11 C5
Balmoral Gro. N7 10 F3
Balmoral Ms. W12 22 B4
Balmoral Rd. E7 13 F1
Balmoral Rd. NW2 8 D3
Balmuir Gdns. SW15 36 E2
Balnacraig Ave. NW10 8 A1
Balniel Gate SW1 31 D1
Baltic St. EC1 18 B3
Balvernie Gro. SW18 37 A5
Bamborough Gdns. W12 22 E3
Bamford Rd., Bark. 14 E3
Banbury Ct. WC2 43 E3
Banbury Rd. E9 12 B4
Banbury St. SW11 30 F5
Banchory Rd. SE3 34 E3
Bancroft Rd. E1 19 B2
Bangalore St. SW15 36 E1
Banim St. W6 22 D5
Banister Rd. W10 15 F2
Bank End SE1 44 E5
Bank La. SW15 36 A3
Bankhurst Rd. SE6 40 D5
Bankside SE1 44 D4
Bankton Rd. SW2 38 G2
Bankwell Rd. SE13 41 B2
Banner St. EC1 18 B3
Bannerman Ho. SW8 31 F2
Banning St. SE10 34 B1
Bannockburn Rd. SE18 28 G5
Banstead St. SE15 40 A1
Bantry St. SE5 32 C3
Barb Ms. W6 22 E4
Barber's All. E13 20 E2
Barbers Rd. E15 19 F1
Barbican, The EC2 18 B4
Barchard St. SW18 37 C3
Barchester St. E14 19 F4
Barclay Clo. SW6 30 B3
Barclay Rd. E13 20 F3
Barclay Rd. SW6 30 B3
Bard Rd. W10 22 F1
Barden St. SE18 35 G3
Bardolph Rd. N7 10 E1
Bardsey Pl. E1 19 A4
Bardsley La. SE10 33 G2
Barfett St. W10 16 A3
Barford St. N1 10 G5
Barforth Rd. SE15 39 G1
Barge Ho. Rd. E16 28 D3
Barge Ho. St. SE1 44 A5
Baring Rd. SE12 41 D5
Baring St. N1 11 C5
Bark Pl. W2 23 C1
Barker Dr. NW1 10 C4
Barker St. SW10 30 D2
Barking Rd. E6 20 G1
Barking Rd. E13 20 D3
Barking Rd. E16 20 B4
Barkston Gdns. SW5 23 C5
Barlborough St. SE14 33 B3
Barlby Gdns. W10 15 F3
Barlby Rd. W10 15 E4
Barleycorn Way E14 26 D1
Barlow Rd. NW6 9 A3
Barmouth Rd. SW18 37 D4
Barn Elms Pk. SW15 29 E5
Barnabas Rd. E9 12 B2
Barnaby Pl. SW7 23 E5
Barnard Clo. SE18 28 C4
Barnard Ms. SW11 37 F2
Barnard Rd. SW11 37 F2
Barnard's Inn EC1 43 J1
Barnby St. E15 13 B5
Barnby St. NW1 17 C2
Barnes Ave. SW13 29 C3
Barnes Bri. SW13 29 A5
Barnes Bri. W4 29 A5
Barnes Clo. E12 13 G1
Barnes High St. SW13 29 B5
Barnes Rd., Ilf. 14 E2
Barnes St. E14 19 C5
Barnes Ter. SE8 33 D1
Barnesbury Ho. SW4 38 D4
Barnet Gro. E2 18 F2
Barney Clo. SE7 34 F1
Barnfield Pl. E14 26 E5
Barnfield Rd. SE18 35 D2
Barnham St. SE1 25 D3
Barnsbury Gro. N7 10 F3
Barnsbury Pk. N1 10 G4
Barnsbury Rd. N1 17 G1
Barnsbury Sq. N1 10 G4
Barnsbury St. N1 10 G4
Barnsbury Ter. N1 10 F4
Barnsdale Ave. E14 26 F5
Barnsdale Rd. W9 16 A3
Barnsley St. E1 18 G3
Barnwell Rd. SW2 38 G3
Barnwood Clo. W9 16 C3
Baron St. N1 17 G1
Barons Ct. Rd. W14 29 G1
Barons Keep W14 29 G1
Barons Pl. SE1 24 G3
Baronsmead Rd. SW13 29 C4
Barrett St. W1 17 A5
Barretts Gro. N16 11 D2
Barriedale SE14 33 C5
Barrier App. SE7 27 G4
Barrington Rd. E12 14 C3
Barrington Rd. SW9 39 A1
Barrington Vill. SE18 35 C4
Barrow Hill Rd. NW8 16 F1
Barry Rd. E6 21 A5
Barry Rd. SE22 39 F4
Barset Rd. SE15 40 A1
Barter St. WC1 17 E4
Barth Rd. SE18 28 G5
Bartholomew Clo. EC1 18 B4
Bartholomew Clo. SW18 37 D2
Bartholomew La. EC2 44 G2
Bartholomew Rd. NW5 10 C3
Bartholomew Sq. EC1 18 B3
Bartholomew St. SE1 25 C4
Bartholomew Vill. NW5 10 C3
Bartle Ave. E6 21 A1
Bartle Rd. W11 15 G5
Bartlett Clo. E14 19 E5
Bartlett Ct. EC4 44 A1
Barton Rd. W14 29 G1
Bartram Rd. SE4 40 C3
Barwick Rd. E7 13 E1
Baseing Clo. E6 28 C1
Basil Ave. E6 21 A1
Basil St. SW3 23 G4
Basing Ct. SE15 32 E4
Basing St. W11 16 A5
Basingdon Way SE5 39 C2
Basinghall Ave. EC2 18 C4
Basinghall St. EC2 44 F1
Basire St. N1 11 B5
Baskerville Rd. SW18 37 F5
Basket Gdns. SE9 42 A3
Basnett Rd. SW11 38 A1
Bassano St. SE22 39 E3
Bassein Pk. Rd. W12 22 B3
Bassett Rd. W10 15 F5
Bassett St. NW5 10 A3
Bassingham Rd. SW18 37 D5
Bastable Ave., Bark. 21 G1
Bastwick St. EC1 18 B3
Basuto Rd. SW6 30 B4
Batavia Rd. SE14 33 C3
Batchelor St. N1 17 G1
Bateman St. W1 43 C2
Bateman's Bldgs. W1 43 C2
Bateman's Row EC2 18 D3
Bath Rd. E7 13 G3
Bath Rd. W4 22 A5
Bath St. EC1 18 B2
Bath Ter. SE1 25 B4
Bathurst Gdns. NW10 15 D1
Bathurst St. W2 23 E1
Bathway SE18 28 C5
Batman Clo. W12 22 D2
Batoum Gdns. W6 22 E4
Batson St. W12 22 C3
Batten St. SW11 37 F1
Battersea Bri. SW3 30 E3
Battersea Bri. SW11 30 F3
Battersea Bri. Rd. SW11 30 F3
Battersea Ch. Rd. SW11 30 E4
Battersea High St. SW11 30 E4
Battersea Pk. SW11 30 G3
Battersea Pk. Rd. SW8 31 B4
Battersea Pk. Rd. SW11 30 F5
Battersea Ri. SW11 37 E3
Battery Rd. SE28 28 G3
Battle Bri. La. SE1 44 H6
Battle Bri. Rd. NW1 17 E1
Battledean Rd. N5 11 A2
Batty St. E1 18 F5
Baulk, The SW18 37 B5
Bavent Rd. SE5 32 B5
Bawdale Rd. SE22 39 E3
Bawtree Rd. SE14 33 C3
Baxendale St. E2 18 F2
Baxter Rd. E16 20 F5
Baxter Rd. N1 11 C3
Baxter Rd. NW10 15 A3
Baxter Rd., Ilf. 14 D2
Bayfield Rd. SE9 41 G2
Bayford Rd. NW10 15 F2
Bayford St. E8 11 G4
Bayham Pl. NW1 10 C5
Bayham St. NW1 10 C5
Bayley St. WC1 17 D4
Baylis Rd. SE1 24 G3
Baynes St. NW1 10 C4
Bayonne Rd. W6 29 G2
Bayswater Rd. W2 23 C1
Baythorne St. E3 19 D4
Baytree Rd. SW2 38 F2
Bazely St. E14 26 G1
Beacham Clo. SE7 34 G1
Beachy Rd. E3 12 E4
Beacon Hill N7 10 E2
Beacon Rd. SE13 41 A4
Beaconsfield Clo. SE3 34 D2
Beaconsfield Rd. E16 20 C3
Beaconsfield Rd. NW10 8 B3
Beaconsfield Rd. SE3 34 C3
Beaconsfield Rd. SE17 32 C2
Beaconsfield Ter. Rd. W14 22 G4
Beadon Rd. W6 22 E5
Beak St. W1 43 B3
Beale Pl. E3 19 D1
Beale Rd. E3 12 D5
Beanacre Clo. E9 12 D3
Bear All. EC4 44 B1
Bear Gdns. SE1 44 D5
Bear La. SE1 44 C6
Bear St. WC2 43 D3
Bearstead Ri. SE4 40 D3
Beatrice Pl. W8 23 C4
Beatrice Rd. SE1 25 F5
Beatson Wk. SE16 26 C2
Beatty Rd. N16 11 D1
Beatty St. NW1 17 C1
Beauchamp Pl. SW3 23 F4
Beauchamp Rd. E7 13 E4
Beauchamp Rd. SW11 37 F2
Beauclerc Rd. W6 22 D4
Beaufort Clo. SW15 36 D5
Beaufort Gdns. SW3 23 F4
Beaufort St. SW3 30 E2
Beaufoy Wk. SE11 24 F5
Beaulieu Clo. SE5 39 C1
Beaumont Ave. W14 30 A1
Beaumont Cres. W14 30 A1
Beaumont Gro. E1 19 B3
Beaumont Pl. W1 17 C3
Beaumont Rd. E13 20 E2
Beaumont Rd. SW19 36 G5
Beaumont Sq. E1 19 B3
Beaumont St. W1 17 A4
Beaumont Wk. NW3 9 G4
Beauval Rd. SE22 39 E4
Beavor La. W6 22 C5
Bebbington Rd. SE18 28 G5
Beccles Dr., Bark. 14 G3
Beccles St. E14 26 D1
Beck Clo. SE13 33 F4
Beck Rd. E8 11 G5
Becket Ave. E6 21 C2
Becklow Rd. W12 22 B3
Beckton Retail Pk. E6 21 C4
Beckton Rd. E16 20 C4
Beckway St. SE17 25 C5
Beckwith Rd. SE24 39 C4
Bective Rd. E7 13 D1
Bective Rd. SW15 36 G2
Bedale St. SE1 44 F6
Bedford Ave. WC1 17 D4
Bedford Ct. WC2 43 E4
Bedford Gdns. W8 23 B2
Bedford Ho. SW4 38 E2
Bedford Pl. WC1 17 E4
Bedford Rd. E6 14 C5
Bedford Rd. SW4 38 E1
Bedford Row WC1 17 F4
Bedford Sq. WC1 17 D4
Bedford St. WC2 43 E3
Bedford Way WC1 17 D3
Bedfordbury WC2 43 E4
Bedgebury Rd. SE9 41 G2
Beeby Rd. E16 20 E4
Beech Ave. W3 22 A2
Beech Clo. SW15 36 C5

Beech Ct. SE9	42	A4
Beech St. EC2	18	B4
Beechdale Rd. SW2	38	F4
Beechhill Rd. SE9	42	C3
Beechmore Rd. SW11	30	G4
Beechwood Rd. E8	11	E3
Beecroft Rd. SE4	40	C3
Beehive Pas. EC3	**44**	**H2**
Beehive Pl. SW9	38	G1
Beeston Pl. SW1	24	B4
Beethoven St. W10	15	G2
Begbie Rd. SE3	34	F4
Beira St. SW12	38	B5
Belfont Wk. N7	10	E1
Belford Gro. SE18	28	C5
Belfort Rd. SE15	33	A5
Belgrade Rd. N16	11	D1
Belgrave Gdns. NW8	9	C5
Belgrave Ms. N. SW1	24	A4
Belgrave Ms. S. SW1	24	A4
Belgrave Ms. W. SW1	24	A4
Belgrave Pl. SW1	24	A4
Belgrave Rd. E13	20	F2
Belgrave Rd. SW1	24	B5
Belgrave Rd. SW13	29	B3
Belgrave Sq. SW1	24	A4
Belgrave St. E1	19	B4
Belgravia Ho. SW4	38	D4
Belgrove St. WC1	17	E2
Belinda Rd. SW9	39	A1
Belitha Vill. N1	10	F4
Bell Dr. SW18	36	G5
Bell Inn Yd. EC3	**44**	**G2**
Bell La. E1	18	E4
Bell La. E16	27	D2
Bell St. NW1	16	F4
Bell Water Gate SE18	28	C4
Bell Wf. La. EC4	**44**	**E3**
Bell Yd. WC2	**43**	**J2**
Bellamy St. SW12	38	B5
Bellefields Rd. SW9	38	F1
Bellegrove Rd., Well.	35	G5
Bellenden Rd. SE15	39	E1
Belleville Rd. SW11	37	F3
Bellevue Rd. SW13	29	C5
Bello Clo. SE24	39	A5
Bellot St. SE10	34	B1
Bells All. SW6	30	B5
Bellwood Rd. SE15	40	B2
Belmont Ave., Well.	35	G5
Belmont Clo. SW4	38	C1
Belmont Gro. SE13	41	A1
Belmont Hill SE13	40	G1
Belmont Pk. SE13	41	A2
Belmont Rd. SW4	38	C1
Belmont St. NW1	10	A4
Belmore La. N7	10	D2
Belmore St. SW8	31	D4
Beloe Clo. SW15	36	C1
Belsham St. E9	12	A3
Belsize Ave. NW3	9	E3
Belsize Cres. NW3	9	E2
Belsize Gro. NW3	9	F3
Belsize La. NW3	9	E3
Belsize Pk. NW3	9	E3
Belsize Pk. Gdns. NW3	9	F3
Belsize Rd. NW6	9	C5
Belsize Sq. NW3	9	E3
Belsize Ter. NW3	9	E3
Belson Rd. SE18	28	B5
Belthorn Cres. SW12	38	C5
Belton Rd. E7	13	E4
Belton Rd. E11	13	B1
Belton Rd. NW2	8	C3
Belton Way E3	19	E4
Beltran Rd. SW6	30	C5
Belvedere Ms. SE15	40	A1
Belvedere Rd. SE1	24	F3
Belvoir Rd. SE22	39	F5
Bembridge Clo. NW6	8	G4
Bemerton Est. N1	10	E4
Bemerton St. N1	10	F5
Bemish Rd. SW15	36	F1
Ben Jonson Rd. E1	19	B4
Benbow Rd. W6	22	D4
Benbow St. SE8	33	E2
Bendemeer Rd. SW15	36	F1
Bendish Rd. E6	14	A4
Bendon Valley SW18	37	C5
Benedict Rd. SW9	38	F1
Bengal Rd., Ilf.	14	D1
Bengeworth Rd. SE5	39	B1
Benham Clo. SW11	37	E1
Benhill Rd. SE5	32	C3
Benin St. SE13	41	A5
Benjamin Clo. E8	11	F5
Benjamin St. EC1	18	A4
Benledi St. E14	20	A5
Benn St. E9	12	C3
Bennerley Rd. SW11	37	F3
Bennet's Hill EC4	**44**	**C3**
Bennett Gro. SE13	33	F4
Bennett Pk. SE3	41	C1
Bennett Rd. E13	20	F3
Bennett Rd. N16	11	D1
Bennett St. SW1	**43**	**A5**
Bennett St. W4	29	A2
Bensbury Clo. SW15	36	E5
Benson Ave. E6	20	F1
Bentham Rd. E9	12	B3
Bentinck St. W1	17	A5
Bentworth Rd. W12	15	D5
Benwell Rd. N7	10	G1
Benwick Clo. SE16	25	G5
Benworth St. E3	19	D2
Berber Rd. SW11	37	G3
Berens Rd. NW10	15	F2
Beresford Rd. N5	11	C2
Beresford Sq. SE18	28	D5
Beresford St. SE18	28	D4
Beresford Ter. N5	11	B2
Berestede Rd. W6	29	B1
Berger Rd. E9	12	B3
Bering Wk. E16	20	G5
Berkeley Rd. SW13	29	C4
Berkeley Sq. W1	24	B1
Berkeley St. W1	24	B2
Berkley Rd. E12	14	A2
Berkley Rd. NW1	9	G4
Berkshire Rd. E9	12	D3
Bermans Way NW10	8	A1
Bermondsey St. SE1	**44**	**H6**
Bermondsey Wall E. SE16	25	F3
Bermondsey Wall W. SE16	25	F3
Bernard Ashley Dr. SE7	34	E1
Bernard Cassidy St. E16	20	C4
Bernard St. WC1	17	E3
Bernays Gro. SW9	38	F2
Berners Ms. W1	17	C4
Berners Pl. W1	**43**	**B1**
Berners Rd. N1	10	G5
Berners St. W1	17	C4
Berry Clo. NW10	8	A4
Berry St. EC1	18	A3
Berryfield Rd. SE17	32	A1
Berryhill SE9	42	D2
Berryhill Gdns. SE9	42	D2
Berthon St. SE8	33	E3
Bertie Rd. NW10	8	C3
Bertrand St. SE13	40	F1
Berwick Cres., Sid.	42	G4
Berwick Rd. E16	20	E5
Berwick St. W1	**43**	**B1**
Beryl Ave. E6	21	A4
Beryl Rd. W6	29	F1
Besant Rd. NW2	8	G1
Bessborough Gdns. SW1	31	D1
Bessborough Pl. SW1	31	D1
Bessborough St. SW1	31	D1
Bessemer Rd. SE5	32	B5
Bessie Lansbury Clo. E6	21	C5
Besson St. SE14	33	A4
Bestwood St. SE8	26	B5
Bethell Ave. E16	20	C3
Bethnal Grn. Rd. E1	18	E3
Bethnal Grn. Rd. E2	18	E3
Bethwin Rd. SE5	32	A3
Betterton St. WC2	**43**	**E2**
Bettons Pk. E15	13	B5
Bettridge Rd. SW6	30	A5
Bevan St. N1	11	B5
Bevenden St. N1	18	C2
Beverley Clo. SW13	29	B5
Beverley Ct. SE4	40	D1
Beverley Gdns. SW13	36	B1
Beverley Path SW13	29	B5
Beverley Rd. E6	20	G2
Beverley Rd. SW13	36	B1
Beverley Rd. W4	29	B1
Beverstone Rd. SW2	38	F3
Bevin Clo. SE16	26	C2
Bevington Rd. W10	15	G4
Bevington St. SE16	25	F3
Bevis Marks EC3	**44**	**J1**
Bewdley St. N1	10	G4
Bewick St. SW8	31	B5
Bewley St. E1	25	G1
Bexhill Rd. SE4	40	D4
Bexley Rd. SE9	42	D3
Bianca Rd. SE15	32	E2
Bibury Clo. SE15	32	D2
Bickenhall St. W1	16	G4
Bicknell Rd. SE5	39	B1
Bidborough St. WC1	17	E2
Bidder St. E16	20	B4
Biddestone Rd. N7	10	F1
Biddulph Rd. W9	16	C2
Bidwell St. SE15	32	G4
Biggerstaff Rd. E15	12	G5
Bigland St. E1	18	G5
Bignell Rd. SE18	35	D1
Bignold Rd. E7	13	D1
Billing Pl. SW10	30	C3
Billing Rd. SW10	30	C3
Billing St. SW10	30	C3
Billingford Clo. SE4	40	B2
Billington Rd. SE14	33	B3
Billiter Sq. EC3	**44**	**J2**
Billiter St. EC3	**44**	**J2**
Billson St. E14	26	G5
Bina Gdns. SW5	23	D5
Binden Rd. W12	22	B4
Binfield Rd. SW4	31	E4
Bingfield St. N1	10	E5
Bingham St. N1	11	C3
Bingley Rd. E16	20	F5
Binney St. W1	17	A5
Binns Rd. W4	29	A1
Birch Clo. E16	20	B4
Birch Clo. SE15	32	F5
Birch Gro. SE12	41	C5
Birchdale Rd. E7	13	F2
Birches, The SE7	34	E2
Birchfield St. E14	26	E1
Birchin La. EC3	**44**	**G2**
Birchington Rd. NW6	9	B5
Birchlands Ave. SW12	37	G5
Birchmere Row SE3	34	C5
Bird in Bush Rd. SE15	32	F3
Birdbrook Rd. SE3	41	F1
Birdcage Wk. SW1	24	C3
Birdhurst Rd. SW18	37	D2
Birdlip Clo. SE15	32	D2
Birdsfield La. E3	12	D5
Birkbeck Rd. E8	11	E2
Birkenhead St. WC1	17	E2
Birkwood Clo. SW12	38	D5
Birley St. SW11	31	A5
Birse Cres. NW10	8	A1
Biscay Rd. W6	29	F1
Biscoe Way SE13	41	A1
Bishop Kings Rd. W14	22	G5
Bishop St. N1	11	B5
Bishop Way NW10	8	A4
Bishop's Ave. E13	13	E5
Bishops Ave. SW6	29	F5
Bishops Bri. W2	16	D4
Bishops Bri. Rd. W2	16	C5
Bishop's Ct. EC4	**44**	**B1**
Bishop's Ct. WC2	**43**	**J1**
Bishop's Pk. Rd. SW6	29	F5
Bishops Rd. SW6	29	G4
Bishops Ter. SE11	24	G5
Bishops Way E2	18	G1
Bishopsgate Chyd. EC2	**44**	**H1**
Bisson Rd. E15	19	G1
Black Friars Ct. EC4	**44**	**B3**
Black Friars La. EC4	**44**	**B3**
Black Lion La. W6	22	C5
Black Prince Rd. SE1	24	F5
Black Prince Rd. SE11	24	F5
Blackburn Rd. NW6	9	C3
Blackburne's Ms. W1	24	A1
Blackdown Ter. SE18	35	B3
Blackett St. SW15	36	F1
Blackfen Rd., Sid.	42	G4
Blackfriars Bri. EC4	**44**	**B4**
Blackfriars Bri. SE1	**44**	**B4**
Blackfriars Pas. EC4	**44**	**B3**
Blackfriars Rd. SE1	**44**	**B5**
Blackheath Ave. SE10	34	A3
Blackheath Gro. SE3	34	C5
Blackheath Hill SE10	33	G4
Blackheath Pk. SE3	41	C1
Blackheath Ri. SE13	33	G5
Blackheath Rd. SE10	33	F4
Blackheath Vale SE3	34	B5
Blackheath Village SE3	34	C5
Blackhorse Rd. SE8	33	C1
Blackland Ter. SW3	23	G5
Blackpool Rd. SE15	32	G5
Blackstone Est. E8	11	F4
Blackstone Rd. NW2	8	E2
Blackthorn St. E3	19	E3
Blacktree Ms. SW9	38	G1
Blackwall La. SE10	34	B1
Blackwall Tunnel E14	27	A2
Blackwall Tunnel App. SE10	27	B3
Blackwall Tunnel Northern App. E3	19	E1
Blackwall Tunnel Northern App. E14	19	G3
Blackwall Way E14	26	G1
Blackwater St. SE22	39	E3
Blackwell Clo. E5	12	C1
Blackwood St. SE17	32	C1
Blagdon Rd. SE13	40	F4
Blagrove Rd. W10	15	G4
Blair Clo. N1	11	B3
Blair Clo., Sid.	42	G3
Blair St. E14	19	G5
Blake Ave., Bark.	14	G5
Blake Clo. W10	15	E4

Blake Clo., Well.	35	G4
Blake Gdns. SW6	30	C4
Blake Rd. E16	20	C3
Blaker Rd. E15	12	G5
Blakes Rd. SE15	32	D3
Blanchard Way E8	11	F3
Blanche St. E16	20	C3
Blanchedowne SE5	39	C2
Bland St. SE9	41	G2
Blandfield Rd. SW12	38	A4
Blandford Rd. W4	22	A4
Blandford Sq. NW1	16	F3
Blandford St. W1	16	G5
Blaney Cres. E6	21	D2
Blann Clo. SE9	41	G4
Blantyre St. SW10	30	E3
Blashford NW3	9	G4
Blashford St. SE13	41	A5
Blasker Wk. E14	33	E1
Blendon Ter. SE18	35	E1
Blenheim Cres. W11	22	G1
Blenheim Gdns. NW2	8	E3
Blenheim Gdns. SW2	38	F4
Blenheim Gro. SE15	32	F5
Blenheim Rd. E6	20	G2
Blenheim Rd. E15	13	B1
Blenheim Rd. NW8	16	D1
Blenheim Rd. W4	22	A4
Blenheim Ter. NW8	16	D1
Blenkarne Rd. SW11	37	G4
Blessington Clo. SE13	41	A1
Blessington Rd. SE13	41	A2
Bletchley St. N1	18	B1
Blissett St. SE10	33	G4
Blithfield St. W8	23	C4
Bloemfontein Ave. W12	22	D2
Bloemfontein Rd. W12	22	D1
Blomfield Rd. W9	16	C4
Blomfield St. EC2	18	C4
Blomfield Vill. W2	16	C4
Blondel St. SW11	31	A5
Blondin St. E3	19	E1
Bloom Pk. Rd. SW6	30	A3
Bloomfield Rd. SE18	35	D1
Bloomfield Ter. SW1	31	A1
Bloomsbury Ho. SW4	38	D4
Bloomsbury Sq. WC1	17	E4
Bloomsbury St. WC1	17	D4
Bloomsbury Way WC1	**43**	**E1**
Blore Ct. W1	**43**	**C3**
Blossom St. E1	18	D3
Blount St. E14	19	C4
Bloxam Gdns. SE9	42	A3
Blucher Rd. SE5	32	B3
Blue Anchor La. SE16	25	F5
Blue Anchor Yd. E1	25	F1
Blue Ball Yd. SW1	**43**	**A6**
Blundell St. N7	10	E4
Blunts Rd. SE9	42	C3
Blurton Rd. E5	12	A1
Blythe Clo. SE6	40	D5
Blythe Hill SE6	40	D5
Blythe Hill La. SE6	40	D5
Blythe Rd. W14	22	F4
Blythe St. E2	18	G2
Boathouse Wk. SE15	32	E3
Bobbin Clo. SW4	38	C1
Bocking St. E8	11	G5
Bodney Rd. E8	11	G2
Bohemia Pl. E8	12	A3
Boileau Rd. SW13	29	C3
Bolden St. SE8	33	F5
Boleyn Rd. E6	20	G1
Boleyn Rd. E7	13	D4
Boleyn Rd. N16	11	D2
Bolina Rd. SE16	33	A1
Bolingbroke Gro. SW11	37	G4
Bolingbroke Rd. W14	22	F4
Bolingbroke Wk. SW11	30	E4
Bolney St. SW8	31	F3
Bolsover St. W1	17	B3
Bolt Ct. EC4	**44**	**A2**
Bolton Cres. SE5	32	A2
Bolton Gdns. NW10	15	F1
Bolton Gdns. SW5	30	C1
Bolton Gdns. Ms. SW10	30	C1
Bolton Rd. E15	13	C3
Bolton Rd. NW8	9	C5
Bolton Rd. NW10	8	A5
Bolton St. W1	24	B2
Boltons, The SW10	30	D1
Bombay St. SE16	25	G5
Bomore Rd. W11	22	G1
Bonar Rd. SE15	32	F3
Bonchurch Rd. W10	15	G4
Bond Ct. EC4	**44**	**F2**
Bond St. E15	13	B2
Bondway SW8	31	E2
Boneta Rd. SE18	28	B4
Bonfield Rd. SE13	40	G2
Bonham Rd. SW2	38	F3
Bonhill St. EC2	18	C3
Bonner Rd. E2	19	A1
Bonner St. E2	19	A1
Bonneville Gdns. SW4	38	C4
Bonnington Sq. SW8	31	F2
Bonny St. NW1	10	C4
Bonsor St. SE5	32	D3
Book Ms. WC2	**43**	**D2**
Boone St. SE13	41	B2
Boones Rd. SE13	41	B2
Boord St. SE10	27	B4
Boot St. N1	18	D2
Bordon Wk. SW15	36	C5
Boreham Ave. E16	20	D5
Borer's Pas. E1	**44**	**J1**
Borgard Rd. SE18	28	B5
Borland Rd. SE15	40	A2
Borneo St. SW15	36	E1
Borough High St. SE1	25	B3
Borough Rd. SE1	25	A4
Borrodaile Rd. SW18	37	C4
Borthwick Rd. E15	13	B1
Borthwick St. SE8	33	E1
Boscobel Pl. SW1	24	A5
Boscobel St. NW8	16	E3
Boscombe Clo. E5	12	C2
Boscombe Rd. W12	22	C2
Boston Gdns. W4	29	A2
Boston Pl. NW1	16	G3
Boston Rd. E6	21	A2
Boswell St. WC1	17	E4
Bosworth Rd. W10	15	G3
Botha Rd. E13	20	E4
Bothwell Clo. E16	20	C4
Botolph All. EC3	**44**	**H3**
Botolph La. EC3	**44**	**H3**
Boughton Rd. SE28	28	G4
Boulcott St. E1	19	B5
Boultwood Rd. E6	21	B5
Boundary La. E13	20	G2
Boundary La. SE17	32	B2
Boundary Rd. E13	20	F1
Boundary Rd. NW8	9	C5
Boundary Rd., Bark.	14	F5
Boundary Rd., Sid.	42	G3
Boundary St. E2	18	E3
Bourchier St. W1	**43**	**C3**
Bourdon St. W1	24	B1
Bourke Clo. SW4	38	E4
Bournbrook Rd. SE3	41	G1
Bourne Est. EC1	17	G4
Bourne St. SW1	24	A5
Bourne Ter. W2	16	C4
Bournemouth Rd. SE15	32	F5
Bournville Rd. SE6	40	E5
Bousfield Rd. SE14	33	B5
Boutflower Rd. SW11	37	F2
Bouverie Pl. W2	16	E5
Bouverie St. EC4	**44**	**A2**
Boveney Rd. SE23	40	B5
Bovill Rd. SE23	40	B5
Bovingdon Rd. SW6	30	C4
Bow Bri. Est. E3	19	F1
Bow Chyd. EC4	**44**	**E2**
Bow Common La. E3	19	C3
Bow Ind. Est. E15	12	F4
Bow La. EC4	**44**	**E2**
Bow Rd. E3	19	D2
Bow St. E15	13	B2
Bow St. WC2	**43**	**F2**
Bowater Clo. SW2	38	E4
Bowater Pl. SE3	34	E3
Bowater Rd. SE18	27	G4
Bowden St. SE11	31	G1
Bowditch SE8	33	D1
Bowen St. E14	19	F5
Bower Ave. SE10	34	B4
Bower St. E1	19	B5
Bowerdean St. SW6	30	C4
Bowerman Ave. SE14	33	C2
Bowes Rd. W3	22	A1
Bowfell Rd. W6	29	E2
Bowhill Clo. SW9	31	G3
Bowie Clo. SW4	38	D5
Bowland Rd. SW4	38	D2
Bowling Grn. Clo. SW15	36	D5
Bowling Grn. Ct. EC2	18	D3
Bowling Grn. La. EC1	17	G3
Bowling Grn. Pl. SE1	25	C3
Bowling Grn. St. SE11	31	G2
Bowman Ave. E16	27	C1
Bowmans Lea SE23	40	A5
Bowness Rd. SE6	40	F5
Bowood Rd. SW11	38	A3
Bowyer Clo. E6	21	B4
Bowyer Pl. SE5	32	B3
Bowyer St. SE5	32	B3
Boxall Rd. SE21	39	D4
Boxley St. E16	27	E2
Boyard Rd. SE18	35	D1
Boyce St. SE1	**43**	**J6**
Boyce Way E13	20	D3
Boyd St. E1	18	F5
Boyfield St. SE1	25	A3
Boyle St. W1	**43**	**A3**
Boyne Rd. SE13	40	G1
Boyne Ter. Ms. W11	23	A2
Boyson Rd. SE17	32	C2
Brabant Ct. EC3	**44**	**H3**
Brabazon St. E14	19	F5
Brabourn Gro. SE15	33	A5
Bracewell Rd. W10	15	E4
Bracken Ave. SW12	38	A4
Bracken Clo. E6	21	B4
Bracken Gdns. SW13	29	C5
Brackenbury Gdns. W6	22	D4
Brackenbury Rd. W6	22	D4
Brackley Rd. W4	29	A1
Brackley Ter. W4	29	A1
Bracklyn St. N1	18	C1
Bracknell Gdns. NW3	9	C1
Bracknell Gate NW3	9	C2
Bracknell Way NW3	9	C1
Brad St. SE1	**44**	**A6**
Bradbourne St. SW6	30	B5
Bradbury St. N16	11	D2
Braddyll St. SE10	34	B1
Bradenham Clo. SE17	32	C2
Bradfield Rd. E16	27	D3
Bradgate Rd. SE6	40	E4
Brading Rd. SW2	38	F5
Bradiston Rd. W9	16	A2
Bradmead SW8	31	B3
Bradmore Pk. Rd. W6	22	D5
Bradstock Rd. E9	12	B3
Bradwell St. E1	19	B2
Brady St. E1	18	G3
Braemar Rd. E13	20	C3
Braes St. N1	11	A4
Braganza St. SE17	32	A1
Braham St. E1	18	E5
Braid Ave. W3	15	A5
Braidwood St. SE1	**44**	**H6**
Brailsford Rd. SW2	38	G3
Braintree St. E2	19	A3
Bramah Grn. SW9	31	G4
Bramber Rd. W14	30	A2
Bramblebury Rd. SE18	35	E1
Bramcote Gro. SE16	33	A1
Bramcote Rd. SW15	36	D2
Bramerton St. SW3	30	F2
Bramfield Rd. SW11	37	F4
Bramford Rd. SW18	37	D2
Bramham Gdns. SW5	30	C1
Bramhope La. SE7	34	E2
Bramlands Clo. SW11	37	F1
Bramley Rd. W10	22	F1
Brampton Rd. E6	20	G3
Bramshaw Rd. E9	12	B3
Bramshill Rd. NW10	15	A1
Bramshot Ave. SE7	34	D2
Bramston Rd. NW10	15	C1
Brancaster Rd. E12	14	B1
Branch Pl. N1	11	C5
Branch Rd. E14	26	C1
Brand St. SE10	33	G3
Brandlehow Rd. SW15	37	A2
Brandon Est. SE17	32	A2
Brandon Rd. N7	10	E4
Brandon St. SE17	25	B5
Brandram Rd. SE13	41	B1
Brandreth Rd. E6	21	B5
Brangton Rd. SE11	31	F1
Branksea St. SW6	29	G3
Branksome Rd. SW2	38	E2
Branscombe St. SE13	40	F1
Brantwood Rd. SE24	39	B3
Brassey Rd. NW6	9	A3
Brassey Sq. SW11	38	A1
Brassie Ave. W3	15	A5
Brathway Rd. SW18	37	B5
Bravington Rd. W9	16	A2
Braxfield Rd. SE4	40	C2
Bray NW3	9	F4
Bray Pl. SW3	23	G5
Brayards Rd. SE15	32	G5
Braybrook St. W12	15	B4
Brayburne Ave. SW4	31	C5
Braywood Rd. SE9	42	F2
Bread St. EC4	**44**	**E3**
Breakspears Rd. SE4	40	D1
Bream Gdns. E6	21	C2
Bream St. E3	12	E4
Bream's Bldgs. EC4	**43**	**J1**
Breasley Clo. SW15	36	D2
Brecknock Rd. N7	10	D2
Brecknock Rd. N19	10	C1
Brecknock Rd. Est. N7	10	C1
Brecon Rd. W6	29	G2
Brede Clo. E6	21	C2
Bredon Rd. SE5	39	B1

Breer St. SW6	37	C1
Brenchley Gdns. SE23	40	A4
Brendon Ave. NW10	8	A1
Brendon St. W1	16	F5
Brenley Gdns. SE9	41	G2
Brent Rd. E16	20	D4
Brent Rd. SE18	35	D3
Brenthouse Rd. E9	12	A3
Brenthurst Rd. NW10	8	B3
Brenton St. E14	19	C5
Bressenden Pl. SW1	24	B4
Brett Rd. E8	11	G2
Brewer St. W1	**43**	**B3**
Brewery Rd. N7	10	E4
Brewery Rd. SE18	35	F1
Brewhouse La. E1	25	G2
Brewhouse Rd. SE18	28	B5
Brewhouse St. SW15	36	G1
Brewhouse Wk. SE16	26	C2
Brewster Gdns. W10	15	E4
Brewster Ho. E14	26	D1
Briant St. SE14	33	B4
Briar Rd. NW2	8	E1
Briar Wk. SW15	36	D2
Briarwood Rd. SW4	38	D3
Brick Ct. EC4	**43**	**J2**
Brick La. E1	18	E3
Brick La. E2	18	E2
Brick St. W1	24	B2
Brickfield Rd. E3	19	F3
Bride Ct. EC4	**44**	**B2**
Bride La. EC4	**44**	**B2**
Bride St. N7	10	F3
Bridewell Pl. EC4	**44**	**B2**
Bridge App. NW1	10	A4
Bridge Ave. W6	29	D1
Bridge La. SW11	30	F4
Bridge Pk. SW18	37	B3
Bridge Pl. SW1	24	B5
Bridge Rd. E6	14	B4
Bridge Rd. E15	13	A5
Bridge Rd. NW10	8	A3
Bridge St. SW1	24	E3
Bridge Ter. E15	13	A4
Bridge Vw. W6	29	E1
Bridge Yd. SE1	**44**	**G5**
Bridgefoot SE1	31	E1
Bridgeland Rd. E16	27	D1
Bridgeman Rd. N1	10	F4
Bridgeman St. NW8	16	F1
Bridgend Rd. SW18	37	D2
Bridges Ct. SW11	37	E1
Bridges Pl. SW6	30	A4
Bridgeway St. NW1	17	C1
Bridgwater Rd. E15	12	G5
Bridle La. W1	**43**	**B3**
Bridport Pl. N1	11	C5
Brief St. SE5	32	A4
Brierley Rd. E11	13	A1
Bright St. E14	19	F5
Brightfield Rd. SE12	41	C3
Brightling Rd. SE4	40	D4
Brightlingsea Pl. E14	26	D1
Brighton Rd. E6	21	C2
Brighton Rd. N16	11	D1
Brighton Ter. SW9	38	F2
Brightside Rd. SE13	41	A4
Brill Pl. NW1	17	D1
Brindley St. SE14	33	D4
Brinklow Cres. SE18	35	D3
Brinklow Ho. W2	16	C4
Brinkworth Way E9	12	D3
Brinton Wk. SE1	**44**	**B6**
Brion Pl. E14	19	G4
Brisbane St. SE5	32	C3
Briset Rd. SE9	41	G1
Bristol Gdns. W9	16	C3
Bristol Rd. E7	13	F3
Britannia Rd. E14	26	E5
Britannia Rd. SW6	30	C3
Britannia Row N1	11	A5
Britannia St. WC1	17	F2
British Gro. W4	29	B1
British Gro. Pas. W4	29	B1
British St. E3	19	D2
Britten St. SW3	30	F1
Britton St. EC1	18	A3
Brixham Gdns., Ilf.	14	G2
Brixham St. E16	28	B2
Brixton Hill SW2	38	E5
Brixton Oval SW2	38	G2
Brixton Rd. SW9	38	G1
Brixton Sta. Rd. SW9	38	G1
Brixton Water La. SW2	38	G3
Broad Ct. WC2	**43**	**F2**
Broad La. EC2	18	D4
Broad Sanctuary SW1	24	D3
Broad Wk. SE3	34	F5
Broad Wk. W1	24	A2
Broad Wk., The W8	23	D2
Broadbridge Clo. SE3	34	D3
Broadfield La. NW1	10	E4
Broadfield Rd. SE6	41	B5
Broadfields Way NW10	8	B2
Broadgate E13	20	F1
Broadhinton Rd. SW4	38	B1
Broadhurst Gdns. NW6	9	C3
Broadley St. NW8	16	E4
Broadley Ter. NW1	16	F3
Broadwall SE1	**44**	**A5**
Broadwater Rd. SE28	28	E4
Broadway E15	13	A4
Broadway SW1	24	D4
Broadway, Bark.	14	E4
Broadway, The E13	20	E1
Broadway Mkt. E8	11	G5
Broadwick St. W1	**43**	**B3**
Brock Pl. E3	19	F3
Brock Rd. E13	20	E4
Brockenhurst Gdns., Ilf.	14	E2
Brockham St. SE1	25	B4
Brockill Cres. SE4	40	C2
Brocklebank Rd. SE7	27	E5
Brocklebank Rd. SW18	37	D5
Brocklehurst St. SE14	33	B3
Brockley Footpath SE15	40	A2
Brockley Gdns. SE4	33	D5
Brockley Gro. SE4	40	D3
Brockley Hall Rd. SE4	40	C3
Brockley Ms. SE4	40	C3
Brockley Pk. SE23	40	C5
Brockley Ri. SE23	40	C5
Brockley Rd. SE4	40	D1
Brockley Vw. SE23	40	C5
Brockley Way SE4	40	B3
Brockwell Pk. Gdns. SE24	38	G5
Brockworth Clo. SE15	32	D2
Brodlove La. E1	26	B1
Broken Wf. EC4	**44**	**D3**
Brokesley St. E3	19	D2
Bromar Rd. SE5	39	D1
Brome Rd. SE9	42	B1
Bromell's Rd. SW4	38	C2
Bromfelde Rd. SW4	38	D1
Bromfelde Wk. SW4	31	E5
Bromfield St. N1	17	G1
Bromley Hall Rd. E14	19	G4
Bromley High St. E3	19	F2
Bromley St. E1	19	B4
Brompton Pk. Cres. SW6	30	C2
Brompton Pl. SW3	23	F4
Brompton Rd. SW1	23	G3
Brompton Rd. SW3	23	F5
Brompton Rd. SW7	23	F4
Brompton Sq. SW3	23	F4
Brompton Ter. SE18	35	C4
Bromyard Ave. W3	22	A1
Brondesbury Ct. NW2	8	F3
Brondesbury Pk. NW2	8	E4
Brondesbury Pk. NW6	8	F4
Brondesbury Rd. NW6	16	A1
Brondesbury Vill. NW6	16	A1
Bronsart Rd. SW6	29	G3
Bronte Ho. NW6	16	B2
Bronti Clo. SE17	32	B1
Bronze St. SE8	33	E3
Brook Dr. SE11	24	G4
Brook Gdns. SW13	36	B1
Brook Grn. W6	22	E4
Brook La. SE3	34	E5
Brook St. W1	24	A1
Brook St. W2	23	E1
Brookbank Rd. SE13	40	E1
Brookdale Rd. SE6	40	F4
Brooke St. EC1	17	G4
Brookfield Rd. E9	12	C3
Brookhill Clo. SE18	35	D1
Brookhill Rd. SE18	28	D5
Brooking Rd. E7	13	D2
Brooklands Pk. SE3	41	D1
Brooklands St. SW8	31	D4
Brookmill Rd. SE8	33	E4
Brooks Ave. E6	21	B3
Brook's Ms. W1	24	B1
Brooks Rd. E13	13	D5
Brooksbank St. E9	12	A3
Brooksby St. N1	10	G4
Brooksby's Wk. E9	12	B2
Brooksville Ave. NW6	8	G5
Brookville Rd. SW6	30	A3
Brookway SE3	41	D1
Brookwood Ave. SW13	36	B1
Broome Way SE5	32	B3
Broomfield St. E14	19	E4
Broomgrove Rd. SW9	31	F5
Broomhill Rd. SW18	37	B3
Broomhouse La. SW6	30	B5
Broomhouse Rd. SW6	30	B5
Broomsleigh St. NW6	9	A2
Broomwood Rd. SW11	37	G4
Brougham Rd. E8	11	F5
Broughton Dr. SW9	38	G2
Broughton Rd. SW6	30	C5
Broughton St. SW8	31	A5
Brown Hart Gdns. W1	24	A1
Brown St. W1	16	G5
Brownfield St. E14	19	F5
Brownhill Rd. SE6	40	F5
Browning Clo., Well.	35	G4
Browning Est. SE17	32	B1
Browning Rd. E12	14	B3
Browning St. SE17	32	B1
Brownlow Ms. WC1	17	F3
Brownlow Rd. E8	11	E5
Brownlow Rd. NW10	8	A4
Brown's Bldgs. EC3	**44**	**J2**
Browns La. NW5	10	B2
Broxash Rd. SW11	38	A4
Broxwood Way NW8	9	F5
Bruce Rd. E3	19	F2
Bruckner St. W10	16	A2
Brune St. E1	18	E4
Brunel Est. W2	16	B4
Brunel Rd. SE16	26	A3
Brunel Rd. W3	15	A4
Brunswick Ct. SE1	25	D3
Brunswick Gdns. W8	23	B2
Brunswick Pk. SE5	32	C4
Brunswick Pl. N1	18	C2
Brunswick Quay SE16	26	B4
Brunswick Rd. E14	19	G5
Brunswick Sq. WC1	17	E3
Brunswick Vill. SE5	32	D4
Brunton Pl. E14	19	C5
Brushfield St. E1	18	D4
Brussels Rd. SW11	37	E2
Bruton La. W1	24	B1
Bruton Pl. W1	24	B1
Bruton St. W1	24	B1
Bryan Ave. NW10	8	D4
Bryan Rd. SE16	26	D3
Bryanston Pl. W1	16	G4
Bryanston Sq. W1	16	G4
Bryanston St. W1	16	G5
Bryant St. E15	13	A4
Bryantwood Rd. N7	10	G2
Brydges Pl. WC2	**43**	**E4**
Brydges Rd. E15	13	A2
Brymay Clo. E3	19	E1
Brynmaer Rd. SW11	30	G4
Bryony Rd. W12	22	C1
Buchan Rd. SE15	40	A1
Buchanan Gdns. NW10	15	D1
Bucharest Rd. SW18	37	D5
Buck St. NW1	10	B4
Buckfast St. E2	18	F2
Buckhold Rd. SW18	37	B4
Buckhurst St. E1	18	G3
Buckingham Arc. WC2	**43**	**F4**
Buckingham Ave., Well.	42	G2
Buckingham Gate SW1	24	B4
Buckingham La. SE23	40	C5
Buckingham Palace Rd. SW1	24	B5
Buckingham Rd. E15	13	C2
Buckingham Rd. N1	11	D3
Buckingham Rd. NW10	15	B1
Buckingham St. WC2	**43**	**F4**
Buckland Cres. NW3	9	E4
Buckland St. N1	18	C1
Bucklersbury EC4	**44**	**F2**
Buckley Rd. NW6	9	A4
Buckley St. SE1	**43**	**J6**
Buckmaster Rd. SW11	37	F2
Bucknall St. WC2	**43**	**D1**
Bucknell Clo. SW2	38	F2
Buckner Rd. SW2	38	F2
Buckstone Clo. SE23	40	A4
Buckters Rents SE16	26	C2
Buckthorne Rd. SE4	40	C4
Budge Row EC4	**44**	**F3**
Budge's Wk. W2	23	E1
Buer Rd. SW6	29	G5
Bugsby's Way SE7	27	D5
Bugsby's Way SE10	27	C5
Bulinga St. SW1	24	D5
Bull Inn Ct. WC2	**43**	**F4**
Bull Rd. E15	20	C1
Bull Wf. La. EC4	**44**	**E3**
Bullards Pl. E2	19	B2
Bullen St. SW11	30	F5
Buller Clo. SE15	32	F3

Buller Rd., Bark.	14	G4
Bullivant St. E14	19	G5
Bull's Head Pas. EC3	**44**	**H2**
Bulmer Pl. W11	23	B2
Bulow Ct. SW6	30	C5
Bulstrode St. W1	17	A5
Bulwer St. W12	22	E2
Bunhill Row EC1	18	C3
Bunhouse Pl. SW1	31	A1
Bunning Way N7	10	E4
Burbage Clo. SE1	25	C4
Burbage Rd. SE21	39	C5
Burbage Rd. SE24	39	B4
Burcham St. E14	19	F5
Burchell Rd. SE15	32	G4
Burcote Rd. SW18	37	E5
Burder Clo. N1	11	D3
Burdett Rd. E3	19	C3
Burdett Rd. E14	19	D4
Burford Rd. E6	21	A2
Burford Rd. E15	13	A4
Burges Ct. E6	14	C4
Burges Rd. E6	14	A4
Burgess Hill NW2	9	B1
Burgess Rd. E15	13	B1
Burgess St. E14	19	E4
Burgh St. N1	18	A1
Burghley Rd. NW5	10	B1
Burghley Twr. W3	22	B1
Burgon St. EC4	**44**	**C2**
Burgos Gro. SE10	33	F4
Burgoyne Rd. SW9	38	F1
Burke Clo. SW15	36	A2
Burke St. E16	20	C5
Burland Rd. SW11	37	G3
Burleigh Pl. SW15	36	F3
Burleigh St. WC2	**43**	**F3**
Burley Rd. E16	20	F4
Burlington Arc. W1	**43**	**A4**
Burlington Clo. W9	16	A3
Burlington Gdns. W1	**43**	**A4**
Burlington La. W4	29	A3
Burlington Rd. SW6	29	G5
Burma Ms. N16	11	C1
Burma Rd. N16	11	C1
Burnaby St. SW10	30	D3
Burne Jones Ho. W14	23	A5
Burne St. NW1	16	F4
Burnels Ave. E6	21	C2
Burnett Clo. E9	12	A2
Burney St. SE10	33	G3
Burnfoot Ave. SW6	29	G4
Burnham NW3	9	F4
Burnham St. E2	19	A2
Burnley Rd. NW10	8	B2
Burnley Rd. SW9	31	F5
Burns Rd. NW10	8	B5
Burns Rd. SW11	30	G5
Burnsall St. SW3	30	F1
Burnside Clo. SE16	26	B2
Burnt Ash Hill SE12	41	C4
Burnt Ash Rd. SE12	41	C3
Burnthwaite Rd. SW6	30	A3
Burrage Gro. SE18	28	E5
Burrage Pl. SE18	35	D1
Burrage Rd. SE18	28	E5
Burrard Rd. E16	20	E5
Burrard Rd. NW6	9	B2
Burrell St. SE1	**44**	**B5**
Burrells Wf. Sq. E14	33	F1
Burrows Rd. NW10	15	E2
Burslem St. E1	18	F5
Burstock Rd. SW15	36	G2
Burston Rd. SW15	36	F3
Burt Rd. E16	27	F2
Burton La. SW9	31	G5
Burton Rd. NW6	9	A4
Burton Rd. SW9	32	A5
Burton St. WC1	17	D2
Burwash Rd. SE18	35	F1
Burwell Wk. E3	19	E3
Burwood Pl. W2	16	F5
Bury Ct. EC3	**44**	**J1**
Bury Pl. WC1	17	E4
Bury St. EC3	**44**	**J2**
Bury St. SW1	**43**	**B5**
Bury Wk. SW3	23	F5
Busby Ms. NW5	10	D3
Busby Pl. NW5	10	D3
Bush Ct. W12	22	F3
Bush La. EC4	**44**	**F3**
Bush Rd. E8	11	G5
Bush Rd. SE8	26	B5
Bushberry Rd. E9	12	C3
Bushey Hill Rd. SE5	32	D4
Bushey Rd. E13	20	F1
Bushmoor Cres. SE18	35	E3
Bushwood Dr. SE1	25	E5
Butcher Row E1	26	B1
Butcher Row E14	26	B1
Butchers Rd. E16	20	D5
Bute Gdns. W6	22	F5
Bute St. SW7	23	E5
Butterfly La. SE9	42	D4
Buttermere Dr. SW15	36	G3
Buttermere Wk. E8	11	E3
Butterwick W6	22	E5
Buttesland St. N1	18	C2
Buttmarsh Clo. SE18	35	D1
Buttsbury Rd., Ilf.	14	E2
Buxted Clo. E8	11	E4
Buxton Rd. E6	21	A2
Buxton Rd. E15	13	B2
Buxton Rd. NW2	8	D3
Buxton Rd. SW14	36	A1
Buxton St. E1	18	E3
Byam St. SW6	30	D5
Bye, The W3	15	A5
Byfeld Gdns. SW13	29	C4
Byford Clo. E15	13	B4
Bygrove St. E14	19	F5
Byng Pl. WC1	17	D3
Byng St. E14	26	E3
Byron Ave. E12	14	A3
Byron Clo. E8	11	F5
Bythorn St. SW9	38	F2
Byward St. EC3	**44**	**J4**
Bywater Pl. SE16	26	C2
Bywater St. SW3	30	G1

C

Cabbell St. NW1	16	F4
Cable St. E1	25	F1
Cabot Sq. E14	26	E2
Cabul Rd. SW11	30	F5
Cade Rd. SE10	34	A4
Cader Rd. SW18	37	D4
Cadet Dr. SE1	32	E1
Cadet Pl. SE10	34	B1
Cadiz St. SE17	32	B1
Cadogan Gdns. SW3	23	G5
Cadogan Gate SW1	23	G5
Cadogan La. SW1	24	A4
Cadogan Pl. SW1	23	G4
Cadogan Sq. SW1	23	G4
Cadogan St. SW3	23	G5
Cadogan Ter. E9	12	D3
Caedmon Rd. N7	10	F1
Cahir St. E14	26	F5
Caird St. W10	15	G2
Cairns Rd. SW11	37	F3
Caistor Pk. Rd. E15	13	C5
Caistor Rd. SW12	38	B5
Caithness Rd. W14	22	F4
Calabria Rd. N5	11	A3
Calais St. SE5	32	A4
Calbourne Rd. SW12	37	G5
Caldecot Rd. SE5	32	B5
Calderon Rd. E11	12	G1
Caldervale Rd. SW4	38	D3
Calderwood St. SE18	28	C5
Caldwell St. SW9	31	F3
Cale St. SW3	30	F1
Caledon Rd. E6	14	A5
Caledonia St. N1	17	E1
Caledonian Rd. N1	17	E1
Caledonian Rd. N7	10	F1
Caledonian Wf. Rd. E14	27	A5
Caletock Way SE10	34	C1
Callcott Rd. NW6	9	A4
Callendar Rd. SW7	23	E4
Callow St. SW3	30	E2
Calmington Rd. SE5	32	D1
Calshot St. N1	17	F1
Calthorpe St. WC1	17	F3
Calton Ave. SE21	39	D4
Calvert Ave. E2	18	D2
Calvert Rd. SE10	34	C1
Calverton Rd. E6	14	C5
Calvert's Bldgs. SE1	**44**	**F6**
Calvin St. E1	18	E3
Calydon Rd. SE7	34	E1
Calypso Way SE16	26	D5
Cam Rd. E15	13	A5
Cambalt Rd. SW15	36	F3
Cambert Way SE3	41	E2
Camberwell Ch. St. SE5	32	C4
Camberwell Glebe SE5	32	D4
Camberwell Grn. SE5	32	C4
Camberwell Gro. SE5	32	C4
Camberwell New Rd. SE5	31	G2
Camberwell Rd. SE5	32	B2
Camberwell Sta. Rd. SE5	32	B4
Camborne Rd. SW18	37	B5
Cambria Rd. SE5	39	B1
Cambria St. SW6	30	C3
Cambridge Ave. NW6	16	B1
Cambridge Barracks Rd. SE18	28	B5
Cambridge Circ. WC2	**43**	**D2**
Cambridge Cres. E2	18	G1
Cambridge Dr. SE12	41	D3
Cambridge Gdns. NW6	16	B1
Cambridge Gdns. W10	15	F5
Cambridge Gro. W6	22	D5
Cambridge Heath Rd. E1	18	G3
Cambridge Heath Rd. E2	19	A3
Cambridge Pl. W8	23	C3
Cambridge Rd. NW6	16	B2
Cambridge Rd. SW11	30	G4
Cambridge Rd. SW13	29	B5
Cambridge Rd., Bark.	14	E4
Cambridge Row SE18	35	D1
Cambridge Sq. W2	16	F5
Cambridge St. SW1	24	B5
Cambus Rd. E16	20	D4
Camden Est. SE15	32	E4
Camden High St. NW1	10	B5
Camden La. N7	10	D3
Camden Ms. NW1	10	C4
Camden Pk. Rd. NW1	10	D3
Camden Pas. N1	11	A5
Camden Rd. N7	10	E1
Camden Rd. NW1	10	C4
Camden Row SE3	34	B5
Camden Sq. NW1	10	D3
Camden St. NW1	10	C4
Camden Wk. N1	11	A5
Camdenhurst St. E14	19	C5
Camel Rd. E16	27	G2
Camellia St. SW8	31	E3
Camelot Clo. SE28	28	F3
Camera Pl. SW10	30	E2
Camilla Rd. SE16	25	G5
Camlet St. E2	18	E3
Camley St. NW1	10	D4
Camomile St. EC3	**44**	**H1**
Campana Rd. SW6	30	B4
Campbell Rd. E3	19	E2
Campbell Rd. E6	14	A5
Campden Gro. W8	23	B3
Campden Hill W8	23	B3
Campden Hill Gdns. W8	23	B2
Campden Hill Rd. W8	23	B2
Campden Hill Sq. W8	23	A2
Campden St. W8	23	B2
Campfield Rd. SE9	41	G5
Campion Clo. E6	28	B1
Campion Rd. SW15	36	E2
Campion Ter. NW2	8	F1
Camplin St. SE14	33	B3
Campshill Rd. SE13	40	G3
Canada Est. SE16	26	A4
Canada Sq. E14	26	F2
Canada St. SE16	26	B3
Canada Way W12	22	D1
Canada Yd. S. SE16	26	B4
Canal App. SE8	33	C1
Canal Clo. E1	19	C3
Canal Gro. SE15	32	F2
Canal Rd. E3	19	C3
Canal St. SE5	32	C2
Canal Wk. N1	11	C5
Canal Way W10	15	F3
Canary Wf. E14	26	E2
Canberra Rd. SE7	34	F2
Cancell Rd. SW9	31	G4
Candahar Rd. SW11	30	F5
Candy St. E3	12	D5
Canfield Gdns. NW6	9	C4
Canford Rd. SW11	38	A3
Canham Rd. W3	22	A3
Cann Hall Rd. E11	13	B1
Canning Cross SE5	32	D5
Canning Pl. W8	23	D4
Canning Rd. E15	20	B1
Cannon Dr. E14	26	E1
Cannon Hill NW6	9	B2
Cannon Pl. SE7	35	A1
Cannon St. EC4	**44**	**D2**
Cannon St. Rd. E1	18	G5
Canon Beck Rd. SE16	26	A3
Canon Row SW1	24	E3
Canon St. N1	11	B5
Canonbie Rd. SE23	40	A5
Canonbury Cres. N1	11	B4
Canonbury Gro. N1	11	B4
Canonbury La. N1	11	A4
Canonbury Pk. N. N1	11	B3
Canonbury Pk. S. N1	11	B3
Canonbury Pl. N1	11	A3
Canonbury Rd. N1	11	A3
Canonbury Sq. N1	11	A4
Canonbury St. N1	11	B4
Canonbury Vill. N1	11	A4
Canrobert St. E2	18	G2
Cantelowes Rd. NW1	10	D3
Canterbury Cres. SW9	38	G1
Canterbury Pl. SE17	25	A5
Canterbury Rd. NW6	16	A1

Canterbury Ter. NW6	16	B1
Canton St. E14	19	E5
Cantrell Rd. E3	19	D3
Cantwell Rd. SE18	35	D3
Canute Gdns. SE16	26	B5
Canvey St. SE1	**44**	**C5**
Capel Ct. EC2	**44**	**G2**
Capel Pt. E7	13	E1
Capel Rd. E7	13	E1
Capel Rd. E12	13	G1
Capland St. NW8	16	E3
Caple Rd. NW10	15	B1
Capper St. WC1	17	C3
Capstan Rd. SE8	26	D5
Capstan Sq. E14	26	G3
Capstan Way SE16	26	C2
Caradoc Clo. W2	16	B5
Caradoc St. SE10	34	B1
Carbis Rd. E14	19	D5
Carburton St. W1	17	B4
Carden Rd. SE15	39	G1
Cardiff St. SE18	35	G3
Cardigan Rd. E3	19	D1
Cardigan Rd. SW13	29	C5
Cardigan St. SE11	31	G1
Cardinal Bourne St. SE1	25	C4
Cardinal Pl. SW15	36	F2
Cardine Ms. SE15	32	G3
Cardington St. NW1	17	C2
Cardozo Rd. N7	10	E2
Cardross St. W6	22	D4
Cardwell Rd. N7	10	E1
Cardwell Rd. SE18	28	B5
Carew St. SE5	32	B5
Carey Gdns. SW8	31	C4
Carey La. EC2	**44**	**D1**
Carey St. WC2	**43**	**H2**
Carker's La. NW5	10	B2
Carleton Rd. N7	10	D2
Carlile Clo. E3	19	D1
Carlingford Rd. NW3	9	E1
Carlisle Ave. W3	15	A5
Carlisle La. SE1	24	F4
Carlisle Ms. NW8	16	E4
Carlisle Pl. SW1	24	C4
Carlisle Rd. NW6	8	G5
Carlisle St. W1	**43**	**C2**
Carlos Pl. W1	24	A1
Carlton Ct. SW9	32	A4
Carlton Dr. SW15	36	F3
Carlton Gdns. SW1	**43**	**C6**
Carlton Gro. SE15	32	G4
Carlton Hill NW8	16	C1
Carlton Ho. Ter. SW1	**43**	**C6**
Carlton Rd. E12	13	G1
Carlton St. SW1	**43**	**C4**
Carlton Twr. Pl. SW1	23	G4
Carlton Vale NW6	16	B1
Carlyle Pl. SW15	36	F2
Carlyle Rd. E12	14	A1
Carlyle Sq. SW3	30	E1
Carmalt Gdns. SW15	36	E2
Carmelite St. EC4	**44**	**A3**
Carmen St. E14	19	F5
Carnaby St. W1	**43**	**A2**
Carnarvon Rd. E15	13	C3
Carnbrook Rd. SE3	41	G1
Carnecke Gdns. SE9	42	A3
Carnegie St. N1	10	F5
Carnoustie Dr. N1	10	F4
Carnwath Rd. SW6	37	B1
Carol St. NW1	10	C5
Caroline Gdns. SE15	32	G3
Caroline Pl. SW11	31	A5
Caroline Pl. W2	23	C1
Caroline St. E1	19	B5
Caroline Ter. SW1	24	A5
Carpenters Pl. SW4	38	D2
Carpenters Rd. E15	12	E3
Carr St. E14	19	C4
Carriage Dr. E. SW11	31	A3
Carriage Dr. N. SW11	30	G3
Carriage Dr. S. SW11	30	G4
Carriage Dr. W. SW11	30	G3
Carrol Clo. NW5	10	B1
Carroll Clo. E15	13	C2
Carron Clo. E14	19	F5
Carronade Pl. SE28	28	E4
Carroun Rd. SW8	31	F3
Carslake Rd. SW15	36	E4
Carson Rd. E16	20	D3
Carston Clo. SE12	41	C3
Carswell Rd. SE6	40	G5
Carter La. EC4	**44**	**C2**
Carter Pl. SE17	32	B1
Carter Rd. E13	13	E5
Carter St. SE17	32	B2
Carteret St. SW1	24	D3
Carteret Way SE8	26	C5
Carthew Rd. W6	22	D4
Carthew Vill. W6	22	D4
Carthusian St. EC1	18	B4
Cartier Circle E14	26	F2
Carting La. WC2	**43**	**F4**
Cartwright Gdns. WC1	17	E2
Cartwright St. E1	25	E1
Carver Rd. SE24	39	B4
Cary Rd. E11	13	B1
Casella Rd. SE14	33	B3
Casino Ave. SE24	39	C3
Caspian St. SE5	32	C3
Cassidy Rd. SW6	30	B3
Cassland Rd. E9	12	B4
Casslee Rd. SE6	40	D5
Casson St. E1	18	F4
Castellain Rd. W9	16	C3
Castello Ave. SW15	36	E3
Castelnau SW13	29	C4
Casterbridge NW6	9	C5
Casterbridge Rd. SE3	41	D1
Castile Rd. SE18	28	C5
Castle Baynard St. EC4	**44**	**C3**
Castle Ct. EC3	**44**	**G2**
Castle La. SW1	24	C4
Castle Pt. E6	20	F1
Castle Rd. NW1	10	B3
Castle St. E6	20	F1
Castle Yd. SE1	**44**	**C5**
Castlecombe Dr. SW19	36	F5
Castlehaven Rd. NW1	10	B4
Castlemaine Twr. SW11	30	G5
Castletown Rd. W14	29	G1
Castlewood Dr. SE9	35	B5
Castor La. E14	26	F1
Caterham Rd. SE13	40	G1
Catesby St. SE17	25	C5
Catford Bdy. SE6	40	F5
Catford Rd. SE6	40	E5
Cathay St. SE16	25	G3
Cathcart Rd. SW10	30	C2
Cathcart St. NW5	10	B3
Cathedral Pl. EC4	**44**	**D2**
Cathedral St. SE1	**44**	**F5**
Catherine Gro. SE10	33	F4
Catherine Pl. SW1	24	C4
Catherine St. WC2	**43**	**G3**
Catherine Wheel Yd. SW1	**43**	**A6**
Cathles Rd. SW12	38	B4
Cathnor Hill Ct. W12	22	D4
Cathnor Rd. W12	22	D3
Catlin St. SE16	32	F1
Cato Rd. SW4	38	D1
Cator St. SE15	32	E2
Catton St. WC1	17	F4
Caulfield Rd. E6	14	A5
Caulfield Rd. SE15	32	G5
Causeway, The SW18	37	C3
Causton St. SW1	24	D5
Cautley Ave. SW4	38	C3
Cave Rd. E13	20	E1
Cavell St. E1	18	G4
Cavendish Ave. NW8	16	E1
Cavendish Clo. NW8	16	E2
Cavendish Ct. EC3	**44**	**J1**
Cavendish Gdns., Bark.	14	G2
Cavendish Pl. W1	17	B5
Cavendish Rd. E4	19	G5
Cavendish Rd. NW6	8	G4
Cavendish Rd. SW12	38	B4
Cavendish Sq. W1	17	B5
Cavendish St. N1	18	C1
Caversham Rd. NW5	10	C3
Caversham St. SW3	30	G2
Caverswall St. W12	15	E5
Caxton Gro. E3	19	E2
Caxton Rd. W12	22	F2
Caxton St. SW1	24	C4
Cearns Ho. E6	13	G5
Cecil Ave., Bark.	14	F4
Cecil Ct. WC2	**43**	**E4**
Cecil Rd. E13	13	D5
Cecil Rd. NW10	8	A5
Cecil Rd., Ilf.	14	D1
Cecilia Rd. E8	11	E2
Cedar Ct. E8	11	E4
Cedar Ct. SE9	42	A4
Cedar Rd. NW2	8	E1
Cedar Way NW1	10	D4
Cedarhurst Dr. SE9	41	F3
Cedarne Rd. SW6	30	C3
Cedars Rd. E15	13	B3
Cedars Rd. SW4	38	B1
Cedars Rd. SW13	29	B5
Celandine Clo. E14	19	E4
Celandine Way E15	20	B2
Celestial Gdns. SE13	41	A2
Celia Rd. N19	10	C1
Celtic St. E14	19	F4
Cemetery La. SE7	35	A2
Cemetery Rd. E7	13	C1
Centaur St. SE1	24	F4
Central Ave. SW11	31	A3
Central Mkts. EC1	18	B4
Central Pk. Rd. E6	20	G1
Central St. EC1	18	B2
Centre St. E2	18	G1
Centurion Clo. N7	10	F4
Cephas Ave. E1	19	A3
Cephas St. E1	19	A3
Cerise Rd. SE15	32	F4
Ceylon Rd. W14	22	F4
Chadbourn St. E14	19	F4
Chadd Grn. E13	13	D5
Chadwell St. EC1	17	G2
Chadwick Rd. NW10	8	B5
Chadwick Rd. SE15	32	E5
Chadwick St. SW1	24	D4
Chadwin Ms. E13	20	E4
Chadwin Rd. E13	20	E4
Chagford St. NW1	16	G3
Chalcot Cres. NW1	9	G5
Chalcot Gdns. NW3	9	G3
Chalcot Rd. NW1	10	A4
Chalcot Sq. NW1	10	A4
Chalcroft Rd. SE13	41	B3
Chaldon Rd. SW6	29	G3
Chale Rd. SW2	38	E4
Chalk Fm. Rd. NW1	10	A4
Chalk Rd. E13	20	E4
Challoner St. W14	30	A1
Chalsey Rd. SE4	40	D2
Chalton St. NW1	17	C1
Chamber St. E1	25	E1
Chamberlayne Rd. NW10	8	E5
Chambers La. NW10	8	D4
Chambers Rd. N7	10	E1
Chambers St. SE16	25	F3
Chambord St. E2	18	E2
Champion Gro. SE5	39	C1
Champion Hill SE5	39	C1
Champion Hill Est. SE5	39	D1
Champion Pk. SE5	32	C5
Chance St. E1	18	E3
Chance St. E2	18	E3
Chancel St. SE1	**44**	**B6**
Chancellors Rd. W6	29	E1
Chancellors St. W6	29	E1
Chancery La. WC2	**43**	**J1**
Chandler Ave. E16	20	D4
Chandlers Ms. E14	26	E3
Chandlers Way SW2	38	G5
Chandos Pl. WC2	**43**	**E4**
Chandos Rd. E15	13	A2
Chandos Rd. NW2	8	E2
Chandos Rd. NW10	15	A3
Chandos St. W1	17	B4
Change All. EC3	**44**	**G2**
Channelsea Rd. E15	13	A5
Chant Sq. E15	13	A4
Chant St. E15	13	A4
Chantrey Rd. SW9	38	F1
Chantry Pt. W9	16	A3
Chantry St. N1	11	A5
Chapel Ho. St. E14	33	F1
Chapel Mkt. N1	17	G1
Chapel Pl. W1	17	B5
Chapel Side W2	23	C1
Chapel St. E15	13	A4
Chapel St. NW1	16	F4
Chapel St. SW1	24	A4
Chaplin Clo. SE1	24	G3
Chaplin Rd. E15	13	B5
Chaplin Rd. NW2	8	C3
Chapman Rd. E9	12	D3
Chapman St. E1	25	G1
Chapmans Pk. Ind. Est. NW10	8	B3
Chapone Pl. W1	**43**	**C2**
Chapter Ho. Ct. EC4	**44**	**C2**
Chapter Rd. NW2	8	C2
Chapter Rd. SE17	32	A1
Chapter St. SW1	24	D5
Charecroft Way W12	22	F3
Charford Rd. E16	20	D4
Chargeable La. E13	20	C3
Chargeable St. E16	20	C3
Charing Cross WC2	**43**	**E5**
Charing Cross Rd. WC2	**43**	**D2**
Charlbert St. NW8	16	F1
Charlemont Rd. E6	21	B2
Charles Barry Clo. SW4	38	C1
Charles Dickens Ho. E2	18	G2
Charles Grinling Wk. SE18	28	C5
Charles II St. SW1	**43**	**C5**
Charles St. E16	27	G2
Charles St. SW13	29	A5
Charles St. W1	24	B2
Charleston St. SE17	25	B5
Charleville Rd. W14	29	G1
Charlotte Despard Ave. SW11	31	A4
Charlotte Rd. EC2	18	D3
Charlotte Rd. SW13	29	B4
Charlotte St. W1	17	C4
Charlotte Ter. N1	10	F5

Charlton Ch. La. SE7	34	F1
Charlton Dene SE7	34	F3
Charlton Kings Rd. NW5	10	D2
Charlton La. SE7	34	G1
Charlton Pk. La. SE7	34	G3
Charlton Pk. Rd. SE7	34	G2
Charlton Pl. N1	18	A1
Charlton Rd. NW10	8	A5
Charlton Rd. SE3	34	E3
Charlton Rd. SE7	34	F2
Charlton Way SE3	34	B4
Charlwood Pl. SW1	24	C5
Charlwood Rd. SW15	36	F2
Charlwood St. SW1	31	C1
Charnwood Gdns. E14	26	E5
Charrington St. NW1	17	D1
Chart St. N1	18	C2
Charterhouse Sq. EC1	18	A4
Charterhouse St. EC1	17	G4
Charteris Rd. NW6	9	A5
Chartfield Ave. SW15	36	D3
Chase, The E12	13	G1
Chase, The SW4	38	B1
Chaseley St. E14	19	C5
Chatfield Rd. SW11	37	D1
Chatham Pl. E9	12	A3
Chatham Rd. SW11	37	G4
Chatham St. SE17	25	C5
Chatsworth Rd. E15	13	C2
Chatsworth Rd. NW2	8	F3
Chatto Rd. SW11	37	G3
Chaucer Ct. N16	11	D1
Chaucer Dr. SE1	25	E5
Chaucer Rd. E7	13	D3
Chaucer Rd. SE24	38	G3
Chaundrye Clo. SE9	42	A4
Cheapside EC2	**44**	**D2**
Cheesemans Ter. W14	30	A1
Chelmer Rd. E9	12	B2
Chelmsford Clo. W6	29	F2
Chelmsford Sq. NW10	8	E5
Chelsea Bri. SW1	31	B2
Chelsea Bri. SW8	31	B2
Chelsea Bri. Rd. SW1	31	A1
Chelsea Embk. SW3	30	F2
Chelsea Harbour Dr. SW10	30	D4
Chelsea Manor Gdns. SW3	30	F1
Chelsea Manor St. SW3	30	F1
Chelsea Pk. Gdns. SW3	30	E2
Chelsea Sq. SW3	30	E1
Chelsham Rd. SW4	38	D1
Chelsworth Dr. SE18	35	F2
Cheltenham Gdns. E6	21	A1
Cheltenham Rd. SE15	40	A2
Cheltenham Ter. SW3	30	G1
Chelverton Rd. SW15	36	F2
Chelwood Wk. SE4	40	C2
Chenappa Clo. E13	20	D2
Cheney Rd. NW1	17	E1
Chenies Pl. NW1	17	D1
Chenies St. WC1	17	D4
Cheniston Gdns. W8	23	C4
Chepstow Cres. W11	23	B1
Chepstow Pl. W2	16	B5
Chepstow Rd. W2	16	B5
Chepstow Vill. W11	23	A1
Cherbury St. N1	18	C1
Cheriton Dr. SE18	35	F3
Cherry Gdn. St. SE16	25	G3
Cherrywood Dr. SW15	36	F3
Chertsey Rd., Ilf.	14	F1
Cheryls Clo. SW6	30	C4
Chesham Ms. SW1	24	A4
Chesham Pl. SW1	24	A4
Chesham St. SW1	24	A4
Cheshire Clo. SE4	33	D5
Cheshire St. E2	18	E3
Cheshunt Rd. E7	13	E3
Chesilton Rd. SW6	30	A4
Chesley Gdns. E6	20	G1
Chesney St. SW11	31	A4
Chesson Rd. W14	30	A2
Chester Clo. SW1	24	B3
Chester Clo. SW13	36	D1
Chester Ct. SE5	32	C3
Chester Gate NW1	17	B2
Chester Ms. SW1	24	B4
Chester Rd. E7	13	G4
Chester Rd. E16	20	B3
Chester Rd. NW1	17	A2
Chester Rd., Sid.	42	G3
Chester Row SW1	24	A5
Chester Sq. SW1	24	A5
Chester St. E2	18	F3
Chester St. SW1	24	A4
Chester Way SE11	24	G5
Chesterfield Gdns. W1	24	B2
Chesterfield Gro. SE22	39	E3
Chesterfield Hill W1	24	B2
Chesterfield St. W1	24	B2
Chesterfield Wk. SE10	34	A4
Chesterfield Way SE15	33	A3
Chesterford Gdns. NW3	9	C1
Chesterford Rd. E12	14	B2
Chesterton Rd. E13	20	D2
Chesterton Rd. W10	15	F4
Chesterton Ter. E13	20	D2
Chestnut Ave. E7	13	E1
Chestnut Gro. SW12	38	A5
Chestnut Ri. SE18	35	G1
Chetwynd Rd. NW5	10	B1
Cheval Pl. SW7	23	F4
Cheval St. E14	26	E4
Chevening Rd. NW6	15	F1
Chevening Rd. SE10	34	C1
Chevron Clo. E16	20	D5
Cheyne Gdns. SW3	30	F2
Cheyne Row SW3	30	F2
Cheyne Wk. SW3	30	F2
Cheyne Wk. SW10	30	E3
Chichele Rd. NW2	8	F2
Chicheley St. SE1	24	F3
Chichester Clo. E6	21	A5
Chichester Clo. SE3	34	F4
Chichester Rents WC2	**43**	**J1**
Chichester Rd. NW6	16	B1
Chichester Rd. W2	16	C4
Chichester St. SW1	31	C1
Chichester Way E14	27	A5
Chicksand St. E1	18	E4
Chiddingstone St. SW6	30	B5
Childeric Rd. SE14	33	C3
Childers St. SE8	33	C2
Child's Pl. SW5	23	B5
Child's St. SW5	23	B5
Chiltern St. W1	17	A4
Chilton Gro. SE8	26	B5
Chilton St. E2	18	E3
Chiltonian Ind. Est. SE12	41	C4
Chilver St. SE10	34	C1
Chilworth Ms. W2	16	E5
Chilworth St. W2	16	D5
Ching Ct. WC2	**43**	**E2**
Chipka St. E14	26	G3
Chippenham Gdns. NW6	16	B2
Chippenham Ms. W9	16	B3
Chippenham Rd. W9	16	B3
Chipstead St. SW6	30	B4
Chisenhale Rd. E3	19	C1
Chiswell St. EC1	18	C4
Chiswick La. W4	29	A1
Chiswick La. S. W4	29	B1
Chiswick Mall W4	29	B2
Chiswick Mall W6	29	C1
Chiswick Wf. W4	29	B2
Chitty St. W1	17	C4
Chivalry Rd. SW11	37	F3
Chobham Rd. E15	13	A2
Cholmondeley Ave. NW10	15	C1
Choumert Gro. SE15	32	F5
Choumert Rd. SE15	39	E1
Choumert Sq. SE15	32	F5
Chrisp St. E14	19	F4
Christchurch Ave. NW6	8	F5
Christchurch St. SW3	30	G2
Christchurch Way SE10	34	B1
Christian Ct. SE16	26	D2
Christian St. E1	18	F5
Christie Rd. E9	12	C3
Christopher Clo. SE16	26	B3
Christopher St. EC2	18	C3
Chryssell Rd. SW9	31	G3
Chubworthy St. SE14	33	C2
Chudleigh Cres., Ilf.	14	G1
Chudleigh Rd. NW6	8	F4
Chudleigh Rd. SE4	40	D3
Chudleigh St. E1	19	B5
Chumleigh St. SE5	32	D2
Church Cres. E9	12	B4
Church Gate SW6	36	G1
Church Gro. SE13	40	F2
Church Hill SE18	28	B4
Church Path N5	11	A2
Church Path NW10	8	A4
Church Pl. SW1	**43**	**B4**
Church Rd. E12	14	A2
Church Rd. NW10	8	A4
Church Rd. SW13	29	B5
Church Rd., Bark.	14	E3
Church Row NW3	9	D1
Church St. E15	20	B1
Church St. E16	28	D2
Church St. NW8	16	E4
Church St. W2	16	E4
Church St. W4	29	B2
Church St. Est. NW8	16	E3
Church St. N. E15	13	B5
Church Ter. SE13	41	B1
Church Ter. SW8	31	D5
Church Wk. N16	11	C1
Church Wk. SW13	29	C4
Churchbury Rd. SE9	41	G5
Churchill Gdns. Est. SW1	31	C1
Churchill Gdns. Rd. SW1	31	B1
Churchill Pl. E14	26	F2
Churchill Rd. E16	20	F5
Churchill Rd. NW2	8	D3
Churchill Rd. NW5	10	B1
Churchill Wk. E9	12	A2
Churchmead Rd. NW10	8	C3
Churchway NW1	17	D2
Churston Ave. E13	13	E5
Churton St. SW1	24	C5
Cicada Rd. SW18	37	D4
Cicely Rd. SE15	32	F4
Cinnamon Row SW11	37	D1
Cinnamon St. E1	25	G2
Circular Way SE18	35	B2
Circus Rd. NW8	16	E2
Circus St. SE10	33	G3
Cirencester St. W2	16	C4
City Gdn. Row N1	18	A1
City Rd. EC1	18	A1
Clabon Ms. SW1	23	G4
Clack St. SE16	26	A3
Clacton Rd. E6	20	G2
Claire Pl. E14	26	E4
Clancarty Rd. SW6	30	B5
Clandon St. SE8	33	E5
Clanricarde Gdns. W2	23	B1
Clapham Common N. Side SW4	37	G2
Clapham Common S. Side SW4	38	B4
Clapham Common W. Side SW4	37	G2
Clapham Cres. SW4	38	D2
Clapham High St. SW4	38	D2
Clapham Junct. Est. SW11	37	F2
Clapham Manor St. SW4	38	C1
Clapham Pk. Est. SW4	38	D4
Clapham Pk. Rd. SW4	38	D2
Clapham Rd. SW9	38	E1
Clapham Rd. Est. SW4	38	D1
Claps Gate La., Bark.	21	D3
Clapton Sq. E5	12	A2
Clapton Way E5	11	F1
Clara Pl. SE18	28	C5
Clare Cor. SE9	42	D5
Clare Gdns. E7	13	D1
Clare La. N1	11	B4
Clare Mkt. WC2	**43**	**G2**
Clare Rd. NW10	8	C4
Clare Rd. SE14	33	D5
Clare St. E2	18	G1
Claredale St. E2	18	G1
Claremont Clo. E16	28	C2
Claremont Clo. N1	17	G1
Claremont Rd. E7	13	E2
Claremont Rd. W9	16	A1
Claremont Sq. N1	17	G1
Claremont St. E16	28	C2
Claremont St. SE10	33	F2
Clarence Ave. SW4	38	D5
Clarence Cres. SW4	38	D4
Clarence Gdns. NW1	17	B2
Clarence La. SW15	36	A4
Clarence Ms. E5	11	G2
Clarence Pl. E5	11	G2
Clarence Rd. E5	11	G1
Clarence Rd. E12	13	G2
Clarence Rd. E16	20	B3
Clarence Rd. NW6	9	A4
Clarence Wk. SW4	31	E5
Clarence Way NW1	10	B4
Clarence Way Est. NW1	10	B4
Clarendon Dr. SW15	36	E1
Clarendon Gdns. W9	16	D3
Clarendon Pl. W2	23	F1
Clarendon Ri. SE13	40	G1
Clarendon Rd. W11	22	G1
Clarendon St. SW1	31	B1

Clareville Gro. SW7 23 D5
Clareville St. SW7 23 D5
Clarges Ms. W1 24 B2
Clarges St. W1 24 B2
Claribel Rd. SW9 32 A5
Clarissa St. E8 11 E5
Clark St. E1 18 G4
Clarks Pl. EC2 44 H1
Clarkson Rd. E16 20 C5
Clarkson St. E2 18 G2
Clarksons, The, Bark. 21 E1
Claude Rd. E13 13 E5
Claude Rd. SE15 32 G5
Claude St. E14 26 E5
Claudia Jones Way SW2 38 E4
Claughton Rd. E13 20 F1
Clavell St. SE10 33 G2
Claverdale Rd. SW2 38 F5
Clavering Ave. SW13 29 D2
Claverton St. SW1 31 C1
Claxton Gro. W6 29 F1
Claybrook Rd. W6 29 F2
Claylands Pl. SW8 31 G3
Claylands Rd. SW8 31 F2
Claymill Ho. SE18 35 E1
Claypole Rd. E15 19 G1
Clays La. E15 12 F2
Clays La. Clo. E15 12 F2
Clayton Rd. SE15 32 F4
Clayton St. SE11 31 G2
Cleanthus Rd. SE18 35 D4
Clearwell Dr. W9 16 C3
Cleaver Sq. SE11 31 G1
Cleaver St. SE11 31 G1
Clegg St. E13 20 D1
Clem Attlee Ct. SW6 30 A2
Clematis St. W12 22 C1
Clemence St. E14 19 D4
Clement Clo. NW6 8 E4
Clements Ave. E16 27 D1
Clement's Inn WC2 43 H2
Clement's Inn Pas. WC2 43 H2
Clements La. EC4 44 G3
Clements Rd. E6 14 A4
Clements Rd. SE16 25 F4
Clephane Rd. N1 11 B3
Clerkenwell Clo. EC1 17 G3
Clerkenwell Grn. EC1 17 G3
Clerkenwell Rd. EC1 17 G3
Clermont Rd. E9 12 A5
Cleve Rd. NW6 9 B4
Cleveland Ave. W4 22 B5
Cleveland Gdns. SW13 29 B5
Cleveland Gdns. W2 16 D5
Cleveland Pl. SW1 43 B5
Cleveland Rd. N1 11 C4
Cleveland Rd. SW13 29 B5
Cleveland Row SW1 43 A6
Cleveland Sq. W2 16 D5
Cleveland St. W1 17 C3
Cleveland Ter. W2 16 D5
Cleveland Way E1 19 A3
Cleveley Clo. SE7 27 G5
Cleverley Est. W12 22 C2
Cleves Rd. E6 13 G5
Clichy Est. E1 19 A4
Clifden Rd. E5 12 A2
Cliff Rd. NW1 10 D3
Cliff Ter. SE8 33 E5
Cliff Vill. NW1 10 D3
Cliff Wk. E16 20 C3
Clifford Dr. SW9 39 A2
Clifford Gdns. NW10 15 E1
Clifford Rd. E16 20 C3
Clifford St. W1 43 A4
Clifford Way NW10 8 B1
Clifford's Inn Pas. EC4 43 J2
Cliffview Rd. SE13 40 E1
Clifton Ave. W12 22 B3
Clifton Cres. SE15 32 G3
Clifton Gdns. W9 16 D3
Clifton Gro. E8 11 F3
Clifton Hill NW8 16 C1
Clifton Pl. W2 16 E5
Clifton Ri. SE14 33 C3
Clifton Rd. E7 13 G3
Clifton Rd. E16 20 B4
Clifton Rd. NW10 15 C1
Clifton Rd. W9 16 D3
Clifton St. EC2 18 D4
Clifton Vill. W9 16 D4
Clifton Way SE15 33 A3
Clink St. SE1 44 F5
Clinton Rd. E3 19 C2
Clinton Rd. E7 13 D1
Clipper Way SE13 40 G2
Clipstone Ms. W1 17 C4
Clipstone St. W1 17 B4
Clissold Cres. N16 11 C1
Clitheroe Rd. SW9 31 E5
Cliveden Pl. SW1 24 A5
Cloak La. EC4 44 F3
Clock Twr. Pl. N7 10 E3
Clockhouse Ave., Bark. 14 E5
Cloisters, The SW9 31 G4
Clonbrock Rd. N16 11 D1
Cloncurry St. SW6 29 F5
Clonmell Rd. SW6 30 A3
Cloth Fair EC1 18 A4
Clothworkers Rd. SE18 35 F3
Cloudesley Pl. N1 10 G5
Cloudesley Rd. N1 10 G5
Cloudesley Sq. N1 10 G5
Cloudesley St. N1 10 G5
Clova Rd. E7 13 C3
Clove Cres. E14 27 A1
Club Row E1 18 E3
Club Row E2 18 E3
Clunbury St. N1 18 C1
Cluny Ms. SW5 23 B5
Clutton St. E14 19 F4
Clyde St. SE8 33 D2
Clydesdale Rd. W11 16 A5
Clyston St. SW8 31 C5
Coach & Horses Yd. W1 43 A3
Coach Ho. Ms. SE23 40 A4
Coalecroft Rd. SW15 36 E2
Coate St. E2 18 F1
Cobb St. E1 18 E4
Cobbett Rd. SE9 42 A1
Cobbett St. SW8 31 F3
Cobbold Est. NW10 8 B3
Cobbold Rd. NW10 8 B3
Cobbold Rd. W12 22 B3
Cobham Clo. SW11 37 F4
Coborn Rd. E3 19 D2
Coborn St. E3 19 D2
Cobourg Rd. SE5 32 E2
Cobourg St. NW1 17 C2
Cochrane St. NW8 16 E1
Cock La. EC1 18 A4
Cockspur Ct. SW1 43 D5
Cockspur St. SW1 43 D5
Code St. E1 18 E3
Codrington Hill SE23 40 C5
Cody Rd. E16 20 B3
Coin St. SE1 43 J5
Coity Rd. NW5 10 A3
Coke St. E1 18 F5
Colbeck Ms. SW7 23 C5
Cold Blow La. SE14 33 B3
Cold Harbour E14 26 G3
Coldbath St. SE13 33 F4
Coldharbour La. SE5 39 B1
Coldharbour La. SW9 38 G2
Coldstream Gdns. SW18 37 A4
Cole St. SE1 25 B3
Colebeck Ms. N1 11 A3
Colebert Ave. E1 19 A3
Colebrooke Row N1 18 A1
Coleford Rd. SW18 37 D3
Colegrave Rd. E15 13 A2
Colegrove Rd. SE15 32 E2
Coleherne Ct. SW5 30 C1
Coleherne Ms. SW10 30 C1
Coleherne Rd. SW10 30 C1
Colehill La. SW6 29 G4
Coleman Flds. N1 11 B5
Coleman Rd. SE5 32 D3
Coleman St. EC2 44 F1
Colenso Rd. E5 12 A1
Colepits Wd. Rd. SE9 42 F3
Coleraine Rd. SE3 34 C2
Coleridge Ave. E12 14 A3
Coleridge Clo. SW8 31 B5
Colestown St. SW11 30 F5
Colet Gdns. W14 29 F1
Coley St. WC1 17 F3
Colin Rd. NW10 8 C3
Colinette Rd. SW15 36 E2
Coliston Rd. SW18 37 B5
College App. SE10 33 G2
College Cres. NW3 9 E3
College Cross N1 10 G4
College Hill EC4 44 E3
College La. NW5 10 B1
College Pk. Clo. SE13 41 A2
College Pl. NW1 10 C5
College Rd. NW10 15 E1
College Rd. SE21 39 D5
College St. EC4 44 F3
College Ter. E3 19 D2
Collent St. E9 12 A3
Collett Rd. SE16 25 F4
Collier St. N1 17 F1
Collingbourne Rd. W12 22 D2
Collingham Gdns. SW5 23 C5
Collingham Pl. SW5 23 C5
Collingham Rd. SW5 23 C5
Collingwood St. E1 18 G3
Collins Rd. N5 11 B1
Collins St. SE3 34 B5
Colls Rd. SE15 33 A4
Colman Rd. E16 20 F4
Colmore Ms. SE15 32 G4
Colnbrook St. SE1 25 A4
Colne Ho., Bark. 14 D3
Colne Rd. E5 12 C1
Cologne Rd. SW11 37 E2
Colomb St. SE10 34 B1
Colombo St. SE1 44 B6
Colonnade WC1 17 E3
Colston Rd. E7 13 G3
Columbia Rd. E2 18 E2
Columbia Rd. E13 20 C3
Columbine Ave. E6 21 A4
Columbine Way SE13 33 G5
Colvestone Cres. E8 11 E2
Colville Est. N1 11 D5
Colville Gdns. W11 16 A5
Colville Hos. W11 16 A5
Colville Rd. W11 16 A5
Colville Sq. W11 16 A5
Colville Ter. W11 16 A5
Colvin Rd. E6 14 A4
Colwell Rd. SE22 39 E3
Colwith Rd. W6 29 E2
Colyton Rd. SE22 39 G3
Combe Ave. SE3 34 C3
Combe Ms. SE3 34 C3
Combedale Rd. SE10 34 D1
Combemartin Rd. SW18 36 G5
Comber Gro. SE5 32 B3
Combermere Rd. SW9 38 F1
Comeragh Rd. W14 29 G1
Comerford Rd. SE4 40 C2
Comet Pl. SE8 33 E3
Comet St. SE8 33 E3
Commercial Rd. E1 18 F5
Commercial Rd. E14 19 C5
Commercial St. E1 18 E3
Commercial Way SE15 32 E3
Commerell St. SE10 34 B1
Commodore Sq. SW10 30 D4
Commodore St. E1 19 C3
Common Rd. SW13 36 C1
Commondale SW15 36 E1
Commonwealth Ave. W12 22 D1
Community Rd. E15 13 A2
Compayne Gdns. NW6 9 C4
Compton Ave. E6 20 G1
Compton Ave. N1 11 A3
Compton Rd. N1 11 A3
Compton Rd. NW10 15 F2
Compton St. EC1 18 A3
Compton Ter. N1 11 A3
Comus Pl. SE17 25 D5
Comyn Rd. SW11 37 F2
Comyns Clo. E16 20 C4
Concanon Rd. SW2 38 F2
Concert Hall App. SE1 43 H6
Concorde Dr. E6 21 B4
Condell Rd. SW8 31 C4
Conder St. E14 19 C5
Conderton Rd. SE5 39 B1
Condover Cres. SE18 35 D3
Condray Pl. SW11 30 F3
Conduit Ct. WC2 43 E3
Conduit Ms. W2 16 E5
Conduit Pl. W2 16 E5
Conduit Rd. SE18 35 D1
Conduit St. W1 24 B1
Coney Way SW8 31 F2
Congleton Gro. SE18 35 E1
Congo Rd. SE18 35 F1
Congreve Rd. SE9 42 B1
Congreve St. SE17 25 D5
Coniger Rd. SW6 30 B5
Coningham Rd. W12 22 D2
Conington Rd. SE13 33 F5
Coniston Ave., Bark. 14 G4
Coniston Ave., Well. 42 G1
Conistone Way N7 10 E4
Conlan St. W10 15 G3
Conley Rd. NW10 8 A3
Connaught Bri. E16 27 G1
Connaught Pl. W2 23 G1
Connaught Rd. NW10 8 A5
Connaught Rd. SE18 35 C1
Connaught Sq. W2 16 G5
Connaught St. W2 16 F5
Conrad Ho. N16 11 D2
Consort Rd. SE15 32 G4
Constantine Rd. NW3 9 F1
Constitution Hill SW1 24 B3
Constitution Ri. SE18 35 C4
Content St. SE17 25 B5
Conway Rd. SE18 28 F5
Conway St. E13 20 D3

Conway St. W1	17	C3
Conyer St. E3	19	C1
Cook's Rd. E15	19	F1
Cooks Rd. SE17	32	A2
Coolfin Rd. E16	20	D5
Coombe Rd. W4	29	A1
Coombs St. N1	18	A1
Coomer Pl. SW6	30	A2
Cooper Rd. NW10	8	C2
Coopers Clo. E1	19	A3
Coopers La. NW1	17	D1
Coopers Rd. SE1	32	E1
Coopersale Rd. E9	12	B2
Cope Pl. W8	23	B4
Cope St. SE16	26	B5
Copeland Dr. E14	26	E5
Copeland Rd. SE15	32	F5
Copenhagen Pl. E14	19	D5
Copenhagen St. N1	10	E5
Copleston Pas. SE15	32	E5
Copleston Rd. SE15	39	E1
Coppelia Rd. SE3	41	C2
Copperas St. SE8	33	F2
Copperfield Rd. E3	19	C3
Copperfield St. SE1	25	A3
Coppice Dr. SW15	36	C4
Coppock Clo. SW11	30	F5
Copse Clo. SE7	34	E2
Copthall Ave. EC2	**44**	**G1**
Copthall Bldgs. EC2	**44**	**G1**
Copthall Clo. EC2	**44**	**F1**
Copthorne Ave. SW12	38	D5
Coptic St. WC1	17	E4
Coral St. SE1	24	G3
Coram St. WC1	17	E3
Corbet Ct. EC3	**44**	**G2**
Corbiere Ho. N1	11	D5
Corbridge Cres. E2	18	G1
Corbylands Rd., Sid.	42	G5
Cordelia St. E14	19	F5
Cordella Clo. SE24	39	A2
Cordova Rd. E3	19	C2
Cordwell Rd. SE13	41	B3
Corelli Rd. SE3	35	A4
Corfield St. E2	18	G2
Coriander Ave. E14	20	A5
Corinne Rd. N19	10	C1
Cork St. W1	**43**	**A4**
Cork St. Ms. W1	**43**	**A4**
Cormont Rd. SE5	32	A4
Cormorant Rd. E7	13	C2
Cornelia St. N7	10	F3
Corner Grn. SE3	34	D5
Corner Ho. St. WC2	**43**	**E5**
Corney Rd. W4	29	A2
Cornflower Ter. SE22	39	G4
Cornhill EC3	**44**	**G2**
Cornmill La. SE13	40	G1
Cornmow Dr. NW10	8	C1
Cornwall Ave. E2	19	A2
Cornwall Ave., Well.	42	G1
Cornwall Cres. W11	15	G5
Cornwall Gdns. NW10	8	D3
Cornwall Gdns. SW7	23	C4
Cornwall Gro. W4	29	A1
Cornwall Ms. S. SW7	23	D4
Cornwall Rd. SE1	**43**	**J5**
Cornwallis Wk. SE9	42	B1
Cornwood Dr. E1	19	A5
Corona Rd. SE12	41	D5
Coronation Rd. E13	20	F2
Coronet St. N1	18	D2
Corporation Row EC1	17	G3
Corporation St. E15	20	B1
Corporation St. N7	10	E2
Corrance Rd. SW2	38	E2
Corsham St. N1	18	C2
Corsica St. N5	11	A3
Cortayne Rd. SW6	30	A5
Cortis Rd. SW15	36	D4
Cortis Ter. SW15	36	D4
Corunna Rd. SW8	31	C4
Corunna Ter. SW8	31	C4
Cosbycote Ave. SE24	39	B3
Cosmur Clo. W12	22	B4
Cossall Wk. SE15	32	G4
Cosser St. SE1	24	G4
Costa St. SE15	32	F5
Cosway St. NW1	16	F4
Cotall St. E14	19	E5
Cotleigh Rd. NW6	9	B4
Cotswold Gdns. E6	20	G2
Cottage Grn. SE5	32	C3
Cottage Gro. SW9	38	E1
Cottage Pl. SW3	23	F4
Cottage St. E14	26	F1
Cottesmore Gdns. W8	23	C4
Cottingham Rd. SW8	31	F3
Cottington Clo. SE11	25	A5
Cotton Row SW11	37	E1
Cotton St. E14	26	G1
Cottons La. SE1	**44**	**G5**
Coulgate St. SE4	40	C1
Coulson St. SW3	30	G1
Coulter Rd. W6	22	D4
Councillor St. SE5	32	B3
Counter Ct. SE1	**44**	**F6**
Counter St. SE1	**44**	**H6**
Countess Rd. NW5	10	C2
County Gro. SE5	32	B4
County Rd. E6	21	D4
County St. SE1	25	B4
Coupland Pl. SE18	35	E1
Courland Gro. SW8	31	D5
Courland St. SW8	31	D4
Court La. SE21	39	D4
Court La. Gdns. SE21	39	D5
Court Rd. SE9	42	B4
Court Yd. SE9	42	B4
Courtenay St. SE11	31	G1
Courtfield Gdns. SW5	23	C5
Courtfield Rd. SW7	23	D5
Courthill Rd. SE13	40	G2
Courthope Rd. NW3	9	G1
Courtlands Ave. SE12	41	E3
Courtmead Clo. SE24	39	B4
Courtnell St. W2	16	B5
Courtrai Rd. SE23	40	C4
Courtyard, The E1	25	G1
Cousin La. EC4	**44**	**F4**
Couthurst Rd. SE3	34	E2
Covent Gdn. WC2	**43**	**F3**
Coventry Rd. E1	18	G3
Coventry Rd. E2	18	G3
Coventry St. W1	**43**	**C4**
Coverdale Rd. NW2	8	F4
Coverdale Rd. W12	22	D3
Coverdales, The, Bark.	21	F1
Coverley Clo. E1	18	F4
Cowbridge La., Bark.	14	D4
Cowcross St. EC1	18	A4
Cowley Rd. SW9	31	G4
Cowley Rd. SW14	36	A1
Cowley Rd. W3	22	B2
Cowper Ave. E6	14	A4
Cowper Rd. N16	11	D2
Cowper St. EC2	18	C3
Cowthorpe Rd. SW8	31	D4
Coxmount Rd. SE7	34	G1
Coxwell Rd. SE18	35	F1
Crabtree La. SW6	29	F3
Craigerne Rd. SE3	34	E3
Craigholm SE18	35	C5
Craignair Rd. SW2	38	G5
Craigs Ct. SW1	**43**	**E5**
Craigton Rd. SE9	42	B2
Cramond Clo. W6	29	G2
Crampton St. SE17	25	B5
Cranberry La. E16	20	B3
Cranborne Rd., Bark.	14	F5
Cranbourn All. WC2	**43**	**D3**
Cranbourn St. WC2	**43**	**D3**
Cranbourne Rd. E15	12	G1
Cranbrook Est. E2	19	B1
Cranbrook Pt. E16	27	D2
Cranbrook Rd. SE8	33	E4
Cranbrook Rd. W4	29	A1
Cranbury Rd. SW6	30	C5
Crane Ct. EC4	**44**	**A2**
Crane Gro. N7	10	G3
Crane Mead SE16	26	B5
Cranfield Rd. SE4	40	D1
Cranford St. E1	26	B1
Cranhurst Rd. NW2	8	E2
Cranleigh Gdns., Bark.	14	F4
Cranleigh Ms. SW11	30	F5
Cranleigh St. NW1	17	C1
Cranley Gdns. SW7	30	D1
Cranley Ms. SW7	30	D1
Cranley Pl. SW7	23	E5
Cranley Rd. E13	20	E4
Cranmer Ct. SW4	38	D1
Cranmer Rd. E7	13	E1
Cranmer Rd. SW9	31	G3
Cranston Est. N1	18	C1
Cranswick Rd. SE16	32	G1
Cranwell Clo. E3	19	F3
Cranwood St. EC1	18	C2
Cranworth Gdns. SW9	31	G4
Craster Rd. SW2	38	F5
Crathie Rd. SE12	41	E4
Craven Gdns., Bark.	21	G1
Craven Hill W2	23	D1
Craven Hill Gdns. W2	23	D1
Craven Hill Ms. W2	23	D1
Craven Pk. NW10	8	A5
Craven Pk. Ms. NW10	8	A5
Craven Pk. Rd. NW10	8	A5
Craven Pas. WC2	**43**	**E5**
Craven Rd. W2	16	D5
Craven St. WC2	**43**	**E5**
Craven Ter. W2	23	D1
Crawford Est. SE5	32	B5
Crawford Pl. W1	16	F5
Crawford Rd. SE5	32	B4
Crawford St. W1	16	G4
Crawthew Gro. SE22	39	E2
Crayford Rd. N7	10	D1
Crealock St. SW18	37	C4
Crebor St. SE22	39	F4
Crediton Hill NW6	9	C2
Crediton Rd. NW10	8	F5
Credon Rd. E13	20	F1
Credon Rd. SE16	32	G1
Creechurch La. EC3	**44**	**J2**
Creechurch Pl. EC3	**44**	**J2**
Creed La. EC4	**44**	**C2**
Creek Rd. SE8	33	E2
Creek Rd. SE10	33	F2
Creekside SE8	33	F3
Crefeld Clo. W6	29	F2
Creighton Ave. E6	20	G1
Creighton Rd. NW6	15	F1
Cremer St. E2	18	E1
Cremorne Rd. SW10	30	D3
Crescent, The SW13	29	B5
Crescent, The W3	15	A5
Crescent Gro. SW4	38	C2
Crescent La. SW4	38	C2
Crescent Pl. SW3	23	F5
Crescent Rd. E6	13	F5
Crescent Rd. E13	13	D5
Crescent Rd. SE18	35	D1
Crescent St. N1	10	F4
Crescent Way SE4	40	E1
Cresford Rd. SW6	30	C4
Cresset Rd. E9	12	A3
Cresset St. SW4	38	D1
Cressfield Clo. NW5	10	A2
Cressingham Rd. SE13	40	G1
Cresswell Gdns. SW5	30	D1
Cresswell Pk. SE3	41	C1
Cresswell Pl. SW10	30	D1
Cressy Ct. W6	22	D4
Cressy Pl. E1	19	A4
Cressy Rd. NW3	9	G2
Crestfield St. WC1	17	E2
Crestway SW15	36	C4
Creton St. SE18	28	C4
Crewdson Rd. SW9	31	G3
Crewe Pl. NW10	15	B2
Crews St. E14	26	E5
Crewys Rd. SE15	32	G5
Cricketfield Rd. E5	11	G1
Cricklewood La. NW2	8	F1
Crieff Rd. SW18	37	D4
Crimscott St. SE1	25	D4
Crimsworth Rd. SW8	31	D4
Crinan St. N1	17	E1
Cringle St. SW8	31	C3
Crisp Rd. W6	29	E1
Crispian Clo. NW10	8	A1
Crispin St. E1	18	E4
Cristowe Rd. SW6	30	A5
Croft, The NW10	15	B1
Croft St. SE8	26	C5
Crofters Ct. SE8	26	C5
Crofters Way NW1	10	D5
Crofton Pk. Rd. SE4	40	D4
Crofton Rd. E13	20	E3
Crofton Rd. SE5	32	D4
Croftongate Way SE4	40	C3
Crofts St. E1	25	F1
Croftway NW3	9	B1
Crogsland Rd. NW1	10	A4
Cromer St. WC1	17	E2
Cromer Vill. Rd. SW18	37	A4
Cromford Rd. SW18	37	B3
Crompton St. W2	16	E3
Cromwell Ave. W6	22	D5
Cromwell Cres. SW5	23	B5
Cromwell Gdns. SW7	23	E4
Cromwell Gro. W6	22	E4
Cromwell Ms. SW7	23	E5
Cromwell Pl. SW7	23	E5
Cromwell Rd. E7	13	F4
Cromwell Rd. SW5	23	C5
Cromwell Rd. SW7	23	C5
Cromwell Rd. SW9	32	A4
Crondace Rd. SW6	30	B4
Crondall St. N1	18	C1
Crooke Rd. SE8	33	C1
Crookham Rd. SW6	30	A4
Crookston Rd. SE9	42	C1
Croombs Rd. E16	20	F4
Crooms Hill SE10	33	G3
Crooms Hill Gro. SE10	33	G3
Cropley St. N1	18	C1
Crosby Rd. E7	13	D3
Crosby Row SE1	25	C3
Crosby Sq. EC3	**44**	**H2**
Crosby Wk. SW2	38	G5
Cross Ave. SE10	34	A2
Cross La. EC3	**44**	**H4**
Cross Rd. SE5	32	D5
Cross St. N1	11	A5
Cross St. SW13	29	A5
Crossbrook Rd. SE3	35	A5
Crossfield Rd. NW3	9	E3
Crossfield St. SE8	33	E3
Crossford St. SW9	31	E5
Crossley St. N7	10	G3

Crossthwaite Ave. SE5	39	C2
Crosswall EC3	25	E1
Crossway N16	11	D2
Croston St. E8	11	F5
Crowder St. E1	25	G1
Crowhurst Clo. SW9	31	G5
Crowland Ter. N1	11	C4
Crown Clo. E3	12	E5
Crown Ct. EC2	**44**	**E2**
Crown Ct. SE12	41	E4
Crown Ct. WC2	**43**	**F2**
Crown Ms. W6	22	C5
Crown Office Row EC4	**43**	**J3**
Crown Pas. SW1	**43**	**B6**
Crown St. SE5	32	B3
Crown Wds. La. SE9	35	E5
Crown Wds. La. SE18	35	D5
Crown Wds. Way SE9	42	F3
Crowndale Rd. NW1	17	C1
Crownfield Rd. E15	13	A1
Crownhill Rd. NW10	8	B5
Crownstone Rd. SW2	38	G3
Crows Rd. E15	20	A2
Crowthorne Rd. W10	15	F5
Croxley Rd. W9	16	A2
Croxted Clo. SE21	39	B5
Croxted Rd. SE21	39	B5
Croxted Rd. SE24	39	B5
Croyde Clo., Sid.	42	F5
Croydon Rd. E13	20	C3
Crozier Ter. E9	12	B2
Crucifix La. SE1	25	D3
Cruden St. N1	11	A5
Cruikshank Rd. E15	13	B1
Cruikshank St. WC1	17	G2
Crutched Friars EC3	**44**	**J3**
Crystal Palace Rd. SE22	39	E4
Cuba St. E14	26	E3
Cubitt St. WC1	17	F2
Cubitt Ter. SW4	38	C1
Cubitts Yd. WC2	**43**	**F3**
Cudham St. SE6	40	G5
Cudworth St. E1	18	G3
Cuff Cres. SE9	41	G4
Culford Gdns. SW3	23	G5
Culford Gro. N1	11	D3
Culford Rd. N1	11	D4
Cullingworth Rd. NW10	8	C2
Culloden St. E14	19	G5
Cullum St. EC3	**44**	**H3**
Culmore Rd. SE15	32	G3
Culmstock Rd. SW11	38	A3
Culross St. W1	24	A1
Culvert Pl. SW11	31	A5
Culvert Rd. SW11	30	G4
Cumberland Ave., Well.	42	G1
Cumberland Clo. E8	11	E3
Cumberland Cres. W14	22	G5
Cumberland Gate W1	23	G1
Cumberland Mkt. NW1	17	B2
Cumberland Rd. E12	13	G1
Cumberland Rd. E13	20	E4
Cumberland Rd. SW13	29	B4
Cumberland St. SW1	31	B1
Cumming St. N1	17	F1
Cunard Pl. EC3	**44**	**J2**
Cundy Rd. E16	20	F5
Cundy St. SW1	24	A5
Cunningham Pl. NW8	16	E3
Cupar Rd. SW11	31	B4
Cureton St. SW1	24	D5
Curlew St. SE1	25	E3
Curricle St. W3	22	A2
Cursitor St. EC4	**43**	**J1**
Curtain Rd. EC2	18	D2
Curtis St. SE1	25	E5
Curtis Way SE1	25	E5
Curve, The W12	22	C1
Curwen Rd. W12	22	C3
Curzon Cres. NW10	8	A4
Curzon St. W1	24	A2
Cut, The SE1	24	G3
Cutcombe Rd. SE5	32	B5
Cuthbert St. W2	16	E3
Cutler St. E1	**44**	**J1**
Cutlers Gdns. E1	**44**	**J1**
Cyclops Ms. E14	26	E5
Cynthia St. N1	17	F1
Cyprus Pl. E2	19	A1
Cyprus Pl. E6	28	C1
Cyprus St. E2	19	A1
Cyrena Rd. SE22	39	E4
Cyril Mans. SW11	30	G4
Cyrus St. EC1	18	A3
Czar St. SE8	33	E2

D

Dabin Cres. SE10	33	G4
Dacca St. SE8	33	D2
Dace Rd. E3	12	E5
Dacre Gdns. SE13	41	B2
Dacre Pk. SE13	41	B1
Dacre Pl. SE13	41	B1
Dacre Rd. E13	13	E5
Dacre St. SW1	24	D4
Daffodil St. W12	22	B1
Dagmar Gdns. NW10	15	F1
Dagmar Rd. SE5	32	D4
Dagmar Ter. N1	11	A5
Dagnall St. SW11	30	G5
Dagnan Rd. SW12	38	B5
Dairsie Rd. SE9	42	C1
Dairy Ms. SW9	38	E1
Daisy La. SW6	37	B1
Dalberg Rd. SW2	38	G3
Dalby Rd. SW18	37	D2
Dalby St. NW5	10	B3
Dale Clo. SE3	41	D1
Dale Rd. SE17	32	A2
Dale St. W4	29	A1
Daleham Gdns. NW3	9	E2
Daleham Ms. NW3	9	E3
Dalehead NW1	17	C1
Daley St. E9	12	B3
Daley Thompson Way SW8	38	B1
Dalgarno Gdns. W10	15	E4
Dalgarno Gdns. Est. W10	15	E3
Dalgarno Way W10	15	E3
Dalgleish St. E14	19	C5
Daling Way E3	19	C1
Dallin Rd. SE18	35	D3
Dalling Rd. W6	22	D5
Dallinger Rd. SE12	41	C4
Dallington St. EC1	18	A3
Dalmeny Ave. N7	10	D1
Dalmeyer Rd. NW10	8	B3
Dalrymple Rd. SE4	40	C2
Dalston La. E8	11	E3
Dalwood St. SE5	32	D4
Dalyell Rd. SW9	38	F1
Dame St. N1	18	B1
Damien St. E1	18	G5
Danbury St. N1	18	A1
Danby St. SE15	39	E1
Dancer Rd. SW6	30	A4
Dando Cres. SE3	41	E1
Dandridge Clo. SE10	34	C1
Dane Rd., Ilf.	14	E2
Danebury Ave. SW15	36	A4
Danecroft Rd. SE24	39	B3
Danehurst St. SW6	29	G4
Danemere St. SW15	36	E1
Danesdale Rd. E9	12	C3
Daneville Rd. SE5	32	C4
Daniel Gdns. SE15	32	E3
Daniels Rd. SE15	40	A1
Dansey Pl. W1	**43**	**C3**
Dante Rd. SE11	25	A5
Danvers St. SW3	30	E2
Daphne St. SW18	37	D4
D'Arblay St. W1	**43**	**B2**
Darfield Rd. SE4	40	D3
Darfield Way W10	15	F5
Darfur St. SW15	36	F1
Darien Rd. SW11	37	E1
Darlan Rd. SW6	30	A3
Darley Rd. SW11	37	G4
Darling Rd. SE4	40	E1
Darling Row E1	18	G3
Darnley Rd. E9	12	A3
Darrell Rd. SE22	39	F3
Darsley Dr. SW8	31	E4
Dart St. W10	15	G2
Dartford St. SE17	32	B2
Dartmouth Clo. W11	16	B5
Dartmouth Gro. SE10	33	G4
Dartmouth Hill SE10	33	G4
Dartmouth Pk. Rd. NW5	10	B1
Dartmouth Pl. W4	29	A2
Dartmouth Rd. NW2	8	F3
Dartmouth Row SE10	33	G4
Dartmouth St. SW1	24	D3
Darwell Clo. E6	21	C1
Darwin St. SE17	25	C5
Datchelor Pl. SE5	32	C4
Date St. SE17	32	B1
Daubeney Rd. E5	12	C1
Daubeney Twr. SE8	26	D5
Dault Rd. SW18	37	D4
Davenant St. E1	18	F4
Davenport Rd. SE6	40	G4
Daventry St. NW1	16	F4
Davern Clo. SE10	27	C5
Davey Clo. N7	10	F3
Davey St. SE15	32	E2
David St. E15	13	A3
Davidge St. SE1	25	A3
Davidson Gdns. SW8	31	E3
Davies St. W1	24	B1
Davis Rd. W3	22	B2
Davis St. E13	20	E1
Davisville Rd. W12	22	C3
Dawes Rd. SW6	29	G3
Dawes St. SE17	32	C1
Dawlish Dr., Ilf.	14	G1
Dawlish Rd. NW2	8	F3
Dawson Clo. SE18	28	E5
Dawson Heights Est. SE22	39	F5
Dawson Pl. W2	23	B1
Dawson Rd. NW2	8	E2
Dawson St. E2	18	E1
Daylesford Ave. SW15	36	C2
Days La., Sid.	42	G5
Dayton Gro. SE15	33	A4
De Beauvoir Cres. N1	11	D5
De Beauvoir Est. N1	11	C5
De Beauvoir Rd. N1	11	D5
De Beauvoir Sq. N1	11	D4
De Crespigny Pk. SE5	32	C5
De Laune St. SE17	32	A1
De Morgan Rd. SW6	37	C1
De Vere Gdns. W8	23	D3
Deacon Rd. NW2	8	C2
Deacon Way SE17	25	B5
Deal Porters Way SE16	26	A4
Deal St. E1	18	F4
Dealtry Rd. SW15	36	E2
Dean Bradley St. SW1	24	E4
Dean Farrar St. SW1	24	D4
Dean Rd. NW2	8	E3
Dean Ryle St. SW1	24	E5
Dean Stanley St. SW1	24	E4
Dean St. E7	13	D2
Dean St. W1	**43**	**C1**
Deancross St. E1	19	A5
Deanery Rd. E15	13	B3
Deanery St. W1	24	A2
Deans Bldgs. SE17	25	C5
Deans Ct. EC4	**44**	**C2**
Dean's Pl. SW1	31	D1
Decima St. SE1	25	D4
Dee St. E14	19	G5
Deeley Rd. SW8	31	D4
Deepdene Gdns. SW2	38	F5
Deepdene Rd. SE5	39	C2
Deerdale Rd. SE24	39	B2
Deerhurst Rd. NW2	8	F3
Dekker Rd. SE21	39	D4
Delafield Rd. SE7	34	E1
Delaford Rd. SE16	32	G1
Delaford St. SW6	29	G3
Delamere Ter. W2	16	C4
Delancey St. NW1	10	B5
Delaware Rd. W9	16	C3
Delawyk Cres. SE24	39	B4
Delhi St. N1	10	E5
Delia St. SW18	37	C5
Dell Clo. E15	13	A5
Dellow St. E1	25	G1
Delme Cres. SE3	34	E5
Deloraine St. SE8	33	E4
Delorme St. W6	29	F2
Delverton Rd. SE17	32	A1
Delvino Rd. SW6	30	B4
Dempster Rd. SW18	37	D3
Denbigh Clo. NW10	8	A4
Denbigh Clo. W11	23	A1
Denbigh Pl. SW1	31	C1
Denbigh Rd. E6	20	G2
Denbigh Rd. W11	23	A1
Denbigh St. SW1	24	C5
Denbigh Ter. W11	23	A1
Dene Clo. SE4	40	C1
Denham St. SE10	34	D1
Denham Way, Bark.	14	G5
Denholme Rd. W9	16	A2
Denman Rd. SE15	32	E4
Denman St. W1	**43**	**C4**
Denmark Gro. N1	17	G1
Denmark Hill SE5	32	C4
Denmark Hill Est. SE5	39	C2
Denmark Pl. WC2	**43**	**D1**
Denmark Rd. NW6	16	A1
Denmark Rd. SE5	32	B4
Denmark St. E13	20	E4
Denmark St. WC2	**43**	**D2**
Denne Ter. E8	11	E5
Dennetts Rd. SE14	33	A4
Denning Clo. NW8	16	D2
Denning Rd. NW3	9	E1
Dennington Pk. Rd. NW6	9	B3
Dennison Pt. E15	12	G4
Denny St. SE11	31	G1
Densham Rd. E15	13	B5
Denton St. SW18	37	C4
Dents Rd. SW11	37	G4
Denyer St. SW3	23	F5
Denzil Rd. NW10	8	B2

Deodar Rd. SW15	36	G2
Deptford Bri. SE8	33	E4
Deptford Bdy. SE8	33	E4
Deptford Ch. St. SE8	33	E2
Deptford Ferry Rd. E14	26	E5
Deptford Grn. SE8	33	E2
Deptford High St. SE8	33	E2
Deptford Strand SE8	26	D5
Deptford Wf. SE8	26	D5
Derby Rd. E7	13	G4
Derby Rd. E9	12	B5
Derbyshire St. E2	18	F2
Dericote St. E8	11	F5
Derifall Clo. E6	21	B4
Dering St. W1	17	B5
Dermody Gdns. SE13	41	A3
Dermody Rd. SE13	41	A3
Derry St. W8	23	C3
Dersingham Ave. E12	14	B1
Derwent Gro. SE22	39	E2
Derwent St. SE10	34	B1
Desenfans Rd. SE21	39	D4
Desford Rd. E16	20	B3
Desmond St. SE14	33	C2
Devalls Clo. E6	28	C1
Devas St. E3	19	F3
Devenay Rd. E15	13	C4
Deverell St. SE1	25	C4
Devereux Ct. WC2	**43**	**J2**
Devereux Rd. SW11	37	G4
Devon Rd., Bark.	14	G5
Devon St. SE15	32	G2
Devonia Rd. N1	18	A1
Devonport Rd. W12	22	D3
Devonport St. E1	19	B5
Devons Est. E3	19	F2
Devons Rd. E3	19	E4
Devonshire Clo. E15	13	B1
Devonshire Clo. W1	17	B4
Devonshire Dr. SE10	33	F3
Devonshire Gro. SE15	32	G2
Devonshire Ms. S. W1	17	B4
Devonshire Ms. W. W1	17	A3
Devonshire Pl. W1	17	A3
Devonshire Pl. W4	29	A1
Devonshire Rd. E16	20	E5
Devonshire Rd. W4	29	A1
Devonshire St. W1	17	B4
Devonshire St. W4	29	A1
Devonshire Ter. W2	16	D5
Dewar St. SE15	39	F1
Dewberry Gdns. E6	21	A4
Dewberry St. E14	19	G4
Dewey Rd. N1	17	G1
Dewhurst Rd. W14	22	F4
Dewsbury Rd. NW10	8	C2
D'Eynsford Rd. SE5	32	C4
Diadem Ct. W1	**43**	**C2**
Diamond St. SE15	32	D3
Diamond Ter. SE10	33	G4
Diana Ho. SW13	29	B4
Diana Pl. NW1	17	B3
Dibden St. N1	11	B5
Dicey Ave. NW2	8	E1
Dickens Est. SE1	25	E3
Dickens Est. SE16	25	E3
Dickens Rd. E6	20	G1
Dickens Sq. SE1	25	B4
Dickens St. SW8	31	B5
Dickson Rd. SE9	42	A1
Digby Rd. E9	12	B2
Digby St. E2	19	A2
Dighton Rd. SW18	37	D3
Dilke St. SW3	30	G2
Dimond Clo. E7	13	D1
Dingle Gdns. E14	26	E1
Dingley Pl. EC1	18	B2
Dingley Rd. EC1	18	B2
Dingwall Rd. SW18	37	D5
Dinsdale Rd. SE3	34	C2
Dinsmore Rd. SW12	38	B5
Dirleton Rd. E15	13	C5
Disbrowe Rd. W6	29	G2
Disraeli Rd. E7	13	D3
Disraeli Rd. SW15	36	G2
Diss St. E2	18	E2
Distaff La. EC4	**44**	**D3**
Distillery Rd. W6	29	E1
Ditch All. SE10	33	F4
Ditchburn St. E14	26	G1
Dixon Rd. SE14	33	C4
Dobell Rd. SE9	42	B3
Dobree Ave. NW10	8	D4
Dobson Clo. NW6	9	E4
Dock Hill Ave. SE16	26	B3
Dock Rd. E16	27	C1
Dock St. E1	25	F1
Dockers Tanner Rd. E14	26	E5
Dockhead SE1	25	E3
Dockland St. E16	28	C2
Dockley Rd. SE16	25	F4
Docwra's Bldgs. N1	11	D3
Dod St. E14	19	E5
Doddington Gro. SE17	32	A2
Doddington Pl. SE17	32	A2
Dodson St. SE1	24	G3
Dog Kennel Hill SE22	39	D1
Dog Kennel Hill Est. SE22	39	D1
Dog La. NW10	8	A1
Doggett Rd. SE6	40	E5
Doherty Rd. E13	20	D3
Dolben St. SE1	**44**	**C6**
Dolby Rd. SW6	30	A5
Dolland St. SE11	31	F1
Dollis Hill La. NW2	8	B1
Dolman St. SW4	38	F2
Dolphin La. E14	26	F1
Dolphin Sq. SW1	31	C1
Dolphin Sq. W4	29	A3
Dombey St. WC1	17	F4
Domett Clo. SE5	39	C2
Don Phelan Clo. SE5	32	C4
Donald Rd. E13	13	E5
Donaldson Rd. NW6	9	A5
Donaldson Rd. SE18	35	C4
Donegal St. N1	17	F1
Doneraile St. SW6	29	F5
Dongola Rd. E13	20	E2
Donkey All. SE22	39	F5
Donne Pl. SW3	23	F5
Donnington Rd. NW10	8	D4
Doon St. SE1	**43**	**J5**
Dora St. E14	19	D5
Doran Gro. SE18	35	G3
Doran Wk. E15	12	G4
Dorchester Ct. SE24	39	B3
Dorchester Dr. SE24	39	B3
Dorchester Gro. W4	29	A1
Dordrecht Rd. W3	22	A2
Dore Ave. E12	14	C2
Doria Rd. SW6	30	A5
Doric Way NW1	17	D2
Doris Rd. E7	13	D4
Dorking Clo. SE8	33	D2
Dorlcote Rd. SW18	37	F5
Dorman Way NW8	9	E5
Dormay St. SW18	37	C3
Dormer Clo. E15	13	C3
Dornberg Clo. SE3	34	D3
Dorncliffe Rd. SW6	29	G5
Dorney NW3	9	F4
Dornfell St. NW6	9	A2
Dorothy Rd. SW11	37	G1
Dorrington St. EC1	17	G4
Dorset Bldgs. EC4	**44**	**B2**
Dorset Est. E2	18	E2
Dorset Pl. E15	13	A3
Dorset Ri. EC4	**44**	**B2**
Dorset Rd. E7	13	F4
Dorset Rd. SW8	31	E3
Dorset Sq. NW1	16	G3
Dorset St. W1	16	G4
Dorville Cres. W6	22	D4
Dorville Rd. SE12	41	C3
Dothill Rd. SE18	35	F3
Doughty Ms. WC1	17	F3
Doughty St. WC1	17	F3
Douglas Rd. E16	20	D4
Douglas Rd. N1	11	B4
Douglas Rd. NW6	9	A5
Douglas St. SW1	24	D5
Douglas Way SE8	33	D3
Douro Pl. W8	23	C4
Douro St. E3	19	E1
Dove App. E6	21	A4
Dove Ct. EC2	**44**	**F2**
Dove Ms. SW5	23	D5
Dove Rd. N1	11	C3
Dove Row E2	11	F5
Dovedale Rd. SE22	39	G3
Dovehouse Mead, Bark.	21	F1
Dovehouse St. SW3	30	E1
Dover Ho. Rd. SW15	36	C2
Dover Pk. Dr. SW15	36	D4
Dover St. W1	24	B1
Dovercourt Rd. SE21	39	D4
Dovercourt Rd. SE22	39	D4
Doverfield Rd. SW2	38	E4
Dowdeswell Clo. SW15	36	A2
Dowgate Hill EC4	**44**	**F3**
Dowland St. W10	15	G2
Dowlas St. SE5	32	D3
Down Pl. W6	29	D1
Down St. W1	24	B2
Downfield Clo. W9	16	C3
Downham Rd. N1	11	C4
Downing St. SW1	24	E3
Downings E6	21	C5
Downman Rd. SE9	42	A1
Downs Pk. Rd. E5	11	F2
Downs Pk. Rd. E8	11	E2
Downs Rd. E5	11	F1
Downsell Rd. E15	12	G1
Downshire Hill NW3	9	E1
Downside Cres. NW3	9	F2
Downtown Rd. SE16	26	C3
Dowson Clo. SE5	39	C2
Doyle Gdns. NW10	8	C5
D'Oyley St. SW1	24	A5
Draco St. SE17	32	B2
Dragoon Rd. SE8	33	D1
Drake Rd. SE4	40	E1
Drakefell Rd. SE4	40	C1
Drakefell Rd. SE14	33	B5
Drapers Rd. E15	13	A1
Drawdock Rd. SE10	27	A2
Drawell Clo. SE18	35	G1
Dray Gdns. SW2	38	F3
Draycott Ave. SW3	23	F5
Draycott Pl. SW3	23	G5
Draycott Ter. SW3	23	G5
Drayford Clo. W9	16	A3
Drayson Ms. W8	23	B3
Drayton Gdns. SW10	30	D1
Drayton Pk. N5	10	G2
Drayton Rd. NW10	8	B5
Dreadnought St. SE10	27	B4
Dressington Ave. SE4	40	E4
Drew Rd. E16	28	A2
Driffield Rd. E3	19	C1
Dromore Rd. SW15	36	G4
Droop St. W10	15	G3
Drover La. SE15	32	G3
Drovers Pl. SE15	32	G3
Druce Rd. SE21	39	D4
Druid St. SE1	25	D3
Drummond Cres. NW1	17	D2
Drummond Gate SW1	31	D1
Drummond Rd. SE16	25	G4
Drummond St. NW1	17	C3
Drury La. WC2	**43**	**F1**
Dryad St. SW15	36	F1
Dryburgh Rd. SW15	36	D1
Dryden Rd., Well.	35	G4
Dryden St. WC2	**43**	**F2**
Drysdale St. N1	18	D2
Du Cane Rd. W12	15	B5
Dublin Cres. E8	11	F5
Duchess of Bedford's Wk. W8	23	B3
Duchess St. W1	17	B4
Duchy St. SE1	**44**	**A5**
Ducie St. SW4	38	F2
Duck La. W1	**43**	**C2**
Duckett St. E1	19	B3
Dudden Hill La. NW10	8	B1
Dudley Rd. NW6	15	G1
Dudley Rd., Ilf.	14	D1
Duff St. E14	19	F5
Dufferin St. EC1	18	B3
Dufour's Pl. W1	**43**	**B2**
Duke Humphrey Rd. SE3	34	B4
Duke of Wellington Pl. SW1	24	A3
Duke of York St. SW1	**43**	**B5**
Duke St. SW1	**43**	**B5**
Duke St. W1	17	A5
Duke St. Hill SE1	**44**	**G5**
Dukes Ct. E6	14	C5
Dukes La. W8	23	C3
Dukes Pl. EC3	**44**	**J2**
Dukes Rd. E6	14	C5
Duke's Rd. WC1	17	D2
Dulford St. W11	22	G1
Dulka Rd. SW11	37	G3
Dulwich Rd. SE24	38	G3
Dulwich Village SE21	39	D4
Dumbarton Rd. SW2	38	E4
Dumbreck Rd. SE9	42	B2
Dunbar Rd. E7	13	D3
Dunblane Rd. SE9	35	A5
Dunboyne Rd. NW3	9	G2
Dunbridge St. E2	18	F3
Duncan Gro. W3	15	A5
Duncan Rd. E8	11	G5
Duncan St. N1	18	A1
Duncan Ter. N1	18	A1
Duncannon St. WC2	**43**	**E4**
Duncombe Hill SE23	40	C5
Duncrievie Rd. SE13	41	A4
Duncroft SE18	35	G3
Dundalk Rd. SE4	40	C1
Dundas Rd. SE15	33	A5
Dundee Rd. E13	20	E1
Dundee St. E1	25	G2
Dundonald Rd. NW10	8	F5
Dunelm St. E1	19	B5
Dunford Rd. N7	10	F1
Dungarvan Ave. SW15	36	C2
Dunlace Rd. E5	12	A1
Dunloe St. E2	18	E1

Dunlop Pt. E16 27 D2
Dunmore Rd. NW6 8 G5
Dunmow Rd. E15 13 A1
Dunn St. E8 11 E2
Dunnock Rd. E6 21 A5
Dunns Pas. WC1 43 F1
Dunollie Rd. NW5 10 C2
Dunoon Rd. SE23 40 A5
Dunraven Rd. W12 22 C2
Dunsany Rd. W14 22 F4
Dunstans Gro. SE22 39 G4
Dunstans Rd. SE22 39 F5
Dunster Ct. EC3 44 H3
Dunster Gdns. NW6 9 A4
Dunston Rd. E8 11 E5
Dunston Rd. SW11 38 A1
Dunston St. E8 11 E5
Dunton Rd. SE1 25 E5
Dunvegan Rd. SE9 42 B2
Dupree Rd. SE7 34 E1
Durand Gdns. SW9 31 F4
Durant St. E2 18 F2
Durban Rd. E15 20 B2
Durham Ho. St. WC2 43 F4
Durham Ri. SE18 35 E1
Durham Rd. E12 13 G1
Durham Rd. E16 20 B3
Durham Row E1 19 C4
Durham St. SE11 31 F1
Durham Ter. W2 16 C5
Durrell Rd. SW6 30 A4
Durrington Rd. E5 12 C1
Dursley Clo. SE3 34 F5
Dursley Gdns. SE3 34 G4
Dursley Rd. SE3 34 F5
Durward St. E1 18 G4
Duthie St. E14 26 G1
Dutton St. SE10 33 G4
Dye Ho. La. E3 12 E5
Dyers La. SW15 36 D2
Dylan Rd. SE24 39 A2
Dylways SE5 39 C2
Dymock St. SW6 37 C1
Dyne Rd. NW6 8 G4
Dynham Rd. NW6 9 B4
Dyott St. WC1 43 D1
Dyson Rd. E15 13 C3

E

Eagle Ct. EC1 18 A4
Eagle Pl. SW1 43 B4
Eagle St. WC1 17 F4
Eagle Wf. Rd. N1 18 B1
Eaglesfield Rd. SE18 35 D5
Ealdham Sq. SE9 41 F2
Eamont St. NW8 16 F1
Eardley Cres. SW5 30 B1
Earl Ri. SE18 28 F5
Earl Rd. SE1 32 E1
Earl St. EC2 18 C4
Earldom Rd. SW15 36 E2
Earlham Gro. E7 13 C2
Earlham St. WC2 43 D2
Earls Ct. Gdns. SW5 23 C5
Earls Ct. Rd. SW5 23 B5
Earls Ct. Rd. W8 23 B5
Earls Ct. Sq. SW5 30 C1
Earls Ter. W8 23 A4
Earls Wk. W8 23 B4
Earlsferry Way N1 10 F4
Earlshall Rd. SE9 42 B2
Earlsmead Rd. NW10 15 E2
Earlsthorpe Ms. SW12 38 A4
Earlston Gro. E9 11 G5
Earlswood St. SE10 34 B1
Earnshaw St. WC2 43 D1
Earsby St. W14 22 G5

East Acton La. W3 22 A1
East Arbour St. E1 19 B5
East Ave. E12 14 A4
East Cross Route E3 12 D4
East Dulwich Gro. SE22 39 D3
East Dulwich Rd. SE15 39 F2
East Dulwich Rd. SE22 39 E2
East Ferry Rd. E14 26 F5
East Ham Ind. Est. E6 20 G3
East Ham Manor Way E6 21 C5
East Harding St. EC4 44 A1
East Hill SW18 37 C3
East India Dock Rd. E14 19 E5
East India Dock Wall Rd. E14 27 A1
East La. SE16 25 F3
East Mt. St. E1 18 G4
East Rd. E15 13 D5
East Rd. N1 18 C2
East Rochester Way SE9 42 F2
East Rochester Way, Sid. 42 G2
East Row W10 15 G3
East Smithfield E1 25 E1
East St. SE17 32 B1
East St., Bark. 14 E4
East Surrey Gro. SE15 32 E3
East Tenter St. E1 18 E5
Eastbourne Ms. W2 16 D5
Eastbourne Rd. E6 21 C2
Eastbourne Rd. E15 13 B5
Eastbourne Ter. W2 16 D5
Eastbrook Rd. SE3 34 E4
Eastbury Ave., Bark. 14 G5
Eastbury Ct., Bark. 14 G5
Eastbury Gro. W4 29 A1
Eastbury Rd. E6 21 C3
Eastbury Ter. E1 19 B3
Eastcastle St. W1 43 A1
Eastcheap EC3 44 G3
Eastcombe Ave. SE7 34 E2
Eastcote Rd., Well. 35 F5
Eastcote St. SW9 31 F5
Eastdown Pk. SE13 41 A2
Eastern Rd. E13 20 E1
Eastern Rd. SE4 40 E2
Eastlake Rd. SE5 32 B5
Eastlands Cres. SE21 39 E4
Eastmoor St. SE7 27 G4
Eastney St. SE10 34 A1
Eastview Ave. SE18 35 G3
Eastway E9 12 D3
Eastway E10 12 E1
Eaton Clo. SW1 24 A5
Eaton Dr. SW9 39 A2
Eaton Gate SW1 24 A5
Eaton La. SW1 24 B4
Eaton Ms. N. SW1 24 A4
Eaton Ms. S. SW1 24 A5
Eaton Ms. W. SW1 24 A5
Eaton Pl. SW1 24 A4
Eaton Row SW1 24 B4
Eaton Sq. SW1 24 A5
Eaton Ter. SW1 24 A5
Ebbisham Dr. SW8 31 F2
Ebbsfleet Rd. NW2 8 G2
Ebdon Way SE3 41 E1
Ebner St. SW18 37 C3
Ebor St. E1 18 E3
Ebsworth St. SE23 40 B5
Ebury Bri. SW1 31 B1

Ebury Bri. Est. SW1 31 B1
Ebury Bri. Rd. SW1 31 A1
Ebury Ms. SW1 24 B5
Ebury Sq. SW1 24 A5
Ebury St. SW1 24 A5
Eccles Rd. SW11 37 G2
Ecclesbourne Rd. N1 11 B4
Eccleston Bri. SW1 24 B5
Eccleston Ms. SW1 24 A4
Eccleston Pl. SW1 24 B5
Eccleston Sq. SW1 24 B5
Eccleston St. SW1 24 B5
Eckford St. N1 17 G1
Eckstein Rd. SW11 37 F2
Eclipse Rd. E13 20 E4
Edbrooke Rd. W9 16 B3
Eddiscombe Rd. SW6 30 A5
Eddystone Rd. SE4 40 C3
Eden Gro. N7 10 F2
Edenbridge Rd. E9 12 B4
Edenhurst Ave. SW6 37 A1
Edensor Gdns. W4 29 A3
Edensor Rd. W4 29 A3
Edenvale St. SW6 30 C5
Edgar Rd. E3 19 F2
Edgarley Ter. SW6 29 G4
Edge Hill SE18 35 D2
Edgeley Rd. SW4 38 D1
Edgeworth Rd. SE9 41 F2
Edgware Rd. W2 16 E3
Edinburgh Gate SW1 23 G3
Edinburgh Ho. W9 16 C2
Edinburgh Rd. E13 20 E1
Edis St. NW1 10 A5
Edith Gro. SW10 30 D2
Edith Rd. E6 13 G4
Edith Rd. W14 22 G5
Edith Row SW6 30 C4
Edith Ter. SW10 30 D3
Edith Vill. W14 30 A1
Edithna St. SW9 38 E1
Edmeston Clo. E9 12 C3
Edmund St. SE5 32 C3
Edna St. SW11 30 F4
Edric Rd. SE14 33 B3
Edrich Ho. SW4 31 E4
Edward Pl. SE8 33 D2
Edward St. E16 20 D3
Edward St. SE8 33 D2
Edward St. SE14 33 C3
Edward Temme Ave. E15 13 C4
Edwardes Sq. W8 23 A4
Edwards Ms. W1 17 A5
Edwin Ave. E6 21 C1
Edwin St. E1 19 A3
Edwin St. E16 20 D4
Effie Pl. SW6 30 B3
Effie Rd. SW6 30 B3
Effingham Rd. SE12 41 B3
Effra Par. SW2 38 G3
Effra Rd. SW2 38 G2
Egan Way SE16 32 G1
Egbert St. NW1 10 A5
Egerton Cres. SW3 23 F5
Egerton Dr. SE10 33 F4
Egerton Gdns. NW10 8 E5
Egerton Gdns. SW3 23 F5
Egerton Gdns. Ms. SW3 23 F4
Egerton Pl. SW3 23 F4
Egerton Ter. SW3 23 F4
Egham Rd. E13 20 E4
Eglantine Rd. SW18 37 D3
Eglinton Hill SE18 35 D2
Eglinton Rd. SE18 35 D2
Egliston Ms. SW15 36 E1
Egliston Rd. SW15 36 E1
Egmont St. SE14 33 B3
Eighth Ave. E12 14 B1

Eisenhower Dr. E6 21 A
Elaine Gro. NW5 10 A
Elam Clo. SE5 32 A
Elam St. SE5 32 A
Eland Rd. SW11 37 G
Elbe St. SW6 30 D
Elbury Dr. E16 20 D
Elcho St. SW11 30 F
Elcot Ave. SE15 32 F
Elder St. E1 18 E
Elderfield Rd. E5 12 B
Elderslie Rd. SE9 42 C
Eldon Gro. NW3 9 E
Eldon Rd. W8 23 C
Eldon St. EC2 18 C
Eldred Rd., Bark. 14 G
Eleanor Clo. SE16 26 B
Eleanor Gro. SW13 36 A
Eleanor Rd. E8 11 G
Eleanor Rd. E15 13 C
Eleanor St. E3 19 E
Electric Ave. SW9 38 G
Electric La. SW9 38 G
Elephant & Castle SE1 25 A
Elephant La. SE16 26 A
Elephant Rd. SE17 25 B
Elf Row E1 26 A
Elfindale Rd. SE24 39 B
Elford Clo. SE3 41 F
Elfort Rd. N5 10 G
Elgar St. SE16 26 C
Elgin Ave. W9 16 B
Elgin Cres. W11 22 G
Elgin Est. W9 16 B
Elia Ms. N1 18 A
Elia St. N1 18 A
Elias Pl. SW8 31 G
Elibank Rd. SE9 42 B
Elim Est. SE1 25 C
Elim Way E13 20 C
Eliot Gdns. SW15 36 C
Eliot Hill SE13 33 G
Eliot Pk. SE13 33 G
Eliot Pl. SE3 34 B
Eliot Vale SE3 34 A
Elizabeth Ave. N1 11 B
Elizabeth Bri. SW1 24 B
Elizabeth Est. SE17 32 C
Elizabeth Gdns. W3 22 B
Elizabeth Ms. NW3 9 G
Elizabeth Rd. E6 13 G
Elizabeth St. SW1 24 A
Elizabeth Ter. SE9 42 B
Elkington Rd. E13 20 E
Elkstone Rd. W10 16 A
Ellaline Rd. W6 29 F
Elland Rd. SE15 40 A
Ellen St. E1 18 F
Ellenborough Pl. SW15 36 C
Ellerby St. SW6 29 F
Ellerdale Rd. NW3 9 D
Ellerdale St. SE13 40 F
Ellerslie Gdns. NW10 8 C
Ellerslie Rd. W12 22 D
Ellerslie Sq. Ind. Est. SW2 38 E
Ellerton Rd. SW13 29 C
Ellery St. SE15 32 G
Ellesmere Rd. E3 19 C
Ellesmere Rd. NW10 8 C
Ellesmere St. E14 19 F
Ellingfort Rd. E8 11 G
Ellingham Rd. E15 13 A
Ellingham Rd. W12 22 C
Ellington St. N7 10 G
Elliot Clo. E15 13 B
Elliott Rd. SW9 32 A
Elliott Rd. W4 22 A

Elliott Sq. NW3	9	F4
Elliotts Row SE11	25	A5
Ellis Ms. SE7	34	F2
Ellis St. SW1	23	G5
Elliscombe Rd. SE7	34	F1
Ellisfield Dr. SW15	36	B5
Ellison Rd. SW13	29	B5
Ellsworth St. E2	18	G2
Elm Bank Gdns. SW13	29	A5
Elm Ct. EC4	**43**	**J3**
Elm Grn. W3	15	A5
Elm Gro. NW2	8	F1
Elm Gro. SE15	32	E5
Elm Gro. Rd. SW13	29	C5
Elm Pk. SW2	38	F4
Elm Pk. Gdns. SW10	30	E1
Elm Pk. La. SW3	30	E1
Elm Pk. Rd. SW3	30	E2
Elm Pl. SW7	30	E1
Elm Quay Ct. SW8	31	D2
Elm Rd. E7	13	C3
Elm St. WC1	17	F3
Elm Ter. SE9	42	C4
Elm Tree Clo. NW8	16	E2
Elm Tree Rd. NW8	16	E2
Elm Way NW10	8	A1
Elmbrook Gdns. SE9	42	A2
Elmcroft St. E5	12	A1
Elmdene Rd. SE18	35	D1
Elmer Rd. SE6	40	G5
Elmhurst Rd. E7	13	E4
Elmhurst St. SW4	38	D1
Elmington Est. SE5	32	C3
Elmington Rd. SE5	32	C4
Elmira St. SE13	40	F1
Elmley St. SE18	28	F5
Elmore St. N1	11	C4
Elms, The SW13	36	B1
Elms Cres. SW4	38	C4
Elms Ms. W2	23	E1
Elms Rd. SW4	38	C3
Elms Wk. SE3	41	C2
Elmshaw Rd. SW15	36	C3
Elmstone Rd. SW6	30	B4
Elmwood Rd. SE24	39	C3
Elrington Rd. E8	11	F3
Elsa St. E1	19	C4
Elsdale St. E9	12	A3
Elsenham Rd. E12	14	C2
Elsham Rd. W14	22	G3
Elsham Ter. W14	22	G3
Elsie Rd. SE22	39	E2
Elsiemaud Rd. SE4	40	D3
Elsley Rd. SW11	37	G1
Elspeth Rd. SW11	37	G2
Elsted St. SE17	25	C5
Elstow Clo. SE9	42	C3
Elstree Gdns., Ilf.	14	E2
Elswick Rd. SE13	33	F5
Elswick St. SW6	30	D5
Elsworthy Ri. NW3	9	F4
Elsworthy Rd. NW3	9	F5
Elsworthy Ter. NW3	9	F4
Elsynge Rd. SW18	37	E3
Eltham Grn. SE9	41	F3
Eltham Grn. Rd. SE9	41	F2
Eltham High St. SE9	42	B4
Eltham Hill SE9	41	G3
Eltham Palace Rd. SE9	41	F4
Eltham Pk. Gdns. SE9	42	C2
Eltham Rd. SE9	41	F3
Eltham Rd. SE12	41	D3
Elthiron Rd. SW6	30	B4
Elthruda Rd. SE13	41	A4
Eltisley Rd., Ilf.	14	D1
Elton Ho. E3	12	D5
Elton Pl. N16	11	D2
Eltringham St. SW18	37	D2
Elvaston Ms. SW7	23	D4
Elvaston Pl. SW7	23	D4
Elverson Rd. SE8	33	F5
Elverton St. SW1	24	D5
Elvis Rd. NW2	8	E3
Elwin St. E2	18	F2
Elwyn Gdns. SE12	41	D5
Elystan Pl. SW3	30	F1
Elystan St. SW3	23	F5
Emba St. SE16	25	F3
Embankment SW15	29	F5
Embankment Gdns. SW3	30	G2
Embankment Pl. WC2	**43**	**F5**
Embleton Rd. SE13	40	F2
Emden St. SW6	30	C4
Emerald Clo. E16	21	A5
Emerald St. WC1	17	F4
Emerson St. SE1	**44**	**D5**
Emery Hill St. SW1	24	C4
Emily Pl. N7	10	G1
Emlyn Gdns. W12	22	A3
Emlyn Rd. W12	22	A3
Emma Rd. E13	20	C1
Emma St. E2	18	G1
Emmott Clo. E1	19	C3
Emperor's Gate SW7	23	C4
Empire Wf. Rd. E14	27	A5
Empress Pl. SW6	30	B1
Empress St. SE17	32	B2
Empson St. E3	19	F3
Emu Rd. SW8	31	B5
Enbrook St. W10	15	G2
Endell St. WC2	**43**	**E1**
Enderby St. SE10	34	B1
Endlesham Rd. SW12	38	A5
Endsleigh Gdns. WC1	17	D3
Endsleigh Pl. WC1	17	D3
Endsleigh St. WC1	17	D3
Endwell Rd. SE4	33	C5
Endymion Rd. SW2	38	F4
Enfield Rd. N1	11	D4
Enford St. W1	16	G4
Engate St. SE13	40	G2
Engineer Clo. SE18	35	C2
Englands La. NW3	9	G3
Englefield Rd. N1	11	C4
Engleheart Rd. SE6	40	F5
Englewood Rd. SW12	38	B4
English Grds. SE1	**44**	**H6**
English St. E3	19	D3
Enid St. SE16	25	E4
Enmore Rd. SW15	36	E2
Ennerdale Ho. E3	19	D3
Ennersdale Rd. SE13	41	A3
Ennis Rd. SE18	35	E2
Ennismore Ave. W4	22	B5
Ennismore Gdns. SW7	23	F3
Ennismore Gdns. Ms. SW7	23	F4
Ennismore Ms. SW7	23	F4
Ennismore St. SW7	23	F4
Ensign St. E1	25	F1
Enslin Rd. SE9	42	C5
Enterprise Way NW10	15	C2
Enterprise Way SW18	37	B2
Enterprize Way SE8	26	D5
Epirus Rd. SW6	30	A3
Epping Clo. E14	26	E5
Epple Rd. SW6	30	A4
Epworth St. EC2	18	C3
Erasmus St. SW1	24	D5
Erconwald St. W12	15	B5
Eresby Pl. NW6	9	B4
Eric Clo. E7	13	D1
Eric Rd. E7	13	D1
Eric St. E3	19	D3
Erica St. W12	22	C1
Ericcson Clo. SW18	37	B3
Erindale SE18	35	F2
Erindale Ter. SE18	35	F2
Erlanger Rd. SE14	33	B4
Ermine Rd. SE13	40	F2
Ernald Ave. E6	21	A1
Ernest St. E1	19	B3
Erpingham Rd. SW15	36	E1
Errington Rd. W9	16	A3
Errol St. EC1	18	B3
Erskine Rd. NW3	9	G4
Erwood Rd. SE7	35	A1
Escreet Gro. SE18	28	C5
Esk Rd. E13	20	D3
Esmeralda Rd. SE1	25	F5
Esmond Rd. NW6	9	A5
Esmond St. SW15	36	G2
Esparto St. SW18	37	C5
Essendine Rd. W9	16	B2
Essex Ct. EC4	**43**	**J2**
Essex Ct. SW13	29	B5
Essex Pk. Ms. W3	22	A2
Essex Rd. E12	14	A2
Essex Rd. N1	11	A5
Essex Rd. NW10	8	A4
Essex Rd., Bark.	14	F4
Essex St. E7	13	D2
Essex St. WC2	**43**	**J3**
Essex Vill. W8	23	B3
Essian St. E1	19	C4
Estcourt Rd. SW6	30	A3
Este Rd. SW11	37	F1
Estelle Rd. NW3	9	G1
Esterbrooke St. SW1	24	D5
Etchingham Rd. E15	12	G1
Eternit Wk. SW6	29	E4
Ethel Rd. E16	20	E5
Ethelburga St. SW11	30	F4
Ethelden Rd. W12	22	D2
Etherow St. SE22	39	F4
Ethnard Rd. SE15	32	G2
Eton Ave. NW3	9	E4
Eton College Rd. NW3	9	G3
Eton Gro. SE13	41	B1
Eton Rd. NW3	9	G4
Eton Rd., Ilf.	14	E2
Eton Vill. NW3	9	G3
Etta St. SE8	33	C2
Ettrick St. E14	19	G5
Eugenia Rd. SE16	26	A5
Europe Rd. SE18	28	B4
Eustace Rd. E6	21	A2
Eustace Rd. SW6	30	B3
Euston Gro. NW1	17	D2
Euston Rd. NW1	17	B3
Euston Sq. NW1	17	D2
Euston St. NW1	17	C2
Evandale Rd. SW9	31	G5
Evangelist Rd. NW5	10	B1
Eve Rd. E11	13	B1
Eve Rd. E15	20	B1
Evelina Rd. SE15	40	A1
Eveline Lowe Est. SE16	25	F4
Evelyn Dennington Rd. E6	21	B4
Evelyn Fox Ct. W10	15	E4
Evelyn Gdns. SW7	30	E1
Evelyn St. SE8	33	C1
Evelyn Wk. N1	18	C1
Evelyn Yd. W1	**43**	**C1**
Evenwood Clo. SW15	36	G3
Everdon Rd. SW13	29	C2
Everest Pl. E14	19	G4
Everest Rd. SE9	42	B3
Everilda St. N1	10	F5
Everington St. W6	29	F2
Eversholt St. NW1	17	C1
Eversleigh Rd. E6	13	G5
Eversleigh Rd. SW11	37	G1
Eversley Rd. SE7	34	E2
Everthorpe Rd. SE15	39	E1
Evesham Rd. E15	13	C4
Evesham St. W11	22	F1
Evesham Wk. SW9	31	G5
Evesham Way SW11	38	A1
Ewald Rd. SW6	30	A5
Ewart Pl. E3	19	D1
Ewart Rd. SE23	40	B5
Ewe Clo. N7	10	E3
Ewen Cres. SW2	38	G5
Ewer St. SE1	**44**	**D6**
Ewhurst Rd. SE4	40	D4
Excel Ct. WC2	**43**	**D4**
Excelsior Gdns. SE13	33	G5
Exchange Arc. EC2	18	D4
Exchange Ct. WC2	**43**	**F4**
Exchange Pl. EC2	18	D4
Exchange Sq. EC2	18	D4
Exeter Rd. E16	20	D4
Exeter Rd. NW2	8	G2
Exeter Rd. SE15	32	E4
Exeter St. WC2	**43**	**F3**
Exeter Way SE14	33	D3
Exhibition Clo. W12	22	E1
Exhibition Rd. SW7	23	E3
Exmoor St. W10	15	F4
Exmouth Mkt. EC1	17	G3
Exmouth Pl. E8	11	G4
Exning Rd. E16	20	C3
Exon St. SE17	25	D5
Exton St. SE1	**43**	**J6**
Eynella Rd. SE22	39	E5
Eynham Rd. W12	15	E5
Eyot Gdns. W6	29	B1
Eythorne Rd. SW9	31	G4
Ezra St. E2	18	E2

F

Fabian Rd. SW6	30	A3
Fabian St. E6	21	B3
Factory Pl. E14	33	F1
Factory Rd. E16	28	A2
Fairacres SW15	36	C3
Fairbairn Grn. SW9	31	G4
Fairby Rd. SE12	41	E3
Fairclough St. E1	18	F5
Faircross Ave., Bark.	14	E3
Fairdale Gdns. SW15	36	D2
Fairfax Gdns. SE3	34	F4
Fairfax Pl. NW6	9	D4
Fairfax Rd. NW6	9	D4
Fairfax Rd. W4	22	A4
Fairfield Ct. NW10	8	C5
Fairfield Dr. SW18	37	C3
Fairfield Gro. SE7	34	G2
Fairfield Rd. E3	19	E1
Fairfield Rd., Ilf.	14	D3
Fairfield St. SW18	37	C3
Fairfoot Rd. E3	19	E3
Fairhazel Gdns. NW6	9	C3
Fairholme Rd. W14	29	G1
Fairland Rd. E15	13	C3
Fairlawn SE7	34	F2
Fairlie Gdns. SE23	40	A5
Fairlight Ave. NW10	15	A1
Fairmount Rd. SW2	38	F4
Fairoak Dr. SE9	42	F3
Fairthorn Rd. SE7	34	D1
Fairview Pl. SW2	38	F5
Fairway, The W3	15	A5
Fairway Gdns., Ilf.	14	E2
Fakruddin St. E1	18	F3
Falcon Clo. SE1	**44**	**C5**

Falcon Gro. SW11	37	F1
Falcon La. SW11	37	F1
Falcon Rd. SW11	30	F5
Falcon St. E13	20	C3
Falcon Ter. SW11	37	F1
Falcon Trd. Est. NW10	8	A1
Falcon Way E14	26	F5
Falconberg Ct. W1	**43**	**D1**
Falconberg Ms. W1	**43**	**C1**
Falconwood Ave., Well.	35	F5
Falconwood Par., Well.	42	G2
Falkirk Ho. W9	16	C2
Falkirk St. N1	18	D1
Falkland Rd. NW5	10	C2
Falmouth Clo. SE12	41	C3
Falmouth Rd. SE1	25	B4
Falmouth St. E15	13	A2
Fann St. EC1	18	B3
Fanshaw St. N1	18	D2
Fanshawe Ave., Bark.	14	E3
Fanthorpe St. SW15	36	E1
Faraday Rd. E15	13	C3
Faraday Rd. W10	15	G4
Faraday Way SE18	27	G4
Fareham St. W1	**43**	**C1**
Faringford Rd. E15	13	B4
Farjeon Rd. SE3	34	G4
Farleigh Rd. N16	11	E1
Farley Rd. SE6	40	G5
Farlow Rd. SW15	36	E1
Farlton Rd. SW18	37	C5
Farm La. SW6	30	B2
Farm St. W1	24	B1
Farmdale Rd. SE10	34	D1
Farmers Rd. SE5	32	A3
Farnaby Rd. SE9	41	F2
Farncombe St. SE16	25	F3
Farnham Pl. SE1	**44**	**C6**
Farnham Royal SE11	31	F1
Faroe Rd. W14	22	F4
Farrance St. E14	19	E5
Farrier St. NW1	10	B4
Farringdon La. EC1	17	G3
Farringdon Rd. EC1	17	G3
Farringdon St. EC4	**44**	**B1**
Farrins Rents SE16	26	C2
Farrow La. SE14	33	A3
Fashion St. E1	18	E4
Fassett Rd. E8	11	F3
Fassett Sq. E8	11	F3
Faulkner St. SE14	33	A4
Favart Rd. SW6	30	B4
Faversham Rd. SE6	40	D5
Fawcett Clo. SW11	30	E5
Fawcett Rd. NW10	8	B4
Fawcett St. SW10	30	C2
Fawe Pk. Rd. SW15	37	A2
Fawe St. E14	19	F4
Fawley Rd. NW6	9	C2
Fawn Rd. E13	20	F1
Fawnbrake Ave. SE24	39	A3
Fearon St. SE10	34	D1
Feathers Pl. SE10	34	A2
Featherstone St. EC1	18	C3
Featley Rd. SW9	39	A1
Felday Rd. SE13	40	F4
Felden St. SW6	30	A4
Felgate Ms. W6	22	D5
Felixstowe Rd. NW10	15	D2
Fellbrigg Rd. SE22	39	E3
Fellows Rd. NW3	9	E4
Felltram Way SE7	27	D5
Felsberg Rd. SW2	38	E4
Felsham Rd. SW15	36	F1
Felstead St. E9	12	D3
Felsted Rd. E16	20	G5
Felton St. N1	11	C5
Fen Ct. EC3	**44**	**H3**
Fenchurch Ave. EC3	**44**	**H2**
Fenchurch Bldgs. EC3	**44**	**J2**
Fenchurch Pl. EC3	**44**	**J3**
Fenchurch St. EC3	**44**	**H3**
Fendall St. SE1	25	D4
Fenelon Pl. W14	23	A5
Fenham Rd. SE15	32	F3
Fenn St. E9	12	A2
Fennel St. SE18	35	C2
Fentiman Rd. SW8	31	E2
Fenton Clo. SW9	31	F5
Fentons Ave. E13	20	E1
Fenwick Gro. SE15	39	F1
Fenwick Pl. SW9	38	E1
Fenwick Rd. SE15	39	F1
Ferdinand St. NW1	10	A4
Fermoy Rd. W9	16	A3
Fern St. E3	19	E3
Fernbrook Rd. SE13	41	B4
Ferncliff Rd. E8	11	F2
Ferndale Ct. SE3	34	C3
Ferndale Rd. E7	13	E4
Ferndale Rd. SW4	38	F2
Ferndale Rd. SW9	38	E2
Ferndale St. E6	28	D1
Ferndene Rd. SE24	39	B2
Ferndown Rd. SE9	41	G5
Fernhead Rd. W9	16	A2
Fernhill St. E16	28	B2
Fernholme Rd. SE15	40	B3
Fernhurst Rd. SW6	29	G4
Ferns Rd. E15	13	C3
Fernshaw Rd. SW10	30	D2
Ferntower Rd. N5	11	C2
Ferranti Clo. SE18	27	G4
Ferrier St. SW18	37	C2
Ferris Rd. SE22	39	F2
Ferry App. SE18	28	C4
Ferry La. SW13	29	B2
Ferry Rd. SW13	29	C3
Ferry St. E14	33	G1
Festing Rd. SW15	36	F1
Fetter La. EC4	**44**	**A2**
Ffinch St. SE8	33	E3
Field Rd. E7	13	D1
Field Rd. W6	29	G1
Field St. WC1	17	F2
Fieldgate St. E1	18	F4
Fielding Ho. NW6	16	B2
Fielding Rd. W14	22	F4
Fielding St. SE17	32	B2
Fields Est. E8	11	F4
Fieldway Cres. N5	10	G2
Fife Rd. E16	20	D4
Fifth Ave. E12	14	B1
Fifth Ave. W10	15	G2
Filmer Rd. SW6	29	G4
Finborough Rd. SW10	30	C1
Finch La. EC3	**44**	**G2**
Finchley Pl. NW8	16	E1
Finchley Rd. NW3	9	C2
Finchley Rd. NW8	9	E4
Finck St. SE1	24	F3
Finden Rd. E7	13	E2
Findhorn St. E14	19	G5
Findon Rd. W12	22	C3
Fingal St. SE10	34	C1
Finland Quay SE16	26	C4
Finland Rd. SE4	40	C1
Finland St. SE16	26	C4
Finlay St. SW6	29	F4
Finnis St. E2	18	G2
Finsbury Circ. EC2	18	C4
Finsbury Est. EC1	17	G2
Finsbury Mkt. EC2	18	D3
Finsbury Pavement EC2	18	C4
Finsbury Sq. EC2	18	C4
Finsbury St. EC2	18	C4
Finsen Rd. SE5	39	B1
Finstock Rd. W10	15	F5
Fir Trees Clo. SE16	26	C2
Firbank Clo. E16	20	G4
Firbank Rd. SE15	32	G5
Firs Clo. SE23	40	B5
First Ave. E12	14	A1
First Ave. E13	20	D2
First Ave. SW14	36	A1
First Ave. W3	22	B2
First Ave. W10	16	A3
First St. SW3	23	F5
Firth Gdns. SW6	29	G4
Fish St. Hill EC3	**44**	**G4**
Fisher St. E16	20	D4
Fisher St. WC1	17	F4
Fishermans Dr. SE16	26	B3
Fisherton St. NW8	16	E3
Fisherton St. Est. NW8	16	E3
Fisons Rd. E16	27	D2
Fitzalan St. SE11	24	F5
Fitzgeorge Ave. W14	22	G5
Fitzgerald Ave. SW14	36	A1
Fitzhardinge St. W1	17	A5
Fitzhugh Gro. SW18	37	E4
Fitzhugh Gro. Est. SW18	37	E4
Fitzjames Ave. W14	22	G5
Fitzjohn's Ave. NW3	9	E2
Fitzmaurice Pl. W1	24	B2
Fitzneal St. W12	15	B5
Fitzroy Rd. NW1	10	A5
Fitzroy Sq. W1	17	C3
Fitzroy St. W1	17	C3
Fitzwilliam Rd. SW4	38	C1
Five Ways Rd. SW9	31	G5
Flamborough St. E14	19	C5
Flamsteed Rd. SE7	35	A1
Flanchford Rd. W12	22	B4
Flanders Rd. E6	21	B1
Flanders Rd. W4	22	A5
Flanders Way E9	12	B3
Flask Wk. NW3	9	D1
Flaxman Ct. W1	**43**	**C2**
Flaxman Rd. SE5	39	A1
Flaxman Ter. WC1	17	D2
Flaxton Rd. SE18	35	F3
Fleet Rd. NW3	9	F2
Fleet St. EC4	**44**	**A2**
Fleetwood Clo. E16	20	G4
Fleetwood Rd. NW10	8	C2
Fleming Rd. SE17	32	A2
Fletching Rd. SE7	34	F2
Fleur de Lis St. E1	18	D3
Flint St. SE17	25	C5
Flintmill Cres. SE3	35	A5
Flinton St. SE17	32	D1
Flitcroft St. WC2	**43**	**D2**
Flodden Rd. SE5	32	B4
Flood St. SW3	30	F1
Flood Wk. SW3	30	F2
Flora Clo. E14	19	F5
Floral St. WC2	**43**	**E3**
Florence Rd. E6	13	F5
Florence Rd. E13	20	C1
Florence Rd. SE14	33	D4
Florence St. E16	20	C3
Florence St. N1	11	A4
Florence Ter. SE14	33	D4
Florian Rd. SW15	36	G2
Florida St. E2	18	F2
Floss St. SW15	29	E5
Flower Wk., The SW7	23	D3
Floyd Rd. SE7	34	F1
Fludyer St. SE13	41	B2
Foley St. W1	17	C4
Folgate St. E1	18	D4
Foliot St. W12	15	B5
Folkestone Rd. E6	21	C1
Follett St. E14	19	G5
Folly Wall E14	26	G3
Fontarabia Rd. SW11	38	A2
Fontley Way SW15	36	C5
Footscray Rd. SE9	42	C4
Footway, The SE9	42	E5
Ford Rd. E3	12	C5
Ford Sq. E1	18	G4
Ford St. E3	12	C5
Ford St. E16	20	C5
Fordham St. E1	18	F5
Fordingley Rd. W9	16	A2
Fords Pk. Rd. E16	20	D5
Fordwych Rd. NW2	8	G1
Fordyce Rd. SE13	40	G4
Fore St. EC2	18	B4
Foreshore SE8	26	D5
Forest Gro. E8	11	E3
Forest Hill Rd. SE22	39	G3
Forest Hill Rd. SE23	40	A4
Forest La. E7	13	D2
Forest La. E15	13	B3
Forest Rd. E7	13	D1
Forest Rd. E8	11	E3
Forest St. E7	13	D2
Forest Vw. Rd. E12	14	A1
Forest Way, Sid.	42	F5
Forester Rd. SE15	39	G2
Forfar Rd. SW11	31	A4
Formosa St. W9	16	C3
Forset St. W1	16	F5
Forster Rd. SW2	38	E5
Forsyth Gdns. SE17	32	A2
Forsythia Clo., Ilf.	14	D2
Fort Rd. SE1	25	E5
Fort St. E1	18	D4
Fort St. E16	27	E2
Fortess Rd. NW5	10	B2
Forthbridge Rd. SW11	38	A2
Fortis Clo. E16	20	F5
Fortune Gate Rd. NW10	8	A5
Fortune Grn. Rd. NW6	9	B1
Fortune St. EC1	18	B3
Fortune Way NW10	15	C2
Forty Acre La. E16	20	D4
Foskett Rd. SW6	30	A5
Fossdene Rd. SE7	34	E1
Fossil Rd. SE13	40	E1
Foster La. EC2	**44**	**D1**
Foster Rd. E13	20	D3
Foster Rd. W3	22	A1
Fothergill Clo. E13	20	D1
Foubert's Pl. W1	**43**	**A2**
Foulden Rd. N16	11	E1
Foulis Ter. SW7	30	E1
Founders Ct. EC2	**44**	**F1**
Foundry Clo. SE16	26	C2
Fount St. SW8	31	D3
Fountain Ct. EC4	**43**	**J3**
Fountain Pl. SW9	31	G4
Fournier St. E1	18	E4
Fourth Ave. E12	14	B1
Fourth Ave. W10	15	G2
Fowler Clo. SW11	37	E1
Fowler Rd. E7	13	D1
Fownes St. SW11	37	F1
Fox Clo. E1	19	A3
Fox Clo. E16	20	D4
Fox Rd. E16	20	C4
Foxberry Rd. SE4	40	C1
Foxborough Gdns. SE4	40	E4
Foxcroft Rd. SE18	35	D4
Foxes Dale SE3	41	D1
Foxglove St. W12	22	B1

Foxhole Rd. SE9	42	A3
Foxley Rd. SW9	31	G3
Foxmore St. SW11	30	G4
Foxwell St. SE4	40	C1
Foxwood Rd. SE3	41	C2
Foyle Rd. SE3	34	C2
Framfield Rd. N5	11	A2
Frampton Pk. Est. E9	12	A4
Frampton Pk. Rd. E9	12	A3
Frampton St. NW8	16	E3
Francemary Rd. SE4	40	E3
Frances St. SE18	28	B5
Francis Chichester Way SW11	31	A4
Francis St. E15	13	B2
Francis St. SW1	24	C5
Franconia Rd. SW4	38	D3
Frank St. E13	20	D3
Frankfurt Rd. SE24	39	B3
Frankham St. SE8	33	E3
Frankland Clo. SE16	26	A5
Frankland Rd. SW7	23	E4
Franklin's Row SW3	30	G1
Franklyn Rd. NW10	8	B4
Fraser St. W4	29	A1
Frazier St. SE1	24	G3
Frean St. SE16	25	F4
Frederick Clo. W2	23	F1
Frederick Cres. SW9	32	A3
Frederick Pl. SE18	35	D1
Frederick St. WC1	17	F2
Frederick's Pl. EC2	**44**	**F2**
Freedom St. SW11	30	G5
Freegrove Rd. N7	10	E2
Freemasons Rd. E16	20	E4
Freke Rd. SW11	38	A1
Fremantle St. SE17	32	D1
Fremont St. E9	12	A5
Frendsbury Rd. SE4	40	C2
Frensham St. SE15	32	F2
Frere St. SW11	30	F5
Fresh Wf. Rd., Bark.	14	D5
Freston Rd. W10	22	F1
Freston Rd. W11	22	F1
Friar St. EC4	**44**	**C2**
Friars Mead E14	26	G4
Friars Ms. SE9	42	C3
Friars Rd. E6	13	G5
Friary Ct. SW1	**43**	**B6**
Friary Est. SE15	32	F2
Friary Rd. SE15	32	F3
Friday St. EC4	**44**	**D3**
Friend St. EC1	18	A2
Friendly St. SE8	33	E5
Friern Rd. SE22	39	F5
Frimley Way E1	19	B3
Frinton Rd. E6	20	G2
Friston St. SW6	30	C5
Frith Rd. E11	12	G1
Frith St. W1	**43**	**C2**
Frithville Gdns. W12	22	E2
Frobisher Rd. E6	21	B5
Frobisher St. SE10	34	B2
Frogley Rd. SE22	39	E2
Frogmore SW18	37	B3
Frognal NW3	9	D2
Frognal Ct. NW3	9	D3
Frognal Gdns. NW3	9	D1
Frognal La. NW3	9	C2
Frognal Way NW3	9	D1
Froissart Rd. SE9	41	G3
Frome St. N1	18	B1
Froude St. SW8	31	B5
Fry Rd. E6	13	G4
Fry Rd. NW10	8	B5
Fulham Bdy. SW6	30	B3
Fulham High St. SW6	29	G5
Fulham Palace Rd. SW6	29	F2
Fulham Palace Rd. W6	29	E1
Fulham Pk. Gdns. SW6	30	A5
Fulham Pk. Rd. SW6	30	A5
Fulham Rd. SW3	30	E1
Fulham Rd. SW6	29	G5
Fulham Rd. SW10	30	E1
Fullerton Rd. SW18	37	D3
Fulmead St. SW6	30	C4
Fulmer Rd. E16	20	G4
Fulthorp Rd. SE3	34	C5
Furber St. W6	22	D4
Furley Rd. SE15	32	F3
Furlong Rd. N7	10	G3
Furmage St. SW18	37	C5
Furness Rd. NW10	15	C1
Furness Rd. SW6	30	C5
Furnival St. EC4	**43**	**J1**
Furrow La. E9	12	A2
Further Grn. Rd. SE6	41	B5
Furze St. E3	19	E4
Furzefield Rd. SE3	34	E3
Fyfield Ct. E7	13	D3
Fyfield Rd. SW9	38	G1
Fynes St. SW1	24	D5
G		
Gables Clo. SE5	32	D4
Gabriel St. SE23	40	B5
Gabrielle Ct. NW3	9	E3
Gainsborough Ave. E12	14	C2
Gainsborough Rd. E15	20	B2
Gainsborough Rd. W4	22	B5
Gainsford St. SE1	25	E3
Gairloch Rd. SE5	32	D5
Gaisford St. NW5	10	C3
Galata Rd. SW13	29	C3
Galbraith St. E14	26	G4
Gale St. E3	19	E4
Galena Rd. W6	22	D5
Gales Gdns. E2	18	G2
Galesbury Rd. SW18	37	D4
Galleywall Rd. SE16	25	G5
Gallia Rd. N5	11	A2
Gallions Rd. E16	28	D1
Gallions Rd. SE7	27	E5
Gallon Clo. SE7	27	F5
Gallosson Rd. SE18	28	G5
Galloway Rd. W12	22	C2
Gallus Sq. SE3	41	E1
Galsworthy Rd. NW2	8	G1
Galton St. W10	15	G2
Galveston Rd. SW15	37	A3
Galway St. EC1	18	B2
Gambetta St. SW8	31	B5
Gambia St. SE1	**44**	**C6**
Gamlen Rd. SW15	36	F2
Ganton St. W1	**43**	**A3**
Garden Clo. SW15	36	D5
Garden Ct. EC4	**43**	**J3**
Garden Rd. NW8	16	D2
Garden Row SE1	25	A4
Garden St. E1	19	B4
Gardeners La. EC4	**44**	**D3**
Gardeners Rd. E3	19	B1
Gardens, The SE22	39	F2
Gardiner Ave. NW2	8	E2
Gardner Rd. E13	20	E3
Garfield Rd. E13	20	C3
Garfield Rd. SW11	38	A1
Garford St. E14	26	E1
Garibaldi St. SE18	28	G5
Garland Rd. SE18	35	F3
Garlick Hill EC4	**44**	**E3**
Garlinge Rd. NW2	9	A3
Garnet Rd. NW10	8	A3
Garnet St. E1	26	A1
Garnett Clo. SE9	42	B1
Garnett Rd. NW3	9	G2
Garratt La. SW18	37	C3
Garrick Clo. SW18	37	D2
Garrick St. WC2	**43**	**E3**
Garsington Ms. SE4	40	D1
Garthorne Rd. SE23	40	B5
Garton Pl. SW18	37	D4
Gartons Way SW11	37	D1
Garvary Rd. E16	20	E3
Garway Rd. W2	16	C5
Gascoigne Pl. E2	18	E2
Gascoigne Rd., Bark.	14	E5
Gascony Ave. NW6	9	B4
Gascoyne Rd. E9	12	B4
Gaselee St. E14	26	G1
Gaskarth Rd. SW12	38	B4
Gaskell St. SW4	31	E5
Gaskin St. N1	11	A5
Gastein Rd. W6	29	F2
Gataker St. SE16	25	G4
Gate Ms. SW7	23	F3
Gate St. WC2	**43**	**G1**
Gateforth St. NW8	16	F3
Gateley Rd. SW9	38	F1
Gateway SE17	32	B2
Gateway Ind. Est. NW10	15	B2
Gatliff Rd. SW1	31	B1
Gauden Clo. SW4	38	D1
Gauden Rd. SW4	31	D5
Gaunt St. SE1	25	B4
Gautrey Rd. SE15	33	A5
Gaverick St. E14	26	E5
Gavestone Cres. SE12	41	E5
Gavestone Rd. SE12	41	E5
Gavin St. SE18	28	G5
Gawber St. E2	19	A2
Gay Clo. NW2	8	D2
Gay Rd. E15	20	A1
Gaydon Ho. W2	16	C4
Gayfere St. SW1	24	E4
Gayford Rd. W12	22	B3
Gayhurst Rd. E8	11	F4
Gayton Cres. NW3	9	E1
Gayton Rd. NW3	9	E1
Gayville Rd. SW11	37	G4
Geary Rd. NW10	8	C2
Geary St. N7	10	F2
Gedling Pl. SE1	25	E4
Gee St. EC1	18	B3
Geere Rd. E15	13	C5
Geffrye St. E2	18	E1
Geldart Rd. SE15	32	G3
Gellatly Rd. SE14	33	A5
Gelston Pt. E1	18	G5
General Gordon Pl. SE18	28	D5
General Wolfe Rd. SE10	34	A4
Genesta Rd. SE18	35	D2
Geneva Dr. SW9	38	G2
Genoa Ave. SW15	36	E3
Geoffrey Clo. SE5	32	B5
Geoffrey Gdns. E6	21	A1
Geoffrey Rd. SE4	40	D1
George Beard Rd. SE8	26	D5
George Ct. WC2	**43**	**F4**
George Inn Yd. SE1	**44**	**F6**
George La. SE13	40	G4
George Row SE16	25	F3
George St. E16	20	C5
George St. EC4	**44**	**F2**
George St. W1	16	G5
George St., Bark.	14	E4
George Yd. EC3	**44**	**G2**
George Yd. W1	24	A1
Georges Rd. N7	10	F2
Georgiana St. NW1	10	C5
Gerald Rd. E16	20	C3
Gerald Rd. SW1	24	A5
Geraldine Rd. SW18	37	D3
Geraldine St. SE11	25	A4
Gerard Rd. SW13	29	B4
Gerards Clo. SE16	33	A1
Germander Way E15	20	B2
Gernon Rd. E3	19	C1
Gerrard Pl. W1	**43**	**D3**
Gerrard Rd. N1	18	A1
Gerrard St. W1	**43**	**D3**
Gerridge St. SE1	24	G4
Gertrude St. SW10	30	D2
Gervase St. SE15	32	G3
Ghent Way E8	11	E3
Gibbins Rd. E15	12	G4
Gibbon Rd. SE15	33	A5
Gibbon Rd. W3	22	A1
Gibbons Rd. NW10	8	A3
Gibbs Grn. W14	30	A1
Gibraltar Wk. E2	18	E2
Gibson Rd. SE11	24	F5
Gibson Sq. N1	10	G5
Gibson St. SE10	34	B1
Gideon Rd. SW11	38	A1
Giffin St. SE8	33	E3
Gifford St. N1	10	E4
Gift La. E15	13	C5
Gilbert Rd. SE11	24	G5
Gilbert St. E15	13	B1
Gilbert St. W1	17	A5
Gilden Cres. NW5	10	A2
Gilkes Cres. SE21	39	D4
Gilkes Pl. SE21	39	D4
Gill Ave. E16	20	D5
Gill St. E14	26	D1
Gillender St. E3	19	G3
Gillender St. E14	19	G3
Gillett Ave. E6	21	A1
Gillett St. N16	11	D2
Gillfoot NW1	17	C1
Gillian St. SE13	40	F3
Gillies St. NW5	10	A2
Gilling Ct. NW3	9	F3
Gillingham St. SW1	24	C5
Gillman Dr. E15	13	C5
Gilmore Rd. SE13	41	A2
Gilpin Rd. E5	12	C1
Gilstead Rd. SW6	30	C5
Gilston Rd. SW10	30	D1
Giltspur St. EC1	**44**	**C1**
Gipsy La. SW15	36	C1
Giraud St. E14	19	F5
Girdlers Rd. W14	22	F5
Girdwood Rd. SW18	36	G5
Gironde Rd. SW6	30	A3
Gladding Rd. E12	13	G1
Glade, The SE7	34	F3
Gladiator St. SE23	40	C5
Gladstone Ave. E12	14	A4
Gladstone Pk. Gdns. NW2	8	D1
Gladstone St. SE1	25	A4
Gladstone Ter. SW8	31	B4
Gladwyn Rd. SW15	36	F1
Gladys Rd. NW6	9	B4
Glamis Pl. E1	26	A1
Glamis Rd. E1	26	A1
Glanville Rd. SW2	38	E3
Glasbrook Rd. SE9	41	G5
Glasgow Ho. W9	16	C1
Glasgow Rd. E13	20	E1
Glasgow Ter. SW1	31	C1
Glass Yd. SE18	28	C4
Glasshill St. SE1	25	A3
Glasshouse All. EC4	**44**	**A2**
Glasshouse Flds. E1	26	B1

Glasshouse St. W1	**43**	**B4**
Glasshouse Wk. SE11	31	E1
Glastonbury St. NW6	9	A2
Glaucus St. E3	19	F4
Glazbury Rd. W14	22	G5
Glebe, The SE3	41	B1
Glebe Pl. SW3	30	F2
Glebe Rd. NW10	8	B3
Glebe Rd. SW13	29	C5
Glebe St. W4	29	A1
Gledhow Gdns. SW5	23	D5
Gledstanes Rd. W14	29	G1
Glegg Pl. SW15	36	F2
Glen Rd. E13	20	F3
Glenaffric Ave. E14	27	A5
Glenalvon Way SE18	28	A5
Glenarm Rd. E5	12	A2
Glenavon Rd. E15	13	B4
Glenbrook Rd. NW6	9	B2
Glencairne Clo. E16	20	G4
Glendall St. SW9	38	F2
Glendarvon St. SW15	36	F1
Glendower Pl. SW7	23	E5
Glendun Rd. W3	22	A1
Glenelg Rd. SW2	38	E3
Glenesk Rd. SE9	42	C1
Glenfinlas Way SE5	32	A3
Glenforth St. SE10	34	C1
Glengall Gro. E14	26	G4
Glengall Rd. NW6	9	A5
Glengall Rd. SE15	32	E1
Glengall Ter. SE15	32	E2
Glengarnock Ave. E14	26	G5
Glengarry Rd. SE22	39	D3
Glenhouse Rd. SE9	42	C3
Glenhurst Ave. NW5	10	A1
Glenilla Rd. NW3	9	F3
Glenister Rd. SE10	34	C1
Glenister St. E16	28	C2
Glenlea Rd. SE9	42	C3
Glenloch Rd. NW3	9	F3
Glenluce Rd. SE3	34	D2
Glenlyon Rd. SE9	42	C3
Glenmore Rd. NW3	9	F3
Glenny Rd., Bark.	14	E3
Glenparke Rd. E7	13	E3
Glenrosa St. SW6	30	D5
Glenroy St. W12	15	E5
Glensdale Rd. SE4	40	D1
Glenshiel Rd. SE9	42	C3
Glentham Rd. SW13	29	C2
Glenthorne Rd. W6	22	D5
Glenton Rd. SE13	41	B2
Glentworth St. NW1	16	G3
Glenure Rd. SE9	42	C3
Glenville Gro. SE8	33	D3
Glenville Ms. SW18	37	C5
Glenworth Ave. E14	27	A5
Gliddon Rd. W14	22	G5
Globe Pond Rd. SE16	26	C2
Globe Rd. E1	19	B3
Globe Rd. E2	19	A2
Globe Rd. E15	13	C2
Globe St. SE1	25	C3
Gloucester Ave. NW1	10	A4
Gloucester Circ. SE10	33	G3
Gloucester Ct. EC3	**44**	**J4**
Gloucester Cres. NW1	10	B5
Gloucester Gate NW1	17	B1
Gloucester Gro. Est. SE15	32	D2
Gloucester Ho. NW6	16	B1
Gloucester Ms. W2	16	D5
Gloucester Pl. NW1	16	G3
Gloucester Pl. W1	16	G4
Gloucester Rd. SW7	23	D4
Gloucester Sq. W2	16	E5
Gloucester St. SW1	31	C1
Gloucester Ter. W2	16	C5
Gloucester Wk. W8	23	B3
Gloucester Way EC1	17	G2
Glycena Rd. SW11	37	G1
Glyn Rd. E5	12	B1
Glynde St. SE4	40	D4
Glyndon Rd. SE18	28	E5
Glynfield Rd. NW10	8	A4
Godalming Rd. E14	19	F4
Godbold Rd. E15	20	B2
Godfrey Hill SE18	28	A5
Godfrey Rd. SE18	28	B5
Godfrey St. SW3	30	F1
Goding St. SE11	31	E1
Godliman St. EC4	**44**	**D2**
Godman Rd. SE15	32	G5
Godolphin Rd. W12	22	D2
Godwin Rd. E7	13	E1
Goffers Rd. SE3	34	B5
Golborne Rd. W10	15	G4
Golden La. EC1	18	B3
Golden Sq. W1	**43**	**B3**
Goldfinch Rd. SE28	28	F4
Goldhawk Rd. W6	22	B5
Goldhawk Rd. W12	22	C4
Goldhurst Ter. NW6	9	C4
Golding St. E1	18	F5
Goldington Cres. NW1	17	D1
Goldington Cres. Gdns. NW1	17	D1
Goldington St. NW1	17	D1
Goldman Clo. E2	18	F3
Goldney Rd. W9	16	B3
Goldsborough Rd. SW8	31	D4
Goldsmith Ave. E12	14	A3
Goldsmith Rd. SE15	32	F4
Goldsmith St. EC2	**44**	**E1**
Goldsmith's Row E2	18	F1
Goldsmith's Sq. E2	18	F1
Goldsworthy Gdns. SE16	26	A5
Goldwin Clo. SE14	33	A4
Goldwing Clo. E16	20	D5
Gollogly Ter. SE7	34	F1
Gomm Rd. SE16	26	A4
Gondar Gdns. NW6	9	A2
Gonson Pl. SE8	33	E2
Gonson St. SE8	33	F2
Goodge St. W1	17	C4
Goodhall St. NW10	15	A2
Goodhart Pl. E14	26	C1
Goodinge Clo. N7	10	E3
Goodman's Stile E1	18	F5
Goodmans Yd. E1	25	E1
Goodrich Rd. SE22	39	E4
Goods Way NW1	17	E1
Goodson Rd. NW10	8	A4
Goodway Gdns. E14	20	A5
Goodwin Rd. W12	22	C3
Goodwins Ct. WC2	**43**	**E3**
Goodwood Rd. SE14	33	C3
Goosander Way SE28	28	F4
Gooseley La. E6	21	C2
Gophir La. EC4	**44**	**F3**
Gopsall St. N1	11	C5
Gordon Ave. SW14	36	A2
Gordon Ct. W12	15	D5
Gordon Gro. SE5	32	A5
Gordon Ho. Rd. NW5	10	A1
Gordon Pl. W8	23	B3
Gordon Rd. E15	12	G1
Gordon Rd. SE15	32	G5
Gordon Rd., Bark.	14	G5
Gordon Rd., Sid.	42	G3
Gordon Sq. WC1	17	D3
Gordon St. WC1	17	D3
Gordonbrock Rd. SE4	40	E3
Gore Rd. E9	12	A5
Gore St. SW7	23	D4
Gorefield Pl. NW6	16	B1
Goring St. EC3	**44**	**J1**
Gorleston St. W14	22	G5
Gorman Rd. SE18	28	B5
Gorst Rd. SW11	37	G4
Gorsuch St. E2	18	E2
Gosfield St. W1	17	C4
Goslett Yd. WC2	**43**	**D2**
Gosling Way SW9	31	G4
Gospel Oak Est. NW5	9	G2
Gosset St. E2	18	E2
Gosterwood St. SE8	33	C2
Goswell Rd. EC1	18	A1
Gough Rd. E15	13	C1
Gough Sq. EC4	**44**	**A1**
Gough St. WC1	17	F3
Goulston St. E1	18	E5
Goulton Rd. E5	11	G1
Gourock Rd. SE9	42	C3
Govier Clo. E15	13	B4
Gowan Ave. SW6	29	G4
Gowan Rd. NW10	8	D3
Gower Ms. WC1	17	D4
Gower Pl. WC1	17	C3
Gower Rd. E7	13	D3
Gower St. WC1	17	C3
Gower's Wk. E1	18	F5
Gowlett Rd. SE15	39	F1
Gowrie Rd. SW11	38	A1
Grace St. E3	19	F2
Gracechurch St. EC3	**44**	**G3**
Graces Ms. SE5	32	C5
Graces Rd. SE5	32	D5
Grafton Cres. NW1	10	B3
Grafton Pl. NW1	17	D2
Grafton Rd. NW5	10	A2
Grafton Sq. SW4	38	C1
Grafton St. W1	24	B1
Grafton Ter. NW5	9	G2
Grafton Way W1	17	C3
Grafton Way WC1	17	C3
Graham Rd. E8	11	F3
Graham Rd. E13	20	D2
Graham St. N1	18	A1
Graham Ter. SW1	24	A5
Granard Ave. SW15	36	D3
Granard Rd. SW12	37	G5
Granary St. NW1	10	D5
Granby Rd. SE9	35	B5
Granby St. E2	18	E3
Granby Ter. NW1	17	C1
Grand Depot Rd. SE18	35	C1
Grand Union Cres. E8	11	F5
Grandison Rd. SW11	37	G3
Granfield St. SW11	30	E4
Grange, The SE1	25	E4
Grange Ct. E8	11	E4
Grange Ct. WC2	**43**	**H2**
Grange Gro. N1	11	B3
Grange Pl. NW6	9	B4
Grange Pl. SE16	25	F4
Grange Rd. E13	20	C2
Grange Rd. NW10	8	D3
Grange Rd. SE1	25	D4
Grange Rd. SW13	29	C4
Grange Rd., Ilf.	14	D1
Grange Wk. SE1	25	D4
Grange Yd. SE1	25	E4
Grangehill Rd. SE9	42	B2
Grangewood St. E6	13	G5
Gransden Ave. E8	11	G4
Grant Rd. SW11	37	E2
Grant St. E13	20	D2
Grantbridge St. N1	18	A1
Grantham Rd. E12	14	C1
Grantham Rd. SW9	38	E1
Grantham Rd. W4	29	A3
Grantley St. E1	19	B2
Grantully Rd. W9	16	C2
Granville Ct. N1	11	C5
Granville Gro. SE13	40	G1
Granville Pk. SE13	40	G1
Granville Pl. W1	17	A5
Granville Rd. NW6	16	B1
Granville Rd. SW18	37	A5
Granville Sq. WC1	17	F2
Granville St. WC1	17	F2
Grape St. WC2	**43**	**E1**
Grasmere Rd. E13	20	D1
Gratton Rd. W14	22	G4
Gravel Pit La. SE9	42	E3
Gravesend Rd. W12	22	C1
Gray's Inn Rd. WC1	17	E2
Grayshott Rd. SW11	31	A5
Great Bell All. EC2	**44**	**F1**
Great Castle St. W1	17	B5
Great Cen. St. NW1	16	G4
Great Chapel St. W1	**43**	**C1**
Great Ch. La. W6	29	F1
Great College St. SW1	24	E4
Great Cross Ave. SE10	34	B3
Great Cumberland Pl. W1	16	G5
Great Dover St. SE1	25	C3
Great Eastern Rd. E15	13	A4
Great Eastern St. EC2	18	D2
Great George St. SW1	24	D3
Great Guildford St. SE1	**44**	**D6**
Great James St. WC1	17	F4
Great Marlborough St. W1	**43**	**A2**
Great New St. EC4	**44**	**A1**
Great Newport St. WC2	**43**	**D3**
Great Ormond St. WC1	17	E4
Great Percy St. WC1	17	F2
Great Peter St. SW1	24	D4
Great Portland St. W1	17	B3
Great Pulteney St. W1	**43**	**B3**
Great Queen St. WC2	**43**	**F2**
Great Russell St. WC1	**43**	**D1**
Great St. Helens EC3	**44**	**H1**
Great St. Thomas Apostle EC4	**44**	**E3**
Great Scotland Yd. SW1	**43**	**E5**
Great Smith St. SW1	24	D4
Great Spilmans SE22	39	D3
Great Suffolk St. SE1	**44**	**C6**
Great Sutton St. EC1	18	A3
Great Swan All. EC2	**44**	**F1**
Great Titchfield St. W1	17	C4
Great Twr. St. EC3	**44**	**H3**
Great Trinity La. EC4	**44**	**E3**
Great W. Rd. W6	29	C1
Great Western Rd. W9	16	A4

Great Western Rd. W11	16	A4
Great Winchester St. EC2	**44**	**G1**
Great Windmill St. W1	**43**	**C3**
Greatfield Ave. E6	21	B3
Greatfield Clo. SE4	40	E2
Greatfields Rd., Bark.	14	F5
Greatorex St. E1	18	F4
Greek Ct. W1	**43**	**D2**
Greek St. W1	**43**	**D2**
Greek Yd. WC2	**43**	**E3**
Green, The E15	13	B3
Green, The W3	15	A5
Green, The, Well.	42	G2
Green Arbour Ct. EC1	**44**	**B1**
Green Bank E1	25	G2
Green Dale SE22	39	D3
Green Dragon Ct. SE1	**44**	**F5**
Green Hill SE18	35	B1
Green Hill Ter. SE18	35	B1
Green Hundred Rd. SE15	32	F2
Green Pt. E15	13	B3
Green Shield Ind. Est. E16	27	D2
Green St. E7	13	E3
Green St. E13	13	F4
Green St. W1	23	G1
Green Way SE9	41	G3
Greenacres SE9	42	C4
Greenaway Gdns. NW3	9	C1
Greenbay Rd. SE7	34	G3
Greenberry St. NW8	16	F1
Greencoat Pl. SW1	24	C5
Greencroft Gdns. NW6	9	C4
Greenend Rd. W4	22	A3
Greenfell St. SE10	27	B4
Greenfield Rd. E1	18	F4
Greengate St. E13	20	E1
Greenham Clo. SE1	24	G3
Greenhill Gro. E12	14	A1
Greenhill Pk. NW10	8	A5
Greenhill Rd. NW10	8	A5
Greenhithe Clo., Sid.	42	G5
Greenholm Rd. SE9	42	D3
Greenland Quay SE16	26	B5
Greenland Rd. NW1	10	B5
Greenlaw St. SE18	28	C4
Greenman St. N1	11	B4
Green's Ct. W1	**43**	**C3**
Green's End SE18	28	D5
Greenside Rd. W12	22	C4
Greenstead Gdns. SW15	36	C3
Greenvale Rd. SE9	42	B2
Greenwell St. W1	17	B3
Greenwich Ch. St. SE10	33	G2
Greenwich High Rd. SE10	33	F4
Greenwich Ind. Est. SE7	27	E5
Greenwich Mkt. SE10	33	G2
Greenwich Pk. SE10	34	A3
Greenwich Pk. St. SE10	34	A1
Greenwich S. St. SE10	33	F4
Greenwich Vw. Pl. E14	26	F4
Greenwood Rd. E8	11	F3
Greet St. SE1	**44**	**A6**
Gregor Ms. SE3	34	D3
Gregory Cres. SE9	41	G5
Gregory Pl. W8	23	C3
Grenada Rd. SE7	34	F3
Grenade St. E14	26	D1
Grenadier St. E16	28	C2
Grendon St. NW8	16	F3
Grenfell Rd. W11	22	F1
Grenfell Twr. W11	22	F1
Grenville Ms. SW7	23	D5
Grenville Pl. SW7	23	D4
Grenville St. WC1	17	E3
Gresham Rd. E6	21	B1
Gresham Rd. E16	20	E5
Gresham Rd. SW9	38	G1
Gresham St. EC2	**44**	**E1**
Gresse St. W1	**43**	**C1**
Gressenhall Rd. SW18	37	A4
Greswell St. SW6	29	F4
Greville Hall NW6	16	C1
Greville Pl. NW6	16	C1
Greville Rd. NW6	16	C1
Greville St. EC1	17	G4
Grey Eagle St. E1	18	E4
Greycoat Pl. SW1	24	D4
Greycoat St. SW1	24	D4
Greyfriars Pas. EC1	**44**	**C1**
Greyhound Rd. NW10	15	D2
Greyhound Rd. W6	29	F2
Greyhound Rd. W14	29	G2
Greystead Rd. SE23	40	A5
Greystoke Pl. EC4	**43**	**J1**
Grierson Rd. SE23	40	B5
Griffin Clo. NW10	8	D2
Griffin Manor Way SE28	28	F4
Griffin Rd. SE18	35	F1
Grimston Rd. SW6	30	A5
Grinling Pl. SE8	33	E2
Grinstead Rd. SE8	33	C1
Grittleton Rd. W9	16	B3
Grocer's Hall Ct. EC2	**44**	**F2**
Groom Cres. SW18	37	E5
Groom Pl. SW1	24	A4
Groombridge Rd. E9	12	B4
Grosse Way SW15	36	D4
Grosvenor Ave. N5	11	B2
Grosvenor Ave. SW14	36	A1
Grosvenor Cres. SW1	24	A3
Grosvenor Cres. Ms. SW1	24	A3
Grosvenor Est. SW1	24	D5
Grosvenor Gdns. E6	20	G2
Grosvenor Gdns. NW2	8	E2
Grosvenor Gdns. SW1	24	B4
Grosvenor Gdns. SW14	36	A1
Grosvenor Hill W1	24	B1
Grosvenor Pk. SE5	32	B3
Grosvenor Pl. SW1	24	A3
Grosvenor Rd. E6	13	G5
Grosvenor Rd. E7	13	E3
Grosvenor Rd. SW1	31	B2
Grosvenor Sq. W1	24	A1
Grosvenor St. W1	24	B1
Grosvenor Ter. SE5	32	B2
Grosvenor Wf. Rd. E14	27	A5
Grote's Bldgs. SE3	34	B5
Grote's Pl. SE3	34	B5
Grove, The E15	13	B3
Grove Cotts. SW3	30	F2
Grove Ct. SE3	34	D4
Grove Cres. SE5	32	D5
Grove Cres. Rd. E15	13	A3
Grove End Rd. NW8	16	E1
Grove Gdns. E15	13	B3
Grove Hill Rd. SE5	39	D1
Grove La. SE5	32	D5
Grove Mkt. Pl. SE9	42	B4
Grove Ms. W6	22	E4
Grove Pk. SE5	32	D5
Grove Rd. E3	12	B5
Grove Rd. NW2	8	E3
Grove Rd. SW13	29	B5
Grove St. SE8	26	D5
Grove Vale SE22	39	D2
Grove Vill. E14	26	F1
Groveland Ct. EC4	**44**	**E2**
Grovelands Clo. SE5	32	D5
Groveway SW9	31	F4
Grummant Rd. SE15	32	E4
Grundy St. E14	19	F5
Gubyon Ave. SE24	39	A3
Guernsey Gro. SE24	39	B5
Guibal Rd. SE12	41	E5
Guild Rd. SE7	34	G1
Guildford Gro. SE10	33	F4
Guildford Rd. E6	21	B5
Guildford Rd. SW8	31	E4
Guildhall Bldgs. EC2	**44**	**F1**
Guildhouse St. SW1	24	C5
Guilford Pl. WC1	17	F3
Guilford St. WC1	17	E3
Guilsborough Clo. NW10	8	A4
Guinness Bldgs. SE1	25	D5
Guinness Clo. E9	12	C4
Guinness Trust Bldgs. SE11	32	A1
Guinness Trust Est. SW9	39	A2
Guion Rd. SW6	30	A5
Gulliver St. SE16	26	D4
Gun St. E1	18	E4
Gunmakers La. E3	12	C5
Gunner La. SE18	35	C1
Gunning St. SE18	28	G5
Gunpowder Sq. EC4	**44**	**A1**
Gunstor Rd. N16	11	D1
Gunter Gro. SW10	30	D2
Gunterstone Rd. W14	22	G5
Gunthorpe St. E1	18	E4
Gunwhale Clo. SE16	26	B2
Gurdon Rd. SE7	34	D1
Gurney Clo., Bark.	14	D3
Gurney Rd. E15	13	B2
Gutter La. EC2	**44**	**E1**
Guy St. SE1	25	C3
Guyscliff Rd. SE13	40	G3
Gwendolen Ave. SW15	36	F2
Gwendolen Clo. SW15	36	F3
Gwendoline Ave. E13	13	E5
Gwendwr Rd. W14	29	G1
Gwyn Clo. SW6	30	D3
Gwynne Rd. SW11	30	E5
Gylcote Clo. SE5	39	C2

H

Ha-Ha Rd. SE18	35	B2
Haarlem Rd. W14	22	F4
Haberdasher St. N1	18	C2
Hackford Rd. SW9	31	F4
Hackney Rd. E2	18	E2
Hadden Rd. SE28	28	G4
Haddo St. SE10	33	G2
Haddonfield SE8	26	B5
Hadleigh St. E2	19	A2
Hadley St. NW1	10	B3
Hadrian St. SE10	34	B1
Hadyn Pk. Rd. W12	22	C3
Hafer Rd. SW11	37	G2
Haggerston Rd. E8	11	E4
Haig Rd. E. E13	20	F2
Haig Rd. W. E13	20	F2
Haimo Rd. SE9	41	G3
Hainford Clo. SE4	40	B2
Halcomb St. N1	11	D5
Halcrow St. E1	18	G4
Haldane Rd. E6	20	G2
Haldane Rd. SW6	30	A3
Haldon Rd. SW18	37	A3
Hale Rd. E6	21	A3
Hale St. E14	26	F1
Hales St. SE8	33	E3
Halesworth Rd. SE13	40	F1
Half Moon Cres. N1	17	F1
Half Moon La. SE24	39	B4
Half Moon St. W1	24	B2
Halford Rd. SW6	30	B2
Halfway St., Sid.	42	F5
Halkin Pl. SW1	24	A4
Halkin St. SW1	24	A3
Hall, The SE3	41	D1
Hall Pl. W2	16	E3
Hall Rd. E6	14	B5
Hall Rd. E15	13	A1
Hall Rd. NW8	16	D2
Hall St. EC1	18	A2
Hallam Rd. SW15	36	D1
Hallam St. W1	17	B4
Halley Gdns. SE13	41	A2
Halley Rd. E7	13	F3
Halley Rd. E12	13	G3
Halley St. E14	19	C4
Halliford St. N1	11	B4
Halliwell Rd. SW2	38	F4
Hallsville Rd. E16	20	C5
Hallywell Cres. E6	21	B4
Halons Rd. SE9	42	C5
Halsbrook Rd. SE3	41	F1
Halsbury Rd. W12	22	C2
Halsey St. SW3	23	G5
Halsmere Rd. SE5	32	A4
Halston Clo. SW11	37	G4
Halstow Rd. NW10	15	F2
Halstow Rd. SE10	34	D1
Halton Rd. N1	11	A4
Ham Pk. Rd. E7	13	D4
Ham Pk. Rd. E15	13	C4
Ham Yd. W1	**43**	**C3**
Hambalt Rd. SW4	38	C3
Hamble St. SW6	37	C1
Hambledon Rd. SW18	37	A5
Hambledown Rd., Sid.	42	F5
Hambridge Way SW2	38	G5
Hameway E6	21	C3
Hamfrith Rd. E15	13	C3
Hamilton Clo. NW8	16	E2
Hamilton Gdns. NW8	16	D2
Hamilton Pk. N5	11	A1
Hamilton Pk. W. N5	11	A1
Hamilton Pl. W1	24	A2
Hamilton Rd. E15	20	B2
Hamilton Rd. NW10	8	C2
Hamilton Rd. W4	22	A3
Hamilton Rd., Ilf.	14	D1
Hamilton Ter. NW8	16	C1
Hamlea Clo. SE12	41	D3
Hamlet, The SE5	39	C1
Hamlet Gdns. W6	22	C5
Hamlets Way E3	19	D3
Hammersmith Bri. SW13	29	D1
Hammersmith Bri. Rd. W6	29	E1
Hammersmith Bdy. W6	22	E5
Hammersmith Flyover W6	29	E1

Hammersmith Gro. W6 22 E3
Hammersmith Rd. W6 22 F5
Hammersmith Rd. W14 22 F5
Hammersmith Ter. W6 29 C1
Hammond St. NW5 10 C3
Hampson Way SW8 31 F4
Hampstead Grn. NW3 9 F2
Hampstead High St. NW3 9 D1
Hampstead Hill Gdns. NW3 9 E1
Hampstead Rd. NW1 17 C1
Hampton Clo. NW6 16 B2
Hampton Rd. E7 13 E2
Hampton Rd., Ilf. 14 D1
Hampton St. SE1 25 B5
Hampton St. SE17 25 A5
Hanameel St. E16 27 E2
Hanbury St. E1 18 E4
Hancock Rd. E3 19 G2
Handel St. WC1 17 E3
Handen Rd. SE12 41 B3
Handforth Rd. SW9 31 G3
Handley Rd. E9 12 A5
Hankey Pl. SE1 25 C3
Hannell Rd. SW6 29 G3
Hannibal Rd. E1 19 A4
Hannington Rd. SW4 38 B1
Hanover Gdns. SE11 31 G2
Hanover Gate NW1 16 F2
Hanover Pk. SE15 32 F4
Hanover Pl. WC2 43 F2
Hanover Rd. NW10 8 E4
Hanover Sq. W1 17 B5
Hanover St. W1 17 B5
Hanover Ter. NW1 16 F2
Hans Cres. SW1 23 G4
Hans Pl. SW1 23 G4
Hans Rd. SW3 23 G4
Hansler Rd. SE22 39 E3
Hanson Clo. SW12 38 B5
Hanson St. W1 17 C4
Hanway Pl. W1 43 C1
Hanway St. W1 43 C1
Harben Rd. NW6 9 D4
Harberson Rd. E15 13 C5
Harbet Rd. W2 16 E4
Harbinger Rd. E14 26 F5
Harbledown Rd. SW6 30 B4
Harbord St. SW6 29 F4
Harborough Ave., Sid. 42 G5
Harbour Ave. SW10 30 D4
Harbour Ex. Sq. E14 26 F3
Harbour Rd. SE5 39 B1
Harbridge Ave. SW15 36 B5
Harbut Rd. SW11 37 E2
Harcourt Ave. E12 14 B1
Harcourt Rd. E15 20 C1
Harcourt Rd. SE4 40 C2
Harcourt St. W1 16 F4
Harcourt Ter. SW10 30 C1
Hardens Manorway SE7 27 G4
Harders Rd. SE15 32 G5
Hardinge Rd. NW10 8 D5
Hardinge St. E1 19 A5
Hardman Rd. SE7 34 E1
Hardwick St. EC1 17 G2
Hardwicke St., Bark. 14 E5
Hardy Rd. SE3 34 C2
Hare & Billet Rd. SE3 34 A4
Hare Ct. EC4 43 J2
Hare Pl. EC4 44 A2
Hare Row E2 18 G1
Hare St. SE18 28 C4
Hare Wk. N1 18 D1
Harebell Dr. E6 21 C4
Harecourt Rd. N1 11 B3
Haredale Rd. SE24 39 B2
Haredon Clo. SE23 40 A5
Harefield Ms. SE4 40 D1
Harefield Rd. SE4 40 D1
Harewood Ave. NW1 16 F3
Harfield Gdns. SE5 39 D1
Harford St. E1 19 C3
Hargood Rd. SE3 34 F4
Hargwyne St. SW9 38 F1
Harlescott Rd. SE15 40 B2
Harlesden Gdns. NW10 8 B5
Harlesden La. NW10 8 C5
Harlesden Rd. NW10 8 C5
Harley Gdns. SW10 30 D1
Harley Gro. E3 19 D2
Harley Pl. W1 17 B4
Harley Rd. NW3 9 E4
Harley Rd. NW10 15 A1
Harley St. W1 17 B4
Harleyford Rd. SE11 31 F2
Harleyford St. SE11 31 G2
Harmood St. NW1 10 B3
Harmsworth St. SE17 32 A1
Harold Est. SE1 25 D4
Harold Rd. E13 13 E5
Harp All. EC4 44 B1
Harp La. EC3 44 H4
Harper Rd. E6 21 B5
Harper Rd. SE1 25 B4
Harpley Sq. E1 19 A2
Harpour Rd., Bark. 14 E3
Harpsden St. SW11 31 A4
Harpur St. WC1 17 F4
Harraden Rd. SE3 34 F4
Harrier Ms. SE28 28 F4
Harrier Way E6 21 B4
Harriet Clo. E8 11 F5
Harriet Wk. SW1 23 G3
Harrington Gdns. SW7 23 D5
Harrington Rd. SW7 23 E5
Harrington Sq. NW1 17 C1
Harrington St. NW1 17 C2
Harrington Way SE18 27 G4
Harriott Clo. SE10 27 C5
Harris St. SE5 32 C3
Harrison St. WC1 17 E2
Harrow La. E14 26 G1
Harrow Rd. E6 14 A5
Harrow Rd. NW10 15 D2
Harrow Rd. W2 16 B4
Harrow Rd. W9 16 A3
Harrow Rd. W10 15 G3
Harrow Rd., Bark. 14 G5
Harrow Rd., Ilf. 14 E1
Harroway Rd. SW11 30 E5
Harrowby St. W1 16 F5
Harrowgate Rd. E9 12 C3
Hart St. EC3 44 J3
Hartfield Ter. E3 19 E1
Hartham Clo. N7 10 E2
Hartham Rd. N7 10 E2
Hartington Rd. E16 20 E5
Hartington Rd. SW8 31 E4
Hartismere Rd. SW6 30 A3
Hartlake Rd. E9 12 B3
Hartland Rd. E15 13 C4
Hartland Rd. NW1 10 B4
Hartland Rd. NW6 16 A1
Hartley Ave. E6 14 A5
Hartley St. E2 19 A2
Harton St. SE8 33 E4
Harts La. SE14 33 C3
Harts La., Bark. 14 D3
Hartshorn All. EC3 44 J2
Hartshorn Gdns. E6 21 C3
Hartswood Rd. W12 22 B3
Hartsworth Clo. E13 20 C1
Hartville Rd. SE18 28 G5
Harvard Rd. SE13 40 G3
Harvey Gdns. SE7 34 F1
Harvey Rd. SE5 32 C4
Harvey Rd., Ilf. 14 D2
Harvey St. N1 11 C5
Harvist Est. N7 10 G1
Harvist Rd. NW6 15 F1
Harwich La. EC2 18 D4
Harwood Rd. SW6 30 B3
Harwood Ter. SW6 30 C4
Hascombe Ter. SE5 32 C5
Haselrigge Rd. SW4 38 D2
Hasker St. SW3 23 F5
Haslam Clo. N1 10 G4
Hassendean Rd. SE3 34 E2
Hassett Rd. E9 12 B3
Hassop Rd. NW2 8 F1
Hasted Rd. SE7 34 G1
Hastings Clo. SE15 32 F3
Hastings St. WC1 17 E2
Hatcham Pk. Rd. SE14 33 B4
Hatcham Rd. SE15 33 A2
Hatcliffe Clo. SE3 41 C1
Hatfield Clo. SE14 33 B3
Hatfield Rd. E15 13 B2
Hatfields SE1 44 A5
Hathaway Cres. E12 14 B3
Hatherley Gdns. E6 20 G1
Hatherley Gro. W2 16 C5
Hathorne Clo. SE15 32 G5
Hatton Clo. SE18 35 F3
Hatton Gdn. EC1 17 G4
Hatton Pl. EC1 17 G4
Hatton Wall EC1 17 G4
Havannah St. E14 26 E3
Havelock St. N1 10 E5
Havelock Ter. SW8 31 B3
Haverfield Rd. E3 19 C2
Haverstock Hill NW3 9 G3
Haverstock Rd. NW5 10 A2
Haverstock St. N1 18 A1
Havil St. SE5 32 D3
Hawarden Gro. SE24 39 B5
Hawes St. N1 11 A4
Hawgood St. E3 19 E4
Hawkesbury Rd. SW15 36 D3
Hawkshead Rd. NW10 8 B4
Hawkshead Rd. W4 22 A3
Hawkslade Rd. SE15 40 B3
Hawksmoor St. W6 29 F2
Hawkstone Rd. SE16 26 A5
Hawley Cres. NW1 10 B4
Hawley Rd. NW1 10 B4
Hawley St. NW1 10 B4
Hawstead Rd. SE6 40 F4
Hawthorn Rd. NW10 8 C4
Hawthorne Clo. N1 11 D3
Hawtrey Rd. NW3 9 F4
Hay Clo. E15 13 B4
Hay Currie St. E14 19 F5
Hay Hill W1 24 B1
Hay St. E2 11 F5
Haycroft Gdns. NW10 8 C5
Haycroft Rd. SW2 38 E3
Hayday Rd. E16 20 D4
Hayles St. SE11 25 A5
Haymarket SW1 43 C4
Haymarket Arc. SW1 43 C4
Haymerle Rd. SE15 32 F2
Haynes Clo. SE3 41 B1
Hay's La. SE1 44 H6
Hay's Ms. W1 24 B2
Hayter Rd. SW2 38 E3
Hayward Gdns. SW15 36 E4
Hazel Rd. NW10 15 D2
Hazelbourne Rd. SW12 38 B4
Hazeldon Rd. SE4 40 C3
Hazelmere Rd. NW6 9 A5
Hazelwood Cres. W10 15 G3
Hazlebury Rd. SW6 30 C5
Hazlewell Rd. SW15 36 D3
Hazlitt Rd. W14 22 G4
Head St. E1 19 B5
Headfort Pl. SW1 24 A3
Headlam Rd. SW4 38 D4
Headlam St. E1 18 G3
Heald St. SE14 33 D4
Healey St. NW1 10 B3
Hearn St. EC2 18 D3
Heath Dr. NW3 9 C1
Heath Hurst Rd. NW3 9 F1
Heath La. SE3 34 A5
Heath Ri. SW15 36 F4
Heath Rd. SW8 31 B5
Heath Side NW3 9 E1
Heathcote St. WC1 17 F3
Heather Clo. E6 21 D5
Heather Clo. SW8 38 B1
Heatherbank SE9 35 B5
Heathfield Clo. E16 20 G4
Heathfield Pk. NW2 8 E3
Heathfield Rd. SW18 37 D4
Heathfield Sq. SW18 37 E5
Heathfield Ter. SE18 35 G2
Heathlee Rd. SE3 41 C2
Heathmans Rd. SW6 30 A4
Heathstan Rd. W12 15 C5
Heathview Gdns. SW15 36 E5
Heathwall St. SW11 37 G1
Heathway SE3 34 D3
Heathwood Gdns. SE7 28 A5
Heaton Rd. SE15 39 F1
Heavitree Rd. SE18 35 F1
Heber Rd. NW2 8 F2
Heber Rd. SE22 39 E4
Hebron Rd. W6 22 D4
Hector St. SE18 28 G5
Heddington Gro. N7 10 F2
Heddon St. W1 43 A3
Hedgeley St. SE12 41 C3
Hedgers Gro. E9 12 C3
Heigham Rd. E6 14 A4
Heights, The SE7 34 F1
Heiron St. SE17 32 A2
Helby Rd. SW4 38 D4
Helder Gro. SE12 41 C5
Helena Rd. E13 20 C1
Helena Rd. NW10 8 D2
Helix Rd. SW2 38 F4
Helmet Row EC1 18 B3
Helmsley Pl. E8 11 G4
Hemans St. SW8 31 D3
Hemberton Rd. SW9 38 E1
Hemingford Rd. N1 10 F5
Hemlock Rd. W12 22 B1
Hemming St. E1 18 F3
Hemstal Rd. NW6 9 B4
Hemsworth St. N1 18 D1
Henchman St. W12 15 B5
Henderson Rd. E7 13 F3
Henderson Rd. SW18 37 F5
Hendrick Ave. SW12 37 G5
Heneage La. EC3 44 J2
Heneage St. E1 18 E4
Hengist Rd. SE12 41 E5
Hengrave Rd. SE23 40 A5
Henley Dr. SE1 25 E5
Henley Rd. E16 28 B3

Henley Rd. NW10	8	E5
Henley Rd., Ilf.	14	E1
Henley St. SW11	31	A5
Henniker Gdns. E6	20	G2
Henniker Pt. E15	13	B2
Henniker Rd. E15	13	A2
Henning St. SW11	30	F4
Henrietta Pl. W1	17	B5
Henrietta St. E15	12	G2
Henrietta St. WC2	**43**	**F3**
Henriques St. E1	18	F5
Henry Dickens Ct. W11	22	F1
Henry Jackson Rd. SW15	36	F1
Henry Rd. E6	21	A1
Henryson Rd. SE4	40	E3
Henshall St. N1	11	C3
Henshaw St. SE17	25	C5
Henslowe Rd. SE22	39	F3
Henson Ave. NW2	8	E2
Henstridge Pl. NW8	16	F1
Henty Clo. SW11	30	F3
Henty Wk. SW15	36	D3
Henwick Rd. SE9	41	G1
Hepscott Rd. E9	12	E3
Herbal Hill EC1	17	G3
Herbert Gdns. NW10	8	D5
Herbert Rd. E12	14	A1
Herbert Rd. SE18	35	C3
Herbert St. E13	20	D1
Herbert St. NW5	10	A3
Herbrand St. WC1	17	E3
Hercules Rd. SE1	24	F4
Hereford Ho. NW6	16	B1
Hereford Pl. SE14	33	D3
Hereford Rd. W2	16	B5
Hereford Sq. SW7	23	D5
Hereford St. E2	18	F3
Hermit Rd. E16	20	C3
Hermit St. EC1	18	A2
Hermitage, The SW13	29	B4
Hermitage Wall E1	25	F2
Herndon Rd. SW18	37	D3
Herne Hill SE24	39	B3
Herne Hill Rd. SE24	39	B1
Herne Pl. SE24	39	A3
Heron Clo. NW10	8	A3
Heron Pl. SE16	26	C2
Heron Quay E14	26	E2
Heron Rd. SE24	39	B2
Herrick St. SW1	24	D5
Herries St. W10	15	G1
Herringham Rd. SE7	27	F4
Hersant Clo. NW10	8	C5
Herschell Rd. SE23	40	C5
Hersham Clo. SW15	36	C5
Hertford Rd. N1	11	D5
Hertford Rd., Bark.	14	D4
Hertford St. W1	24	A2
Hertsmere Rd. E14	26	E1
Hervey Rd. SE3	34	E4
Hesketh Pl. W11	22	G1
Hesper Ms. SW5	30	C1
Hesperus Cres. E14	26	F5
Hessel St. E1	18	G5
Hester Rd. SW11	30	F3
Hestercombe Ave. SW6	29	G5
Heston St. SE14	33	E4
Hetherington Rd. SW4	38	E2
Hetley Rd. W12	22	D2
Hevelius Clo. SE10	34	C1
Heverham Rd. SE18	28	G5
Hewer St. W10	15	F4
Hewlett Rd. E3	19	C1
Heyford Ave. SW8	31	E3
Heygate St. SE17	25	B5
Heyworth Rd. E5	11	G1
Heyworth Rd. E15	13	C1
Hibbert St. SW11	37	D1
Hichisson Rd. SE15	40	A3
Hickin Clo. SE7	27	G5
Hickling Rd., Ilf.	14	D2
Hickman Clo. E16	20	G4
Hickmore Wk. SW4	38	C1
Hicks Clo. SW11	37	F1
Hicks St. SE8	33	C1
Hide Pl. SW1	24	D5
High Gro. SE18	35	F3
High Holborn WC1	**43**	**E1**
High Rd. (Willesden) NW10	8	B3
High Rd. Leyton E15	12	G1
High Rd. Leytonstone E11	13	B1
High Rd. Leytonstone E15	13	B1
High St. E13	20	D1
High St. E15	19	G1
High St. (Harlesden) NW10	15	B1
High St. SW6	36	G1
High St. N. E6	14	A4
High St. N. E12	14	A2
High St. S. E6	21	B1
High Timber St. EC4	**44**	**D3**
Highbridge Rd., Bark.	14	D5
Highbrook Rd. SE3	41	G1
Highbury Cor. N5	11	A3
Highbury Cres. N5	11	A2
Highbury Est. N5	11	B2
Highbury Gra. N5	11	B1
Highbury Gro. N5	11	A3
Highbury New Pk. N5	11	B2
Highbury Pk. N5	11	A1
Highbury Pl. N5	11	A3
Highbury Sta. Rd. N1	10	G3
Highbury Ter. N5	11	A2
Highbury Ter. Ms. N5	11	A2
Highcliffe Dr. SW15	36	B4
Highcombe SE7	34	E2
Highdown Rd. SW15	36	D4
Highgate Rd. NW5	10	B1
Highlands Heath SW15	36	E5
Highlever Rd. W10	15	E4
Highmore Rd. SE3	34	B3
Highshore Rd. SE15	32	E5
Highway, The E1	25	F1
Highway, The E14	26	B1
Hilary Clo. SW6	30	C3
Hilary Rd. W12	15	B5
Hilda Rd. E6	13	G4
Hilda Rd. E16	20	B3
Hilda Ter. SW9	31	G5
Hildyard Rd. SW6	30	B2
Hiley Rd. NW10	15	E2
Hilgrove Rd. NW6	9	D4
Hill Fm. Rd. W10	15	E4
Hill Rd. NW8	16	D1
Hill St. W1	24	A1
Hill Vw. Dr., Well.	35	G5
Hillbeck Clo. SE15	33	A3
Hillcourt Rd. SE22	39	G4
Hillcroft Rd. E6	21	D4
Hilldrop Cres. N7	10	D2
Hilldrop Est. N7	10	D2
Hilldrop La. N7	10	D2
Hilldrop Rd. N7	10	D2
Hillend SE18	35	D4
Hillersdon Ave. SW13	29	C5
Hillfield Ct. NW3	9	F2
Hillfield Rd. NW6	9	A2
Hillgate Pl. SW12	38	B5
Hillgate Pl. W8	23	B2
Hillgate St. W8	23	B2
Hillier Rd. SW11	37	G4
Hillingdon St. SE5	32	A2
Hillingdon St. SE17	32	A2
Hillman St. E8	11	G3
Hillmarton Rd. N7	10	E2
Hillmead Dr. SW9	39	A2
Hillreach SE18	35	B1
Hills Pl. W1	**43**	**A2**
Hillsborough Rd. SE22	39	D3
Hillside Clo. NW8	16	C1
Hillsleigh Rd. W8	23	A2
Hilltop Rd. NW6	9	B4
Hillworth Rd. SW2	38	G5
Hilly Flds. Cres. SE4	40	E1
Hillyard St. SW9	31	G4
Hilsea St. E5	12	A1
Hinckley Rd. SE15	39	F2
Hind Ct. EC4	**44**	**A2**
Hind Gro. E14	19	E5
Hinde St. W1	17	A5
Hindmans Rd. SE22	39	F3
Hindrey Rd. E5	11	G2
Hinstock Rd. SE18	35	E2
Hinton Rd. SE24	39	A1
Hippodrome Pl. W11	22	G1
Hiroshima Wk. SE7	27	E4
Hitchin Sq. E3	19	C1
Hither Grn. La. SE13	40	G3
Hobart Pl. SW1	24	B4
Hobbes Wk. SW15	36	D3
Hobday St. E14	19	F4
Hobury St. SW10	30	D2
Hockley Ave. E6	21	A1
Hocroft Rd. NW2	9	A1
Hofland Rd. W14	22	F4
Hogarth Clo. E16	20	G4
Hogarth Ct. EC3	**44**	**J3**
Hogarth La. W4	29	A2
Hogarth Rd. SW5	23	C5
Hogarth Roundabout W4	29	A2
Holbeach Gdns., Sid.	42	G4
Holbeach Rd. SE6	40	E5
Holbeck Row SE15	32	F3
Holbein Ms. SW1	31	A1
Holbein Pl. SW1	24	A5
Holberton Gdns. NW10	15	D2
Holborn EC1	17	G4
Holborn Rd. E13	20	E3
Holborn Viaduct EC1	17	G4
Holbrook Rd. E15	20	C1
Holburne Clo. SE3	34	F4
Holburne Gdns. SE3	34	G4
Holburne Rd. SE3	34	F4
Holcombe St. W6	29	D1
Holcroft Rd. E9	12	A4
Holden St. SW11	31	A5
Holdenby Rd. SE4	40	C3
Holford St. WC1	17	G2
Holgate Ave. SW11	37	E1
Holland Gdns. W14	22	G4
Holland Gro. SW9	31	G3
Holland Pk. W11	22	G2
Holland Pk. Ave. W11	22	G2
Holland Pk. Gdns. W14	22	G3
Holland Pk. Ms. W11	23	A2
Holland Pk. Rd. W14	23	A4
Holland Rd. E6	14	B5
Holland Rd. E15	20	B2
Holland Rd. NW10	8	C5
Holland Rd. W14	22	F3
Holland St. SE1	**44**	**C5**
Holland St. W8	23	B3
Holland Vill. Rd. W14	22	G3
Holland Wk. W8	23	A3
Hollen St. W1	**43**	**B1**
Holles St. W1	17	B5
Holley Rd. W3	22	A3
Hollingbourne Rd. SE24	39	B3
Hollington Rd. E6	21	B2
Holloway Rd. E6	21	B2
Holly Bush Hill NW3	9	D1
Holly Clo. NW10	8	A4
Holly Gro. SE15	32	E5
Holly Hedge Ter. SE13	41	A3
Holly Hill NW3	9	D1
Holly St. E8	11	E3
Holly St. Est. E8	11	E4
Holly Wk. NW3	9	D1
Hollybush Gdns. E2	18	G2
Hollybush St. E13	20	E2
Hollybush Wk. SW9	39	A2
Hollydale Rd. SE15	33	A4
Hollydene SE15	32	G4
Hollymount Clo. SE10	33	G4
Hollywood Rd. SW10	30	D2
Holman Rd. SW11	30	E5
Holmbush Rd. SW15	36	G4
Holmcote Gdns. N5	11	B2
Holmdale Rd. NW6	9	B2
Holmdene Ave. SE24	39	B3
Holme Lacey Rd. SE12	41	C4
Holme Rd. E6	14	A5
Holmead Rd. SW6	30	C3
Holmefield Ct. NW3	9	F3
Holmes Rd. NW5	10	B3
Holmes Ter. SE1	24	G3
Holmesley Rd. SE23	40	C4
Holmewood Gdns. SW2	38	F5
Holmewood Rd. SW2	38	E5
Holmside Rd. SW12	38	A4
Holmwood Vill. SE7	34	D1
Holness Rd. E15	13	C3
Holroyd Rd. SW15	36	E2
Holt Rd. E16	28	A2
Holton St. E1	19	B3
Holwood Pl. SW4	38	D2
Holybourne Ave. SW15	36	C5
Holyhead Clo. E3	19	E2
Holyoak Rd. SE11	25	A5
Holyport Rd. SW6	29	E3
Holyrood St. SE1	**44**	**H6**
Holywell Clo. SE3	34	D2
Holywell La. EC2	18	D3
Holywell Row EC2	18	D3
Home Rd. SW11	30	F5
Homefield Rd. W4	29	B1
Homeleigh Rd. SE15	40	B3
Homer Dr. E14	26	E5
Homer Rd. E9	12	C3
Homer Row W1	16	F4
Homer St. W1	16	F4
Homerton Gro. E9	12	B2
Homerton High St. E9	12	A2
Homerton Rd. E9	12	C2
Homerton Row E9	12	A2
Homestall Rd. SE22	40	A3
Homestead Rd. SW6	30	A3
Honey La. EC2	**44**	**E2**
Honeybourne Rd. NW6	9	C2
Honeybrook Rd. SW12	38	C5
Honeyman Clo. NW6	8	F4
Honeywell Rd. SW11	37	F4
Honeywood Rd. NW10	15	B1
Honiton Rd. NW6	16	A1
Honley Rd. SE6	40	F5
Honor Oak Pk. SE23	40	B4
Honor Oak Ri. SE23	40	A4

Hood Ct. EC4	**44**	**A2**
Hooper Rd. E16	20	D5
Hooper St. E1	25	F1
Hop Gdns. WC2	**43**	**E4**
Hope St. SW11	37	E1
Hopedale Rd. SE7	34	E2
Hopefield Ave. NW6	15	G1
Hopewell St. SE5	32	C3
Hopewell Yd. SE5	32	C3
Hopkins St. W1	**43**	**B2**
Hopton Gdns. SE1	**44**	**C5**
Hopton St. SE1	**44**	**C5**
Hopwood Rd. SE17	32	C2
Horace Rd. E7	13	E1
Horatio St. E2	18	F1
Horbury Cres. W11	23	B1
Horder Rd. SW6	29	G4
Horizon Way SE7	27	E5
Hormead Rd. W9	16	A3
Horn La. SE10	27	D5
Horn Pk. Clo. SE12	41	E3
Horn Pk. La. SE12	41	E3
Hornby Clo. NW3	9	E4
Horncastle Clo. SE12	41	D5
Horncastle Rd. SE12	41	D5
Horne Way SW15	29	E5
Hornfair Rd. SE7	34	F2
Hornsey St. N7	10	F2
Hornshay St. SE15	33	A2
Hornton St. W8	23	B3
Horsa Rd. SE12	41	F5
Horse and Dolphin Yd. W1	**43**	**D3**
Horse Guards Ave. SW1	**43**	**E6**
Horse Guards Rd. SW1	**43**	**D6**
Horse Leaze E6	21	C5
Horse Ride SW1	**43**	**C6**
Horseferry Pl. SE10	33	G2
Horseferry Rd. E14	26	B1
Horseferry Rd. SW1	24	D5
Horsell Rd. N5	10	G2
Horselydown La. SE1	25	E3
Horsfeld Gdns. SE9	42	A3
Horsfeld Rd. SE9	41	G3
Horsford Rd. SW2	38	F3
Horsley St. SE17	32	C2
Horsmonden Rd. SE4	40	D3
Hortensia Rd. SW10	30	D3
Horton Ave. NW2	8	G1
Horton Rd. E8	11	G3
Horton St. SE13	40	F1
Hosier La. EC1	18	A4
Hoskins Clo. E16	20	F5
Hoskins St. SE10	34	A1
Hotham Rd. SW15	36	E1
Hotham St. E15	13	B5
Hotspur St. SE11	31	G1
Houghton St. WC2	**43**	**H2**
Houndsditch EC3	**44**	**J1**
Hoveden Rd. NW2	8	G2
Howard Clo. NW2	8	G1
Howard Rd. E6	21	B1
Howard Rd. N16	11	C1
Howard Rd. NW2	8	F1
Howard Rd., Bark.	14	F5
Howard Rd., Ilf.	14	D1
Howards La. SW15	36	D3
Howards Rd. E13	20	D2
Howbury Rd. SE15	40	A1
Howden St. SE15	39	F1
Howick Pl. SW1	24	C4
Howie St. SW11	30	F3
Howitt Rd. NW3	9	F3
Howland St. W1	17	C4
Howland Way SE16	26	C3
Howletts Rd. SE24	39	B4
Howley Pl. W2	16	D4
Hows St. E2	18	E1
Howsman Rd. SW13	29	C2
Howson Rd. SE4	40	C2
Hoxton Sq. N1	18	D2
Hoxton St. N1	11	D5
Hoy St. E16	20	C5
Hoylake Rd. W3	15	A5
Hubbard St. E15	13	B5
Hubert Gro. SW9	38	E1
Hubert Rd. E6	20	G2
Huddart St. E3	19	D4
Huddlestone Rd. E7	13	C1
Huddlestone Rd. NW2	8	D3
Hudson Pl. SE18	35	E1
Huggin Ct. EC4	**44**	**E3**
Huggin Hill EC4	**44**	**E3**
Hugh St. SW1	24	B5
Hughan Rd. E15	13	A2
Hugo Rd. N19	10	C1
Hugon Rd. SW6	37	C1
Huguenot Pl. SW18	37	D3
Hull Clo. SE16	26	B3
Hulse Ave., Bark.	14	F3
Humber Rd. SE3	34	C2
Humberstone Rd. E13	20	F2
Humbolt Rd. W6	29	G2
Hume Pt. E16	20	E4
Humphrey St. SE1	32	E1
Hungerford Bri. SE1	**43**	**G6**
Hungerford Bri. WC2	**43**	**G6**
Hungerford La. WC2	**43**	**F5**
Hungerford Rd. N7	10	D3
Hunsdon Rd. SE14	33	B3
Hunt St. W11	22	F2
Hunter Rd., Ilf.	14	D2
Hunter St. WC1	17	E3
Huntingdon St. E16	20	C5
Huntingdon St. N1	10	F4
Huntingfield Rd. SW15	36	C2
Huntley St. WC1	17	C3
Hunton St. E1	18	F4
Hunt's Clo. SE3	34	D5
Hunt's Ct. WC2	**43**	**D4**
Hunts La. E15	19	G1
Huntsman St. SE17	25	D5
Hurlingham Ct. SW6	37	A1
Hurlingham Gdns. SW6	37	A1
Hurlingham Rd. SW6	30	A5
Hurren Clo. SE3	41	B1
Hurry Clo. E15	13	B4
Hurst St. SE24	39	A4
Hurstbourne Gdns., Bark.	14	G3
Huson Clo. NW3	9	F4
Hutchings St. E14	26	E3
Hutton St. EC4	**44**	**A2**
Huxbear St. SE4	40	D3
Huxley St. W10	15	G2
Hyde Pk. W2	23	F2
Hyde Pk. Cor. W1	24	A3
Hyde Pk. Cres. W2	16	F5
Hyde Pk. Gdns. W2	23	E1
Hyde Pk. Gate SW7	23	D3
Hyde Pk. Sq. W2	16	F5
Hyde Pk. St. W2	16	F5
Hyde Rd. N1	11	D5
Hyde Vale SE10	34	A4
Hyndman St. SE15	32	G2
Hythe Rd. NW10	15	C3

I

Ibbotson Ave. E16	20	C5
Iceland Rd. E3	12	E5
Ida St. E14	19	G5
Idmiston Rd. E15	13	C2
Idol La. EC3	**44**	**H4**
Idonia St. SE8	33	E3
Iffley Rd. W6	22	D4
Ifield Rd. SW10	30	C2
Ilbert St. W10	15	F2
Ilchester Gdns. W2	23	C1
Ilchester Pl. W14	23	A4
Ilderton Rd. SE15	33	A3
Ilderton Rd. SE16	32	G1
Ilex Rd. NW10	8	B3
Iliffe St. SE17	32	A1
Ilkley Rd. E16	20	F4
Ilminster Gdns. SW11	37	F2
Imber St. N1	11	C5
Imperial College Rd. SW7	23	E4
Imperial Rd. SW6	30	C4
Imperial Sq. SW6	30	C4
Imperial St. E3	19	G2
Inca Dr. SE9	42	D5
Indescon Ct. E14	26	E3
India Way W12	22	D1
Indus Rd. SE7	34	F3
Ingal Rd. E13	20	D3
Ingate Pl. SW8	31	B4
Ingelow Rd. SW8	31	B5
Ingersoll Rd. W12	22	D2
Ingestre Pl. W1	**43**	**B2**
Ingestre Rd. E7	13	D1
Ingestre Rd. NW5	10	B1
Ingham Rd. NW6	9	B1
Ingleborough St. SW9	31	G5
Ingledew Rd. SE18	35	F1
Ingleside Gro. SE3	34	C2
Inglethorpe St. SW6	29	F4
Ingleton St. SW9	31	G5
Inglewood Clo. E14	26	E5
Inglewood Rd. NW6	9	B2
Inglis St. SE5	32	A4
Ingrave St. SW11	37	E1
Inigo Jones Rd. SE7	35	A3
Inigo Pl. WC2	**43**	**E3**
Inkerman Rd. NW5	10	B3
Inman Rd. NW10	8	A5
Inman Rd. SW18	37	D5
Inner Circle NW1	17	A2
Inner Temple La. EC4	**43**	**J2**
Innes Gdns. SW15	36	D4
Inniskilling Rd. E13	20	F1
Inverine Rd. SE7	34	E1
Invermore Pl. SE18	28	E5
Inverness Pl. W2	23	C1
Inverness St. NW1	10	B5
Inverness Ter. W2	16	C5
Inverton Rd. SE15	40	B2
Invicta Rd. SE3	34	D3
Inville Rd. SE17	32	C1
Inworth St. SW11	30	F5
Iona Clo. SE6	40	E5
Ireland Yd. EC4	**44**	**C2**
Irene Rd. SW6	30	B4
Iron Mill Rd. SW18	37	C4
Ironmonger La. EC2	**44**	**F2**
Ironmonger Row EC1	18	B2
Irving Gro. SW9	31	F5
Irving Rd. W14	22	F4
Irving St. WC2	**43**	**D4**
Irwin Ave. SE18	35	G3
Irwin Gdns. NW10	8	D5
Isabel St. SW9	31	F4
Isabella Rd. E9	12	A2
Isabella St. SE1	**44**	**B6**
Isambard Ms. E14	26	G4
Isis Clo. SW15	36	E2
Isla Rd. SE18	35	E2
Islington Grn. N1	11	A5
Islington High St. N1	18	A1
Islington Pk. St. N1	10	G4
Islip St. NW5	10	C2
Ismailia Rd. E7	13	E4
Ivanhoe Rd. SE5	39	E1
Ivatt Pl. W14	30	A1
Iveagh Clo. E9	12	B5
Iveley Rd. SW4	31	C5
Iverna Ct. W8	23	B4
Iverna Gdns. W8	23	B4
Iverson Rd. NW6	9	A3
Ives Rd. E16	20	B4
Ives St. SW3	23	F5
Ivestor Ter. SE23	40	A5
Ivimey St. E2	18	F2
Ivor Pl. NW1	16	G3
Ivor St. NW1	10	C4
Ivy Rd. NW2	8	E1
Ivy Rd. SE4	40	D2
Ivy St. N1	18	D1
Ivybridge La. WC2	**43**	**F4**
Ivydale Rd. SE15	40	B1
Ixworth Pl. SW3	23	F5

J

Jack Cornwell St. E12	14	C1
Jack Walker Ct. N5	11	A1
Jackman St. E8	11	G5
Jackson Rd. N7	10	F1
Jackson Rd., Bark.	14	F5
Jackson St. SE18	35	C2
Jacob St. SE1	25	E3
Jacobs Ho. E14	20	F2
Jade Clo. E16	20	G5
Jaggard Way SW12	37	G5
Jago Clo. SE18	35	E2
Jamaica Rd. SE1	25	E3
Jamaica Rd. SE16	25	F4
Jamaica St. E1	19	A4
James Ave. NW2	8	E2
James Sinclair Pt. E13	13	F5
James St. W1	17	A5
James St. WC2	**43**	**F3**
James St., Bark.	14	E4
Jameson St. W8	23	B2
Jamestown Rd. NW1	10	B5
Janet St. E14	26	E4
Janeway St. SE16	25	F3
Janson Rd. E15	13	B2
Jardine Rd. E1	26	B1
Jarrow Rd. SE16	26	A5
Jarrow Way E9	12	D2
Jasmine Clo., Ilf.	14	D2
Jasper Rd. E16	20	G5
Jay Ms. SW7	23	D3
Jebb Ave. SW2	38	E4
Jebb St. E3	19	E1
Jedburgh Rd. E13	20	F2
Jedburgh St. SW11	38	A2
Jeddo Rd. W12	22	B3
Jeffreys Rd. SW4	31	E5
Jeffreys St. NW1	10	C4
Jeffreys Wk. SW4	31	E5
Jeken Rd. SE9	41	F2
Jelf Rd. SW2	38	G3
Jenkins La. E6	21	C1
Jenkins La., Bark.	21	D1
Jenkins Rd. E13	20	E3
Jenner Ho. SE3	34	B2
Jenner Pl. SW13	29	D2
Jennings Rd. SE22	39	E4
Jephson Rd. E7	13	F4
Jephtha Rd. SW18	37	B4
Jeremiah St. E14	19	F5
Jermyn St. SW1	**43**	**B5**
Jerningham Rd. SE14	33	C5
Jerome Cres. NW8	16	F3
Jerrard St. SE13	40	F1
Jersey Rd. E16	20	F5

Jersey Rd., Ilf.	14	D1
Jessica Rd. SW18	37	D4
Jessup Clo. SE18	28	E5
Jewry St. EC3	18	E5
Jew's Row SW18	37	C2
Jeymer Ave. NW2	8	D2
Jeypore Rd. SW18	37	D5
Joan Cres. SE9	41	G5
Joan St. SE1	**44**	**B6**
Jockey's Flds. WC1	17	F4
Jodane St. SE8	26	D5
Jodrell Rd. E3	12	D5
John Adam St. WC2	**43**	**F4**
John Ashby Clo. SW2	38	E4
John Burns Dr., Bark.	14	G4
John Campbell Rd. N16	11	D2
John Carpenter St. EC4	**44**	**A3**
John Cornwall VC Ho. E12	14	C1
John Felton Rd. SE16	25	F3
John Fisher St. E1	25	F1
John Islip St. SW1	31	D1
John Penn St. SE13	33	F4
John Princes St. W1	17	B5
John Roll Way SE16	25	F4
John Ruskin St. SE5	32	A3
John Silkin La. SE8	33	B1
John Spencer Sq. N1	11	A3
John St. E15	13	C5
John St. WC1	17	F3
John Wilson St. SE18	28	C4
John Woolley Clo. SE13	41	A2
John's Ms. WC1	17	F3
Johnson Clo. E8	11	F5
Johnson's Pl. SW1	31	C1
Johnstone Rd. E6	21	B2
Joiner St. SE1	**44**	**G6**
Jonathan St. SE11	31	F1
Joseph St. E3	19	D3
Josephine Ave. SW2	38	F3
Joubert St. SW11	30	G5
Jowett St. SE15	32	E3
Jubilee Cres. E14	26	G4
Jubilee Pl. SW3	30	F1
Jubilee St. E1	19	A5
Judd St. WC1	17	E2
Jude St. E16	20	C5
Juer St. SW11	30	F3
Julian Pl. E14	33	F1
Junction App. SW11	37	F1
Junction Rd. E13	20	E1
Junction Rd. N19	10	C1
Junction Wf. N1	18	B1
Juniper La. E6	21	A4
Juniper Rd., Ilf.	14	D1
Juniper St. E1	26	A1
Juno Way SE14	33	B2
Jupiter Way N7	10	F3
Jupp Rd. E15	13	A4
Jupp Rd. W. E15	12	G5
Jutland Rd. E13	20	D3
Jutland Rd. SE6	40	G5
Juxon St. SE11	24	F5

K

Kambala Rd. SW11	37	E1
Kashmir Rd. SE7	34	G3
Kassala Rd. SW11	30	G4
Katella Trd. Est., Bark.	21	G2
Katherine Gdns. SE9	41	G2
Katherine Rd. E6	13	G4
Katherine Rd. E7	13	F3
Kathleen Rd. SW11	37	G1
Kay Rd. SW9	31	E5
Kay St. E2	18	F1
Kay St. E15	13	A4
Kean St. WC2	**43**	**G2**
Keats Gro. NW3	9	F1
Keats Rd., Well.	35	G4
Keel Clo. SE16	26	B2
Keeley St. WC2	**43**	**G2**
Keeling Rd. SE9	41	G3
Keep, The SE3	34	D5
Keetons Rd. SE16	25	G4
Keevil Dr. SW19	36	F5
Keildon Rd. SW11	37	G2
Keith Gro. W12	22	C3
Keith Rd., Bark.	21	F1
Kelbrook Rd. SE3	35	A5
Kelfield Gdns. W10	15	E5
Kelland Rd. E13	20	D3
Kellaway Rd. SE3	34	F5
Kellerton Rd. SE13	41	B3
Kellett Rd. SW2	38	G2
Kelly St. NW1	10	B3
Kelman Clo. SW4	31	D5
Kelmore Gro. SE22	39	F2
Kelmscott Gdns. W12	22	C4
Kelmscott Rd. SW11	37	F3
Kelross Rd. N5	11	B1
Kelsall Clo. SE3	34	E5
Kelsey St. E2	18	F3
Kelso Pl. W8	23	C4
Kelson Ho. E14	26	G4
Kelvedon Rd. SW6	30	A3
Kelvin Rd. N5	11	A1
Kelvington Rd. SE15	40	B3
Kemble St. WC2	**43**	**G2**
Kemerton Rd. SE5	39	B1
Kemeys St. E9	12	C2
Kempe Rd. NW6	15	F1
Kemplay Rd. NW3	9	E1
Kemp's Ct. W1	**43**	**B2**
Kempsford Gdns. SW5	30	B1
Kempsford Rd. SE11	24	G5
Kempson Rd. SW6	30	B4
Kempt St. SE18	35	C2
Kempthorne Rd. SE8	26	C5
Kempton Rd. E6	14	B5
Kemsing Rd. SE10	34	D1
Kenbury St. SE5	32	B5
Kenchester Clo. SW8	31	E3
Kendal Ave., Bark.	14	G4
Kendal Clo. SW9	32	A3
Kendal Rd. NW10	8	C1
Kendal St. W2	16	F5
Kender St. SE14	33	A4
Kendoa Rd. SW4	38	D2
Kendrick Pl. SW7	23	E5
Kenilford Rd. SW12	38	B5
Kenilworth Ct. SW15	36	F1
Kenilworth Gdns. SE18	35	D5
Kenilworth Rd. E3	19	C1
Kenilworth Rd. NW6	9	A5
Kenmont Gdns. NW10	15	D2
Kenmure Rd. E8	11	G2
Kennard Rd. E15	13	A4
Kennard St. E16	28	B2
Kennard St. SW11	31	A4
Kennedy Clo. E13	20	D1
Kennedy Rd., Bark.	14	G5
Kennel Hill SE22	39	D1
Kennet Rd. W9	16	A3
Kennet St. E1	25	F2
Kennet Wf. La. EC4	**44**	**E3**
Kenneth Ave., Ilf.	14	D1
Kenneth Cres. NW2	8	D2
Kenning Ter. N1	11	D5
Kennings Way SE11	31	G1
Kennington La. SE11	31	E1
Kennington Oval SE11	31	F2
Kennington Pk. Pl. SE11	31	G2
Kennington Pk. Rd. SE11	31	G2
Kennington Rd. SE1	24	G4
Kennington Rd. SE11	24	G4
Kensal Rd. W10	15	F3
Kensington Ave. E12	14	A3
Kensington Ch. Ct. W8	23	C3
Kensington Ch. St. W8	23	B2
Kensington Ch. Wk. W8	23	C3
Kensington Ct. W8	23	C3
Kensington Ct. Pl. W8	23	C4
Kensington Gdns. Sq. W2	16	C5
Kensington Gate W8	23	D4
Kensington Gore SW7	23	D3
Kensington High St. W8	23	B4
Kensington High St. W14	23	A4
Kensington Mall W8	23	B2
Kensington Palace Gdns. W8	23	C2
Kensington Pk. Gdns. W11	23	A1
Kensington Pk. Rd. W11	16	A5
Kensington Pl. W8	23	B2
Kensington Rd. SW7	23	D3
Kensington Rd. W8	23	C3
Kensington Sq. W8	23	C3
Kent St. E2	18	E1
Kent St. E13	20	E2
Kent Ter. NW1	16	F2
Kentish Town Rd. NW1	10	B4
Kentish Town Rd. NW5	10	B3
Kentmere Rd. SE18	28	G5
Kenton Rd. E9	12	B3
Kenton St. WC1	17	E3
Kentwode Grn. SW13	29	C3
Kenward Rd. SE9	41	F3
Kenway Rd. SW5	23	C5
Kenworthy Rd. E9	12	C2
Kenwyn Rd. SW4	38	D2
Kenya Rd. SE7	34	G3
Kenyon St. SW6	29	F4
Keogh Rd. E15	13	B3
Kepler Rd. SW4	38	E2
Keppel Rd. E6	14	B4
Keppel Row SE1	**44**	**D6**
Keppel St. WC1	17	D4
Kerbey St. E14	19	F5
Kerfield Pl. SE5	32	C4
Kerrison Rd. E15	13	A5
Kerrison Rd. SW11	37	F1
Kerry Clo. E16	20	E5
Kersfield Rd. SW15	36	F4
Kersley Ms. SW11	30	G5
Kersley St. SW11	30	G5
Keslake Rd. NW6	15	F1
Keston Rd. SE15	39	F1
Kestrel Ave. SE24	39	A3
Keswick Rd. SW15	36	G3
Kett Gdns. SW2	38	F3
Key Clo. E1	18	G3
Keybridge Ho. SW8	31	E2
Keyes Rd. NW2	8	F2
Keynsham Gdns. SE9	42	A3
Keynsham Rd. SE9	41	G3
Keyworth St. SE1	25	A4
Khartoum Rd. E13	20	E2
Khartoum Rd., Ilf.	14	D2
Khyber Rd. SW11	30	F5
Kibworth St. SW8	31	F3
Kidbrooke Gdns. SE3	34	D5
Kidbrooke Gro. SE3	34	D4
Kidbrooke La. SE9	42	A2
Kidbrooke Pk. Clo. SE3	34	E4
Kidbrooke Pk. Rd. SE3	34	E4
Kidbrooke Way SE3	34	E5
Kidd Pl. SE7	35	A1
Kidderpore Ave. NW3	9	B1
Kidderpore Gdns. NW3	9	B1
Kilburn High Rd. NW6	9	A4
Kilburn La. W9	15	G2
Kilburn La. W10	15	F2
Kilburn Pk. Rd. NW6	16	B2
Kilburn Pl. NW6	9	B5
Kilburn Priory NW6	9	C5
Kildare Gdns. W2	16	B5
Kildare Rd. E16	20	D4
Kildare Ter. W2	16	B5
Kildoran Rd. SW2	38	E3
Kilgour Rd. SE23	40	C4
Kilkie St. SW6	30	D5
Killarney Rd. SW18	37	D4
Killick St. N1	17	F1
Killip Clo. E16	20	C5
Killowen Rd. E9	12	B3
Killyon Rd. SW8	31	C5
Kilmaine Rd. SW6	29	G3
Kilmarsh Rd. W6	22	E5
Kilmington Rd. SW13	29	C2
Kiln Pl. NW5	10	A1
Kilner St. E14	19	E4
Kilravock St. W10	15	G2
Kimbell Gdns. SW6	29	G4
Kimber Rd. SW18	37	B5
Kimberley Ave. E6	21	A1
Kimberley Ave. SE15	32	G5
Kimberley Rd. E16	20	C3
Kimberley Rd. NW6	8	G5
Kimberley Rd. SW9	31	E5
Kimbolton Clo. SE12	41	C4
Kimpton Rd. SE5	32	C4
Kinburn St. SE16	26	B3
Kincaid Rd. SE15	32	G3
King & Queen St. SE17	32	B1
King Arthur Clo. SE15	33	A3
King Charles St. SW1	24	D3
King David La. E1	26	A1
King Edward Ms. SW13	29	C4
King Edward St. EC1	**44**	**D1**
King Edward Wk. SE1	24	G4
King Edwards Rd. E9	11	G5
King Edwards Rd., Bark.	14	F5
King George Ave. E16	20	G5
King George St. SE10	33	G3
King Henry St. N16	11	D2
King Henry's Rd. NW3	9	F4
King Henry's Wk. N1	11	D3
King James St. SE1	25	A3
King John St. E1	19	B4
King St. E13	20	D3
King St. EC2	**44**	**E2**
King St. SW1	**43**	**B6**
King St. W6	22	C5
King St. WC2	**43**	**E3**
King William St. EC4	**44**	**G4**
King William Wk. SE10	33	G2

Kingdon Rd. NW6 9 B3
Kingfield St. E14 26 G5
Kingfisher St. E6 21 A4
Kingham Clo. SW18 37 D5
Kingham Clo. W11 22 G3
Kinglake St. SE17 32 D1
Kingly Ct. W1 43 B3
Kingly St. W1 43 A3
Kings Arms Yd. EC2 44 F1
King's Ave. SW4 38 E3
Kings Bench Wk. EC4 44 A2
Kings College Rd. NW3 9 F4
Kings Ct. E13 13 E5
King's Cross Rd. WC1 17 F2
Kings Gro. SE15 32 G4
Kings Head Yd. SE1 44 F6
Kings Highway SE18 35 G2
King's Ms. WC1 17 F3
King's Orchard SE9 42 A4
King's Reach Twr. SE1 44 A5
Kings Rd. E6 13 F5
Kings Rd. NW10 8 D4
King's Rd. SW1 24 A5
King's Rd. SW3 30 E2
King's Rd. SW6 30 C3
King's Rd. SW10 30 D3
Kingsbridge Rd. W10 15 E5
Kingsbridge Rd., Bark. 21 F1
Kingsbury Rd. N1 11 D3
Kingsbury Ter. N1 11 D3
Kingsclere Clo. SW15 36 C5
Kingscote St. EC4 44 B3
Kingscroft Rd. NW2 9 A3
Kingsdale Gdns. W11 22 F2
Kingsdown Ave. W3 22 A1
Kingsdown Clo. W10 15 F5
Kingsford St. NW5 9 G2
Kingsgate Pl. NW6 9 B4
Kingsgate Rd. NW6 9 B4
Kingsground SE9 42 A5
Kingshold Rd. E9 12 A4
Kingsholm Gdns. SE9 41 G2
Kingshurst Rd. SE12 41 D5
Kingsland Grn. E8 11 D3
Kingsland High St. E8 11 E3
Kingsland Rd. E2 18 D2
Kingsland Rd. E8 11 D5
Kingsland Rd. E13 20 F2
Kingsley Rd. E7 13 D4
Kingsley Rd. NW6 9 A5
Kingsley St. SW11 37 G1
Kingsman St. SE18 28 B4
Kingsmead Way E9 12 C1
Kingsmill Ter. NW8 16 E1
Kingston Rd., Ilf. 14 D1
Kingstown St. NW1 10 A5
Kingsway WC2 43 G1
Kingswood Ave. NW6 8 G5
Kingswood Pl. SE13 41 B2
Kingswood Rd. SW2 38 E4
Kingwood Rd. SW6 29 G3
Kinlet Rd. SE18 35 E4
Kinnear Rd. W12 22 B3
Kinnerton St. SW1 24 A3
Kinnoul Rd. W6 29 G2
Kinsale Rd. SE15 39 F1
Kinveachy Gdns. SE7 35 A1
Kipling Est. SE1 25 C3
Kipling St. SE1 25 C3
Kirby Est. SE16 25 G4
Kirby Gro. SE1 25 D3
Kirk La. SE18 35 E2
Kirkham Rd. E6 21 A5
Kirkham St. SE18 35 G2
Kirkland Clo., Sid. 42 G4
Kirkside Rd. SE3 34 D2
Kirkwall Pl. E2 19 A2
Kirkwood Rd. SE15 32 G5
Kirtling St. SW8 31 C3
Kirton Rd. E13 20 F1
Kirwyn Way SE5 32 A3
Kitcat Ter. E3 19 E2
Kitchener Rd. E7 13 E3
Kitson Rd. SE5 32 C3
Kitson Rd. SW13 29 C4
Kitto Rd. SE14 33 B5
Klea Ave. SW4 38 C4
Knapp Clo. NW10 8 A3
Knapp Rd. E3 19 E3
Knaresborough Pl. SW5 23 C5
Knatchbull Rd. SE5 32 A5
Kneller Rd. SE4 40 C2
Knights Rd. E16 27 D3
Knightsbridge SW1 23 G3
Knightsbridge SW7 23 F3
Knightsbridge Grn. SW1 23 G3
Knivet Rd. SW6 30 B2
Knobs Hill Rd. E15 12 F5
Knockholt Rd. SE9 41 G3
Knoll Rd. SW18 37 D3
Knottisford St. E2 19 A2
Knowle Clo. SW9 38 G1
Knowles Hill Cres. SE13 41 A3
Knowles Wk. SW4 38 C1
Knowsley Rd. SW11 30 G5
Knox Rd. E7 13 C3
Knox St. W1 16 G4
Kossuth St. SE10 34 B1
Kylemore Rd. NW6 9 B4
Kynance Pl. SW7 23 D4
Kyrle Rd. SW11 37 G4

L

Laburnum St. E2 11 E5
Lacey Wk. E3 19 E1
Lackington St. EC2 18 C4
Lacon Rd. SE22 39 F2
Lacy Rd. SW15 36 F2
Ladbroke Gdns. W11 23 A1
Ladbroke Gro. W10 15 F3
Ladbroke Gro. W11 15 G5
Ladbroke Rd. W11 23 A2
Ladbroke Sq. W11 23 A1
Ladbroke Ter. W11 23 A1
Ladbroke Wk. W11 23 A2
Lady Margaret Rd. N19 10 C1
Lady Margaret Rd. NW5 10 C2
Lady Somerset Rd. NW5 10 B1
Ladycroft Rd. SE13 40 F1
Ladysmith Ave. E6 21 A1
Ladysmith Rd. E16 20 C2
Ladysmith Rd. SE9 42 C4
Ladywell Rd. SE13 40 F3
Lafone St. SE1 25 E3
Lagado Ms. SE16 26 B2
Lainson St. SW18 37 B5
Lakedale Rd. SE18 35 G1
Laker Pl. SW15 36 G4
Lakeside Rd. W14 22 F4
Laleham Rd. SE6 40 G5
Lalor St. SW6 29 G5
Lamb La. E8 11 G4
Lamb St. E1 18 E4
Lambert Rd. E16 20 E5
Lambert Rd. SW2 38 E3
Lambert St. N1 10 G4
Lambeth Bri. SE1 24 E5
Lambeth Bri. SW1 24 E5
Lambeth High St. SE1 24 F5
Lambeth Hill EC4 44 D3
Lambeth Palace Rd. SE1 24 F4
Lambeth Rd. SE1 24 F4
Lambeth Wk. SE11 24 F5
Lamble St. NW5 10 A2
Lambolle Pl. NW3 9 F3
Lambolle Rd. NW3 9 F3
Lambourn Rd. SW4 38 B1
Lambourne Rd., Bark. 14 G4
Lambrook Ter. SW6 29 G4
Lamb's Conduit St. WC1 17 F3
Lamb's Pas. EC1 18 C4
Lamerton St. SE8 33 E2
Lamington St. W6 22 D5
Lammas Rd. E9 12 B4
Lammermoor Rd. SW12 38 B5
Lamont Rd. SW10 30 D2
Lampmead Rd. SE12 41 C3
Lamport Clo. SE18 28 B5
Lanark Pl. W9 16 D3
Lanark Rd. W9 16 C1
Lanark Sq. E14 26 F4
Lanbury Rd. SE15 40 B2
Lancaster Ave., Bark. 14 G4
Lancaster Ct. SW6 30 A3
Lancaster Dr. NW3 9 F3
Lancaster Gate W2 23 D1
Lancaster Gro. NW3 9 E3
Lancaster Ms. W2 23 D1
Lancaster Pl. WC2 43 G3
Lancaster Rd. E7 13 D4
Lancaster Rd. NW10 8 C2
Lancaster Rd. W11 15 G5
Lancaster St. SE1 25 A3
Lancaster Ter. W2 23 E1
Lancaster Wk. W2 23 E2
Lancefield St. W10 16 A2
Lancelot Pl. SW7 23 G3
Lancresse Ct. N1 11 D5
Landcroft Rd. SE22 39 E3
Landells Rd. SE22 39 E4
Landford Rd. SW15 36 E1
Landmann Way SE14 33 B2
Landon Pl. SW1 23 G4
Landons Clo. E14 26 G2
Landor Rd. SW9 38 E1
Landor Wk. W12 22 C3
Landridge Rd. SW6 30 A5
Landseer Ave. E12 14 C2
Landstead Rd. SE18 35 F3
Lane, The SE3 41 D1
Lanfranc Rd. E3 19 C1
Lang St. E1 19 A3
Langbrook Rd. SE3 41 G1
Langdale Clo. SE17 32 B2
Langdale Rd. SE10 33 G3
Langdon Ct. NW10 8 A5
Langdon Cres. E6 21 C1
Langdon Rd. E6 14 C5
Langford Clo. E8 11 F2
Langford Grn. SE5 39 D1
Langford Pl. NW8 16 D1
Langham Pl. W1 17 B4
Langham St. W1 17 B4
Langland Gdns. NW3 9 C2
Langler Rd. NW10 15 E1
Langley Ct. SE9 42 C4
Langley Ct. WC2 43 E3
Langley La. SW8 31 E2
Langley St. WC2 43 E2
Langside Ave. SW15 36 C2
Langthorn Ct. EC2 44 G1
Langthorne St. SW6 29 F4
Langton Ave. E6 21 C2
Langton Ri. SE23 39 G5
Langton Rd. SW9 32 A3
Langton St. SW10 30 D2
Langton Way SE3 34 C4
Langtry Rd. NW8 9 C5
Lanhill Rd. W9 16 B3
Lanier Rd. SE13 40 G4
Lanrick Rd. E14 20 A5
Lansbury Est. E14 19 F5
Lansbury Gdns. E14 19 G5
Lansdown Rd. E7 13 F4
Lansdowne Cres. W11 23 A1
Lansdowne Dr. E8 11 F3
Lansdowne Gdns. SW8 31 E4
Lansdowne Gro. NW10 8 A1
Lansdowne La. SE7 34 G1
Lansdowne Ms. SE7 34 G1
Lansdowne Ri. W11 22 G1
Lansdowne Rd. W11 22 G1
Lansdowne Ter. WC1 17 E3
Lansdowne Wk. W11 23 A2
Lansdowne Way SW8 31 D4
Lant St. SE1 25 B3
Lantern Clo. SW15 36 C2
Lanterns Ct. E14 26 E3
Lanvanor Rd. SE15 33 A5
Lapford Clo. W9 16 A3
Lara Clo. SE13 40 G4
Larch Ave. W3 22 A2
Larch Rd. NW2 8 E1
Larcom St. SE17 25 B5
Larden Rd. W3 22 A2
Lark Row E2 12 A5
Larkhall La. SW4 31 D5
Larkhall Ri. SW4 38 C1
Larkhill Ter. SE18 35 C3
Larks Gro., Bark. 14 G4
Larkspur Clo. E6 21 A4
Larnach Rd. W6 29 F2
Larpent Ave. SW15 36 E3
Lassa Rd. SE9 42 A3
Lassell St. SE10 34 A1
Latchmere Rd. SW11 30 G5
Latchmere St. SW11 30 G5
Latham Ho. E1 19 B5
Lathom Rd. E6 14 A4
Latimer Ave. E6 14 B5
Latimer Pl. W10 15 E5
Latimer Rd. E7 13 E1
Latimer Rd. W10 15 E4
Latona Rd. SE15 32 F2
Latymer Ct. W6 22 F5
Lauderdale Rd. W9 16 C2
Launceston Pl. W8 23 D4
Launch St. E14 26 G4
Laundry Rd. W6 29 G2
Laura Pl. E5 12 A1
Laurel Rd. SW13 29 C5
Laurel St. E8 11 E3
Laurence Pountney Hill EC4 44 F3
Laurence Pountney La. EC4 44 F3
Laurie Gro. SE14 33 C4
Lauriston Rd. E9 12 B5
Lausanne Rd. SE15 33 A4
Lavell St. N16 11 C1
Lavender Gdns. SW11 37 G2
Lavender Gro. E8 11 F4
Lavender Hill SW11 37 G2

Lavender Pl., Ilf.	14	D2
Lavender Rd. SE16	26	C2
Lavender Rd. SW11	37	E1
Lavender Sweep SW11	37	G2
Lavender Wk. SW11	37	G2
Laverstoke Gdns. SW15	36	B5
Laverton Pl. SW5	23	C5
Lavington St. SE1	**44**	**C6**
Law St. SE1	25	C4
Lawford Rd. N1	11	D4
Lawford Rd. NW5	10	C3
Lawless St. E14	26	F1
Lawley St. E5	12	A1
Lawn Ho. Clo. E14	26	G3
Lawn La. SW8	31	E2
Lawn Rd. NW3	9	G2
Lawn Ter. SE3	41	B1
Lawnside SE3	41	C2
Lawrence Ave. E12	14	C1
Lawrence Clo. E3	19	E2
Lawrence La. EC2	**44**	**E2**
Lawrence Rd. E6	14	A5
Lawrence Rd. E13	13	E5
Lawrence St. E16	20	C4
Lawrence St. SW3	30	F2
Lawson Clo. E16	20	F4
Lawton Rd. E3	19	C2
Laxley Clo. SE5	32	A3
Layard Rd. SE16	25	G5
Layard Sq. SE16	25	G5
Laycock St. N1	10	G3
Laystall St. EC1	17	G3
Layton Rd. N1	17	G1
Leabank Sq. E9	12	E3
Leacroft Ave. SW12	37	G5
Leadenhall Mkt. EC3	**44**	**H2**
Leadenhall Pl. EC3	**44**	**H2**
Leadenhall St. EC3	**44**	**H2**
Leader Ave. E12	14	C2
Leahurst Rd. SE13	41	A3
Leake St. SE1	24	F3
Leamington Clo. E12	14	B2
Leamington Rd. Vill. W11	16	A4
Leamore St. W6	22	D5
Leamouth Rd. E6	21	A5
Leamouth Rd. E14	20	A5
Leander Ct. SE8	33	E4
Leander Rd. SW2	38	F5
Learoyd Gdns. E6	28	C1
Leather La. EC1	17	G4
Leathermarket St. SE1	25	D3
Leathwaite Rd. SW11	37	G2
Leathwell Rd. SE8	33	F5
Lebanon Gdns. SW18	37	B3
Lebanon Rd. SW18	37	B3
Lebrun Sq. SE3	41	E1
Lechmere Rd. NW2	8	D3
Lecky St. SW7	30	E1
Leconfield Ave. SW13	36	B1
Leconfield Rd. N5	11	C1
Leda Rd. SE18	28	B4
Ledbury Est. SE15	32	G3
Ledbury Rd. W11	16	A5
Ledbury St. SE15	32	F3
Lee Bri. SE13	40	G1
Lee Ch. St. SE13	41	B2
Lee Conservancy Rd. E9	12	D2
Lee Grn. SE12	41	C3
Lee High Rd. SE12	41	C2
Lee High Rd. SE13	41	A2
Lee Pk. SE3	41	C2
Lee Rd. SE3	41	C1
Lee St. E8	11	E5
Lee Ter. SE3	41	B1
Leefern Rd. W12	22	C3
Leegate SE12	41	C3
Leeke St. WC1	17	F2
Leeland Way NW10	8	B1
Leerdam Dr. E14	26	G4
Lees Pl. W1	24	A1
Leeson Rd. SE24	38	G2
Leeway SE8	33	D1
Lefroy Rd. W12	22	B3
Legatt Rd. SE9	41	G3
Leggatt Rd. E15	19	G1
Legge St. SE13	40	G3
Leghorn Rd. NW10	15	B1
Leghorn Rd. SE18	35	F1
Legion Clo. N1	10	G4
Leicester Ct. WC2	**43**	**D3**
Leicester Pl. WC2	**43**	**D3**
Leicester Sq. WC2	**43**	**D4**
Leicester St. WC2	**43**	**D3**
Leigh Gdns. NW10	15	E1
Leigh Rd. E6	14	C3
Leigh Rd. N5	11	A1
Leigh St. WC1	17	E3
Leighton Ave. E12	14	C2
Leighton Gdns. NW10	15	D1
Leighton Gro. NW5	10	C2
Leighton Pl. NW5	10	C2
Leighton Rd. NW5	10	C2
Leinster Gdns. W2	16	D5
Leinster Ms. W2	23	D1
Leinster Pl. W2	16	D5
Leinster Sq. W2	16	B5
Leinster Ter. W2	23	D1
Leman St. E1	18	E5
Lemmon Rd. SE10	34	B2
Lemonwell Ct. SE9	42	E3
Lena Gdns. W6	22	E4
Lendal Ter. SW4	38	D1
Lenham Rd. SE12	41	C2
Lennon Rd. NW2	8	E3
Lennox Gdns. NW10	8	B1
Lennox Gdns. SW1	23	G4
Lennox Gdns. Ms. SW1	23	G4
Lens Rd. E7	13	F4
Lenthall Rd. E8	11	E4
Lenthorp Rd. SE10	27	C5
Lenton St. SE18	28	F5
Leo St. SE15	32	G3
Leonard Rd. E7	13	D1
Leonard St. E16	28	A2
Leonard St. EC2	18	C3
Leontine Clo. SE15	32	F3
Leopold Rd. NW10	8	A4
Leopold St. E3	19	D4
Leppoc Rd. SW4	38	D3
Leroy St. SE1	25	D5
Leslie Rd. E11	12	G1
Leslie Rd. E16	20	E5
Lessar Ave. SW4	38	B3
Lessing St. SE23	40	C5
Lester Ave. E15	20	B3
Letchford Gdns. NW10	15	C2
Lethbridge Clo. SE13	33	G4
Lett Rd. E15	13	A4
Lettice St. SW6	30	A4
Lettsom St. SE5	32	D5
Levehurst Way SW4	31	E5
Leven Rd. E14	19	G4
Lever St. EC1	18	A2
Leverton St. NW5	10	C2
Levett Rd., Bark.	14	G3
Lewey Ho. E3	19	D3
Lewis Gro. SE13	40	G1
Lewis St. NW1	10	B3
Lewisham High St. SE13	40	F4
Lewisham Hill SE13	33	G5
Lewisham Pk. SE13	40	G3
Lewisham Rd. SE13	33	F4
Lewisham Way SE4	33	E5
Lewisham Way SE14	33	D4
Lexham Gdns. W8	23	B5
Lexham Ms. W8	23	B5
Lexington St. W1	**43**	**B3**
Leybourne Rd. NW1	10	B4
Leybridge Ct. SE12	41	D3
Leyes Rd. E16	20	F5
Leyland Rd. SE12	41	C3
Leylang Rd. SE14	33	B3
Leysfield Rd. W12	22	C4
Leyton Rd. E15	13	A2
Leytonstone Rd. E15	13	B3
Leywick St. E15	20	B1
Liardet St. SE14	33	C2
Liberia Rd. N5	11	A3
Liberty Ms. SW12	38	B4
Liberty St. SW9	31	F4
Libra Rd. E3	12	D5
Libra Rd. E13	20	D1
Library St. SE1	25	A3
Lichfield Rd. E3	19	C2
Lichfield Rd. E6	20	G2
Lichfield Rd. NW2	8	G1
Lidcote Gdns. SW9	31	G5
Liddell Gdns. NW10	15	E1
Liddell Rd. NW6	9	B3
Liddington Rd. E15	13	C5
Liddon Rd. E13	20	E2
Lidfield Rd. N16	11	C1
Lidlington Pl. NW1	17	C1
Liffler Rd. SE18	35	G1
Lifford St. SW15	36	F2
Liffords Pl. SW13	29	B5
Lightermans Rd. E14	26	E3
Lilac Pl. SE11	24	F5
Lilac St. W12	22	C1
Lilburne Gdns. SE9	42	A3
Lilburne Rd. SE9	42	A3
Lilestone St. NW8	16	F3
Lilford Rd. SE5	32	A5
Lilian Barker Clo. SE12	41	D3
Lillian Rd. SW13	29	C2
Lillie Rd. SW6	29	F2
Lillie Yd. SW6	30	B2
Lillieshall Rd. SW4	38	B1
Lily Pl. EC1	17	G4
Lilyville Rd. SW6	30	A4
Limburg Rd. SW11	37	G2
Lime Clo. E1	25	F2
Lime Gro. W12	22	E3
Lime St. EC3	**44**	**H3**
Lime St. Pas. EC3	**44**	**H3**
Limeburner La. EC4	**44**	**B2**
Limeharbour E14	26	F4
Limehouse Causeway E14	26	D1
Limehouse Flds. Est. E14	19	C4
Limerick Clo. SW12	38	C5
Limerston St. SW10	30	D2
Limes Ave. SW13	29	B5
Limes Gdns. SW18	37	B4
Limes Gro. SE13	40	G2
Limes Wk. SE15	39	G2
Limesford Rd. SE15	40	B2
Linacre Ct. W6	29	F1
Linacre Rd. NW2	8	D3
Linchmere Rd. SE12	41	C5
Lincoln Rd. E7	13	G3
Lincoln Rd. E13	20	E3
Lincoln St. SW3	23	G5
Lincoln's Inn Flds. WC2	**43**	**G1**
Lind St. SE8	33	E5
Lindal Rd. SE4	40	D3
Linden Ave. NW10	15	F1
Linden Ct. W12	22	E2
Linden Gdns. W2	23	B1
Linden Gdns. W4	29	A1
Linden Gro. SE15	39	G1
Linden Ms. W2	23	B1
Lindfield Gdns. NW3	9	D2
Lindfield St. E14	19	E5
Lindisfarne Way E9	12	C1
Lindley St. E1	19	A4
Lindore Rd. SW11	37	G2
Lindrop St. SW6	30	D5
Lindsay Sq. SW1	31	D1
Lindsell St. SE10	33	G4
Lindsey Ms. N1	11	B4
Lindsey St. EC1	18	A4
Linford St. SW8	31	C4
Ling Rd. E16	20	D4
Lingards Rd. SE13	40	G2
Lingfield Cres. SE9	42	F2
Lingham St. SW9	31	E5
Linhope St. NW1	16	G3
Link St. E9	12	A2
Linnell Rd. SE5	32	D5
Linnet Ms. SW12	38	A5
Linom Rd. SW4	38	E2
Linscott Rd. E5	12	A1
Linsdell Rd., Bark.	14	E5
Linsey St. SE16	25	F5
Linstead Ct. SE9	42	G4
Linstead St. NW6	9	B4
Linstead Way SW18	36	G5
Linton Gdns. E6	21	A5
Linton Rd., Bark.	14	E4
Linton St. N1	11	B5
Lintons, The, Bark.	14	E4
Linver Rd. SW6	30	A5
Linwood Clo. SE5	32	E5
Lion Clo. SE4	40	E4
Lion Rd. E6	21	B4
Lionel Gdns. SE9	41	G3
Lionel Rd. SE9	41	G3
Liphook Cres. SE23	40	A5
Lisburne Rd. NW3	9	G1
Lisford St. SE15	32	E4
Lisgar Ter. W14	23	A5
Liskeard Gdns. SE3	34	D4
Lisle St. WC2	**43**	**D3**
Lissenden Gdns. NW5	10	A1
Lisson Grn. Est. NW8	16	F2
Lisson Gro. NW1	16	F3
Lisson Gro. NW8	16	E3
Lisson St. NW1	16	F4
Lister Ho. SE3	34	B2
Lister Ms. N7	10	F1
Liston Rd. SW4	38	C1
Litchfield Ave. E15	13	B3
Litchfield Gdns. NW10	8	C3
Litchfield St. WC2	**43**	**D3**
Lithos Rd. NW3	9	D3
Little Argyll St. W1	**43**	**A2**
Little Boltons, The SW10	30	C1
Little Britain EC1	18	A4
Little Chester St. SW1	24	B4
Little Dorrit Ct. SE1	25	B3
Little Essex St. WC2	**43**	**J3**
Little Heath SE7	35	A1
Little Ilford La. E12	14	B1
Little Marlborough St. W1	**43**	**A2**
Little New St. EC4	**44**	**A1**
Little Newport St. WC2	**43**	**D3**
Little Russell St. WC1	17	E4

Little St. James's St. SW1 43 A6
Little Trinity La. EC4 44 E3
Littlebury Rd. SW4 38 D1
Littlecombe SE7 34 E2
Littlecombe Clo. SW15 36 F4
Littlecote Clo. SW19 36 F5
Littlecroft SE9 42 C1
Littlewood SE13 40 G3
Livermere Rd. E8 11 E5
Liverpool Gro. SE17 32 C1
Liverpool Rd. E16 20 B4
Liverpool Rd. N1 10 G4
Liverpool Rd. N7 10 G2
Liverpool St. EC2 18 D4
Livingstone Rd. E15 12 G5
Livingstone Wk. SW11 37 E1
Livonia St. W1 43 B2
Lizard St. EC1 18 B2
Lizban St. SE3 34 E3
Llanover Rd. SE18 35 C2
Lloyd Baker St. WC1 17 F2
Lloyd Rd. E6 14 B5
Lloyd Sq. WC1 17 G2
Lloyd St. WC1 17 G2
Lloyd's Ave. EC3 44 J2
Lloyds Pl. SE3 34 B5
Loampit Hill SE13 33 E5
Loampit Vale SE13 40 F1
Loats Rd. SW2 38 E4
Lochaber Rd. SE13 41 B2
Lochaline St. W6 29 E2
Lochinvar St. SW12 38 B5
Lochnagar St. E14 19 G4
Lock Chase SE3 41 B1
Lockesfield Pl. E14 33 F1
Lockhart Clo. N7 10 F3
Lockhart St. E3 19 D3
Lockhurst St. E5 12 B1
Lockington Rd. SW8 31 B4
Lockmead Rd. SE13 40 G1
Locksley Est. E14 19 D5
Locksley St. E14 19 D4
Lockwood Sq. SE16 25 G4
Loddiges Rd. E9 12 A4
Loder St. SE15 33 A3
Lodge Ave. SW14 36 A1
Lodge Rd. NW8 16 E2
Lodore St. E14 19 G5
Loftie St. SE16 25 F3
Lofting Rd. N1 10 F4
Loftus Rd. W12 22 D2
Logan Ms. W8 23 B5
Logan Pl. W8 23 B5
Lollard St. SE11 24 G5
Loman St. SE1 25 A3
Lomas Ct. E8 11 E4
Lomas St. E1 18 F4
Lombard Ct. EC3 44 G3
Lombard La. EC4 44 A2
Lombard Rd. SW11 30 E5
Lombard St. EC3 44 G2
Lombard Wall SE7 27 E4
Lomond Gro. SE5 32 C3
Loncroft Rd. SE5 32 D2
Londesborough Rd. N16 11 D1
London Bri. EC4 44 G5
London Bri. SE1 44 G5
London Bri. St. SE1 44 G6
London Bri. Wk. SE1 44 G5
London Flds. E8 11 G4
London Flds. E. Side E8 11 G4
London Flds. W. Side E8 11 F4
London Ind. Pk. E6 21 D4
London La. E8 11 G4
London Rd. E13 20 D1
London Rd. SE1 25 A4
London Rd., Bark. 14 D4
London St. EC3 44 J3
London St. W2 16 E5
London Wall EC2 18 B4
Long Acre WC2 43 E3
Long Ct. WC2 43 D4
Long Dr. W3 15 A5
Long La. EC1 18 A4
Long La. SE1 25 C3
Long Pond Rd. SE3 34 B4
Long Reach Ct., Bark. 21 F1
Long Rd. SW4 38 B2
Long St. E2 18 E2
Long Wk. SE18 35 D2
Long Yd. WC1 17 F3
Longbeach Rd. SW11 37 G1
Longbridge Rd., Bark. 14 F3
Longbridge Way SE13 40 G3
Longfield Est. SE1 25 E5
Longfield St. SW18 37 B5
Longford St. NW1 17 B3
Longhedge St. SW11 31 A5
Longhope Clo. SE15 32 D2
Longhurst Rd. SE13 41 A3
Longley St. SE1 25 F5
Longmoore St. SW1 24 C5
Longnor Rd. E1 19 B2
Longridge Rd. SW5 23 B5
Longshore SE8 26 D5
Longstaff Cres. SW18 37 B4
Longstaff Rd. SW18 37 B4
Longstone Ave. NW10 8 B4
Longwood Dr. SW15 36 C4
Lonsdale Ave. E6 20 G2
Lonsdale Rd. NW6 9 A5
Lonsdale Rd. SW13 29 B4
Lonsdale Rd. W4 22 B5
Lonsdale Rd. W11 16 A5
Lonsdale Sq. N1 10 G5
Loraine Rd. N7 10 F1
Lord Hills Rd. W2 16 C4
Lord North St. SW1 24 E4
Lord Roberts Ter. SE18 35 C1
Lord St. E16 28 A2
Lord Warwick St. SE18 28 B4
Lordship La. SE22 39 E4
Lorenzo St. WC1 17 F2
Loris Rd. W6 22 E4
Lorn Rd. SW9 31 F5
Lorne Gdns. W11 22 F3
Lorne Rd. E7 13 E1
Lorrimore Rd. SE17 32 A2
Lorrimore Sq. SE17 32 A2
Lothbury EC2 44 F1
Lothian Rd. SW9 32 A4
Lothrop St. W10 15 G2
Lots Rd. SW10 30 D3
Loudoun Rd. NW8 9 D5
Lough Rd. N7 10 F2
Loughborough Pk. SW9 39 A2
Loughborough Rd. SW9 31 G5
Loughborough St. SE11 31 F1
Louisa St. E1 19 B3
Louise Rd. E15 13 B3
Louvaine Rd. SW11 37 E2
Lovage App. E6 21 A4
Lovat La. EC3 44 H4
Love La. EC2 44 E1
Love La. SE18 28 D5
Love Wk. SE5 32 C5
Lovegrove St. SE1 32 F1
Lovegrove Wk. E14 26 G2
Lovelace Grn. SE9 42 B1
Lovelinch Clo. SE15 33 A2
Lovell Ho. E8 11 F5
Loveridge Rd. NW6 9 A3
Lovers Wk. SE10 34 B3
Lover's Wk. W1 24 A2
Lowbrook Rd., Ilf. 14 D1
Lowden Rd. SE24 39 B2
Lowell St. E14 19 C5
Lower Addison Gdns. W14 22 G3
Lower Belgrave St. SW1 24 B4
Lower Clapton Rd. E5 12 A2
Lower Common S. SW15 36 D1
Lower Grosvenor Pl. SW1 24 B4
Lower James St. W1 43 B3
Lower John St. W1 43 B3
Lower Lea Crossing E14 27 B1
Lower Mall W6 29 D1
Lower Marsh SE1 24 F3
Lower Merton Ri. NW3 9 F4
Lower Richmond Rd. SW15 36 D1
Lower Rd. SE8 26 B5
Lower Robert St. WC2 43 F4
Lower Sloane St. SW1 24 A5
Lower Thames St. EC3 44 G4
Lowfield Rd. NW6 9 B4
Lowman Rd. N7 10 F1
Lowndes Clo. SW1 24 A4
Lowndes Pl. SW1 24 A4
Lowndes Sq. SW1 23 G3
Lowndes St. SW1 23 G4
Lowth Rd. SE5 32 B5
Lowther Hill SE23 40 C5
Lowther Rd. SW13 29 B4
Loxford Ave. E6 20 G1
Loxford La., Ilf. 14 E2
Loxford Rd., Bark. 14 D3
Lubbock St. SE14 33 A3
Lucan Pl. SW3 23 F5
Lucas Ave. E13 13 E5
Lucas St. SE8 33 E4
Lucerne Rd. N5 11 A1
Lucey Rd. SE16 25 F4
Lucknow St. SE18 35 G3
Lucorn Clo. SE12 41 C4
Ludgate Bdy. EC4 44 B2
Ludgate Circ. EC4 44 B2
Ludgate Hill EC4 44 B2
Ludgate Sq. EC4 44 C2
Ludovick Wk. SW15 36 A2
Ludwick Ms. SE14 33 C3
Lugard Rd. SE15 32 G5
Luke Ho. E1 18 G5
Luke St. EC2 18 D3
Lukin St. E1 19 A5
Lulworth Rd. SE15 32 G5
Lumley Ct. WC2 43 F4
Lumley St. W1 17 A5
Lupton St. NW5 10 C1
Lupus St. SW1 31 B1
Lurgan Ave. W6 29 F2
Lurline Gdns. SW11 31 A4
Luscombe Way SW8 31 E3
Lushington Rd. NW10 15 D1
Luton Pl. SE10 33 G3
Luton St. NW8 16 E3
Luttrell Ave. SW15 36 D3
Luxborough St. W1 17 A4
Luxemburg Gdns. W6 22 F5
Luxford St. SE16 26 B5
Luxmore St. SE4 33 D4
Luxor St. SE5 39 B1
Lyal Rd. E3 19 C1
Lyall Ms. SW1 24 A4
Lyall St. SW1 24 A4
Lydden Ct. SE9 42 G4
Lydden Gro. SW18 37 C5
Lydden Rd. SW18 37 C5
Lydeard Rd. E6 14 B4
Lydford Rd. NW2 8 E3
Lydford Rd. W9 16 A3
Lydon Rd. SW4 38 C1
Lyford Rd. SW18 37 E5
Lyham Clo. SW2 38 E4
Lyham Rd. SW2 38 E3
Lyme Fm. Rd. SE12 41 D2
Lyme St. NW1 10 C4
Lymington Rd. NW6 9 C3
Lympstone Gdns. SE15 32 F3
Lyncott Cres. SW4 38 B2
Lyncroft Gdns. NW6 9 B2
Lyndale NW2 9 A1
Lyndale Clo. SE3 34 C2
Lyndhurst Gdns. NW3 9 E2
Lyndhurst Gdns., Bark. 14 G3
Lyndhurst Gro. SE15 32 D5
Lyndhurst Rd. NW3 9 E2
Lyndhurst Sq. SE15 32 E4
Lyndhurst Ter. NW3 9 E2
Lyndhurst Way SE15 32 E4
Lynette Ave. SW4 38 B4
Lynn Rd. SW12 38 B5
Lynne Way NW10 8 A3
Lynsted Gdns. SE9 41 G1
Lynton Rd. NW6 9 A5
Lynton Rd. SE1 25 E5
Lyon Ind. Est., Bark. 21 G1
Lyons Pl. NW8 16 E3
Lyons Wk. W14 22 G5
Lyric Rd. SW13 29 B4
Lysia St. SW6 29 F3
Lysias Rd. SW12 38 B4
Lytcott Gro. SE22 39 E3
Lytham St. SE17 32 C1
Lytton Gro. SW15 36 F3
Lyveden Rd. SE3 34 E3

M

Mabledon Pl. WC1 17 D2
Mablethorpe Rd. SW6 29 G3
Mabley St. E9 12 C2
Macarthur Ter. SE7 34 G2
Macaulay Ct. SW4 38 B1
Macaulay Rd. E6 20 G1
Macaulay Rd. SW4 38 B1
Macaulay Sq. SW4 38 B2
Macauley Ms. SE13 33 G4
Macbean St. SE18 28 D4
Macbeth St. W6 29 D1
Macclesfield Bri. NW1 16 F1
Macclesfield Rd. EC1 18 B2
Macclesfield St. W1 43 D3
Macdonald Rd. E7 13 D1
Macduff Rd. SW11 31 A4
Mace St. E2 19 B1
Macfarlane Rd. W12 22 E2
Macgregor Rd. E16 20 F4
Machell Rd. SE15 40 A1

Mackay Rd. SW4	38	B1
Mackennal St. NW8	16	F1
Mackenzie Rd. N7	10	F3
Mackeson Rd. NW3	9	G1
Mackie Rd. SW2	38	G5
Macklin St. WC2	**43**	**F1**
Macks Rd. SE16	25	F5
Mackworth St. NW1	17	C2
Maclean Rd. SE23	40	C4
Macleod St. SE17	32	B1
Maclise Rd. W14	22	G4
Macoma Rd. SE18	35	F2
Macoma Ter. SE18	35	F2
Maconochies Rd. E14	33	F1
Macquarie Way E14	26	F5
Macroom Rd. W9	16	A2
Maddams St. E3	19	F3
Maddox St. W1	24	B1
Madras Pl. N7	10	G3
Madras Rd., Ilf.	14	D1
Madrid Rd. SW13	29	C4
Madrigal La. SE5	32	A3
Madron St. SE17	32	D1
Mafeking Ave. E6	21	A1
Mafeking Rd. E16	20	C3
Magdalen St. SE1	**44**	**H6**
Magdalene Gdns. E6	21	C3
Magee St. SE11	31	G2
Magnolia Pl. SW4	38	E3
Magpie All. EC4	**44**	**A2**
Magpie Clo. E7	13	C2
Maguire St. SE1	25	E3
Mahogany Clo. SE16	26	C2
Maida Ave. W2	16	D4
Maida Vale W9	16	C1
Maiden La. NW1	10	D4
Maiden La. SE1	**44**	**E5**
Maiden La. WC2	**43**	**F3**
Maiden Rd. E15	13	B4
Maidenstone Hill SE10	33	G4
Maidstone Bldgs. SE1	**44**	**F6**
Maitland Clo. SE10	33	F3
Maitland Pk. Est. NW3	9	G3
Maitland Pk. Rd. NW3	9	G3
Maitland Pk. Vill. NW3	9	G3
Maitland Rd. E15	13	C3
Majendie Rd. SE18	35	F1
Major Rd. E15	13	A2
Makins St. SW3	23	F5
Malabar St. E14	26	E3
Malbrook Rd. SW15	36	D2
Malcolm Pl. E2	19	A3
Malcolm Rd. E1	19	A3
Malden Cres. NW1	10	A3
Malden Rd. NW5	9	G2
Maldon Clo. N1	11	B5
Maldon Clo. SE5	39	D1
Malet Pl. WC1	17	D3
Malet St. WC1	17	D3
Malfort Rd. SE5	39	D1
Mall Rd. W6	29	D1
Mallard Clo. E9	12	D3
Mallet Rd. SE13	41	A4
Mallinson Rd. SW11	37	F3
Mallord St. SW3	30	E2
Mallory Clo. SE4	40	C2
Mallory St. NW8	16	F3
Malmesbury Rd. E3	19	D2
Malmesbury Rd. E16	20	B4
Malmesbury Ter. E16	20	C4
Malpas Rd. E8	11	G3
Malpas Rd. SE4	33	D5
Malt St. SE1	32	F2
Maltby St. SE1	25	E4
Maltings Pl. SW6	30	C4
Malton St. SE18	35	G2
Maltravers St. WC2	**43**	**H3**
Malvern Clo. W10	16	A4
Malvern Ct. SW7	23	E5
Malvern Gdns. NW6	16	A1
Malvern Pl. NW6	16	A2
Malvern Rd. E6	14	A5
Malvern Rd. E8	11	F4
Malvern Rd. NW6	16	B2
Malvern Ter. N1	10	G5
Malwood Rd. SW12	38	B4
Malyons Rd. SE13	40	F4
Malyons Ter. SE13	40	F3
Manaton Clo. SE15	39	G1
Manbey Gro. E15	13	B3
Manbey Pk. Rd. E15	13	B3
Manbey Rd. E15	13	B3
Manbey St. E15	13	B3
Manborough Ave. E6	21	B2
Manbre Rd. W6	29	E2
Manchester Dr. W10	15	G3
Manchester Gro. E14	33	G1
Manchester Rd. E14	33	G1
Manchester Sq. W1	17	A5
Manchester St. W1	17	A4
Manchuria Rd. SW11	38	A4
Manciple St. SE1	25	C3
Mandalay Rd. SW4	38	C3
Mandela Rd. E16	20	D5
Mandela St. NW1	10	C5
Mandela St. SW9	31	G3
Mandela Way SE1	25	D5
Mandeville Pl. W1	17	A5
Mandrell Rd. SW2	38	E3
Manette St. W1	**43**	**D2**
Manfred Rd. SW15	37	A3
Manger Rd. N7	10	E3
Manilla St. E14	26	E3
Manley St. NW1	10	A5
Manor Ave. SE4	33	D5
Manor Est. SE16	25	G5
Manor Flds. SW15	36	F4
Manor Gro. SE15	33	A2
Manor Ho. Dr. NW6	8	F4
Manor La. SE12	41	B4
Manor La. SE13	41	B3
Manor La. Ter. SE13	41	B2
Manor Ms. SE4	33	D5
Manor Pk. SE13	41	A3
Manor Pk. Rd. E12	13	G1
Manor Pk. Rd. NW10	8	B5
Manor Pl. SE17	32	A1
Manor Rd. E15	20	B1
Manor Rd. E16	20	B3
Manor Way SE3	41	C2
Manorbrook SE3	41	D2
Manresa Rd. SW3	30	F1
Mansell St. E1	18	E5
Mansergh Clo. SE18	35	A3
Mansfield Rd. NW3	9	G2
Mansfield St. W1	17	B4
Mansford St. E2	18	F1
Mansion Ho. Pl. EC4	**44**	**F2**
Manson Ms. SW7	23	D5
Manson Pl. SW7	23	E5
Manstone Rd. NW2	8	G2
Manthorp Rd. SE18	35	E1
Mantle Rd. SE4	40	C1
Mantua St. SW11	37	E1
Mantus Rd. E1	19	A3
Manwood Rd. SE4	40	D3
Manwood St. E16	28	B2
Mape St. E2	18	G3
Mapesbury Rd. NW2	8	G4
Maple Ave. W3	22	A2
Maple Clo. SW4	38	D4
Maple St. W1	17	C4
Mapledene Rd. E8	11	F4
Maplestead Rd. SW2	38	F5
Mapleton Cres. SW18	37	C4
Mapleton Rd. SW18	37	B4
Maplin Rd. E16	20	D5
Maplin St. E3	19	D2
Marban Rd. W9	16	A2
Marble Arch W1	23	G1
Marble Quay E1	25	F2
Marchbank Rd. W14	30	A2
Marchmont St. WC1	17	E3
Marchwood Clo. SE5	32	D3
Marcia Rd. SE1	25	D5
Marcilly Rd. SW18	37	E3
Marco Rd. W6	22	D4
Marcon Pl. E8	11	G2
Marcus Ct. E15	13	B5
Marcus Garvey Way SE24	38	G2
Marcus St. E15	13	B5
Marcus St. SW18	37	C4
Marcus Ter. SW18	37	C4
Marden Sq. SE16	25	G4
Mardon St. E14	19	C4
Mare St. E8	11	G5
Maresfield Gdns. NW3	9	D2
Margaret Ct. W1	**43**	**A1**
Margaret St. W1	17	B5
Margaretta Ter. SW3	30	F2
Margate Rd. SW2	38	E3
Margery Pk. Rd. E7	13	D3
Margery St. WC1	17	G2
Margravine Gdns. W6	29	F1
Margravine Rd. W6	29	F1
Maria Ter. E1	19	B3
Marian Pl. E2	18	G1
Marian Way NW10	8	B4
Marigold All. SE1	**44**	**B4**
Marigold St. SE16	25	G3
Marina Dr., Well.	35	G5
Marine Dr. SE18	28	B5
Marinefield Rd. SW6	30	C5
Mariners Ms. E14	27	A5
Marischal Rd. SE13	41	A1
Maritime St. E3	19	D3
Marjorie Gro. SW11	37	G2
Mark La. EC3	**44**	**J3**
Market Ct. W1	**43**	**A1**
Market Hill SE18	28	C4
Market Pl. W1	**43**	**A1**
Market Rd. N7	10	E3
Market St. E6	21	B1
Market St. SE18	28	C5
Markham Pl. SW3	30	G1
Markham Sq. SW3	30	G1
Markham St. SW3	30	F1
Marl Rd. SW18	37	C2
Marlborough Ave. E8	11	F5
Marlborough Bldgs. SW3	23	F5
Marlborough Ct. W8	23	B5
Marlborough Gro. SE1	32	F1
Marlborough Hill NW8	9	D5
Marlborough La. SE7	34	F2
Marlborough Pl. NW8	16	D1
Marlborough Rd. E7	13	F4
Marlborough Rd. SW1	**43**	**B6**
Marlborough St. SW3	23	F5
Marloes Rd. W8	23	C4
Marlow Ct. NW6	8	F4
Marlow Rd. E6	21	B2
Marlow Way SE16	26	B3
Marlowe Gdns. SE9	42	C4
Marlowes, The NW8	9	E5
Marmion Rd. SW11	38	A2
Marmont Rd. SE15	32	F4
Marmora Rd. SE22	40	A4
Marne St. W10	15	G2
Marney Rd. SW11	38	A2
Marnham Ave. NW2	8	G1
Marnock Rd. SE4	40	D3
Maroon St. E14	19	C4
Marquess Est. N1	11	B3
Marquess Rd. N1	11	C3
Marquis Rd. NW1	10	D3
Marrick Clo. SW15	36	C2
Marriott Rd. E15	13	B5
Marsala Rd. SE13	40	F2
Marsden Rd. SE15	39	E1
Marsden St. NW5	10	A3
Marsh Hill E9	12	C2
Marsh Wall E14	26	E2
Marshall St. W1	**43**	**B2**
Marshall's Gro. SE18	28	A5
Marshalsea Rd. SE1	25	B3
Marsham St. SW1	24	D4
Marshbrook Clo. SE3	41	G1
Marshfield St. E14	26	G4
Marshgate La. E15	12	F4
Marsland Clo. SE17	32	A1
Mart St. WC2	**43**	**F3**
Martello St. E8	11	G4
Martello Ter. E8	11	G4
Martha Rd. E15	13	B3
Martha St. E1	18	G5
Martin Bowes Rd. SE9	42	B1
Martin La. EC4	**44**	**G3**
Martindale Rd. SW12	38	B5
Martineau Est. E1	26	A1
Martineau Rd. N5	11	A1
Martlett Ct. WC2	**43**	**F2**
Marville Rd. SW6	30	A3
Mary Ann Gdns. SE8	33	E2
Mary Datchelor Clo. SE5	32	C4
Mary Grn. NW8	9	C5
Mary Pl. W11	22	G1
Mary St. N1	11	B5
Marybank SE18	28	B5
Maryland Pk. E15	13	B2
Maryland Rd. E15	13	A2
Maryland Sq. E15	13	B2
Maryland St. E15	13	A2
Marylands Rd. W9	16	B3
Marylebone High St. W1	17	A4
Marylebone La. W1	17	A5
Marylebone Ms. W1	17	B4
Marylebone Pas. W1	**43**	**B1**
Marylebone Rd. NW1	16	F4
Marylebone St. W1	17	A4
Marylee Way SE11	24	F5
Maryon Gro. SE7	28	A5
Maryon Rd. SE7	28	A5
Maryon Rd. SE18	28	A5
Masbro Rd. W14	22	F4
Mascalls Rd. SE7	34	F2
Mascotte Rd. SW15	36	F2
Masefield Gdns. E6	21	C3
Mashie Rd. W3	15	A5
Maskelyn Clo. SW11	30	F4
Mason Clo. E16	27	D1
Mason St. SE17	25	C5
Masons Ave. EC2	**44**	**F1**
Masons Hill SE18	28	D5
Mason's Pl. EC1	18	B2
Mason's Yd. SW1	**43**	**B5**
Massingham St. E1	19	B3
Mast Ho. Ter. E14	26	E5
Master Gunner Pl. SE18	35	A3
Masterman Rd. E6	21	A2
Masters St. E1	19	B4
Mastmaker Rd. E14	26	E3
Matham Gro. SE22	39	E2
Matheson Rd. W14	23	A5
Mathews Pk. Ave. E15	13	C3
Matilda St. N1	10	F5

Matlock Clo. SE24	39	B2
Matlock St. E14	19	C5
Matthew Clo. W10	15	F3
Matthew Parker St. SW1	24	D3
Matthews Ave. E6	21	C1
Matthews St. SW11	30	G5
Matthews Yd. WC2	**43**	**E2**
Matthias Rd. N16	11	C2
Maud Gdns. E13	13	C5
Maud Rd. E13	20	C1
Maud St. E16	20	C4
Maude Rd. SE5	32	D4
Maudslay Rd. SE9	42	B1
Mauleverer Rd. SW2	38	E3
Maunsel St. SW1	24	D5
Maurice St. W12	15	D5
Mauritius Rd. SE10	27	B5
Maverton Rd. E3	12	E5
Mawbey Est. SE1	32	E1
Mawbey Pl. SE1	32	E1
Mawbey St. SW8	31	E3
Maxey Rd. SE18	28	E5
Maxted Rd. SE15	39	E1
Maxwell Rd. SW6	30	C3
May Rd. E13	20	D1
Mayall Rd. SE24	39	A3
Maybury Gdns. NW10	8	D3
Maybury Rd. E13	20	F3
Mayday Gdns. SE3	35	A5
Mayerne Rd. SE9	41	G3
Mayfair Pl. W1	24	B2
Mayfield Ave. W4	22	A5
Mayfield Clo. SW4	38	D3
Mayfield Rd. E8	11	E4
Mayfield Rd. E13	20	C3
Mayfield Rd. W12	22	A3
Mayflower Rd. SW9	38	E1
Mayford Clo. SW12	37	G5
Mayford Rd. SW12	37	G5
Maygood St. N1	17	F1
Maygrove Rd. NW6	9	A3
Mayhill Rd. SE7	34	E2
Mayo Rd. NW10	8	A3
Mayola Rd. E5	12	A1
Mayplace La. SE18	35	D3
Mays Ct. WC2	**43**	**E4**
Maysoule Rd. SW11	37	E2
Mayville Rd., Ilf.	14	D2
Maze Hill SE3	34	B3
Maze Hill SE10	34	B2
Mazenod Ave. NW6	9	B4
McAuley Clo. SE1	24	G4
McAuley Clo. SE9	42	D3
McCall Cres. SE7	35	A1
McDermott Clo. SW11	37	F1
McDermott Rd. SE15	39	F1
McDowall Rd. SE5	32	B4
McDowell Clo. E16	20	C4
McEwan Way E15	13	A5
McGrath Rd. E15	13	C2
McGregor Rd. W11	16	A4
McKerrell Rd. SE15	32	F4
McLeod's Ms. SW7	23	C5
McMillan St. SE8	33	E2
McNeil Rd. SE5	32	D5
Mead Pl. E9	12	A3
Meadcroft Rd. SE11	32	A2
Meadow Ms. SW8	31	F2
Meadow Pl. SW8	31	E3
Meadow Rd. SW8	31	F3
Meadow Row SE1	25	B4
Meadowbank NW3	9	G4
Meadowbank SE3	41	C1
Meadowbank Clo. SW6	29	E3
Meadowcourt Rd. SE3	41	C2
Meadowside SE9	41	F2
Meadway, Ilf.	14	G1
Meakin Est. SE1	25	D4
Meanley Rd. E12	14	A1
Meard St. W1	**43**	**C2**
Meath Rd. E15	20	C1
Meath St. SW11	31	B4
Mecklenburgh Pl. WC1	17	F3
Mecklenburgh Sq. WC1	17	F3
Medburn St. NW1	17	D1
Medebourne Clo. SE3	41	D1
Medfield St. SW15	36	C5
Median Rd. E5	12	A2
Medlar St. SE5	32	B4
Medley Rd. NW6	9	B3
Medora Rd. SW2	38	F5
Medusa Rd. SE6	40	F4
Medway Rd. E3	19	C1
Medway St. SW1	24	D4
Medwin St. SW4	38	F2
Meerbrook Rd. SE3	41	F1
Meeson Rd. E15	13	C5
Meeson St. E5	12	C1
Meeting Ho. La. SE15	32	G4
Mehetabel Rd. E9	12	A3
Melba Way SE13	33	F4
Melbourne Gro. SE22	39	D2
Melbourne Ms. SE6	40	G5
Melbourne Ms. SW9	31	G4
Melbourne Pl. WC2	**43**	**H2**
Melbourne Rd. E6	14	B5
Melbury Ct. W8	23	A4
Melbury Rd. W14	23	A4
Melbury Ter. NW1	16	F3
Melcombe Pl. NW1	16	G4
Melcombe St. NW1	16	G3
Melford Ave., Bark.	14	G3
Melford Rd. E6	21	B3
Melford Rd. SE22	39	F5
Melgund Rd. N5	10	G2
Melina Pl. NW8	16	E2
Melina Rd. W12	22	D3
Melior St. SE1	25	C3
Melling St. SE18	35	G2
Mellish St. E14	26	E4
Mellitus St. W12	15	B5
Melody Rd. SW18	37	D3
Melon Rd. SE15	32	F4
Melrose Ave. NW2	8	D2
Melrose Gdns. W6	22	E4
Melrose Rd. SW13	29	B5
Melrose Rd. SW18	37	A4
Melrose Ter. W6	22	E3
Melthorpe Gdns. SE3	34	G4
Melton Ct. SW7	23	E5
Melton St. NW1	17	C2
Melville Rd. SW13	29	C4
Memorial Ave. E15	20	B2
Mendip Rd. SW11	37	D1
Mendora Rd. SW6	29	G3
Menelik Rd. NW2	8	G1
Mentmore Ter. E8	11	G4
Mepham St. SE1	**43**	**J6**
Merbury Clo. SE13	41	A3
Merbury Rd. SE28	28	G3
Mercator Rd. SE13	41	A2
Mercer St. WC2	**43**	**E2**
Merceron St. E1	18	G3
Mercers Clo. SE10	27	C5
Mercers Pl. W6	22	E5
Merchant St. E3	19	D2
Mercia Gro. SE13	40	G2
Mercier Rd. SW15	36	G3
Mercury Way SE14	33	B2
Mercy Ter. SE13	40	F2
Mere Clo. SW15	36	F5
Meredith Ave. NW2	8	E2
Meredith St. E13	20	D2
Meredyth Rd. SW13	29	C5
Meretone Clo. SE4	40	C2
Mereworth Dr. SE18	35	D3
Meridian Gate E14	26	G3
Meridian Rd. SE7	34	G3
Meridian Trd. Est. SE7	27	E5
Merifield Rd. SE9	41	F2
Merivale Rd. SW15	36	G2
Mermaid Ct. SE1	25	C3
Mermaid Ct. SE16	26	D2
Merredene St. SW2	38	F4
Merrick Sq. SE1	25	B4
Merriman Rd. SE3	34	F4
Merrington Rd. SW6	30	B2
Merritt Rd. SE4	40	D3
Merrow St. SE17	32	B2
Merryfield SE3	34	C5
Mersea Ho., Bark.	14	D3
Merthyr Ter. SW13	29	D2
Merton Ave. W4	22	B5
Merton Ri. NW3	9	F4
Merton Rd. SW18	37	B3
Merttins Rd. SE15	40	B3
Mervan Rd. SW2	38	G2
Messent Rd. SE9	41	F3
Messeter Pl. SE9	42	C4
Messina Ave. NW6	9	B4
Meteor St. SW11	38	A2
Methley St. SE11	31	G1
Methwold Rd. W10	15	F4
Mews St. E1	25	F2
Mexfield Rd. SW15	37	A3
Meymott St. SE1	**44**	**B6**
Meynell Cres. E9	12	B4
Meynell Gdns. E9	12	B4
Meynell Rd. E9	12	B4
Meyrick Rd. NW10	8	C3
Meyrick Rd. SW11	37	E1
Micawber St. N1	18	B2
Michael Rd. SW6	30	C4
Michaels Clo. SE13	41	B2
Micheldever Rd. SE12	41	B4
Michigan Ave. E12	14	B1
Micklethwaite Rd. SW6	30	B2
Middle Fld. NW8	9	E5
Middle Pk. Ave. SE9	41	G4
Middle Row W10	15	G3
Middle Temple La. EC4	**43**	**J2**
Middle Yd. SE1	**44**	**H5**
Middlesex St. E1	18	D4
Middleton Dr. SE16	26	B3
Middleton Gro. N7	10	E2
Middleton Rd. E8	11	E4
Middleton St. E2	18	G2
Middleton Way SE13	41	A2
Midland Rd. NW1	17	D1
Midland Ter. NW10	15	A3
Midlothian Rd. E3	19	C4
Midstrath Rd. NW10	8	A1
Miers Clo. E6	14	C5
Milborne Gro. SW10	30	D1
Milborne St. E9	12	A3
Milborough Cres. SE12	41	B4
Milcote St. SE1	25	A3
Mildenhall Rd. E5	12	A1
Mildmay Ave. N1	11	C3
Mildmay Gro. N1	11	C2
Mildmay Pk. N1	11	C2
Mildmay Rd. N1	11	C2
Mildmay St. N1	11	C3
Mile End Pl. E1	19	B3
Mile End Rd. E1	19	A4
Mile End Rd. E3	19	C3
Miles St. SW8	31	E2
Milfoil St. W12	22	C1
Milford La. WC2	**43**	**J3**
Milk St. E16	28	D2
Milk St. EC2	**44**	**E1**
Milk Yd. E1	26	A1
Milkwell Yd. SE5	32	B4
Milkwood Rd. SE24	39	A3
Mill Hill Rd. SW13	29	C5
Mill La. NW6	8	G2
Mill La. SE18	35	C1
Mill Rd. E16	27	E2
Mill Row N1	11	D5
Mill Shot Clo. SW6	29	E4
Mill St. SE1	25	E3
Mill St. W1	**43**	**A3**
Millais Ave. E12	14	C2
Millais Rd. E11	12	G1
Millbank SW1	24	E5
Millbank Twr. SW1	24	E5
Millbank Way SE12	41	D3
Millbrook Ave., Well.	42	F2
Millbrook Rd. SW9	39	A1
Millender Wk. SE16	26	A5
Miller St. NW1	17	C1
Miller's Ave. E8	11	E2
Miller's Ter. E8	11	E2
Millers Way W6	22	E3
Millfields Rd. E5	12	A1
Millgrove St. SW11	31	A4
Millharbour E14	26	F4
Millman Ms. WC1	17	F3
Millman St. WC1	17	F3
Millmark Gro. SE14	33	C5
Millstream Rd. SE1	25	E3
Millwall Dock Rd. E14	26	E4
Milman Rd. NW6	15	F1
Milmans St. SW10	30	E2
Milne Gdns. SE9	42	A3
Milner Pl. N1	10	G5
Milner Rd. E15	20	B2
Milner Sq. N1	11	A4
Milner St. SW3	23	G5
Milo Rd. SE22	39	E4
Milroy Wk. SE1	**44**	**B5**
Milson Rd. W14	22	F4
Milton Ave. E6	13	G4
Milton Clo. SE1	25	E5
Milton Ct. Rd. SE14	33	C2
Milton Gro. N16	11	C1
Milton Rd. SE24	39	A4
Milton St. EC2	18	C4
Milverton Rd. NW6	8	E4
Milverton St. SE11	31	G1
Mimosa St. SW6	30	A4
Mina Rd. SE17	32	D1
Minard Rd. SE6	41	B5
Mincing La. EC3	**44**	**H3**
Minera Ms. SW1	24	A5
Mineral St. SE18	28	G5
Minerva Clo. SW9	31	G3
Minerva St. E2	18	G1
Minet Ave. NW10	15	A1
Minet Gdns. NW10	15	A1
Minet Rd. SW9	32	A5
Minford Gdns. W14	22	F3
Ming St. E14	26	E1
Minories EC3	18	E5
Minson Rd. E9	12	B5
Minstead Gdns. SW15	36	B5
Minster Rd. NW2	8	G2
Mintern St. N1	18	C1
Mirabel Rd. SW6	30	A3
Mirfield St. SE7	27	G4
Miriam Rd. SE18	35	G1
Mission Pl. SE15	32	F4
Mitcham Rd. E6	21	A2
Mitchell St. EC1	18	B3

Mitchison Rd. N1	11	C3
Mitre Ct. EC2	**44**	**E1**
Mitre Ct. EC4	**44**	**A2**
Mitre Rd. E15	20	B1
Mitre Rd. SE1	24	G3
Mitre Sq. EC3	**44**	**J2**
Mitre St. EC3	**44**	**J2**
Mitre Way NW10	15	D3
Moat Pl. SW9	38	F1
Moberley Rd. SW4	38	D5
Moiety Rd. E14	26	E3
Moira Rd. SE9	42	B2
Molesford Rd. SW6	30	B4
Molesworth St. SE13	40	G2
Molly Huggins Clo. SW12	38	C5
Molyneux St. W1	16	F4
Mona Rd. SE15	33	A5
Mona St. E16	20	C4
Monarch Dr. E16	20	G4
Monck St. SW1	24	D4
Monclar Rd. SE5	39	C2
Moncrieff St. SE15	32	F5
Monega Rd. E7	13	F3
Monega Rd. E12	13	G3
Monier Rd. E3	12	E4
Monk Dr. E16	20	D5
Monk St. SE18	28	C5
Monkton St. SE11	24	G5
Monmouth Rd. E6	21	B2
Monmouth Rd. W2	16	B5
Monmouth St. WC2	**43**	**E3**
Monnow Rd. SE1	32	F1
Monson Rd. NW10	15	C1
Monson Rd. SE14	33	B3
Montacute Rd. SE6	40	D5
Montagu Ms. N. W1	16	G4
Montagu Pl. W1	16	G4
Montagu Sq. W1	16	G4
Montagu St. W1	16	G5
Montague Ave. SE4	40	D2
Montague Clo. SE1	**44**	**F5**
Montague Pl. WC1	17	D4
Montague Rd. E8	11	F2
Montague St. EC1	18	B4
Montague St. WC1	17	E4
Montcalm Rd. SE7	34	G3
Monteagle Ave., Bark.	14	E3
Monteagle Way SE15	39	G1
Montefiore St. SW8	31	B5
Monteith Rd. E3	12	D5
Montem Rd. SE23	40	D5
Montford Pl. SE11	31	G1
Montholme Rd. SW11	37	G4
Montolieu Gdns. SW15	36	D3
Montpelier Gdns. E6	20	G2
Montpelier Gro. NW5	10	C2
Montpelier Pl. SW7	23	F4
Montpelier Rd. SE15	32	G4
Montpelier Row SE3	34	C5
Montpelier Sq. SW7	23	F3
Montpelier St. SW7	23	F4
Montpelier Vale SE3	34	C5
Montpelier Wk. SW7	23	F4
Montreal Pl. WC2	**43**	**G3**
Montrose Ave. NW6	15	G1
Montrose Ave., Well.	42	F1
Montrose Ct. SW7	23	E3
Montrose Pl. SW1	24	A3
Montserrat Rd. SW15	36	G2
Monument Gdns. SE13	40	G3
Monument St. EC3	**44**	**G3**
Monza St. E1	26	A1
Moodkee St. SE16	26	A4
Moody St. E1	19	B2
Moon St. N1	11	A5
Moor La. EC2	18	C4
Moor St. W1	**43**	**D2**
Moordown SE18	35	C4
Moore Pk. Rd. SW6	30	C3
Moore St. SW3	23	G5
Moorehead Way SE3	41	E1
Moorfields EC2	18	C4
Moorgate EC2	18	C4
Moorgate Pl. EC2	**44**	**F1**
Moorhouse Rd. W2	16	B5
Moorland Rd. SW9	39	A2
Moorlands Est. SW9	38	G2
Mora Rd. NW2	8	E1
Mora St. EC1	18	B2
Morant St. E14	26	E1
Morat St. SW9	31	F4
Moravian St. E2	19	A2
Mordaunt St. SW9	38	F1
Morden Clo. SE13	33	G5
Morden Hill SE13	33	G5
Morden La. SE13	33	G4
Morden Rd. SE3	34	D5
Morden Rd. Ms. SE3	34	D5
Morden St. SE13	33	F4
Morden Wf. Rd. SE10	27	B4
More Clo. E16	20	C5
More Clo. W14	22	F5
Morecambe Clo. E1	19	B4
Morecambe St. SE17	25	B5
Moreland St. EC1	18	A2
Morella Rd. SW12	37	G5
Morena St. SE6	40	F5
Moresby Wk. SW8	31	B5
Moreton Pl. SW1	31	C1
Moreton St. SW1	31	C1
Moreton Ter. SW1	31	C1
Morgan Rd. N7	10	G2
Morgan Rd. W10	16	A4
Morgan St. E3	19	C2
Morgan St. E16	20	C4
Morgans La. SE1	**44**	**H6**
Moriatri Clo. N7	10	E1
Morie St. SW18	37	C2
Morley Rd. E15	20	C1
Morley Rd. SE13	40	G2
Morley Rd., Bark.	14	F5
Morley St. SE1	24	G4
Morna Rd. SE5	32	B5
Morning La. E9	12	A3
Mornington Ave. W14	23	A5
Mornington Cres. NW1	17	C1
Mornington Gro. E3	19	E2
Mornington Ms. SE5	32	B4
Mornington Rd. SE8	33	D3
Mornington St. NW1	17	B1
Mornington Ter. NW1	17	B1
Morocco St. SE1	25	D3
Morpeth Gro. E9	12	B5
Morpeth Rd. E9	12	A5
Morpeth St. E2	19	B2
Morpeth Ter. SW1	24	C4
Morris Ave. E12	14	B2
Morris Gdns. SW18	37	B5
Morris Rd. E14	19	F4
Morris Rd. E15	13	A1
Morris St. E1	18	G5
Morrish Rd. SW2	38	E5
Morrison St. SW11	38	A1
Morse Clo. E13	20	D2
Morshead Rd. W9	16	B2
Morten Clo. SW4	38	D4
Mortham St. E15	13	B5
Mortimer Cres. NW6	9	C5
Mortimer Est. NW6	9	C5
Mortimer Pl. NW6	9	C5
Mortimer Rd. E6	21	B2
Mortimer Rd. N1	11	D4
Mortimer Rd. NW10	15	E2
Mortimer St. W1	**43**	**A1**
Mortlake Rd. E16	20	E5
Mortlake Rd., Ilf.	14	E1
Morton Rd. E15	13	C4
Morton Rd. N1	11	B4
Morval Rd. SW2	38	G3
Morville St. E3	19	E1
Moscow Rd. W2	23	C1
Mossbury Rd. SW11	37	F1
Mossford St. E3	19	D3
Mossop St. SW3	23	F5
Mostyn Gdns. NW10	15	F2
Mostyn Gro. E3	19	E1
Mostyn Rd. SW9	31	G4
Motcomb St. SW1	24	A4
Moulins Rd. E9	12	A4
Mount Adon Pk. SE22	39	F5
Mount Pleasant WC1	17	G3
Mount Pleasant Rd. NW10	8	E4
Mount Pleasant Rd. SE13	40	G4
Mount Rd., Ilf.	14	D2
Mount Row W1	24	B1
Mount St. W1	24	A1
Mount Vernon NW3	9	D1
Mountague Pl. E14	26	G1
Mountbatten Clo. SE18	35	G2
Mountfield Rd. E6	21	C1
Mounts Pond Rd. SE3	34	A5
Mountsfield Ct. SE13	41	A4
Movers La., Bark.	14	F5
Mowbray Rd. NW6	8	G4
Mowlem St. E2	18	G1
Mowll St. SW9	31	G3
Moxon St. W1	17	A4
Moylan Rd. W6	29	G2
Mozart St. W10	16	A2
Mudlarks Way SE7	27	E4
Mudlarks Way SE10	27	C4
Muir Rd. E5	11	F1
Muirfield W3	15	A5
Mulberry Clo. SE7	34	G2
Mulberry Clo. SE22	39	F4
Mulberry Wk. SW3	30	E2
Mulgrave Rd. NW10	8	B1
Mulgrave Rd. SW6	30	A2
Muller Rd. SW4	38	D4
Multon Rd. SW18	37	E5
Mulvaney Way SE1	25	C3
Mumford Ct. EC2	**44**	**E1**
Muncaster Rd. SW11	37	G3
Mund St. W14	30	A1
Mundania Rd. SE22	39	G4
Munday Rd. E16	20	D5
Munden St. W14	22	G5
Mundy St. N1	18	D2
Munro Ms. W10	15	G4
Munro Ter. SW10	30	E2
Munster Rd. SW6	29	G3
Munster Sq. NW1	17	B2
Munton Rd. SE17	25	B5
Murdock St. SE15	32	G2
Muriel St. N1	10	F5
Murillo Rd. SE13	41	A2
Murphy St. SE1	24	G3
Murray Gro. N1	18	B1
Murray Ms. NW1	10	D4
Murray Sq. E16	20	D5
Murray St. NW1	10	D4
Mursell Est. SW8	31	F4
Musard Rd. W6	29	G2
Musbury St. E1	19	A5
Muscal W6	29	G2
Muschamp Rd. SE15	39	E1
Muscovy St. EC3	**44**	**J4**
Museum St. WC1	17	E4
Musgrave Cres. SW6	30	B3
Musgrove Rd. SE14	33	B4
Mutrix Rd. NW6	9	B5
Myatt Rd. SW9	32	A4
Myatt's Flds. S. SW9	31	G5
Mycenae Rd. SE3	34	D3
Myddelton Sq. EC1	17	G2
Myddelton St. EC1	17	G2
Myers La. SE14	33	B2
Mylne St. EC1	17	G1
Myrdle St. E1	18	F4
Myron Pl. SE13	40	G1
Myrtle Rd. E6	14	A5
Myrtle Wk. N1	18	D1
Mysore Rd. SW11	37	G1

N

Nadine St. SE7	34	F1
Nagasaki Wk. SE7	27	F4
Nairn St. E14	19	G4
Nairne Gro. SE24	39	C3
Naish Ct. N1	10	E5
Nankin St. E14	19	E5
Nansen Rd. SW11	38	A2
Nantes Clo. SW18	37	D2
Napier Ave. E14	33	E1
Napier Ave. SW6	37	A1
Napier Gro. N1	18	B1
Napier Pl. W14	23	A4
Napier Rd. E6	14	C5
Napier Rd. E11	13	B1
Napier Rd. E15	20	B1
Napier Rd. NW10	15	D2
Napier Rd. W14	22	G4
Napier Ter. N1	11	A3
Narbonne Ave. SW4	38	C3
Narborough St. SW6	30	C5
Narcissus Rd. NW6	9	B2
Narrow St. E14	26	C1
Nascot St. W12	15	E5
Nash Rd. SE4	40	C2
Nasmyth St. W6	22	D4
Nassau Rd. SW13	29	B4
Nassau St. W1	17	C4
Nassington Rd. NW3	9	F1
Natal Rd., Ilf.	14	D1
Nathan Way SE28	28	G4
Naval Row E14	26	G1
Navarino Gro. E8	11	F3
Navarino Rd. E8	11	F3
Navarre Rd. E6	21	A1
Navarre St. E2	18	E3
Navy St. SW4	38	D1
Naylor Rd. SE15	32	G3
Nazrul St. E2	18	E2
Neal St. WC2	**43**	**E2**
Nealden St. SW9	38	F1
Neal's Yd. WC2	**43**	**E2**
Neasden Clo. NW10	8	A2
Neasden La. NW10	8	A1
Neate St. SE5	32	D2
Neatscourt Rd. E6	20	G4
Neckinger SE16	25	E4
Neckinger Est. SE16	25	E4
Neckinger St. SE1	25	E3
Nectarine Way SE13	33	F5
Needleman St. SE16	26	B3
Nelgarde Rd. SE6	40	E5
Nella Rd. W6	29	F2
Nelldale Rd. SE16	26	A5
Nelson Gdns. E2	18	F2
Nelson Mandela Rd. SE3	41	F1
Nelson Pas. EC1	18	B2
Nelson Pl. N1	18	A1
Nelson Rd. SE10	33	G2
Nelson Sq. SE1	25	A3
Nelson St. E1	18	G5
Nelson St. E6	21	B1
Nelson Ter. N1	18	A1

Nelson's Row SW4 38 D2
Nepean St. SW15 36 C4
Neptune St. SE16 26 A4
Nesbit Rd. SE9 41 G2
Nesham St. E1 25 F2
Netheravon Rd. N. W4 22 B5
Netheravon Rd. S. W4 29 B1
Netherby Rd. SE23 40 A5
Netherfield Gdns., Bark. 14 F3
Netherford Rd. SW4 31 C5
Netherhall Gdns. NW3 9 D3
Netherton Gro. SW10 30 D2
Netherwood Rd. W14 22 F4
Netherwood St. NW6 9 A4
Nettleton Rd. SE14 33 B4
Nevada St. SE10 33 G2
Nevern Pl. SW5 23 B5
Nevern Rd. SW5 23 B5
Nevern Sq. SW5 23 B5
Nevill Rd. N16 11 D1
Neville Clo. NW6 16 A1
Neville Clo. SE15 32 F3
Neville Gill Clo. SW18 37 C4
Neville Rd. E7 13 D4
Neville Rd. NW6 16 A1
Neville St. SW7 30 E1
Neville Ter. SW7 30 E1
New Barn St. E13 20 D3
New Bond St. W1 17 B5
New Bri. St. EC4 44 B2
New Burlington Ms. W1 43 A3
New Burlington Pl. W1 43 A3
New Burlington St. W1 43 A3
New Butt La. SE8 33 E3
New Butt La. N. SE8 33 E3
New Cavendish St. W1 17 A4
New Change EC4 44 D2
New Ch. Rd. SE5 32 C3
New City Rd. E13 20 F2
New Compton St. WC2 43 D2
New Ct. EC4 43 J3
New Covent Gdn. Mkt. SW8 31 D3
New Coventry St. W1 43 D4
New Cross Rd. SE14 33 A3
New End NW3 9 D1
New End Sq. NW3 9 E1
New Fetter La. EC4 44 A1
New Globe Wk. SE1 44 D5
New Inn Pas. WC2 43 H2
New Inn Yd. EC2 18 D3
New Kent Rd. SE1 25 B4
New King St. SE8 33 E2
New Kings Rd. SW6 30 A5
New London St. EC3 44 J3
New Lydenburgh St. SE7 27 F4
New Mt. St. E15 13 A4
New N. Rd. N1 11 B4
New N. St. WC1 17 F4
New Oxford St. WC1 43 D1
New Pk. Ct. SW2 38 E5
New Pl. Sq. SE16 25 G4
New Plaistow Rd. E15 13 B5
New Quebec St. W1 16 G5
New Rd. E1 18 G4
New Row WC2 43 E3
New Sq. WC2 43 H1
New St. EC2 18 D4
New St. Sq. EC4 44 A1
New Union Clo. E14 26 G4
New Union St. EC2 18 C4
New Wf. Rd. N1 17 E1
Newark Knok E6 21 C4
Newark St. E1 18 G4
Newburgh St. W1 43 A2
Newburn St. SE11 31 F1
Newby Pl. E14 26 G1
Newby St. SW8 38 B1
Newcastle Clo. EC4 44 B1
Newcastle Pl. W2 16 E4
Newcomen Rd. SW11 37 E1
Newcomen St. SE1 25 C3
Newcourt St. NW8 16 F1
Newell St. E14 19 D5
Newent Clo. SE15 32 D3
Newgate St. EC1 44 C1
Newham Way E6 21 C3
Newham Way E16 20 C4
Newhaven Gdns. SE9 41 G2
Newhaven La. E16 20 C3
Newington Butts SE1 25 A5
Newington Butts SE11 25 A5
Newington Causeway SE1 25 A4
Newington Grn. N1 11 C2
Newington Grn. N16 11 C2
Newington Grn. Rd. N1 11 C3
Newland St. E16 28 A2
Newlands Ct. SE9 42 C4
Newlands Quay E1 26 A1
Newman Rd. E13 20 E2
Newman St. W1 17 C4
Newman Yd. W1 43 B1
Newman's Ct. EC3 44 G2
Newmarket Grn. SE9 41 G5
Newport Ct. WC2 43 D3
Newport Pl. WC2 43 D3
Newport Rd. SW13 29 C4
Newport St. SE11 24 F5
Newstead Rd. SE12 41 C5
Newton Gro. W4 22 A5
Newton Rd. E15 13 A2
Newton Rd. W2 16 C5
Newton St. WC2 43 F1
Nicholas La. EC4 44 G3
Nicholas Rd. E1 19 A3
Nicholl St. E2 11 F5
Nicholson St. SE1 44 B6
Nicoll Rd. NW10 8 A5
Nicosia Rd. SW18 37 F5
Nigel Ms., Ilf. 14 D1
Nigel Rd. E7 13 F2
Nigel Rd. SE15 39 F1
Nigeria Rd. SE7 34 F3
Nightingale Gro. SE13 41 A3
Nightingale La. SW4 38 B4
Nightingale La. SW12 37 G5
Nightingale Pl. SE18 35 C2
Nightingale Rd. NW10 15 B1
Nightingale Sq. SW12 38 A5
Nightingale Vale SE18 35 C2
Nightingale Wk. SW4 38 B4
Nightingale Way E6 21 A4
Nile Rd. E13 20 F1
Nile St. N1 18 C2
Nile Ter. SE15 32 E1
Nine Acres Clo. E12 14 A2
Nine Elms La. SW8 31 C3
Nithdale Rd. SE18 35 D3
Niton St. SW6 29 F3
Noble St. EC2 44 D1
Noel Rd. E6 21 A3
Noel Rd. N1 18 A1
Noel St. W1 43 B2
Nolan Way E5 11 F1
Norbiton Rd. E14 19 D5
Norbroke St. W12 22 B1
Norcroft Gdns. SE22 39 F5
Norfolk Cres. W2 16 F5
Norfolk Cres., Sid. 42 G5
Norfolk Ho. SE3 34 B2
Norfolk Pl. W2 16 E5
Norfolk Rd. E6 14 B5
Norfolk Rd. NW8 9 E5
Norfolk Rd. NW10 8 A4
Norfolk Rd., Bark. 14 G4
Norfolk Row SE1 24 F4
Norfolk Sq. W2 16 E5
Norfolk St. E7 13 D2
Norland Pl. W11 22 G2
Norland Rd. W11 22 F2
Norland Sq. W11 22 G2
Norman Gro. E3 19 C1
Norman Rd. E6 21 B3
Norman Rd. SE10 33 F3
Norman Rd., Ilf. 14 D2
Normanby Rd. NW10 8 B1
Normand Rd. W14 30 A2
Normandy Rd. SW9 31 G4
Normandy Ter. E16 20 E5
Norris St. SW1 43 C4
Norroy Rd. SW15 36 F2
North Audley St. W1 24 A1
North Bank NW8 16 F2
North Carriage Dr. W2 23 F1
North Circular Rd. NW10 8 A1
North Colonnade E14 26 E2
North Cross Rd. SE22 39 E3
North End Cres. W14 23 A5
North End Ho. W14 22 G5
North End Rd. SW6 30 A2
North End Rd. W14 22 G5
North Gower St. NW1 17 C2
North Ms. WC1 17 F3
North Pk. SE9 42 C4
North Pas. SW18 37 B3
North Peckham Est. SE15 32 D3
North Pole Rd. W10 15 E4
North Ride W2 23 F2
North Rd. N7 10 E3
North Rd. SE18 28 G5
North Row W1 23 G1
North St. E13 20 E1
North St. SW4 38 C1
North St., Bark. 14 D3
North Tenter St. E1 18 E5
North Vw. Cres. NW10 8 B1
North Vill. NW1 10 D3
North Wf. Rd. W2 16 E4
North Woolwich Rd. E16 27 D2
Northampton Pk. N1 11 B3
Northampton Rd. EC1 17 G3
Northampton Sq. EC1 18 A2
Northampton St. N1 11 B4
Northbourne Rd. SW4 38 D2
Northbrook Rd. SE13 41 A3
Northburgh St. EC1 18 A3
Northchurch Rd. N1 11 C4
Northchurch Ter. N1 11 D4
Northcote Rd. NW10 8 A4
Northcote Rd. SW11 37 F3
Northdown St. N1 17 E1
Northern Relief Rd., Bark. 14 D4
Northern Rd. E13 20 E1
Northey St. E14 26 C1
Northfield Rd. E6 14 B4
Northfields SW18 37 B2
Northiam St. E9 11 G5
Northington St. WC1 17 F3
Northlands St. SE5 32 B5
Northolme Rd. N5 11 B1
Northport St. N1 11 C5
Northumberland All. EC3 44 J2
Northumberland Ave. WC2 43 E5
Northumberland Ave., Well. 42 F2
Northumberland Pl. W2 16 B5
Northumberland Rd. E6 21 A5
Northumberland St. WC2 43 E5
Northumbria St. E14 19 E5
Northway Rd. SE5 39 B1
Northwick Ter. NW8 16 E3
Norton Folgate E1 18 D4
Norway Gate SE16 26 C4
Norway St. SE10 33 F2
Norwich Rd. E7 13 D2
Norwich St. EC4 43 J1
Notley St. SE5 32 C3
Notre Dame Est. SW4 38 C2
Notting Barn Rd. W10 15 F3
Notting Hill Gate W11 23 B2
Nottingham Ave. E16 20 F4
Nottingham Ct. WC2 43 E2
Nottingham Pl. W1 17 A4
Nottingham St. W1 17 A4
Novello St. SW6 30 B4
Nowell Rd. SW13 29 C2
Nuding Clo. SE13 40 E1
Nugent Ter. NW8 16 D1
Nun Ct. EC2 44 F1
Nunhead Cres. SE15 39 G1
Nunhead Grn. SE15 39 G1
Nunhead Gro. SE15 39 G1
Nunhead La. SE15 39 G1
Nursery Clo. SW15 36 F2
Nursery La. E7 13 D3
Nursery La. W10 15 E4
Nursery Rd. SW9 38 F2
Nutbourne St. W10 15 G2
Nutbrook St. SE15 39 F1
Nutcroft Rd. SE15 32 G3
Nutfield Rd. E15 12 G1
Nutfield Rd. SE22 39 E3
Nutford Pl. W1 16 F5
Nuthatch Gdns. SE28 28 F3
Nutley Ter. NW3 9 D3
Nutmeg La. E14 20 A5
Nutt St. SE15 32 E3
Nuttall St. N1 18 D1
Nyanza St. SE18 35 F2
Nynehead St. SE14 33 C3

O

Oak Cres. E16 20 B4
Oak Gro. NW2 8 F1
Oak Hill Ave. NW3 9 C1
Oak Hill Pk. NW3 9 C1
Oak Hill Pk. Ms. NW3 9 D1
Oak Hill Way NW3 9 D1
Oak La. E14 26 D1
Oak Pk. Gdns. SW19 36 F5
Oak Tree Rd. NW8 16 F2
Oak Village NW5 10 A1
Oak Way W3 22 A2
Oakbank Gro. SE24 39 B2
Oakbury Rd. SW6 30 C5
Oakcroft Rd. SE13 34 A5
Oakdale Rd. E7 13 E4
Oakdale Rd. SE15 40 A1
Oakden St. SE11 24 G5
Oake Ct. SW15 36 G3
Oakfield Rd. E6 14 A5
Oakfield St. SW10 30 D2

Oakford Rd. NW5	10	C1
Oakhill Rd. SW15	37	A3
Oakhurst Gro. SE22	39	F2
Oakington Rd. W9	16	B3
Oaklands Est. SW4	38	C4
Oaklands Gro. W12	22	C2
Oaklands Rd. NW2	8	F1
Oakley Gdns. SW3	30	F2
Oakley Pl. SE1	32	E1
Oakley Rd. N1	11	C4
Oakley Sq. NW1	17	C1
Oakley St. SW3	30	F2
Oaks, The SE18	35	E1
Oakshaw Rd. SW18	37	C5
Oakways SE9	42	D4
Oakwood Ct. W14	23	A4
Oakwood La. W14	23	A4
Oakworth Rd. W10	15	E4
Oat La. EC2	**44**	**E1**
Oban Rd. E13	20	F2
Oban St. E14	20	A5
Oberstein Rd. SW11	37	E2
Oborne Clo. SE24	39	A3
Observatory Gdns. W8	23	B3
Occupation La. SE18	35	D4
Occupation Rd. SE17	32	B1
Ocean Est. E1	19	B3
Ocean St. E1	19	B4
Ockenden Rd. N1	11	C3
Octavia St. SW11	30	F4
Octavius St. SE8	33	E3
Odessa Rd. E7	13	C1
Odessa Rd. NW10	15	C1
Odessa St. SE16	26	D3
Odger St. SW11	30	G5
Odhams Wk. WC2	**43**	**E2**
Offerton Rd. SW4	38	C1
Offley Rd. SW9	31	G3
Offord Rd. N1	10	F4
Offord St. N1	10	F4
Ogilby St. SE18	28	B5
Oglander Rd. SE15	39	E2
Ogle St. W1	17	C4
Ohio Rd. E13	20	C3
Okehampton Rd. NW10	8	E5
Olaf St. W11	22	F1
Old Bailey EC4	**44**	**C2**
Old Bethnal Grn. Rd. E2	18	F2
Old Bond St. W1	**43**	**A4**
Old Brewers Yd. WC2	**43**	**E2**
Old Broad St. EC2	**44**	**G2**
Old Brompton Rd. SW5	30	C1
Old Brompton Rd. SW7	30	C1
Old Bldgs. WC2	**43**	**J1**
Old Burlington St. W1	**43**	**A3**
Old Castle St. E1	18	E5
Old Cavendish St. W1	17	B5
Old Ch. Rd. E1	19	B5
Old Ch. St. SW3	30	E1
Old Compton St. W1	**43**	**C3**
Old Ct. Pl. W8	23	C3
Old Devonshire Rd. SW12	38	B5
Old Dover Rd. SE3	34	D3
Old Fish St. Hill EC4	**44**	**D3**
Old Fleet La. EC4	**44**	**B1**
Old Ford Rd. E2	19	A1
Old Ford Rd. E3	19	B1
Old Gloucester St. WC1	17	E4
Old Jamaica Rd. SE16	25	F4
Old James St. SE15	39	G1
Old Jewry EC2	**44**	**F2**
Old Kent Rd. SE1	25	D5
Old Kent Rd. SE15	32	G2
Old Marylebone Rd. NW1	16	F4
Old Mill La. W6	29	C1
Old Mill Rd. SE18	35	F2
Old Montague St. E1	18	F4
Old Nichol St. E2	18	E3
Old Oak Common La. NW10	15	A3
Old Oak Common La. W3	15	A4
Old Oak La. NW10	15	B2
Old Oak Rd. W3	22	B1
Old Palace Yd. SW1	24	E4
Old Paradise St. SE11	24	F5
Old Pk. Ave. SW12	38	A4
Old Pk. La. W1	24	A2
Old Pye St. SW1	24	D4
Old Quebec St. W1	16	G5
Old Queen St. SW1	24	D3
Old Rd. SE13	41	B2
Old Seacoal La. EC4	**44**	**B2**
Old S. Lambeth Rd. SW8	31	E3
Old Sq. WC2	**43**	**H1**
Old St. E13	20	E1
Old St. EC1	18	B3
Old Town SW4	38	C1
Old Woolwich Rd. SE10	34	A1
Old York Rd. SW18	37	C3
Oldbury Pl. W1	17	A4
Oldfield Gro. SE16	26	B5
Oldfield Rd. NW10	8	B4
Oldridge Rd. SW12	38	A5
O'Leary Sq. E1	19	A4
Oliphant St. W10	15	F2
Olive Rd. E13	20	F2
Olive Rd. NW2	8	E1
Oliver Gdns. E6	21	A5
Ollerton Grn. E3	12	D5
Ollgar Clo. W12	22	B2
Olliffe St. E14	26	G4
Olmar St. SE1	32	F2
Olney Rd. SE17	32	A2
Olven Rd. SE18	35	E2
Olympia Way W14	22	G4
Oman Ave. NW2	8	D1
O'Meara St. SE1	**44**	**E6**
Omega St. SE14	33	E4
Ommaney Rd. SE14	33	B4
Ondine Rd. SE15	39	E2
One Tree Clo. SE23	40	A4
Onega Gate SE16	26	C4
Ongar Rd. SW6	30	B2
Onslow Gdns. SW7	30	E1
Onslow Sq. SW7	23	E5
Opal Clo. E16	20	G5
Opal St. SE11	25	A5
Ophir Ter. SE15	32	F4
Oppenheim Rd. SE13	33	G5
Oppidans Rd. NW3	9	G4
Orange St. WC2	**43**	**D4**
Orange Yd. W1	**43**	**D2**
Orangery La. SE9	42	B3
Orb St. SE17	25	C5
Orbain Rd. SW6	29	G3
Orbel St. SW11	30	F4
Orchard, The SE3	34	A5
Orchard Clo. W10	15	G4
Orchard Dr. SE3	34	B5
Orchard Pl. E14	27	B1
Orchard Ri. E., Sid.	42	G3
Orchard Ri. W., Sid.	42	G3
Orchard Rd. SE18	28	F5
Orchard St. W1	17	A5
Orchardson St. NW8	16	E3
Orchid Clo. E6	21	A4
Orchid St. W12	22	C1
Orde Hall St. WC1	17	F4
Ordell Rd. E3	19	D1
Ordnance Cres. SE10	27	B3
Ordnance Hill NW8	9	E5
Ordnance Rd. E16	20	C4
Ordnance Rd. SE18	35	C2
Oregano Dr. E14	20	A5
Oregon Ave. E12	14	B1
Oriel Rd. E9	12	B3
Oriental Rd. E16	27	G2
Orissa Rd. SE18	35	G1
Orkney St. SW11	31	A5
Orlando Rd. SW4	38	C1
Orleston Ms. N7	10	G3
Orleston Rd. N7	10	G3
Orlop St. SE10	34	B1
Orme Ct. W2	23	C1
Orme La. W2	23	C1
Ormeley Rd. SW12	38	B5
Ormiston Gro. W12	22	D2
Ormiston Rd. SE10	34	D1
Ormond Yd. SW1	**43**	**B5**
Ormonde Gate SW3	30	G1
Ormonde Ter. NW8	9	G5
Ormsby St. E2	18	E1
Ormside St. SE15	33	A2
Ornan Rd. NW3	9	F2
Orpheus St. SE5	32	C4
Orsett St. SE11	31	F1
Orsett Ter. W2	16	C5
Orsman Rd. N1	11	D5
Orville Rd. SW11	30	E5
Orwell Ct. N5	11	B1
Orwell Rd. E13	13	F5
Osberton Rd. SE12	41	D3
Osborn Clo. E8	11	F5
Osborn La. SE23	40	C5
Osborn St. E1	18	E4
Osborne Rd. E7	13	E2
Osborne Rd. E9	12	D3
Osborne Rd. NW2	8	D3
Oscar St. SE8	33	E4
Oseney Cres. NW5	10	C3
O'Shea Gro. E3	12	D5
Osier St. E1	19	A3
Osiers Rd. SW18	37	B2
Osnaburgh St. NW1	17	B3
Ospringe Ct. SE9	42	F4
Ospringe Rd. NW5	10	C1
Ossington St. W2	23	C1
Ossory Rd. SE1	32	F2
Ossulston St. NW1	17	D1
Ostade Rd. SW2	38	F5
Osterley Rd. N16	11	D1
Oswin St. SE11	25	A5
Oswyth Rd. SE5	32	D5
Otford Cres. SE4	40	D4
Otis St. E3	19	G2
Otley Rd. E16	20	F5
Otto St. SE17	32	A2
Outer Circle NW1	16	F2
Outgate Rd. NW10	8	B4
Outram Pl. N1	10	E5
Outram Rd. E6	14	A5
Outwich St. EC3	**44**	**J1**
Oval, The E2	18	G1
Oval Pl. SW8	31	F3
Oval Rd. NW1	10	B5
Oval Way SE11	31	F1
Overbury St. E5	12	B1
Overcliff Rd. SE13	40	E1
Overhill Rd. SE22	39	F5
Overmead, Sid.	42	F5
Oversley Ho. W2	16	B4
Overstone Rd. W6	22	E4
Overton Rd. SW9	31	G5
Ovex Clo. E14	26	G3
Ovington Gdns. SW3	23	F4
Ovington Ms. SW3	23	F4
Ovington Sq. SW3	23	F4
Ovington St. SW3	23	F5
Owens Way SE23	40	C5
Oxberry Ave. SW6	29	G5
Oxendon St. SW1	**43**	**C4**
Oxenford St. SE15	39	E1
Oxenholme NW1	17	C1
Oxestalls Rd. SE8	33	C1
Oxford Circ. Ave. W1	**43**	**A2**
Oxford Ct. EC4	**44**	**F3**
Oxford Gdns. W10	15	F5
Oxford Gate W6	22	F5
Oxford Rd. E15	13	A3
Oxford Rd. NW6	16	B1
Oxford Rd. SW15	36	G2
Oxford Rd., Ilf.	14	E2
Oxford Sq. W2	16	F5
Oxford St. W1	17	A5
Oxleas E6	21	D5
Oxleas Clo., Well.	35	F5
Oxley Clo. SE1	32	E1
Oxonian St. SE22	39	E2
Ozolins Way E16	20	D5

P

Pacific Rd. E16	20	D5
Packington Sq. N1	11	B5
Packington St. N1	11	A5
Packmores Rd. SE9	42	F3
Paddenswick Rd. W6	22	C4
Paddington Grn. W2	16	E4
Paddington St. W1	17	A4
Paddock Clo. SE3	41	D1
Padfield Rd. SE5	39	B1
Pagden St. SW8	31	B4
Page St. SW1	24	D5
Pageant Masters Ct. EC4	**44**	**B2**
Pages Wk. SE1	25	D5
Paget Ri. SE18	35	C2
Paget Rd., Ilf.	14	D1
Paget Ter. SE18	35	C2
Pagnell St. SE14	33	D3
Pagoda Gdns. SE3	34	A5
Pakenham St. WC1	17	F2
Palace Ave. W8	23	C2
Palace Ct. NW3	9	C2
Palace Ct. W2	23	C1
Palace Gdn. Ms. W8	23	B2
Palace Gdns. Ter. W8	23	B2
Palace Gate W8	23	D3
Palace Grn. W8	23	C3
Palace St. SW1	24	C4
Palatine Rd. N16	11	D1
Palermo Rd. NW10	15	C1
Palfrey Pl. SW8	31	F3
Palgrave Rd. W12	22	B4
Pall Mall SW1	**43**	**B6**
Pall Mall E. SW1	**43**	**D5**
Pall Mall Pl. SW1	**43**	**B6**
Pallet Way SE18	35	A4
Palliser Rd. W14	29	G1
Palmer Pl. N7	10	G2
Palmer Rd. E13	20	E3
Palmer St. SW1	24	D4
Palmers Rd. E2	19	B1
Palmerston Cres. SE18	35	E2
Palmerston Rd. E7	13	E2
Palmerston Rd. NW6	9	A4
Pancras La. EC4	**44**	**E2**
Pancras Rd. NW1	17	D1
Pandora Rd. NW6	9	B3
Pangbourne Ave. W10	15	E4
Panmure Clo. N5	11	A1
Pansy Gdns. W12	22	C1
Panton St. SW1	**43**	**C4**
Panyer All. EC4	**44**	**D1**

Papillons Wk. SE3 41 D1
Papworth Way SW2 38 G5
Parade, The SW11 30 G3
Paradise Rd. SW4 31 E5
Paradise St. SE16 25 G3
Paradise Wk. SW3 30 G2
Paragon, The SE3 34 C5
Paragon Pl. SE3 34 C5
Paragon Rd. E9 12 A3
Parbury Rd. SE23 40 C4
Pardoner St. SE1 25 C4
Parfett St. E1 18 F4
Parfrey St. W6 29 E2
Paris Gdn. SE1 44 B5
Parish Gate Dr., Sid. 42 G4
Park Ave. E6 14 C5
Park Ave. E15 13 B3
Park Ave. NW2 8 D3
Park Ave., Bark. 14 E3
Park Ave. N. NW10 8 D2
Park Clo. W14 23 A4
Park Cres. W1 17 B3
Park Dr. SE7 35 A2
Park Dr. Clo. SE7 35 A1
Park Gro. E15 13 D5
Park Hill SW4 38 D3
Park La. W1 23 G1
Park Par. NW10 15 B1
Park Pl. E14 26 E2
Park Pl. SW1 43 A6
Park Pl. Vill. W2 16 D4
Park Rd. E6 13 F5
Park Rd. E15 13 D5
Park Rd. NW1 16 G3
Park Rd. NW8 16 F2
Park Rd. NW10 8 A5
Park Row SE10 34 A2
Park Sq. E. NW1 17 B3
Park Sq. Ms. NW1 17 B3
Park Sq. W. NW1 17 B3
Park St. SE1 44 D5
Park St. W1 24 A1
Park Vw. Est. E2 19 B1
Park Vw. Rd. NW10 8 B1
Park Village E. NW1 17 B1
Park Village W. NW1 17 B1
Park Vista SE10 34 A2
Park Wk. SW10 30 D2
Parkcroft Rd. SE12 41 C5
Parkdale Rd. SE18 35 G1
Parke Rd. SW13 29 C4
Parker Clo. E16 28 A2
Parker Ms. WC2 43 F1
Parker St. E16 28 A2
Parker St. WC2 43 F1
Parkfield Ave. SW14 36 A2
Parkfield Rd. NW10 8 C4
Parkfield Rd. SE14 33 D4
Parkfield St. N1 17 G1
Parkfields SW15 36 E2
Parkgate SE3 41 C1
Parkgate Rd. SW11 30 F3
Parkham St. SW11 30 E4
Parkhill Rd. NW3 9 G2
Parkhill Wk. NW3 9 G2
Parkholme Rd. E8 11 F3
Parkhouse St. SE5 32 C3
Parkhurst Rd. E12 14 C1
Parkhurst Rd. N7 10 E1
Parkmead SW15 36 D4
Parkside SE3 34 C3
Parkside Rd. SW11 31 A4
Parkstead Rd. SW15 36 C3
Parkthorne Rd. SW12 38 D5
Parkville Rd. SW6 30 A3
Parkway NW1 10 B5
Parliament Hill NW3 9 F1
Parliament Sq. SW1 24 E3
Parliament St. SW1 24 E3
Parma Cres. SW11 37 G2
Parmiter St. E2 18 G1
Parnell Rd. E3 12 D5
Parr Rd. E6 13 G5
Parr St. N1 18 C1
Parry Ave. E6 21 B5
Parry Pl. SE18 28 D5
Parry St. SW8 31 E2
Parsifal Rd. NW6 9 B2
Parsonage St. E14 26 G5
Parsons Grn. SW6 30 B5
Parsons Grn. La. SW6 30 B4
Parthenia Rd. SW6 30 B4
Parvin St. SW8 31 D4
Pascal St. SW8 31 D3
Pascoe Rd. SE13 41 A3
Passey Pl. SE9 42 B4
Passmore St. SW1 31 A1
Paston Cres. SE12 41 E5
Pastor St. SE11 25 A5
Patcham Ter. SW8 31 B4
Pater St. W8 23 B4
Paternoster Row EC4 44 D2
Paternoster Sq. EC4 44 C1
Patience Rd. SW11 30 F5
Patio Clo. SW4 38 D4
Patmore Est. SW8 31 C4
Patmore St. SW8 31 C4
Patmos Rd. SW9 32 A3
Paton Clo. E3 19 E2
Patrick Pas. SW11 30 F5
Patrick Rd. E13 20 F2
Patriot Sq. E2 18 G1
Patrol Pl. SE6 40 F4
Patshull Rd. NW5 10 C3
Patten Rd. SW18 37 F5
Patterdale Rd. SE15 33 A3
Paul St. E15 13 B5
Paul St. EC2 18 C3
Paulet Rd. SE5 32 A5
Paultons Sq. SW3 30 E2
Paultons St. SW3 30 E2
Paveley Dr. SW11 30 F3
Paveley St. NW8 16 F3
Pavement, The SW4 38 C2
Pavilion Rd. SW1 23 G4
Paxton Rd. W4 29 A2
Paxton Ter. SW1 31 B2
Payne Rd. E3 19 F1
Payne St. SE8 33 D2
Peabody Est. SE1 44 A6
Peabody Est. SE24 39 B5
Peabody Est. W6 29 E1
Peabody Sq. SE1 25 A3
Peabody Trust SE1 44 D6
Peach Rd. W10 15 F2
Peachum Rd. SE3 34 C2
Pear Tree Ct. EC1 17 G3
Pear Tree St. EC1 18 A3
Peardon St. SW8 31 B5
Pearl Clo. E6 21 C5
Pearman St. SE1 24 G4
Pearscroft Ct. SW6 30 C4
Pearscroft Rd. SW6 30 C4
Pearson St. E2 18 E1
Peckford Pl. SW9 31 G5
Peckham Gro. SE15 32 D3
Peckham High St. SE15 32 F4
Peckham Hill St. SE15 32 F3
Peckham Pk. Rd. SE15 32 F3
Peckham Rd. SE5 32 D4
Peckham Rd. SE15 32 E4
Peckham Rye SE15 39 F1
Peckham Rye SE22 39 F2
Peckwater St. NW5 10 C2
Pedlars Wk. N7 10 E3
Pedley St. E1 18 F3
Peel Gro. E2 19 A1
Peel Prec. NW6 16 B1
Peel Rd. NW6 16 A2
Peel St. W8 23 B2
Peerless St. EC1 18 C2
Pegwell St. SE18 35 G3
Pekin St. E14 19 E5
Pelham Clo. SE5 39 D1
Pelham Cres. SW7 23 F5
Pelham Pl. SW7 23 F5
Pelham St. SW7 23 E5
Pelican Est. SE15 32 E4
Pellant Rd. SW6 29 G3
Pellatt Rd. SE22 39 E3
Pellerin Rd. N16 11 D2
Pelling St. E14 19 E5
Pellipar Gdns. SE18 35 B1
Pelly Rd. E13 13 D5
Pelter St. E2 18 E2
Pelton Rd. SE10 34 B1
Pember Rd. NW10 15 F2
Pemberton Row EC4 44 A1
Pembridge Cres. W11 23 B1
Pembridge Gdns. W2 23 B1
Pembridge Ms. W11 23 B1
Pembridge Pl. W2 23 B1
Pembridge Rd. W11 23 B1
Pembridge Sq. W2 23 B1
Pembridge Vill. W11 23 B1
Pembroke Clo. SW1 24 A3
Pembroke Gdns. W8 23 A5
Pembroke Gdns. Clo. W8 23 A4
Pembroke Pl. W8 23 B4
Pembroke Rd. E6 21 B4
Pembroke Rd. W8 23 B5
Pembroke Sq. W8 23 B4
Pembroke St. N1 10 E4
Pembroke Studios W8 23 A4
Pembroke Vill. W8 23 B5
Pembroke Wk. W8 23 B5
Pembury Pl. E5 11 G2
Pembury Rd. E5 11 G2
Penang St. E1 25 G2
Penarth St. SE15 33 A2
Pencraig Way SE15 32 G2
Penderyn Way N7 10 D1
Pendrell Rd. SE4 33 C5
Pendrell St. SE18 35 F2
Penfold Pl. NW1 16 F4
Penfold St. NW1 16 F4
Penfold St. NW8 16 G3
Penford Gdns. SE9 41 G1
Penford St. SE5 32 A5
Penge Rd. E13 13 F5
Penhall Rd. SE7 27 G5
Penn Rd. N7 10 E2
Penn St. N1 11 C5
Pennack Rd. SE15 32 E2
Pennant Ms. W8 23 C5
Pennard Rd. W12 22 E3
Pennethorne Rd. SE15 32 G3
Pennington St. E1 25 F1
Pennyfields E14 26 E1
Pennyroyal Ave. E6 21 C5
Penpoll Rd. E8 11 G3
Penrith Clo. SW15 36 G3
Penrose Gro. SE17 32 B1
Penrose St. SE17 32 B1
Penryn St. NW1 17 D1
Pensbury Pl. SW8 31 C5
Pensbury St. SW8 31 C5
Penshurst Rd. E9 12 B4
Pentland St. SW18 37 D4
Pentlow St. SW15 36 E1
Penton Pl. SE17 32 A1
Penton Ri. WC1 17 F2
Penton St. N1 17 G1
Pentonville Rd. N1 17 F1
Pentridge St. SE15 32 E3
Penywern Rd. SW5 30 B1
Penzance Pl. W11 22 G2
Penzance St. W11 22 G2
Peony Gdns. W12 22 C1
Peploe Rd. NW6 15 F1
Pepper Clo. E6 21 B4
Pepper St. E14 26 F4
Pepys Rd. SE14 33 B4
Pepys St. EC3 44 J3
Perceval Ave. NW3 9 F2
Perch St. E8 11 E1
Percival St. EC1 18 A3
Percy Circ. WC1 17 F2
Percy Rd. E16 20 B4
Percy Rd. W12 22 C3
Percy St. W1 17 D4
Peregrine Ho. EC1 18 A2
Perham Rd. W14 29 G1
Peridot St. E6 21 A4
Periton Rd. SE9 41 G2
Perkin's Rents SW1 24 D4
Perkins Sq. SE1 44 E5
Perpins Rd. SE9 42 F4
Perrers Rd. W6 22 D5
Perrins La. NW3 9 D1
Perrin's Wk. NW3 9 D1
Perryman Ho., Bark. 14 E5
Perrymead St. SW6 30 B4
Perrys Pl. W1 43 C1
Perth Rd. E13 20 E1
Perth Rd., Bark. 14 F5
Peter Ave. NW10 8 D4
Peter St. W1 43 C3
Peterborough Ms. SW6 30 B5
Peterborough Rd. SW6 30 B5
Peterborough Vill. SW6 30 C4
Petergate SW11 37 D2
Peters Clo., Well. 35 G5
Peters Hill EC4 44 D3
Petersham La. SW7 23 D4
Petersham Ms. SW7 23 D4
Petersham Pl. SW7 23 D4
Petherton Rd. N5 11 B2
Petley Rd. W6 29 E2
Peto Pl. NW1 17 B3
Petrie Clo. NW2 8 G3
Pett St. SE18 28 A5
Pettiward Clo. SW15 36 E2
Pettman Cres. SE28 28 F4
Petty France SW1 24 C4
Petworth St. SW11 30 F4
Petyward SW3 23 F5
Pevensey Rd. E7 13 C1
Peyton Pl. SE10 33 G3
Phelp St. SE17 32 C2
Phene St. SW3 30 F2
Philbeach Gdns. SW5 30 B1
Philip St. E13 20 D3
Philip Wk. SE15 39 G1
Philippa Gdns. SE9 41 G3
Phillimore Gdns. NW10 8 E5
Phillimore Gdns. W8 23 B3
Phillimore Pl. W8 23 B3
Phillimore Wk. W8 23 B4
Phillipp St. N1 11 D5
Philpot La. EC3 44 H3
Philpot St. E1 18 G5
Phineas Pett Rd. SE9 42 A1
Phipp St. EC2 18 D3
Phoebeth Rd. SE4 40 E3
Phoenix Pl. WC1 17 F3
Phoenix Rd. NW1 17 D2

Phoenix St. WC2	**43**	**D2**													

Phoenix St. WC2 43 D2
Piccadilly W1 24 B2
Piccadilly Arc. SW1 43 A5
Piccadilly Circ. W1 43 C4
Piccadilly Pl. W1 43 B4
Pickering Pl. SW1 43 B6
Pickets St. SW12 38 B5
Pickford Wf. N1 18 B1
Pickwick Rd. SE21 39 C5
Picton St. SE5 32 C3
Piedmont Rd. SE18 35 F1
Pier Rd. E16 28 C3
Pier St. E14 26 G5
Pier Way SE28 28 F4
Piermont Grn. SE22 39 G3
Piermont Rd. SE22 39 G3
Piggot St. E14 19 E5
Pilgrim St. EC4 44 B2
Pilgrimage St. SE1 25 C3
Pilgrims Ct. SE3 34 D4
Pilgrim's La. NW3 9 E1
Pilkington Rd. SE15 32 G5
Pimlico Rd. SW1 31 A1
Pinchin St. E1 25 F1
Pindar St. EC2 18 D4
Pine Ave. E15 13 A2
Pine Rd. NW2 8 E1
Pine St. EC1 17 G3
Pinefield Clo. E14 26 E1
Pinnell Pl. SE9 41 G2
Pinnell Rd. SE9 41 G2
Pinto Way SE3 41 E2
Piper Clo. N7 10 F2
Pirie St. E16 27 E2
Pitchford St. E15 13 A4
Pitfield St. N1 18 D2
Pitfold Clo. SE12 41 D4
Pitfold Rd. SE12 41 D4
Pitman St. SE5 32 B3
Pitsea St. E1 19 B5
Pitt St. SE15 32 E3
Pitt St. W8 23 B3
Pittman Gdns., Ilf. 14 E2
Pitt's Head Ms. W1 24 A2
Pixley St. E14 19 D5
Plaistow Gro. E15 13 C5
Plaistow Pk. Rd. E13 20 E1
Plaistow Rd. E15 13 C5
Plantation, The SE3 34 D5
Plashet Gro. E6 13 F5
Plashet Rd. E13 13 D5
Plassy Rd. SE6 40 F5
Plato Rd. SW2 38 E2
Platt, The SW15 36 F1
Platt St. NW1 17 D1
Platt's La. NW3 9 B1
Playfield Cres. SE22 39 E3
Playhouse Yd. EC4 44 B2
Pleasance, The SW15 36 D2
Pleasance Rd. SW15 36 D3
Pleasant Pl. N1 11 A4
Plender St. NW1 10 C5
Pleshey Rd. N7 10 D1
Plevna St. E14 26 G4
Pleydell Ave. W6 22 B5
Pleydell St. EC4 44 A2
Plough Ct. EC3 44 G3
Plough La. SE22 39 E4
Plough Pl. EC4 44 A1
Plough Rd. SW11 37 E1
Plough Ter. SW11 37 E2
Plough Way SE16 26 B5
Plough Yd. EC2 18 D3
Plover Way SE16 26 C4
Plum La. SE18 35 D3
Plumbers Row E1 18 F4
Plummer Rd. SW4 38 D5
Plumstead Common Rd. SE18 35 D2
Plumstead High St. SE18 28 F5
Plumstead Rd. SE18 28 D5
Plumtree Ct. EC4 44 B1
Plymouth Rd. E16 20 D4
Plymouth Wf. E14 27 A5
Plympton Ave. NW6 9 A4
Plympton Rd. NW6 9 A4
Plympton St. NW8 16 F3
Pocock St. SE1 25 A3
Podmore Rd. SW18 37 D2
Poets Rd. N5 11 C2
Point Hill SE10 33 G3
Point Pleasant SW18 37 B2
Pointers Clo. E14 33 F1
Poland St. W1 43 B1
Polebrook Rd. SE3 41 F1
Polesworth Ho. W2 16 B4
Pollard Clo. E16 27 D1
Pollard Clo. N7 10 F1
Pollard Row E2 18 F2
Pollard St. E2 18 F2
Pollen St. W1 43 A2
Polsted Rd. SE6 40 D5
Polthorne Gro. SE18 28 E5
Polygon Rd. NW1 17 D1
Polytechnic St. SE18 28 C5
Pomeroy St. SE14 33 A4
Pond Clo. SE3 34 C5
Pond Mead SE21 39 C4
Pond Pl. SW3 23 F5
Pond Rd. E15 20 B1
Pond Rd. SE3 34 C5
Pond St. NW3 9 F2
Ponder St. N7 10 F4
Ponler St. E1 18 G5
Ponsard Rd. NW10 15 D2
Ponsford St. E9 12 A2
Ponsonby Pl. SW1 31 D1
Ponsonby Rd. SW15 36 D5
Ponsonby Ter. SW1 31 D1
Pont St. SW1 23 G4
Pont St. Ms. SW1 23 G4
Ponton Rd. SW8 31 D2
Poole Rd. E9 12 B3
Poole St. N1 11 C5
Poolmans St. SE16 26 B3
Pope St. SE1 25 D3
Popes Rd. SW9 38 G1
Popham Rd. N1 11 B5
Popham St. N1 11 B5
Poplar Gro. W6 22 E3
Poplar High St. E14 26 F1
Poplar Pl. W2 23 C1
Poplar Rd. SE24 39 B2
Poplar Wk. SE24 39 B2
Poplars Ave. NW2 8 E3
Poppins Ct. EC4 44 B2
Porchester Gdns. W2 23 C1
Porchester Pl. W2 16 F5
Porchester Rd. W2 16 C4
Porchester Sq. W2 16 C5
Porchester Ter. W2 23 D1
Porchester Ter. N. W2 16 C5
Porden Rd. SW2 38 F2
Porlock St. SE1 25 C3
Portchester Clo. SE5 39 C2
Portelet Rd. E1 19 B2
Porten Rd. W14 22 G4
Porter Rd. E6 21 B5
Porter St. SE1 44 E5
Porteus Rd. W2 16 D4
Portgate Clo. W9 16 A3
Portia Way E3 19 D3
Portinscale Rd. SW15 36 G3
Portland Gro. SW8 31 F4
Portland Ms. W1 43 B2
Portland Pl. W1 17 B4
Portland Rd. W11 22 G1
Portland St. SE17 32 C1
Portman Clo. W1 16 G5
Portman Ms. S. W1 17 A5
Portman Pl. E2 19 A2
Portman Sq. W1 17 A5
Portman St. W1 17 A5
Portnall Rd. W9 16 A1
Portobello Rd. W10 15 G4
Portobello Rd. W11 16 A5
Portpool La. EC1 17 G4
Portree St. E14 20 A5
Portslade Rd. SW8 31 C5
Portsmouth Rd. SW15 36 D5
Portsmouth St. WC2 43 G2
Portsoken St. E1 25 E1
Portugal St. WC2 43 G2
Portway E15 13 C5
Post Office App. E7 13 E2
Post Office Ct. EC3 44 G2
Post Office Way SW8 31 D3
Potier St. SE1 25 C4
Pott St. E2 18 G2
Pottery St. SE16 25 G3
Poulett Rd. E6 21 B1
Poultry EC2 44 F2
Pound La. NW10 8 C3
Pound Pk. Rd. SE7 27 G5
Pound Pl. SE9 42 C4
Pountney Rd. SW11 38 A1
Powell's Wk. W4 29 A2
Powerscroft Rd. E5 12 A1
Powis Gdns. W11 16 A5
Powis Pl. WC1 17 E3
Powis Rd. E3 19 F2
Powis Sq. W11 16 A5
Powis St. SE18 28 C4
Powis Ter. W11 16 A5
Pownall Rd. E8 11 F5
Poynders Gdns. SW4 38 C5
Poynders Rd. SW4 38 C4
Poyntz Rd. SW11 30 G5
Poyser St. E2 18 G1
Praed St. W2 16 E5
Pragel St. E13 20 E1
Prague Pl. SW2 38 E3
Prairie St. SW8 31 A5
Pratt St. NW1 10 C5
Pratt Wk. SE11 24 F5
Prebend Gdns. W4 22 B5
Prebend Gdns. W6 22 B5
Prebend St. N1 11 B5
Prendergast Rd. SE3 41 B1
Prentiss Ct. SE7 27 G5
Prescot St. E1 25 E1
Prescott Pl. SW4 38 D1
Prestbury Rd. E7 13 F4
Preston Pl. NW2 8 C3
Prestons Rd. E14 26 G3
Pretoria Rd. E16 20 C3
Pretoria Rd., Ilf. 14 D2
Prideaux Pl. WC1 17 F2
Prideaux Rd. SW9 38 E1
Priest Ct. EC2 44 D1
Priests Bri. SW14 36 A1
Prima Rd. SW9 31 G3
Primrose Gdns. NW3 9 F3
Primrose Hill EC4 44 A2
Primrose Hill Ct. NW3 9 G4
Primrose Hill Rd. NW3 9 G4
Primrose St. EC2 18 D4
Primula St. W12 15 C5
Prince Albert Rd. NW1 10 A5
Prince Albert Rd. NW8 16 F2
Prince Arthur Rd. NW3 9 D2
Prince Charles Rd. SE3 34 C5
Prince Consort Rd. SW7 23 D4
Prince Edward Rd. E9 12 D3
Prince George Rd. N16 11 D1
Prince Henry Rd. SE7 34 G3
Prince Imperial Rd. SE18 35 B4
Prince John Rd. SE9 42 A3
Prince of Wales Dr. SW8 31 B3
Prince of Wales Dr. SW11 30 F4
Prince of Wales Gate SW7 23 F3
Prince of Wales Rd. E16 20 F5
Prince of Wales Rd. NW5 10 A3
Prince of Wales Rd. SE3 34 C4
Prince of Wales Ter. W4 29 A1
Prince Regent La. E13 20 E2
Prince Regent La. E16 20 F4
Prince Rupert Rd. SE9 42 B2
Prince St. SE8 33 D2
Princedale Rd. W11 22 G2
Princelet St. E1 18 E4
Prince's Arc. SW1 43 B5
Princes Ct. E1 25 G1
Princes Gdns. SW7 23 E4
Princes Gate SW7 23 F3
Princes Gate Ms. SW7 23 E4
Princes Pl. SW1 43 B5
Princes Pl. W11 22 G2
Princes Ri. SE13 33 G5
Princes Sq. W2 23 C1
Princes St. EC2 44 F2
Princes St. W1 17 B5
Princes Ter. E13 13 E5
Princes Way SW19 36 F5
Princess Ct. SE16 26 D4
Princess May Rd. N16 11 D1
Princess Rd. NW1 10 A5
Princess Rd. NW6 16 B1
Princess St. SE1 25 A4
Princethorpe Ho. W2 16 C4
Princeton St. WC1 17 F4
Printer St. EC4 44 A1
Priolo Rd. SE7 34 F1
Prior Bolton St. N1 11 A3
Prior St. SE10 33 G3
Prioress St. SE1 25 C4
Priory, The SE3 41 C2
Priory Ave. W4 22 A5
Priory Ct. SW8 31 D4
Priory Gdns. SW13 36 B1
Priory Gdns. W4 22 A5
Priory Grn. Est. N1 17 F1
Priory Gro. SW8 31 E4
Priory La. SW15 36 A4
Priory Ms. SW8 31 E4
Priory Pk. SE3 41 C1
Priory Pk. Rd. NW6 9 A5
Priory Rd. E6 13 G5
Priory Rd. NW6 9 C5
Priory Rd., Bark. 14 F4
Priory Ter. NW6 9 C5
Priory Wk. SW10 30 D1
Pritchard's Rd. E2 18 F1
Priter Rd. SE16 25 F4
Probert Rd. SW2 38 G3
Procter St. WC1 17 F4
Promenade, The W4 29 A4
Promenade App. Rd. W4 29 A3
Prospect Pl. E1 26 A2

Prospect Vale SE18	28	A5
Prothero Rd. SW6	29	G3
Prout Gro. NW10	8	A1
Providence Ct. W1	24	A1
Provost Est. N1	18	C1
Provost Rd. NW3	9	G4
Provost St. N1	18	C1
Prudent Pas. EC2	**44**	**F1**
Prusom St. E1	25	G2
Pudding La. EC3	**44**	**G4**
Pudding Mill La. E15	12	F5
Puddle Dock EC4	**44**	**C3**
Pulborough Rd. SW18	37	A5
Pulleyns Ave. E6	21	A2
Pullman Gdns. SW15	36	E4
Pulross Rd. SW9	38	F1
Pulteney Clo. E3	12	D5
Pulteney Ter. N1	10	F5
Pulton Pl. SW6	30	B3
Pump Ct. EC4	**43**	**J2**
Pump La. SE14	33	A3
Pumping Sta. Rd. W4	29	A3
Pundersons Gdns. E2	18	G2
Purcell Cres. SW6	29	F3
Purcell St. N1	18	D1
Purchese St. NW1	17	D1
Purdy St. E3	19	F3
Purneys Rd. SE9	41	G2
Purser's Cross Rd. SW6	30	A4
Purves Rd. NW10	15	D1
Putney Bri. SW6	36	G1
Putney Bri. SW15	36	G1
Putney Bri. App. SW6	36	G1
Putney Bri. Rd. SW15	36	G2
Putney Bri. Rd. SW18	37	B3
Putney Common SW15	36	E1
Putney Heath SW15	36	D5
Putney Heath La. SW15	36	F4
Putney High St. SW15	36	F2
Putney Hill SW15	36	F4
Putney Pk. Ave. SW15	36	C2
Putney Pk. La. SW15	36	D2
Pyrland Rd. N5	11	C2
Pytchley Rd. SE22	39	D1

Q

Quadrant Arc. W1	**43**	**B4**
Quadrant Gro. NW5	9	G2
Quaggy Wk. SE3	41	D2
Quaker St. E1	18	E3
Quality Ct. WC2	**43**	**J1**
Quarrendon St. SW6	30	B5
Quarry Rd. SW18	37	D4
Quarter Mile La. E10	12	F1
Quarterdeck, The E14	26	E3
Quebec Way SE16	26	B3
Queen Anne Rd. E9	12	B3
Queen Anne St. W1	17	B4
Queen Anne's Gdns. W4	22	A4
Queen Anne's Gate SW1	24	D3
Queen Anne's Gro. W4	22	A4
Queen Caroline Est. W6	29	E1
Queen Caroline St. W6	29	E1
Queen Elizabeth St. SE1	25	E3
Queen Elizabeth Wk. SW13	29	C4
Queen Margarets Gro. N1	11	D2
Queen of Denmark Ct. SE16	26	D4
Queen Sq. WC1	17	E3
Queen St. EC4	**44**	**E3**
Queen St. W1	24	B2
Queen St. Pl. EC4	**44**	**E4**
Queen Victoria St. EC4	**44**	**C3**
Queenhithe EC4	**44**	**E3**
Queens Club Gdns. W14	29	G2
Queens Cres. NW5	10	A3
Queens Gdns. W2	16	D5
Queen's Gate SW7	23	D4
Queen's Gate Gdns. SW7	23	D4
Queen's Gate Ms. SW7	23	D4
Queen's Gate Pl. SW7	23	D4
Queen's Gate Pl. Ms. SW7	23	D4
Queen's Gate Ter. SW7	23	D4
Queen's Gro. NW8	9	E5
Queen's Head St. N1	11	A5
Queens Head Yd. SE1	**44**	**F6**
Queens Pk. Ct. W10	15	F2
Queens Ride SW13	36	C1
Queens Ride SW15	36	E1
Queens Rd. E13	13	E5
Queens Rd. SE14	32	G4
Queens Rd. SE15	32	G4
Queens Rd., Bark.	14	E3
Queens Rd., Ilf.	14	E3
Queens Rd. W. E13	20	D1
Queen's Row SE17	32	C2
Queens Ter. E13	13	E5
Queen's Ter. NW8	9	E5
Queen's Wk. SW1	**43**	**A6**
Queensberry Pl. SW7	23	E5
Queensborough Ter. W2	23	C1
Queensbridge Rd. E2	11	E4
Queensbridge Rd. E8	11	E4
Queensbury St. N1	11	B4
Queenscroft Rd. SE9	41	G4
Queensdale Cres. W11	22	F2
Queensdale Pl. W11	22	G2
Queensdale Rd. W11	22	F2
Queensdale Wk. W11	22	G2
Queensdown Rd. E5	11	G1
Queensgate Pl. NW6	9	B4
Queensland Rd. N7	10	G1
Queensmead NW8	9	E5
Queensmill Rd. SW6	29	F3
Queenstown Rd. SW8	31	B2
Queensville Rd. SW12	38	D5
Queensway W2	16	C5
Quemerford Rd. N7	10	F2
Quentin Pl. SE13	41	B1
Quentin Rd. SE13	41	B1
Querrin St. SW6	30	D5
Quex Rd. NW6	9	B5
Quick Rd. W4	29	A1
Quick St. N1	18	A1
Quill La. SW15	36	F2
Quilter St. E2	18	F2
Quixley St. E14	27	A1
Quorn Rd. SE22	39	D2

R

Rabbits Rd. E12	14	A1
Racton Rd. SW6	30	B2
Radbourne Rd. SW12	38	C5
Radcliffe Ave. NW10	15	C1
Radcliffe Sq. SW15	36	F4
Raddington Rd. W10	15	G4
Radfield Way, Sid.	42	F5
Radford Rd. SE13	40	G3
Radipole Rd. SW6	30	A4
Radland Rd. E16	20	C5
Radlett Clo. E7	13	C3
Radlett Pl. NW8	9	F5
Radley Ms. W8	23	B4
Radnor Pl. W2	16	F5
Radnor Rd. NW6	8	G5
Radnor Rd. SE15	32	F3
Radnor St. EC1	18	B2
Radnor Ter. W14	23	A5
Radnor Wk. SW3	30	F1
Radstock St. SW11	30	F3
Raeburn Rd., Sid.	42	G4
Raeburn St. SW2	38	E2
Raglan Ct. SE12	41	D3
Raglan Rd. SE18	35	E1
Raglan St. NW5	10	B3
Railey Ms. NW5	10	C2
Railton Rd. SE24	38	G2
Railway App. SE1	**44**	**G6**
Railway Ave. SE16	26	A3
Railway Side SW13	36	A1
Railway St. N1	17	E1
Rainbow Ave. E14	33	F1
Rainbow St. SE5	32	D3
Raine St. E1	25	G2
Rainham Clo. SE9	42	F4
Rainham Clo. SW11	37	F4
Rainham Rd. NW10	15	E2
Rainhill Way E3	19	E2
Rainsborough Ave. SE8	26	C5
Rainton Rd. SE7	34	D1
Rainville Rd. W6	29	E2
Raleana Rd. E14	26	G2
Raleigh St. N1	11	A5
Ram St. SW18	37	C3
Ramac Ind. Est. SE7	27	D5
Ramac Way SE7	34	E1
Ramilles Clo. SW2	38	E4
Ramillies Pl. W1	**43**	**A2**
Ramillies St. W1	**43**	**A2**
Rampayne St. SW1	31	D1
Ramsay Rd. E7	13	B1
Ramsden Rd. SW12	38	A4
Ramsey St. E2	18	F3
Rancliffe Gdns. SE9	42	A2
Rancliffe Rd. E6	21	A1
Randall Clo. SW11	30	F4
Randall Pl. SE10	33	G3
Randall Rd. SE11	31	F1
Randell's Rd. N1	10	E5
Randolph Ave. W9	16	C1
Randolph Cres. W9	16	D3
Randolph Gdns. NW6	16	C1
Randolph Ms. W9	16	D3
Randolph Rd. W9	16	D3
Randolph St. NW1	10	C4
Ranelagh Ave. SW6	37	A1
Ranelagh Ave. SW13	29	C5
Ranelagh Gdns. SW6	37	A1
Ranelagh Gdns. W6	22	B4
Ranelagh Gro. SW1	31	A1
Ranelagh Rd. E6	14	C5
Ranelagh Rd. E11	13	B1
Ranelagh Rd. E15	13	B5
Ranelagh Rd. NW10	15	B1
Rangers Sq. SE10	34	A4
Rannoch Rd. W6	29	E2
Ranulf Rd. NW2	9	A1
Ranwell St. E3	12	D5
Raphael St. SW7	23	G3
Ratcliff Rd. E7	13	F2
Ratcliffe Cross St. E1	19	B5
Ratcliffe La. E14	19	C5
Ratcliffe Orchard E1	26	B1
Rathbone Pl. W1	17	D4
Rathbone St. E16	20	C4
Rathbone St. W1	17	C4
Rathmell Dr. SW4	38	D4
Rathmore Rd. SE7	34	E1
Rattray Rd. SW2	38	G2
Raul Rd. SE15	32	F4
Raveley St. NW5	10	C1
Raven Row E1	18	G4
Ravenhill Rd. E13	20	F1
Ravenna Rd. SW15	36	F3
Ravens Way SE12	41	D3
Ravensbourne Pk. SE6	40	E5
Ravensbourne Pk. Cres. SE6	40	D5
Ravensbourne Pl. SE13	33	F5
Ravenscourt Ave. W6	22	C5
Ravenscourt Gdns. W6	22	C5
Ravenscourt Pk. W6	22	C4
Ravenscourt Pl. W6	22	D5
Ravenscourt Rd. W6	22	D5
Ravenscourt Sq. W6	22	C4
Ravenscroft Clo. E16	20	D4
Ravenscroft Rd. E16	20	D4
Ravenscroft St. E2	18	E1
Ravensdon St. SE11	31	G1
Ravenshaw St. NW6	9	A2
Ravenslea Rd. SW12	37	G5
Ravensmede Way W4	22	B5
Ravenswood Rd. SW12	38	B5
Ravensworth Rd. NW10	15	D2
Ravent Rd. SE11	24	F5
Ravine Gro. SE18	35	G2
Rawlings St. SW3	23	G5
Rawstorne St. EC1	18	A2
Ray St. EC1	17	G3
Rayford Ave. SE12	41	C5
Rayleas Clo. SE18	35	D4
Raymere Gdns. SE18	35	F3
Raymond Rd. E13	13	F4
Raymouth Rd. SE16	25	G5
Rayners Rd. SW15	36	G3
Raynham Rd. W6	22	D5
Reading La. E8	11	G3
Reardon Path E1	25	G2
Reardon St. E1	25	G2
Reaston St. SE14	33	B3
Reckitt Rd. W4	29	A1
Record St. SE15	33	A2
Rector St. N1	11	B5
Rectory Fld. Cres. SE7	34	F3
Rectory Gdns. SW4	38	C1
Rectory Gro. SW4	38	C1
Rectory Pl. SE18	28	C5
Rectory Rd. E12	14	B2
Rectory Rd. SW13	29	C5
Rectory Sq. E1	19	B4
Reculver Rd. SE16	33	B1
Red Barracks Rd. SE18	28	B5
Red Lion Ct. EC4	**44**	**A2**
Red Lion La. SE18	35	C4
Red Lion Row SE17	32	B2
Red Lion Sq. WC1	17	F4
Red Lion St. WC1	17	F4
Red Post Hill SE21	39	C3
Red Post Hill SE24	39	C2
Redan Pl. W2	16	C5
Redan St. W14	22	F4
Redbridge Gdns. SE5	32	D3
Redburn St. SW3	30	G2

Redcar St. SE5	32	B3
Redcastle Clo. E1	26	A1
Redchurch St. E2	18	E3
Redcliffe Gdns. SW10	30	C1
Redcliffe Ms. SW10	30	C1
Redcliffe Pl. SW10	30	D2
Redcliffe Rd. SW10	30	D1
Redcliffe Sq. SW10	30	C1
Redcliffe St. SW10	30	C2
Redclyffe Rd. E6	13	F5
Redcross Way SE1	25	B3
Reddins Rd. SE15	32	F2
Redesdale St. SW3	30	F2
Redfern Rd. NW10	8	A4
Redfern Rd. SE6	40	G5
Redfield La. SW5	23	B5
Redgrave Rd. SW15	36	F1
Redhill St. NW1	17	B1
Redington Gdns. NW3	9	C1
Redington Rd. NW3	9	C1
Redlands Way SW2	38	F5
Redman's Rd. E1	19	A4
Redmore Rd. W6	22	D5
Redriff Est. SE16	26	C4
Redriff Rd. SE16	26	B4
Redriffe Rd. E13	13	C5
Redruth Rd. E9	12	A5
Redwald Rd. E5	12	B1
Redwood Clo. SE16	26	C2
Reece Ms. SW7	23	E5
Reed Clo. E16	20	D4
Reed Clo. SE12	41	D3
Reedham St. SE15	32	F5
Reedworth St. SE11	24	G5
Rees St. N1	11	B5
Reesland Clo. E12	14	C3
Reeves Ms. W1	24	A1
Reeves Rd. E3	19	F3
Reeves Rd. SE18	35	D2
Reform St. SW11	30	G5
Regan Way N1	18	D1
Regency St. SW1	24	D5
Regent Pl. W1	**43**	**B3**
Regent Rd. SE24	39	A4
Regent Sq. E3	19	F2
Regent Sq. WC1	17	E2
Regent St. SW1	**43**	**C4**
Regent St. W1	17	B5
Regents Bri. Gdns. SW8	31	E3
Regents Pk. NW1	16	G1
Regents Pk. Rd. NW1	9	G4
Regent's Pl. SE3	34	D5
Regents Row E8	11	F5
Reginald Rd. E7	13	D3
Reginald Rd. SE8	33	E3
Reginald Sq. SE8	33	E3
Regis Rd. NW5	10	B2
Reidhaven Rd. SE18	28	G5
Relay Rd. W12	22	E2
Relf Rd. SE15	39	F1
Rembrandt Clo. E14	27	A4
Rembrandt Rd. SE13	41	B2
Remington Rd. E6	21	A5
Remington St. N1	18	A1
Remnant St. WC2	**43**	**G1**
Rendlesham Rd. E5	11	F1
Renforth St. SE16	26	A3
Renfrew Clo. E6	28	C1
Renfrew Rd. SE11	25	A5
Rennets Clo. SE9	42	G3
Rennets Wd. Rd. SE9	42	F3
Rennie Est. SE16	25	G5
Rennie St. SE1	**44**	**B5**
Reporton Rd. SW6	29	G4
Repository Rd. SE18	35	B2
Repton St. E14	19	C5
Reservoir Rd. SE4	33	C5
Restell Clo. SE3	34	B2
Restons Cres. SE9	42	F4
Retreat Pl. E9	12	A3
Revelon Rd. SE4	40	C1
Reverdy Rd. SE1	25	F5
Rewell St. SW6	30	D3
Reynolds Ave. E12	14	C2
Reynolds Pl. SE3	34	E3
Reynolds Rd. SE15	40	A3
Rheidol Ter. N1	11	B5
Rhodesia Rd. SW9	31	E5
Rhodeswell Rd. E14	19	C4
Rhondda Gro. E3	19	C2
Rhyl St. NW5	10	A3
Ricardo St. E14	19	F5
Rich St. E14	26	D1
Richard Clo. SE18	28	A5
Richardson Rd. E15	20	B1
Richborne Ter. SW8	31	F3
Richborough Rd. NW2	8	G1
Richford Rd. E15	13	C5
Richford St. W6	22	E3
Richmond Ave. N1	10	F5
Richmond Ave. NW10	8	E3
Richmond Bldgs. W1	**43**	**C2**
Richmond Cres. N1	10	F5
Richmond Gro. N1	11	A4
Richmond Ms. W1	**43**	**C2**
Richmond Pl. SE18	28	E5
Richmond Rd. E7	13	E2
Richmond Rd. E8	11	E4
Richmond St. E13	20	D1
Richmond Ter. SW1	24	E3
Richmond Way W12	22	F3
Richmond Way W14	22	F3
Richmount Gdns. SE3	41	D1
Rickett St. SW6	30	B2
Rickyard Path SE9	42	A2
Rideout St. SE18	28	B5
Rider Clo., Sid.	42	G4
Ridgdale St. E3	19	E1
Ridgebrook Rd. SE3	41	F1
Ridgeway Rd. SW9	39	A1
Ridgeway W., Sid.	42	G3
Ridgewell Rd. E16	20	F4
Ridgmount Rd. SW18	37	C3
Riding Ho. St. W1	17	C4
Ridley Rd. E7	13	F1
Ridley Rd. E8	11	E2
Ridley Rd. NW10	15	C1
Riefield Rd. SE9	42	E2
Riffel Rd. NW2	8	E2
Rifle Pl. W11	22	F2
Rifle St. E14	19	F4
Rigault Rd. SW6	29	G5
Rigden St. E14	19	F5
Rigeley Rd. NW10	15	C2
Rigge Pl. SW4	38	D2
Riley Rd. SE1	25	E4
Riley St. SW10	30	E3
Rinaldo Rd. SW12	38	B5
Ring, The W2	23	E1
Ringcroft St. N7	10	G2
Ringford Rd. SW18	37	A3
Ringmer Ave. SW6	29	G4
Ringmore Ri. SE23	39	G5
Ringstead Rd. SE6	40	F5
Ripley Rd. E16	20	F5
Ripon Rd. SE18	35	D2
Ripple Rd., Bark.	14	F5
Ripplevale Gro. N1	10	F4
Riseldine Rd. SE23	40	C4
Risinghill St. N1	17	F1
Rita Rd. SW8	31	E2
Ritchie St. N1	17	G1
Ritson Rd. E8	11	F3
Ritter St. SE18	35	C2
Rivaz Pl. E9	12	A3
River Pl. N1	11	B4
River Rd., Bark.	21	G1
River St. EC1	17	G2
River Way SE10	27	C4
Rivercourt Rd. W6	22	D5
Rivermead Ct. SW6	37	A1
Riverside Ct. SW8	31	D2
Riverside Gdns. W6	29	D1
Riverside Rd. E15	19	G1
Riverside Wk. SE1	**43**	**H5**
Riverton Clo. W9	16	A2
Riverview Gdns. SW13	29	D2
Rivington Ct. NW10	8	C5
Rivington St. EC2	18	D2
Rixsen Rd. E12	14	A2
Roach Rd. E3	12	E4
Roan St. SE10	33	F3
Robert Adam St. W1	17	A5
Robert Dashwood Way SE17	25	B5
Robert Lowe Clo. SE14	33	B3
Robert Owen Ho. SW6	29	F4
Robert St. E16	28	D2
Robert St. NW1	17	B2
Robert St. SE18	35	F1
Robert St. WC2	**43**	**F4**
Roberta St. E2	18	F2
Robertson Rd. E15	12	G5
Robertson St. SW8	38	B1
Robin Ct. SE16	25	F5
Robin Cres. E6	21	A4
Robin Hood La. E14	19	G5
Robinson Rd. E2	19	A1
Robsart St. SW9	31	F5
Robson Ave. NW10	8	C5
Rochelle Clo. SW11	37	E2
Rochester Ave. E13	13	F5
Rochester Ms. NW1	10	C4
Rochester Pl. NW1	10	C3
Rochester Rd. NW1	10	C3
Rochester Row SW1	24	C5
Rochester Sq. NW1	10	C4
Rochester St. SW1	24	D4
Rochester Ter. NW1	10	C3
Rochester Wk. SE1	**44**	**F5**
Rochester Way SE3	34	F5
Rochester Way SE9	42	B1
Rochester Way Relief Rd. SE3	34	E4
Rochester Way Relief Rd. SE9	41	F2
Rochford St. NW5	9	G2
Rockells Pl. SE22	39	G4
Rockhall Rd. NW2	8	F1
Rockingham Clo. SW15	36	B2
Rockingham Est. SE1	25	B4
Rockingham St. SE1	25	B4
Rockland Rd. SW15	36	G2
Rockley Rd. W14	22	F3
Rocks La. SW13	36	C1
Rocombe Cres. SE23	40	A5
Rocque La. SE3	41	C1
Rodenhurst Rd. SW4	38	C4
Roderick Rd. NW3	9	G1
Roding Rd. E5	12	C1
Roding Rd. E6	21	D4
Roding Trd. Est., Bark.	14	D4
Rodmarton St. W1	16	G4
Rodmill La. SW2	38	E5
Rodney Pl. SE17	25	B5
Rodney Rd. SE17	25	B5
Rodney St. N1	17	F1
Rodway Rd. SW15	36	C5
Rodwell Rd. SE22	39	E4
Roebourne Way E16	28	C3
Roedean Cres. SW15	36	A4
Roehampton Clo. SW15	36	C2
Roehampton Gate SW15	36	A4
Roehampton High St. SW15	36	C5
Roehampton La. SW15	36	C2
Roffey St. E14	26	G3
Roger St. WC1	17	F3
Rogers Rd. E16	20	C5
Rokeby Rd. SE4	33	D5
Rokeby St. E15	13	A5
Rokesby Clo., Well.	35	F5
Roland Gdns. SW7	30	D1
Roland Way SE17	32	C1
Rollins St. SE15	33	A2
Rolls Bldgs. EC4	**43**	**J1**
Rolls Pas. EC4	**43**	**J1**
Rolls Rd. SE1	32	E1
Rollscourt Ave. SE24	39	B3
Rolt St. SE8	33	C2
Roman Rd. E2	19	A2
Roman Rd. E3	19	C1
Roman Rd. E6	20	G3
Roman Rd. W4	22	B5
Roman Rd., Ilf.	14	D3
Roman Way N7	10	F3
Romborough Gdns. SE13	40	G3
Romborough Way SE13	40	G3
Romero Sq. SE3	41	F2
Romford Rd. E7	13	C2
Romford Rd. E12	14	A1
Romford Rd. E15	13	B3
Romford St. E1	18	F4
Romilly St. W1	**43**	**C3**
Romney Rd. SE10	33	G2
Romney St. SW1	24	E4
Rona Rd. NW3	10	A1
Ronald Ave. E15	20	B2
Ronalds Rd. N5	10	G2
Ronaldstone Rd., Sid.	42	G4
Rondu Rd. NW2	8	G2
Rood La. EC3	**44**	**H3**
Rooke Way SE10	34	C1
Rookery Rd. SW4	38	C2
Rope St. SE16	26	C4
Rope Yd. Rails SE18	28	D4
Ropemaker Rd. SE16	26	C3
Ropemaker St. EC2	18	C4
Roper St. SE9	42	B4
Ropery St. E3	19	D3
Ropley St. E2	18	F1
Rosaline Rd. SW6	29	G3
Rosary Gdns. SW7	23	D5
Rosaville Rd. SW6	30	A3
Rose All. SE1	**44**	**E5**
Rose & Crown Ct. EC2	**44**	**D1**
Rose & Crown Yd. SW1	**43**	**B5**
Rose St. WC2	**43**	**E3**
Rose Way SE12	41	D3
Rosebank Gdns. E3	19	D1
Roseberry Pl. E8	11	E3
Roseberry St. SE16	25	G5
Rosebery Ave. E12	14	A3
Rosebery Ave. EC1	17	G3
Rosebery Ave., Sid.	42	G5
Rosebery Rd. SW2	38	E4
Rosebury Rd. SW6	30	C5
Rosedale Rd. E7	13	F2
Rosedene NW6	8	F5
Rosedew Rd. W6	29	F2
Rosefield Gdns. E14	26	E1
Rosehill Rd. SW18	37	D4
Roseleigh Ave. N5	11	A1
Rosemary Dr. E14	20	A5
Rosemary Rd. SE15	32	E3
Rosemont Rd. NW3	9	D3

Rosemoor St. SW3 23 G5
Rosenau Cres. SW11 30 F4
Rosenau Rd. SW11 30 F4
Rosendale Rd. SE21 39 B5
Rosendale Rd. SE24 39 B5
Roseneath Rd. SW11 38 A4
Rosenthal Rd. SE6 40 F4
Rosenthorpe Rd. SE15 40 B3
Roserton St. E14 26 G3
Rosethorn Clo. SW12 38 D5
Roseway SE21 39 C4
Rosher Clo. E15 13 A4
Rosina St. E9 12 B2
Roskell Rd. SW15 36 F1
Rosmead Rd. W11 22 G1
Rosoman St. EC1 17 G2
Ross Ct. SW15 36 F5
Ross Way SE9 42 A1
Rossdale Rd. SW15 36 E2
Rosse Ms. SE3 34 E4
Rossendale Way NW1 10 C5
Rossetti Rd. SE16 32 G1
Rosslyn Ave. SW13 36 A1
Rosslyn Hill NW3 9 E1
Rosslyn Rd., Bark. 14 F4
Rossmore Rd. NW1 16 F3
Rostrevor Rd. SW6 30 A4
Rothbury Rd. E9 12 D4
Rotherfield St. N1 11 B4
Rotherham Wk. SE1 44 B6
Rotherhithe New Rd. SE16 32 G1
Rotherhithe Old Rd. SE16 26 B5
Rotherhithe St. SE16 26 A3
Rotherhithe Tunnel E1 26 B2
Rotherhithe Tunnel App. E14 26 C1
Rotherhithe Tunnel App. SE16 26 A3
Rotherwood Rd. SW15 36 F1
Rothsay Rd. E7 13 F4
Rothsay St. SE1 25 D4
Rothwell St. NW1 9 G5
Rotten Row SW7 23 F3
Rotterdam Dr. E14 26 G4
Rouel Rd. SE16 25 F4
Roundwood Rd. NW10 8 B3
Rounton Rd. E3 19 E3
Roupell St. SE1 44 A6
Rousden St. NW1 10 C4
Routh Rd. SW18 37 F5
Routh St. E6 21 B4
Rowallan Rd. SW6 29 G3
Rowan Ct. E8 11 E4
Rowan Rd. W6 22 F5
Rowberry Clo. SW6 29 E3
Rowcross St. SE1 32 E1
Rowditch La. SW11 31 A5
Rowdon Ave. NW10 8 D4
Rowe La. E9 12 A2
Rowena Cres. SW11 30 F5
Rowhill Rd. E5 11 G1
Rowington Clo. W2 16 C4
Rowland Ct. E16 20 C3
Rowland Hill St. NW3 9 F2
Rowley Way NW8 9 C5
Rowse Clo. E15 12 G5
Rowstock Gdns. N7 10 D2
Rowton Rd. SE18 35 E3
Roxby Pl. SW6 30 B2
Roxley Rd. SE13 40 F4
Roxwell Rd. W12 22 C3
Royal Albert Dock E16 28 A1
Royal Albert Way E16 27 G1
Royal Arc. W1 43 A4
Royal Ave. SW3 30 G1
Royal College St. NW1 10 C4
Royal Cres. W11 22 F2
Royal Docks Rd. E6 28 D1
Royal Docks Rd., Bark. 21 D5
Royal Ex. EC3 44 G2
Royal Ex. Ave. EC3 44 G2
Royal Ex. Bldgs. EC3 44 G2
Royal Hill SE10 33 G3
Royal Hospital Rd. SW3 30 G2
Royal Mint Ct. EC3 25 E1
Royal Mint St. E1 25 E1
Royal Naval Pl. SE14 33 D3
Royal Oak Pl. SE22 39 G4
Royal Oak Rd. E8 11 G3
Royal Opera Arc. SW1 43 C5
Royal Orchard Clo. SW18 36 G5
Royal Par. SE3 34 C5
Royal Pl. SE10 33 G3
Royal Rd. E16 20 F5
Royal Rd. SE17 32 A2
Royal St. SE1 24 F4
Royal Victor Pl. E3 19 B1
Royal Victoria Dock E16 27 D1
Royalty Ms. W1 43 C2
Roydene Rd. SE18 35 G2
Royston St. E2 19 A1
Rozel Ct. N1 11 D5
Rozel Rd. SW4 38 C1
Ruby St. SE15 32 G2
Ruckholt Rd. E10 12 F1
Rucklidge Ave. NW10 15 B1
Ruddstreet Clo. SE18 28 D5
Rudloe Rd. SW12 38 C5
Rudolph Ct. SE22 39 F5
Rudolph Rd. E13 20 C1
Rudolph Rd. NW6 16 B1
Rufford St. N1 10 E5
Rugby Rd. W4 22 A3
Rugby St. WC1 17 F3
Rugg St. E14 26 E1
Rum Clo. E1 26 A1
Rumbold Rd. SW6 30 C3
Rumsey Rd. SW9 38 F1
Runcorn Pl. W11 22 G1
Rupert Ct. W1 43 C3
Rupert Gdns. SW9 32 A5
Rupert Rd. NW6 16 A1
Rupert Rd. W4 22 A4
Rupert St. W1 43 C3
Ruscoe Rd. E16 20 C5
Rush Gro. St. SE18 28 B5
Rush Hill Rd. SW11 38 A1
Rusham Rd. SW12 37 G4
Rushcroft Rd. SW2 38 G2
Rushey Grn. SE6 40 F5
Rushey Mead SE4 40 E3
Rushford Rd. SE4 40 D4
Rushmore Rd. E5 12 A1
Rusholme Rd. SW15 36 F4
Rushton St. N1 18 C1
Rushworth St. SE1 25 A3
Ruskin Ave. E12 14 A3
Ruskin Pk. Ho. SE5 39 C1
Ruskin Wk. SE24 39 B3
Russell Clo. SE7 34 F3
Russell Ct. SW1 43 B6
Russell Gdns. W14 22 G4
Russell Gdns. Ms. W14 22 G3
Russell Gro. SW9 31 G4
Russell Rd. E16 20 D5
Russell Rd. W14 22 G4
Russell Sq. WC1 17 E3
Russell St. WC2 43 F3
Russia Ct. EC2 44 E2
Russia Dock Rd. SE16 26 C2
Russia La. E2 19 A1
Russia Row EC2 44 E2
Rust Sq. SE5 32 C3
Ruston St. E3 12 D5
Rutherford St. SW1 24 D5
Ruthin Rd. SE3 34 D2
Rutland Gdns. SW7 23 F3
Rutland Gate SW7 23 F3
Rutland Gro. W6 29 D1
Rutland Pk. NW2 8 E3
Rutland Rd. E7 13 G4
Rutland Rd. E9 12 A5
Rutland Rd., Ilf. 14 D1
Rutland St. SW7 23 F4
Rutts Ter. SE14 33 B4
Ruvigny Gdns. SW15 36 F1
Ryan Clo. SE3 41 F2
Rycullf Sq. SE3 34 C5
Ryder Ct. SW1 43 B5
Ryder St. SW1 43 B5
Ryder Yd. SW1 43 B5
Rydons Clo. SE9 42 A1
Rye Hill Est. SE15 40 A2
Rye Hill Pk. SE15 40 A2
Rye La. SE15 32 F5
Rye Pas. SE15 39 F1
Rye Rd. SE15 40 B2
Ryecroft Rd. SE13 40 G3
Ryecroft St. SW6 30 C4
Ryedale SE22 39 G4
Ryelands Cres. SE12 41 F4
Ryland Rd. NW5 10 B3
Rylett Cres. W12 22 B3
Rylett Rd. W12 22 B4
Rylston Rd. SW6 30 A2
Rymer St. SE24 39 A4
Rymill St. E16 28 C2
Rysbrack St. SW3 23 G4

S

Sabine Rd. SW11 37 G1
Sackville St. W1 43 B4
Saffron Ave. E14 27 A1
Saffron Hill EC1 17 G4
Sail St. SE11 24 F5
St. Agnes Pl. SE11 32 A2
St. Aidans Rd. SE22 39 G4
St. Albans Ave. E6 21 B2
St. Albans Gro. W8 23 C4
St. Alban's Pl. N1 11 A5
St. Albans Rd. NW10 8 A5
St. Albans St. SW1 43 C4
St. Alfege Pas. SE10 33 G2
St. Alfege Rd. SE7 34 G2
St. Alphonsus Rd. SW4 38 D2
St. Andrew St. EC4 17 G4
St. Andrew's Hill EC4 44 C3
St. Andrews Rd. E13 20 E2
St. Andrews Rd. NW10 8 D3
St. Andrews Rd. W3 15 A5
St. Andrews Rd. W14 29 G2
St. Andrews Way E3 19 F3
St. Anne's Ct. W1 43 C2
St. Anne's Row E14 19 D5
St. Ann's, Bark. 14 E5
St. Ann's Cres. SW18 37 C4
St. Ann's Hill SW18 37 C3
St. Ann's Pk. Rd. SW18 37 D4
St. Ann's Rd. SW13 29 B5
St. Anns Rd. W11 22 F1
St. Ann's St. SW1 24 D4
St. Ann's Ter. NW8 16 E1
St. Anns Vill. W11 22 F2
St. Antony's Rd. E7 13 E4
St. Asaph Rd. SE4 40 B1
St. Augustines Rd. NW1 10 D4
St. Austell Rd. SE13 33 G5
St. Awdry's Rd., Bark. 14 F4
St. Barnabas St. SW1 31 A1
St. Barnabas Ter. E9 12 B2
St. Barnabas Vill. SW8 31 E4
St. Bartholomew's Rd. E6 21 B1
St. Benet's Pl. EC3 44 G3
St. Bernard's Rd. E6 13 G5
St. Botolph St. EC3 18 E5
St. Bride St. EC4 44 B1
St. Bride's Pas. EC4 44 B2
St. Chad's Pl. WC1 17 E2
St. Chad's St. WC1 17 E2
St. Charles Sq. W10 15 G4
St. Clair Rd. E13 20 E1
St. Clement's La. WC2 43 H2
St. Clements St. N1 10 G3
St. Clements St. N7 10 G3
St. Crispins Clo. NW3 9 F1
St. Cross St. EC1 17 G4
St. Cuthberts Rd. NW2 9 A3
St. Dionis Rd. SW6 30 A5
St. Donatts Rd. SE14 33 D4
St. Dunstan's All. EC3 44 H4
St. Dunstan's Hill EC3 44 H4
St. Dunstan's La. EC3 44 H4
St. Dunstan's Rd. E7 13 F3
St. Dunstans Rd. W6 29 F1
St. Edmunds Ter. NW8 9 F5
St. Elmo Rd. W12 22 B2
St. Elmos Rd. SE16 26 B3
St. Erkenwald Rd., Bark. 14 F5
St. Ervans Rd. W10 16 A4
St. Francis Rd. SE22 39 D2
St. Gabriels Rd. NW2 8 F2
St. George St. W1 24 B1
St. Georges Ave. E7 13 E4
St. Georges Ave. N7 10 D1
St. Georges Circ. SE1 25 A4
St. Georges Ct. E6 21 B3
St. George's Ct. EC4 44 B1
St. George's Dr. SW1 24 B5
St. Georges Flds. W2 16 F5
St. Georges La. EC3 44 G3
St. Georges Rd. E7 13 E3
St. Georges Rd. SE1 24 G4
St. Georges Sq. E7 13 E4
St. Georges Sq. E14 26 C1
St. Georges Sq. SE8 26 D5
St. George's Sq. SW1 31 D1
St. George's Sq. Ms. SW1 31 D1
St. Georges Way SE15 32 D2
St. Gerards Clo. SW4 38 C3
St. German's Pl. SE3 34 D4
St. Giles High St. WC2 43 D1
St. Giles Pas. WC2 43 D2
St. Giles Rd. SE5 32 D3
St. Helena Rd. SE16 26 B5
St. Helens Gdns. W10 15 F4
St. Helens Pl. EC3 44 H1
St. Hildas Clo. NW6 8 F5
St. Hilda's Rd. SW13 29 D2
St. James Ave. E2 19 A1
St. James Gdns. W11 22 G2

St. James Ms. E14 26 G4
St. James Rd. E15 13 C2
St. James St. W6 29 E1
St. James's SE14 33 C4
St. James's Ct. SW1 24 C4
St. James's Cres. SW9 38 G1
St. James's Mkt. SW1 43 C4
St. James's Pk. SW1 24 C3
St. James's Pas. EC3 44 J2
St. James's Pl. SW1 43 A6
St. James's Rd. SE1 32 F1
St. James's Rd. SE16 25 F4
St. James's Sq. SW1 43 B5
St. James's St. SW1 43 A5
St. James's Ter. Ms. NW8 9 G5
St. James's Wk. EC1 18 A3
St. John St. EC1 17 G1
St. John's Ave. NW10 8 B5
St. John's Ave. SW15 36 F3
St. John's Ch. Rd. E9 12 A2
St. John's Cres. SW9 38 G1
St. Johns Est. N1 18 C1
St. Johns Gdns. W11 22 G1
St. John's Hill SW11 37 E2
St. John's Hill Gro. SW11 37 E2
St. John's La. EC1 18 A3
St. John's Pk. SE3 34 C3
St. Johns Rd. E6 14 A5
St. Johns Rd. E16 20 D5
St. John's Rd. SW11 37 F2
St. John's Rd., Bark. 14 G5
St. Johns Ter. E7 13 E3
St. Johns Ter. SE18 35 E2
St. Johns Vale SE8 33 E5
St. John's Wd. High St. NW8 16 E1
St. John's Wd. Pk. NW8 9 E5
St. John's Wd. Rd. NW8 16 E3
St. John's Wd. Ter. NW8 16 E1
St. Joseph's Ct. SE7 34 E2
St. Joseph's Vale SE3 41 A1
St. Jude St. N16 11 D2
St. Jude's Rd. E2 18 G1
St. Julian's Rd. NW6 9 B5
St. Katharine's Way E1 25 F2
St. Katherine's Row EC3 44 J3
St. Laurence Clo. NW6 8 F5
St. Lawrence St. E14 26 G2
St. Lawrence Ter. W10 15 G4
St. Lawrence Way SW9 31 G5
St. Leonards Gdns., Ilf. 14 E2
St. Leonards Rd. E14 19 F4
St. Leonards Sq. NW5 10 A3
St. Leonards St. E3 19 F2
St. Leonard's Ter. SW3 30 G1
St. Loo Ave. SW3 30 F2
St. Luke's Ave. SW4 38 D2
St. Luke's Ave., Ilf. 14 D2
St. Luke's Est. EC1 18 C2
St. Lukes Rd. W11 16 A4
St. Lukes Sq. E16 20 C5
St. Luke's St. SW3 30 F1
St. Luke's Yd. W9 16 A2
St. Margarets, Bark. 14 E5
St. Margaret's Ct. SE1 44 F6
St. Margarets Cres. SW15 36 D3
St. Margaret's Gro. SE18 35 E2
St. Margaret's Rd. NW10 15 E2
St. Margarets Rd. SE4 40 D2
St. Margaret's St. SW1 24 E3
St. Margaret's Ter. SE18 35 E1
St. Mark St. E1 18 E5
St. Marks Cres. NW1 10 A5
St. Mark's Gro. SW10 30 C2
St. Marks Pl. W11 15 G5
St. Marks Ri. E8 11 E2
St. Marks Rd. W10 15 F4
St. Marks Rd. W11 15 G5
St. Martins Ave. E6 20 G1
St. Martin's Clo. NW1 10 C5
St. Martin's Ct. WC2 43 E3
St. Martin's La. WC2 43 E3
St. Martin's Pl. WC2 43 E4
St. Martin's Rd. SW9 31 F5
St. Martin's St. WC2 43 D4
St. Martin's-le-Grand EC1 44 D1
St. Mary Abbots Pl. W8 23 A4
St. Mary Abbots Ter. W14 23 A4
St. Mary at Hill EC3 44 H4
St. Mary Axe EC3 44 H2
St. Mary St. SE18 28 C5
St. Marychurch St. SE16 26 A3
St. Marys, Bark. 14 F5
St. Marys App. E12 14 B2
St. Marys Ct. E6 21 B3
St. Mary's Ct. SE7 34 G3
St. Mary's Gdns. SE11 24 G5
St. Mary's Gro. N1 11 A3
St. Mary's Gro. SW13 36 D1
St. Marys Mans. W2 16 E4
St. Marys Path N1 11 A5
St. Marys Rd. E13 20 E1
St. Marys Rd. NW10 8 A5
St. Mary's Rd. SE15 33 A4
St. Marys Sq. W2 16 E4
St. Marys Ter. W2 16 E4
St. Mary's Wk. SE11 24 G5
St. Matthew's Rd. SW2 38 F2
St. Matthew's Row E2 18 F2
St. Maur Rd. SW6 30 A4
St. Merryn Clo. SE18 35 F3
St. Michael's All. EC3 44 G2
St. Michael's Rd. NW2 8 E1
St. Michael's Rd. SW9 31 F5
St. Michaels St. W2 16 E5
St. Mildred's Ct. EC2 44 F2
St. Mildreds Rd. SE12 41 C5
St. Norbert Grn. SE4 40 C2
St. Norbert Rd. SE4 40 B3
St. Olaf's Rd. SW6 29 G3
St. Olaves Ct. EC2 44 F2
St. Olaves Rd. E6 14 C5
St. Oswald's Pl. SE11 31 F1
St. Pancras Way NW1 10 C4
St. Paul St. N1 11 B5
St. Paul's Ave. NW2 8 E3
St. Paul's Ave. SE16 26 B2
St. Paul's Chyd. EC4 44 C2
St. Paul's Clo. SE7 34 G1
St. Pauls Cres. NW1 10 D4
St. Pauls Dr. E15 13 A2
St. Paul's Pl. N1 11 C3
St. Paul's Rd. N1 11 A3
St. Paul's Rd., Bark. 14 E5
St. Paul's Shrubbery N1 11 C3
St. Pauls St. E3 19 D4
St. Pauls Way E3 19 D4
St. Peter's All. EC3 44 G2
St. Peter's Clo. E2 18 F1
St. Peter's Gro. W6 22 C5
St. Peter's Rd. W6 29 C1
St. Peter's Sq. W6 29 C1
St. Peters St. N1 11 A5
St. Peters Ter. SW6 30 A3
St. Peter's Vill. W6 22 C5
St. Peter's Way N1 11 D4
St. Petersburgh Ms. W2 23 C1
St. Petersburgh Pl. W2 23 C1
St. Philip Sq. SW8 31 B5
St. Philip St. SW8 31 B5
St. Philip's Rd. E8 11 F3
St. Quintin Ave. W10 15 E4
St. Quintin Gdns. W10 15 E4
St. Quintin Rd. E13 20 E1
St. Rule St. SW8 31 C5
St. Saviour's Est. SE1 25 E4
St. Saviour's Rd. SW2 38 F3
St. Silas Pl. NW5 10 A3
St. Silas St. Est. NW5 10 A3
St. Simon's Ave. SW15 36 E3
St. Stephens Ave. W12 22 D3
St. Stephens Clo. NW8 9 F5
St. Stephens Gdns. W2 16 B5
St. Stephens Gro. SE13 40 G1
St. Stephen's Rd. E3 12 C5
St. Stephens Rd. E6 13 F4
St. Stephens Row EC4 44 F3
St. Stephens Ter. SW8 31 F3
St. Swithin's La. EC4 44 F3
St. Swithun's Rd. SE13 41 A3
St. Thomas Gdns., Ilf. 14 E3
St. Thomas Rd. E16 20 D5
St. Thomas St. SE1 44 G6
St. Thomas's Pl. E9 12 A4
St. Thomas's Rd. NW10 8 A5
St. Thomas's Sq. E9 12 A4
St. Thomas's Way SW6 30 A3
St. Winifride's Ave. E12 14 B2
Saints Dr. E7 13 G2
Salamanca St. SE11 24 F5
Salcombe Rd. N16 11 D2
Salcott Rd. SW11 37 F3
Sale Pl. W2 16 F5
Sale St. E2 18 F3
Salehurst Rd. SE4 40 D4
Salem Rd. W2 23 C1
Salisbury Ave., Bark. 14 F4
Salisbury Ct. EC4 44 A2
Salisbury Pl. SW9 32 A3
Salisbury Pl. W1 16 G4
Salisbury Rd. E7 13 D3
Salisbury Rd. E12 13 G2
Salisbury Sq. EC4 44 A2
Salisbury St. NW8 16 F3
Salisbury Ter. SE15 40 A1
Salmen Rd. E13 20 C1
Salmon La. E14 19 C5
Saltcoats Rd. W4 22 A3
Salter Rd. SE16 26 B2
Salter St. E14 26 E1
Salter St. NW10 15 C2
Salters Hall Ct. EC4 44 F3
Salters Rd. W10 15 F3
Saltoun Rd. SW2 38 G2
Saltram Cres. W9 16 A2
Saltwell St. E14 26 E1
Salusbury Rd. NW6 8 G5
Salvin Rd. SW15 36 F1
Salway Rd. E15 13 A3
Sam Bartram Clo. SE7 34 F1
Samford St. NW8 16 F3
Sampson St. E1 25 F2
Samson St. E13 20 F1
Samuel Clo. SE14 33 B2
Samuel Clo. SE18 28 A5
Samuel Lewis Trust Dws. SW6 30 B3
Samuel St. SE18 28 B5
Sancroft St. SE11 31 F1
Sandal St. E15 13 B5
Sandall Rd. NW5 10 C3
Sandbach Pl. SE18 35 E1
Sandbourne Rd. SE4 33 C5
Sandby Grn. SE9 42 A1
Sanderson Clo. NW5 10 B1
Sandford Clo. E6 21 B3
Sandford Rd. E6 21 A2
Sandgate St. SE15 32 G2
Sandilands Rd. SW6 30 C4
Sandison St. SE15 39 E1
Sandland St. WC1 17 F4
Sandmere Rd. SW4 38 E2
Sandpit Pl. SE7 35 A1
Sandringham Dr., Well. 35 G5
Sandringham Rd. E7 13 F2
Sandringham Rd. E8 11 E2
Sandringham Rd. NW2 8 D3
Sandrock Rd. SE13 40 E1
Sand's End La. SW6 30 C4
Sandtoft Rd. SE7 34 E2
Sandwell Cres. NW6 9 B3
Sandwich St. WC1 17 E2
Sandy Hill Ave. SE18 35 D1
Sandy Hill Rd. SE18 35 D1
Sandyhill Rd., Ilf. 14 D1
Sandys Row E1 18 D4
Sanford St. SE14 33 C2
Sangley Rd. SE6 40 F5
Sangora Rd. SW11 37 E2
Sans Wk. EC1 17 G3
Sansom St. SE5 32 C3
Santley St. SW4 38 E2
Santos Rd. SW18 37 B3
Sapphire Clo. E6 21 C5
Sapphire Rd. SE8 33 C1
Saracen St. E14 19 E5
Saratoga Rd. E5 12 A1
Sardinia St. WC2 43 G2
Sark Wk. E16 20 E5
Sarre Rd. NW2 9 A2
Sartor Rd. SE15 40 B2
Saunders Ness Rd. E14 33 G1
Savage Gdns. E6 21 B5
Savage Gdns. EC3 44 J3
Savernake Rd. NW3 9 G1
Savile Row W1 43 A3
Saville Rd. E16 28 A2
Savona Est. SW8 31 C3
Savona St. SW8 31 C3
Savoy Bldgs. WC2 43 G4
Savoy Ct. WC2 43 F4

Savoy Hill WC2	**43**	**G4**
Savoy Pl. WC2	**43**	**F4**
Savoy Row WC2	**43**	**G4**
Savoy Steps WC2	**43**	**G4**
Savoy St. WC2	**43**	**G4**
Savoy Way WC2	**43**	**G4**
Sawley Rd. W12	22	B2
Sawyer St. SE1	25	B3
Saxby Rd. SW2	38	E5
Saxon Rd. E3	19	D1
Saxon Rd. E6	21	B3
Saxon Rd., Ilf.	14	D3
Saxton Clo. SE13	41	A1
Sayes Ct. St. SE8	33	D2
Scala St. W1	17	C4
Scampston Ms. W10	15	F5
Scandrett St. E1	25	G2
Scarsbrook Rd. SE3	41	G1
Scarsdale Vill. W8	23	B4
Scarth Rd. SW13	36	B1
Scawen Rd. SE8	33	C1
Scawfell St. E2	18	E1
Sceaux Est. SE5	32	D4
Sceaux Gdns. SE5	32	E4
Sceptre Rd. E2	19	A2
School Rd. E12	14	B1
Schoolhouse La. E1	26	B1
Schubert Rd. SW15	37	A3
Sclater St. E1	18	E3
Scoresby St. SE1	**44**	**B6**
Scotland Pl. SW1	**43**	**E6**
Scotsdale Rd. SE12	41	E3
Scott Ellis Gdns. NW8	16	E2
Scott Lidgett Cres. SE16	25	F3
Scott St. E1	18	G3
Scotts Rd. W12	22	D3
Scott's Yd. EC4	**44**	**F3**
Scoulding Rd. E16	20	D5
Scout App. NW10	8	A1
Scriven St. E8	11	E5
Scrooby St. SE6	40	F4
Scrubs La. NW10	15	C2
Scrubs La. W10	15	D4
Scrutton Clo. SW12	38	D5
Scrutton St. EC2	18	D3
Scutari Rd. SE22	40	A3
Scylla Rd. SE15	39	G1
Seaford St. WC1	17	F2
Seaforth Cres. N5	11	B2
Seagrave Rd. SW6	30	B2
Seal St. E8	11	E1
Searles Clo. SW11	30	F3
Searles Rd. SE1	25	C5
Sears St. SE5	32	C3
Seaton Ave., Ilf.	14	G2
Sebastian St. EC1	18	A2
Sebbon St. N1	11	A4
Sebert Rd. E7	13	E2
Secker St. SE1	**43**	**J6**
Second Ave. E12	14	A1
Second Ave. SW14	36	A1
Second Ave. W3	22	B2
Second Ave. W10	15	G3
Sedding St. SW1	24	A5
Sedgebrook Rd. SE3	34	G5
Sedgeford Rd. W12	22	B2
Sedgmoor Pl. SE5	32	D3
Sedgwick St. E9	12	B2
Sedleigh Rd. SW18	37	A4
Sedlescombe Rd. SW6	30	A2
Seething La. EC3	**44**	**J3**
Sefton St. SW15	36	E1
Segal Clo. SE23	40	C5
Sekforde St. EC1	18	A3
Selbie Ave. NW10	8	B2
Selby Rd. E13	20	E4
Selby St. E1	18	F3
Selden Rd. SE15	33	A5
Sellons Ave. NW10	8	B5
Selsdon Rd. E13	13	F5
Selsdon Way E14	26	F4
Selsey St. E14	19	E4
Selwood Pl. SW7	30	E1
Selwyn Ct. SE3	41	C1
Selwyn Rd. E3	19	D1
Selwyn Rd. E13	13	E5
Semley Pl. SW1	24	A5
Senate St. SE15	33	A5
Senior St. W2	16	C4
Senrab St. E1	19	B5
Serjeants Inn EC4	**44**	**A2**
Serle St. WC2	**43**	**H1**
Serpentine Rd. W2	23	G2
Settles St. E1	18	F4
Settrington Rd. SW6	30	C5
Sevenoaks Rd. SE4	40	C4
Seventh Ave. E12	14	B1
Severn Way NW10	8	B2
Severnake Clo. E14	26	E5
Severus Rd. SW11	37	F2
Seville St. SW1	23	G3
Sevington St. W9	16	C3
Seward St. EC1	18	A3
Sewardstone Rd. E2	19	A1
Sewdley St. E5	12	B1
Sewell St. E13	20	D2
Sextant Ave. E14	27	A5
Seymour Gdns. SE4	40	C1
Seymour Ms. W1	17	A5
Seymour Pl. W1	16	F4
Seymour Rd. E6	20	G1
Seymour Rd. SW18	37	A5
Seymour St. W1	16	G5
Seymour St. W2	16	G5
Seymour Wk. SW10	30	D2
Seyssel St. E14	26	G5
Shacklewell La. E8	11	E2
Shacklewell Rd. N16	11	E1
Shacklewell Row E8	11	E1
Shacklewell St. E2	18	E2
Shad Thames SE1	25	E3
Shaftesbury Ave. W1	**43**	**C3**
Shaftesbury Ave. WC2	**43**	**C4**
Shaftesbury Rd. E7	13	F4
Shaftesbury St. N1	18	B1
Shaftesburys, The, Bark.	21	E1
Shafton Rd. E9	12	B5
Shakespeare Cres. E12	14	B3
Shakespeare Rd. SE24	39	A3
Shakespeare Wk. N16	11	D1
Shalcomb St. SW10	30	D2
Shalfleet Dr. W10	22	F1
Shamrock St. SW4	38	D1
Shand St. SE1	25	D3
Shandon Rd. SW4	38	C4
Shandy St. E1	19	B4
Shannon Gro. SW9	38	F2
Shardcroft Ave. SE24	39	A3
Shardeloes Rd. SE14	33	D5
Sharon Gdns. E9	12	A5
Sharpleshall St. NW1	9	G4
Sharratt St. SE15	33	A2
Sharsted St. SE17	32	A1
Shavers Pl. SW1	**43**	**C4**
Shawbrooke Rd. SE9	41	F3
Shawbury Rd. SE22	39	E3
Shawfield St. SW3	30	F1
Shawford Ct. SW15	36	C5
Shearling Way N7	10	E3
Shearman Rd. SE3	41	C2
Sheep La. E8	11	G5
Sheepcote La. SW11	30	G5
Sheerwater Rd. E16	20	G4
Sheffield St. WC2	**43**	**G2**
Sheffield Ter. W8	23	B2
Shelburne Rd. N7	10	F1
Shelbury Rd. SE22	39	G3
Sheldon Clo. SE12	41	E3
Sheldon Rd. NW2	8	F1
Sheldrake Pl. W8	23	B3
Shelgate Rd. SW11	37	F3
Shell Rd. SE13	40	F1
Shelley Ave. E12	14	A3
Shelley Dr., Well.	35	G4
Shellgrove Est. N16	11	D2
Shellness Rd. E5	11	G2
Shellwood Rd. SW11	30	G5
Shelmerdine Clo. E3	19	E4
Shelton St. WC2	**43**	**E2**
Shenfield St. N1	18	D1
Shenley Rd. SE5	32	D4
Shepherdess Wk. N1	18	B1
Shepherds Bush Grn. W12	22	E3
Shepherds Bush Pl. W12	22	F3
Shepherds Bush Rd. W6	22	E4
Shepherds La. E9	12	B3
Shepherds Wk. NW3	9	E1
Sheppard Dr. SE16	32	G1
Sheppard St. E16	20	C3
Shepperton Rd. N1	11	B5
Sherard Rd. SE9	42	A3
Sheraton St. W1	**43**	**C2**
Sherborne La. EC4	**44**	**F3**
Sherborne St. N1	11	C5
Sherbrooke Rd. SW6	29	G3
Sherfield Gdns. SW15	36	B4
Sheridan Rd. E12	14	A2
Sheringham Ave. E12	14	B1
Sheringham Rd. N7	10	F3
Sherington Rd. SE7	34	E2
Sherrard Rd. E7	13	F3
Sherrard Rd. E12	13	G3
Sherrick Grn. Rd. NW10	8	D2
Sherriff Rd. NW6	9	B3
Sherrin Rd. E10	12	E1
Sherwin Rd. SE14	33	B4
Sherwood Gdns. E14	26	E5
Sherwood Gdns., Bark.	14	F4
Sherwood Rd., Well.	35	G5
Sherwood St. W1	**43**	**B3**
Shetland Rd. E3	19	D1
Shinfield St. W12	15	E5
Ship St. SE8	33	E4
Ship Tavern Pas. EC3	**44**	**H3**
Shipman Rd. E16	20	E5
Shipton St. E2	18	E1
Shipwright Rd. SE16	26	C3
Shirbutt St. E14	26	F1
Shirebrook Rd. SE3	41	G1
Shirland Ms. W9	16	A2
Shirland Rd. W9	16	A2
Shirley Gdns., Bark.	14	G3
Shirley Gro. SW11	38	A1
Shirley Ho. Dr. SE7	34	F3
Shirley Rd. E15	13	B4
Shirley St. E16	20	C5
Shirlock Rd. NW3	9	G1
Shoe La. EC4	**44**	**A1**
Shoebury Rd. E6	14	B4
Shoot Up Hill NW2	8	G2
Shooter's Hill SE18	35	C4
Shooter's Hill, Well.	35	E5
Shooter's Hill Rd. SE3	34	C4
Shooter's Hill Rd. SE10	34	A4
Shooter's Hill Rd. SE18	34	G4
Shore Pl. E9	12	A4
Shore Rd. E9	12	A4
Shoreditch High St. E1	18	D3
Shorncliffe Rd. SE1	32	E1
Shorrolds Rd. SW6	30	A3
Short Rd. E15	13	A5
Short Rd. W4	29	A2
Short Way SE9	42	A1
Shorter St. E1	25	E1
Shortlands W6	22	F5
Shorts Gdns. WC2	**43**	**E2**
Shottendane Rd. SW6	30	B4
Shottfield Ave. SW14	36	A2
Shouldham St. W1	16	F4
Shrapnel Clo. SE18	35	A3
Shrapnel Rd. SE9	42	B1
Shrewsbury La. SE18	35	D4
Shrewsbury Rd. E7	13	G2
Shrewsbury Rd. W2	16	B5
Shroton St. NW1	16	F4
Shrubland Rd. E8	11	E5
Shuttleworth Rd. SW11	30	E5
Sibella Rd. SW4	31	D5
Sibley Gro. E12	14	A4
Sibthorpe Rd. SE12	41	E4
Sidbury St. SW6	29	G4
Sidcup Rd. SE9	41	F5
Sidcup Rd. SE12	41	E3
Sidmouth Rd. NW2	8	E4
Sidmouth Rd. SE15	32	E4
Sidmouth St. WC1	17	F2
Sidney Est. E1	19	A5
Sidney Rd. SW9	31	F5
Sidney Sq. E1	19	A4
Sidney St. E1	19	A4
Sidworth St. E8	11	G4
Siebert Rd. SE3	34	D2
Siemens Rd. SE18	27	G4
Sigdon Rd. E8	11	F2
Silchester Rd. W10	15	F5
Silex St. SE1	25	A3
Silk Clo. SE12	41	D3
Silk Mills Path SE13	33	G5
Silk St. EC2	18	B4
Silver Pl. W1	**43**	**B3**
Silver Rd. W12	22	F1
Silver Wk. SE16	26	D2
Silverland St. E16	28	B2
Silvermere Rd. SE6	40	F4
Silverthorne Rd. SW8	31	B5
Silverton Rd. W6	29	F2
Silvertown Way E16	20	B5
Silvester Rd. SE22	39	E3
Silwood St. SE16	26	A5
Simmons Rd. SE18	35	D1
Simms Rd. SE1	25	F5
Simnel Rd. SE12	41	E5
Simpson St. SW11	30	F5
Simpsons Rd. E14	26	F1
Sinclair Gdns. W14	22	F3
Sinclair Rd. W14	22	F3
Sir Alexander Clo. W3	22	B2
Sir Alexander Rd. W3	22	B2
Sirdar Rd. W11	22	F1
Sirinham Pt. SW8	31	F2
Sise La. EC4	**44**	**F2**
Sisley Rd., Bark.	14	G5
Sispara Gdns. SW18	37	A4
Sisters Ave. SW11	37	G1
Sisulu Pl. SW9	38	G1
Sivill Ho. E2	18	E2
Sixth Ave. E12	14	B1
Sixth Ave. W10	15	G2
Skardu Rd. NW2	8	G2
Skeena Hill SW18	36	G5
Skeffington Rd. E6	14	B5
Skelgill Rd. SW15	37	A2

Skelley Rd. E15 13 C4
Skelton Rd. E7 13 D3
Skelwith Rd. W6 29 E2
Sketchley Gdns. SE16 33 B1
Skiers St. E15 13 B5
Skinner St. EC1 17 G2
Skinners La. EC4 44 E3
Skipsey Ave. E6 21 B2
Skipworth Rd. E9 12 A5
Slade, The SE18 35 G2
Sladebrook Rd. SE3 41 G1
Sladedale Rd. SE18 35 G1
Slaidburn St. SW10 30 D2
Slaithwaite Rd. SE13 40 G2
Sleaford St. SW8 31 C3
Slingsby Pl. WC2 43 E3
Slippers Pl. SE16 25 G4
Sloane Ave. SW3 23 F5
Sloane Ct. E. SW3 31 A1
Sloane Ct. W. SW3 31 A1
Sloane Gdns. SW1 24 A5
Sloane Sq. SW1 23 G5
Sloane St. SW1 23 G3
Sloane Ter. SW1 23 G5
Smart St. E2 19 B2
Smart's Pl. WC2 43 F1
Smeaton Rd. SW18 37 B5
Smeaton St. E1 25 G2
Smedley St. SW4 31 D5
Smedley St. SW8 31 D5
Smeed Rd. E3 12 E4
Smiles Pl. SE13 33 G5
Smith Clo. SE16 26 B2
Smith Sq. SW1 24 E4
Smith St. SW3 30 G1
Smith Ter. SW3 30 G1
Smith's Ct. W1 43 B3
Smithy St. E1 19 A4
Smugglers Way SW18 37 C2
Smyrks Rd. SE17 32 D1
Smyrna Rd. NW6 9 B4
Smythe St. E14 26 F1
Snarsgate St. W10 15 E4
Sneyd Rd. NW2 8 E1
Snow Hill EC1 18 A4
Snow Hill Ct. EC1 44 C1
Snowbury Rd. SW6 30 C5
Snowden St. EC2 18 D3
Snowman Ho. NW6 9 C4
Snowsfields SE1 25 C3
Snowshill Rd. E12 14 A2
Soames St. SE15 39 E1
Soho Sq. W1 43 C1
Soho St. W1 43 C1
Solebay St. E1 19 C3
Solent Rd. NW6 9 B2
Solna Ave. SW15 36 E3
Solomon's Pas. SE15 39 G2
Solon New Rd. SW4 38 E2
Solon Rd. SW2 38 E2
Solway Rd. SE22 39 F2
Somali Rd. NW2 9 A2
Somerby Rd., Bark. 14 F4
Somerford Gro. N16 11 E1
Somerford St. E1 18 G3
Somerford Way SE16 26 C3
Somerleyton Pas. SW9 39 A2
Somerleyton Rd. SW9 38 G2
Somers Cres. W2 16 F5
Somers Pl. SW2 38 F5
Somers Rd. SW2 38 F4
Somerset Est. SW11 30 E4
Somerset Gdns. SE13 33 F5
Somerset Sq. W14 22 G3
Somerton Rd. SE15 39 G2
Sondes St. SE17 32 C2
Sonia Gdns. NW10 8 B1
Sophia Rd. E16 20 E5
Sorrell Gdns. E6 21 A4
Sotheran Clo. E8 11 F5
Sotheron Rd. SW6 30 C3
Soudan Rd. SW11 30 G4
Souldern Rd. W14 22 F4
South Africa Rd. W12 22 D2
South Audley St. W1 24 A1
South Black Lion La. W6 29 C1
South Bolton Gdns. SW5 30 C1
South Carriage Dr. SW1 23 F3
South Carriage Dr. SW7 23 F3
South Colonnade E14 26 E2
South Cres. WC1 17 D4
South Eaton Pl. SW1 24 A5
South Edwardes Sq. W8 23 A4
South End Clo. NW3 9 F1
South End Rd. NW3 9 F1
South End Row W8 23 C4
South Esk Rd. E7 13 F3
South Hill Pk. NW3 9 F1
South Hill Pk. Gdns. NW3 9 F1
South Island Pl. SW9 31 F3
South Lambeth Pl. SW8 31 E2
South Lambeth Rd. SW8 31 E2
South Molton La. W1 17 B5
South Molton Rd. E16 20 D5
South Molton St. W1 17 B5
South Par. SW3 30 E1
South Pk. Ms. SW6 37 C1
South Pl. EC2 18 C4
South Row SE3 34 C5
South Sea St. SE16 26 D4
South Side W6 22 B4
South St. W1 24 A2
South Tenter St. E1 25 E1
South Ter. SW7 23 F5
South Vill. NW1 10 D3
South W. India Dock Entrance E14 26 G3
South Wf. Rd. W2 16 E5
South Woodford to Barking Relief Rd. E12 14 C1
South Woodford to Barking Relief Rd., Bark. 14 C1
Southall Pl. SE1 25 C3
Southam St. W10 15 G3
Southampton Pl. WC1 17 E4
Southampton Rd. NW5 9 G2
Southampton Row WC1 17 E4
Southampton St. WC2 43 F3
Southampton Way SE5 32 C3
Southborough Rd. E9 12 B4
Southbourne Gdns. SE12 41 E3
Southbourne Gdns., Ilf. 14 E2
Southbrook Ms. SE12 41 C4
Southbrook Rd. SE12 41 C4
Southchurch Rd. E6 21 B1
Southcombe St. W14 22 G5
Southcote Rd. N19 10 C1
Southcroft Ave., Well. 42 G1
Southend Clo. SE9 42 D4
Southend Cres. SE9 42 D4
Southend Rd. E6 14 B4
Southern Gro. E3 19 D2
Southern Rd. E13 20 E1
Southern Row W10 15 G3
Southern St. N1 17 F1
Southerngate Way SE14 33 C3
Southerton Rd. W6 22 E4
Southey Rd. SW9 31 G4
Southfields Rd. SW18 37 B4
Southgate Gro. N1 11 C4
Southgate Rd. N1 11 C5
Southmoor Way E9 12 D3
Southolm St. SW11 31 B4
Southport Rd. SE18 28 F5
Southspring, Sid. 42 F5
Southvale Rd. SE3 34 B5
Southview Ave. NW10 8 B2
Southville SW8 31 D4
Southwark Bri. EC4 44 E4
Southwark Bri. SE1 44 E4
Southwark Bri. Rd. SE1 25 A4
Southwark Gro. SE1 44 D6
Southwark Pk. Est. SE16 25 G5
Southwark Pk. Rd. SE16 25 E5
Southwark St. SE1 44 C5
Southwater Clo. E14 19 D5
Southwell Gdns. SW7 23 D5
Southwell Rd. SE5 39 B1
Southwick Pl. W2 16 F5
Southwick St. W2 16 F5
Sovereign Clo. E1 25 G1
Sowerby Clo. SE9 42 A3
Spa Rd. SE16 25 E4
Spanby Rd. E3 19 E3
Spanish Pl. W1 17 A5
Spanish Rd. SW18 37 D3
Sparrows La. SE9 42 E5
Sparsholt Rd., Bark. 14 G5
Sparta St. SE10 33 G4
Spear Ms. SW5 23 B5
Spearman St. SE18 35 C2
Speke Ho. SE5 32 B3
Speldhurst Rd. E9 12 B4
Spelman St. E1 18 F4
Spencer Gdns. SE9 42 B3
Spencer Pk. SW18 37 E3
Spencer Ri. NW5 10 B1
Spencer Rd. E6 13 G5
Spencer Rd. SW18 37 E2
Spencer St. EC1 18 A2
Spencer Wk. SW15 36 F2
Spenser Gro. N16 11 D1
Spenser Rd. SE24 38 G3
Spenser St. SW1 24 C4
Spert St. E14 26 C1
Spey St. E14 19 G4
Spezia Rd. NW10 15 C1
Spicer Clo. SW9 32 A5
Spindrift Ave. E14 26 E5
Spital Sq. E1 18 D4
Spital St. E1 18 F4
Spitalfields Mkt. E1 18 E4
Sportsbank St. SE6 40 G5
Spray St. SE18 28 D5
Sprimont Pl. SW3 23 G5
Spring Gdns. SW1 43 D5
Spring Path NW3 9 E2
Spring Pl. NW5 10 B2
Spring St. W2 16 E5
Springall St. SE15 32 G3
Springbank Rd. SE13 41 A4
Springdale Rd. N16 11 C1
Springfield Gro. SE7 34 F2
Springfield La. NW6 9 C5
Springfield Rd. E6 14 B4
Springfield Rd. E15 20 B2
Springfield Rd. NW8 9 D5
Springfield Wk. NW6 9 C5
Springhill Clo. SE5 39 C1
Springrice Rd. SE13 41 A4
Springvale Ter. W14 22 F4
Springwater Clo. SE18 35 C4
Springwell Ave. NW10 8 B5
Sprowston Ms. E7 13 D3
Sprowston Rd. E7 13 D2
Sprules Rd. SE4 33 C5
Spur Rd. SW1 24 C3
Spur Rd., Bark. 21 E2
Spurgeon St. SE1 25 C4
Spurling Rd. SE22 39 E2
Spurstowe Ter. E8 11 G2
Square, The W6 29 E1
Squirries St. E2 18 F2
Stable Yd. Rd. SW1 24 C3
Stables Way SE11 31 G1
Stacey St. WC2 43 D2
Stadium Rd. SE18 35 B3
Stadium St. SW10 30 D3
Stafford Clo. NW6 16 B2
Stafford Pl. SW1 24 C4
Stafford Rd. E3 19 D1
Stafford Rd. E7 13 F4
Stafford Rd. NW6 16 B2
Stafford St. W1 43 A5
Stafford Ter. W8 23 B3
Staffordshire St. SE15 32 F4
Stag Pl. SW1 24 C4
Stainer St. SE1 44 G6
Staines Rd., Ilf. 14 F1
Staining La. EC2 44 E1
Stainsby Pl. E14 19 E5
Stainsby Rd. E14 19 E5
Stainton Rd. SE6 41 A4
Stalham St. SE16 25 G4
Stamford Brook Ave. W6 22 B4
Stamford Brook Rd. W6 22 B4
Stamford Rd. E6 14 A5
Stamford Rd. N1 11 D4
Stamford St. SE1 43 J6
Stamp Pl. E2 18 E2
Stanbridge Rd. SW15 36 E1
Stanbury Rd. SE15 32 G4
Standard Ind. Est. E16 28 B3
Standen Rd. SW18 37 A5
Standish Rd. W6 22 C5
Stane Way SE18 35 A3
Stanfield Rd. E3 19 C1
Stanford Rd. W8 23 C4
Stanhope Gdns. SW7 23 D5
Stanhope Gate W1 24 A2
Stanhope Ms. E. SW7 23 D5
Stanhope Ms. W. SW7 23 D5
Stanhope Pl. W2 23 G1
Stanhope St. NW1 17 C2
Stanhope Ter. W2 23 E1
Stanlake Ms. W12 22 E2
Stanlake Rd. W12 22 E2
Stanlake Vill. W12 22 E2
Stanley Clo. SW8 31 F2
Stanley Cres. W11 23 A1
Stanley Gdns. NW2 8 E2
Stanley Gdns. W3 22 A3
Stanley Gdns. W11 23 A1
Stanley Gro. SW8 31 A5
Stanley Rd. E12 14 A2
Stanley Rd. E15 13 A5
Stanley St. SE8 33 D3
Stanmer St. SW11 30 F4
Stannard Rd. E8 11 F3

Stannary St. SE11 31 G2
Stansfeld Rd. E6 20 G4
Stansfield Rd. SW9 38 F1
Stanton Rd. SW13 29 B5
Stanton St. SE15 32 F4
Stanway St. N1 18 D1
Stanwick Rd. W14 23 A5
Stanworth St. SE1 25 E3
Staple St. SE1 25 C3
Staplehurst Rd. SE13 41 B3
Staples Clo. SE16 26 C2
Star La. E16 20 B3
Star Rd. W14 30 A2
Star St. E16 20 C4
Star St. W2 16 F5
Star Yd. WC2 43 J1
Starboard Way E14 26 E4
Starcross St. NW1 17 C2
Starfield Rd. W12 22 C3
Station App. SW6 36 G1
Station Cres. SE3 34 D1
Station Par. NW2 8 E3
Station Par., Bark. 14 E4
Station Rd. E7 13 D1
Station Rd. E12 13 G1
Station Rd. NW10 15 B1
Station Rd. SW13 29 B5
Station St. E15 13 A4
Station St. E16 28 D2
Station Ter. NW10 15 F1
Station Ter. SE5 32 B4
Staunton St. SE8 33 D2
Stave Yd. Rd. SE16 26 C2
Staverton Rd. NW2 8 E4
Stavordale Rd. N5 11 A1
Stayners Rd. E1 19 B3
Stead St. SE17 25 C5
Stean St. E8 11 E5
Stebondale St. E14 33 G1
Stedham Pl. WC1 43 E1
Steele Rd. E11 13 B1
Steeles Rd. NW3 9 G3
Steeple Clo. SW6 29 G5
Steers Way SE16 26 C3
Stephan Clo. E8 11 F5
Stephen St. W1 17 D4
Stephendale Rd. SW6 37 C1
Stephen's Rd. E15 13 B5
Stephenson St. E16 20 B3
Stephenson St. NW10 15 A2
Stephenson Way NW1 17 C3
Stepney Causeway E1 19 B5
Stepney Grn. E1 19 A4
Stepney High St. E1 19 B4
Stepney Way E1 18 G4
Sterling Gdns. SE14 33 C2
Sterndale Rd. W14 22 F4
Sterne St. W12 22 F3
Sternhall La. SE15 39 F1
Sterry St. SE1 25 C3
Stevenage Rd. E6 14 C3
Stevenage Rd. SW6 29 F3
Stevens Ave. E9 12 A3
Stevenson Cres. SE16 32 F1
Steventon Rd. W12 22 B1
Steward St. E1 18 D4
Stewart Rainbird Ho. E12 14 C2
Stewart Rd. E15 12 G1
Stewart St. E14 26 G3
Stewart's Gro. SW3 30 F1
Stewart's Rd. SW8 31 C3
Stillingfleet Rd. SW13 29 C2
Stillington St. SW1 24 C5
Stillness Rd. SE23 40 C4
Stirling Rd. E13 20 E1
Stirling Rd. SW9 31 E5
Stock Orchard Cres. N7 10 F2
Stock Orchard St. N7 10 F2
Stock St. E13 20 D1
Stockholm Rd. SE16 33 A1
Stockhurst Clo. SW15 29 E5
Stockwell Ave. SW9 38 F1
Stockwell Gdns. SW9 31 F4
Stockwell Gdns. Est. SW9 31 E5
Stockwell Grn. SW9 31 F5
Stockwell La. SW9 31 F5
Stockwell Pk. Cres. SW9 31 F5
Stockwell Pk. Est. SW9 31 F5
Stockwell Pk. Rd. SW9 31 F4
Stockwell Pk. Wk. SW9 38 F1
Stockwell Rd. SW9 31 F5
Stockwell St. SE10 33 G2
Stockwell Ter. SW9 31 F4
Stoford Clo. SW19 36 G5
Stoke Newington Rd. N16 11 E2
Stoke Pl. NW10 15 B2
Stokenchurch St. SW6 30 C4
Stokes Rd. E6 21 A3
Stokesley St. W12 15 B5
Stondon Pk. SE23 40 C4
Stone Ho. Ct. EC3 44 J1
Stonecutter St. EC4 44 B1
Stonefield St. N1 10 G5
Stoneleigh Pl. W11 22 F1
Stoneleigh St. W11 22 F1
Stones End St. SE1 25 B3
Stoney All. SE18 35 C5
Stoney St. SE1 44 F5
Stoneycroft Clo. SE12 41 C5
Stonhouse St. SW4 38 D1
Stonor Rd. W14 23 A5
Stopford Rd. E13 13 D5
Stopford Rd. SE17 32 A1
Store Rd. E16 28 C3
Store St. E15 13 A2
Store St. WC1 17 D4
Storers Quay E14 27 A5
Storey St. E16 28 C2
Storey's Gate SW1 24 D3
Stories Ms. SE5 32 D5
Stories Rd. SE5 39 D1
Stork Rd. E7 13 C3
Storks Rd. SE16 25 F4
Stormont Rd. SW11 38 A1
Stour Rd. E3 12 E4
Stourcliffe St. W1 16 G5
Stowage SE8 33 E2
Stowe Rd. W12 22 D3
Stracey Rd. E7 13 D1
Stradbroke Rd. N5 11 B1
Stradella Rd. SE24 39 B4
Strafford St. E14 26 E3
Strahan Rd. E3 19 C2
Straightsmouth SE10 33 G3
Strait Rd. E6 28 A1
Straker's Rd. SE15 39 G2
Strand WC2 43 E4
Strand La. WC2 43 H3
Strandfield Clo. SE18 35 G1
Stranraer Way N1 10 E4
Strasburg Rd. SW11 31 B4
Stratford Gro. SW15 36 F2
Stratford Pl. W1 17 B5
Stratford Rd. E13 13 C5
Stratford Rd. W8 23 B4
Stratford Vill. NW1 10 C4
Strath Ter. SW11 37 F2
Strathan Clo. SW18 36 G4
Strathaven Rd. SE12 41 E4
Strathblaine Rd. SW11 37 E3
Strathearn Pl. W2 23 F1
Stratheden Rd. SE3 34 D4
Strathfield Gdns., Bark. 14 F3
Strathleven Rd. SW2 38 E2
Strathnairn St. SE1 25 F5
Strathray Gdns. NW3 9 F3
Stratton St. W1 24 B2
Strattondale St. E14 26 G4
Streatfield Ave. E6 14 B5
Streatham Pl. SW2 38 E5
Streatham St. WC1 43 E1
Streatley Rd. NW6 9 A4
Streetfield Ms. SE3 41 D1
Streimer Rd. E15 19 G1
Strelley Way W3 22 A1
Strickland Row SW18 37 E5
Strickland St. SE8 33 E4
Stride Rd. E13 20 C1
Strode Rd. E7 13 D1
Strode Rd. NW10 8 C3
Strode Rd. SW6 29 G3
Strone Rd. E7 13 F3
Strone Rd. E12 13 G3
Strongbow Cres. SE9 42 B3
Strongbow Rd. SE9 42 B3
Stronsa Rd. W12 22 B3
Stroudley Wk. E3 19 F2
Strutton Grd. SW1 24 D4
Stuart Rd. NW6 16 B2
Stuart Rd. SE15 40 A2
Stuart Twr. W9 16 D2
Stubbs Dr. SE16 32 G1
Stubbs Pt. E13 20 D3
Studd St. N1 11 A5
Studdridge St. SW6 30 B5
Studholme Ct. NW3 9 B1
Studholme St. SE15 32 G3
Studland St. W6 22 D5
Studley Clo. E5 12 C2
Studley Est. SW4 31 E4
Studley Rd. E7 13 E3
Studley Rd. SW4 31 E4
Stukeley Rd. E7 13 E4
Stukeley St. WC2 43 F1
Sturdy Rd. SE15 32 G5
Sturgeon Rd. SE17 32 A1
Sturry St. E14 19 F5
Sturt St. N1 18 B1
Stutfield St. E1 18 F5
Styles Gdns. SW9 39 A1
Sudbourne Rd. SW2 38 E3
Sudbrooke Rd. SW12 37 G4
Sudbury Ct. E5 12 C1
Sudeley St. N1 18 A1
Sudlow Rd. SW18 37 B3
Suffolk La. EC4 44 F3
Suffolk Pl. SW1 43 D5
Suffolk Rd. E13 20 D2
Suffolk Rd. NW10 8 A4
Suffolk Rd. SW13 29 B3
Suffolk Rd., Bark. 14 F4
Suffolk St. E7 13 D2
Suffolk St. SW1 43 D4
Sugar Bakers Ct. EC3 44 J2
Sugar Ho. La. E15 19 G1
Sugden Rd. SW11 38 A1
Sulgrave Rd. W6 22 E4
Sulina Rd. SW2 38 E5
Sulivan Ct. SW6 30 B5
Sulivan Rd. SW6 37 B1
Sullivan Ave. E16 20 G4
Sullivan Clo. SW11 37 F1
Sullivan Rd. SE11 24 G5
Sultan St. SE5 32 B3
Sumatra Rd. NW6 9 B2
Sumburgh Rd. SW12 38 A4
Summer Rd. SE15 32 E3
Summercourt Rd. E1 19 A5
Summerfield Ave. NW6 15 G1
Summerfield St. SE12 41 C5
Summit Ct. NW2 8 G2
Sumner Est. SE15 32 E3
Sumner Pl. SW7 23 E5
Sumner St. SE1 44 C5
Sumpter Clo. NW3 9 D3
Sun Ct. EC3 44 G2
Sun La. SE3 34 E3
Sun Rd. W14 30 A1
Sun St. EC2 18 C4
Sunbury La. SW11 30 E4
Sunbury St. SE18 28 B4
Sunderland Ct. SE22 39 F5
Sunderland Ter. W2 16 C5
Sundew Ave. W12 22 C1
Sundorne Rd. SE7 34 E1
Sundridge Ave., Well. 35 F5
Sunfields Pl. SE3 34 E3
Sunningdale Ave. W3 22 A1
Sunningdale Ave., Bark. 14 F5
Sunninghill Rd. SE13 33 F5
Sunnydale Rd. SE12 41 E3
Sunnymead Rd. SW15 36 D3
Sunray Ave. SE24 39 C2
Sunset Rd. SE5 39 B2
Surr St. N7 10 E2
Surrendale Pl. W9 16 B3
Surrey Canal Rd. SE14 33 B2
Surrey Canal Rd. SE15 33 A2
Surrey La. SW11 30 F4
Surrey La. Est. SW11 30 F4
Surrey Quays Rd. SE16 26 A4
Surrey Rd. SE15 40 B3
Surrey Rd., Bark. 14 G4
Surrey Row SE1 25 A3
Surrey Sq. SE17 32 D1
Surrey St. E13 20 E2
Surrey St. WC2 43 H3
Surrey Ter. SE17 25 D5
Surrey Water Rd. SE16 26 B2
Susan Rd. SE3 34 E5
Susannah St. E14 19 F5
Sussex Gdns. W2 16 E5
Sussex Pl. NW1 16 G3
Sussex Pl. W2 16 E5
Sussex Pl. W6 29 E1
Sussex Rd. E6 14 C5
Sussex Sq. W2 23 E1
Sussex St. E13 20 E2
Sussex St. SW1 31 B1
Sussex Wk. SW9 39 A2
Sutcliffe Rd. SE18 35 G2
Sutherland Ave. W9 16 B3
Sutherland Ave., Well. 42 G2
Sutherland Gdns. SW14 36 A1
Sutherland Gro. SW18 36 G4
Sutherland Pl. W2 16 B5
Sutherland Rd. W4 29 A2
Sutherland Row SW1 31 B1
Sutherland Sq. SE17 32 B1
Sutherland St. SW1 31 B1
Sutherland Wk. SE17 32 B1
Sutlej Rd. SE7 34 F3
Sutterton St. N7 10 F3
Sutton Ct. Rd. E13 20 F2
Sutton Est. SW3 30 F1
Sutton Est. W10 15 E4
Sutton Pl. E9 12 A2
Sutton Rd. E13 20 C3

Sutton Rd., Bark. 21 G1
Sutton Row W1 43 D1
Sutton St. E1 26 A1
Sutton Way W10 15 E4
Swaffield Rd. SW18 37 C5
Swainson Rd. W3 22 B3
Swallow Clo. SE14 33 B4
Swallow St. E6 21 A4
Swallow St. W1 43 B4
Swallowfield Rd. SE7 34 E1
Swan App. E6 21 A4
Swan La. EC4 44 F4
Swan Mead SE1 25 D4
Swan Ms. SW9 31 F4
Swan Pl. SW13 29 B5
Swan Rd. SE16 26 A3
Swan Rd. SE18 27 G4
Swan St. SE1 25 B4
Swan Wk. SW3 30 G2
Swanage Rd. SW18 37 D4
Swandon Way SW18 37 C2
Swanfield St. E2 18 E2
Swanscombe Rd. W4 29 A1
Swanscombe Rd. W11 22 F2
Swanwick Clo. SW15 36 B5
Swaton Rd. E3 19 E3
Sweden Gate SE16 26 C4
Swedenborg Gdns. E1 25 F1
Sweeney Cres. SE1 25 E3
Swete St. E13 20 D1
Sweyn Pl. SE3 34 D5
Swift St. SW6 30 A4
Swinbrook Rd. W10 15 G4
Swinburne Rd. SW15 36 C2
Swindon St. W12 22 D2
Swinford Gdns. SW9 39 A1
Swingate La. SE18 35 G3
Swinnerton St. E9 12 C2
Swinton Pl. WC1 17 F2
Swinton St. WC1 17 F2
Swiss Ter. NW6 9 E4
Sybil Phoenix Clo. SE8 33 B1
Sycamore Gdns. W6 22 D3
Sycamore Gro. SE6 40 G4
Sydmons Ct. SE23 40 A5
Sydner Rd. N16 11 E1
Sydney Clo. SW3 23 E5
Sydney Pl. SW7 23 E5
Sydney St. SW3 30 F1
Sylvan Gro. SE15 32 G2
Sylvan Rd. E7 13 D3
Sylvester Rd. E8 11 G3
Symons St. SW3 23 G5

T

Tabard Gdn. Est. SE1 25 C3
Tabard St. SE1 25 C3
Tabernacle St. EC2 18 C3
Tableer Ave. SW4 38 C3
Tabley Rd. N7 10 E1
Tabor Rd. W6 22 D4
Tachbrook Est. SW1 31 D1
Tachbrook St. SW1 24 C5
Tack Ms. SE4 40 E1
Tadema Rd. SW10 30 D3
Tadmor St. W12 22 F2
Taeping St. E14 26 F5
Talacre Rd. NW5 10 A3
Talbot Ct. EC3 44 G3
Talbot Pl. SE3 34 B5
Talbot Rd. E6 21 C1
Talbot Rd. E7 13 D1
Talbot Rd. W2 16 B5
Talbot Rd. W11 16 A5
Talbot Sq. W2 16 E5
Talbot Yd. SE1 44 F6
Talfourd Pl. SE15 32 E4
Talfourd Rd. SE15 32 E4
Talgarth Rd. W6 29 F1
Talgarth Rd. W14 29 F1
Tallis Gro. SE7 34 E2
Tallis St. EC4 44 A3
Talma Rd. SW2 38 G2
Talwin St. E3 19 F2
Tamar St. SE7 28 A4
Tamarisk Sq. W12 22 B1
Tamworth St. SW6 30 B2
Tanfield Ave. NW2 8 B1
Tangley Gro. SW15 36 B5
Tanner St. SE1 25 D3
Tanner St., Bark. 14 E3
Tanners Hill SE8 33 D4
Tansy Clo. E6 21 C5
Tant Ave. E16 20 C5
Tanza Rd. NW3 9 G1
Taplow NW3 9 E4
Taplow SE17 32 C1
Taplow St. N1 18 B1
Tapp St. E1 18 G3
Tappesfield Rd. SE15 40 A1
Tarbert Rd. SE22 39 D3
Tarling Rd. E16 20 C5
Tarling St. E1 18 G5
Tarling St. Est. E1 19 A5
Tarnwood Pk. SE9 42 B5
Tarry La. SE8 26 C5
Tarver Rd. SE17 32 A1
Tarves Way SE10 33 F3
Tasker Rd. NW3 9 G2
Tasman Rd. SW9 38 E1
Tasso Rd. W6 29 G2
Tatnell Rd. SE23 40 C4
Tattersall Clo. SE9 42 A3
Tatum St. SE17 25 C5
Taunton Pl. NW1 16 G3
Taunton Rd. SE12 41 B3
Tavern La. SW9 31 G5
Tavistock Cres. W11 16 A4
Tavistock Gdns., Ilf. 14 G1
Tavistock Pl. WC1 17 E3
Tavistock Rd. E7 13 C1
Tavistock Rd. E15 13 C3
Tavistock Rd. NW10 15 B1
Tavistock Rd. W11 16 A5
Tavistock Sq. WC1 17 D3
Tavistock St. WC2 43 F3
Taviton St. WC1 17 D3
Tawny Way SE16 26 B5
Taybridge Rd. SW11 38 A1
Tayburn Clo. E14 19 G5
Taylor Ct. E15 12 G2
Taylors La. NW10 8 A4
Tayport Clo. N1 10 E4
Teak Clo. SE16 26 C2
Teale St. E2 18 F1
Teasel Way E15 20 B2
Tedworth Sq. SW3 30 G1
Tee, The W3 15 A5
Teesdale Clo. E2 18 F1
Teesdale St. E2 18 G1
Teignmouth Clo. SW4 38 D2
Teignmouth Rd. NW2 8 F2
Telegraph Rd. SW15 36 D5
Telegraph St. EC2 44 F1
Telemann Sq. SE3 41 E1
Telford Rd. W10 15 G4
Telford Ter. SW1 31 C2
Telford Way W3 15 A4
Telham Rd. E6 21 C1
Tell Gro. SE22 39 E2
Tellson Ave. SE18 34 G4
Temperley Rd. SW12 38 A5
Templar St. SE5 32 A5
Temple EC4 43 J3
Temple Ave. EC4 44 A3
Temple Clo. SE28 28 E4
Temple La. EC4 44 A2
Temple Mill La. E15 12 E1
Temple Pl. WC2 43 H3
Temple Rd. E6 14 A5
Temple Rd. NW2 8 E1
Temple St. E2 18 G1
Temple W. Ms. SE11 25 A4
Templecombe Rd. E9 12 A5
Templemead Clo. W3 15 A5
Templeton Pl. SW5 23 B5
Tench St. E1 25 G2
Tenison Ct. W1 43 A3
Tenison Way SE1 43 H6
Tennis St. SE1 25 C3
Tennyson Ave. E12 14 A4
Tennyson Rd. E15 13 B4
Tennyson Rd. NW6 9 A5
Tennyson St. SW8 31 B5
Tent St. E1 18 G3
Tenterden St. W1 17 B5
Terminus Pl. SW1 24 B4
Terrace, The NW6 9 B5
Terrace, The SW13 29 A5
Terrace Gdns. SW13 29 B5
Terrace Rd. E9 12 A4
Terrace Rd. E13 13 D5
Terrick St. W12 15 D5
Tetcott Rd. SW10 30 D3
Teversham La. SW8 31 E4
Teviot St. E14 19 G4
Tewkesbury Ave. SE23 39 G5
Tewson Rd. SE18 28 G5
Thackeray Rd. E6 20 G1
Thackeray Rd. SW8 31 B5
Thackeray St. W8 23 C3
Thame Rd. SE16 26 B3
Thames Ave. SW10 30 D4
Thames Pl. SW15 36 F1
Thames Rd. E16 27 G2
Thames Rd., Bark. 21 G2
Thames Rd. Ind. Est. E16 27 G2
Thames St. SE10 33 F2
Thameside Ind. Est. E16 28 A3
Thanet St. WC1 17 E2
Thanington Ct. SE9 42 G4
Thavies Inn EC1 44 A1
Thaxton Rd. W14 30 A2
Thayer St. W1 17 A4
Theatre St. SW11 37 G1
Theberton St. N1 10 G5
Theed St. SE1 44 A6
Thelma Gdns. SE3 34 G4
Theobald's Rd. WC1 17 F4
Theodore Rd. SE13 41 A4
Therapia Rd. SE22 40 A4
Theresa Rd. W6 22 C5
Thermopylae Gate E14 26 F5
Thessaly Rd. SW8 31 C3
Third Ave. E12 14 A1
Third Ave. E13 20 D2
Third Ave. W3 22 B2
Third Ave. W10 15 G2
Thirleby Rd. SW1 24 C4
Thirsk Rd. SW11 38 A1
Thistle Gro. SW10 30 D1
Thomas Baines Rd. SW11 37 E1
Thomas Darby Ct. W11 15 G5
Thomas Doyle St. SE1 25 A4
Thomas La. SE6 40 E5
Thomas More St. E1 25 F1
Thomas Rd. E14 19 D5
Thomas St. SE18 28 D5
Thompson Rd. SE22 39 E4
Thompson's Ave. SE5 32 B3
Thorburn Sq. SE1 25 F5
Thoresby St. N1 18 B2
Thornbury Rd. SW2 38 E4
Thorncliffe Rd. SW2 38 E4
Thorncombe Rd. SE22 39 D3
Thorncroft St. SW8 31 E3
Thorndike Clo. SW10 30 D3
Thorndike St. SW1 24 D5
Thorne Clo. E11 13 B1
Thorne Clo. E16 20 C5
Thorne Pas. SW13 29 A5
Thorne Rd. SW8 31 E3
Thorne St. SW13 36 A1
Thorney Cres. SW11 30 E3
Thorney St. SW1 24 E5
Thornfield Rd. W12 22 D3
Thornford Rd. SE13 40 G3
Thorngate Rd. W9 16 B3
Thorngrove Rd. E13 13 E5
Thornham Gro. E15 13 A2
Thornham St. SE10 33 F2
Thornhaugh St. WC1 17 D4
Thornhill Ave. SE18 35 G3
Thornhill Cres. N1 10 F4
Thornhill Gdns., Bark. 14 G4
Thornhill Rd. N1 10 G4
Thornhill Sq. N1 10 F4
Thornton Ave. W4 22 A5
Thornton Pl. W1 16 G4
Thornton Rd. SW12 38 D5
Thornton Rd., Ilf. 14 D1
Thornton St. SW9 31 G5
Thorntree Rd. SE7 34 G1
Thornville St. SE8 33 E4
Thornwood Rd. SE13 41 B3
Thorogood Gdns. E15 13 B2
Thorparch Rd. SW8 31 D4
Thorpe Rd. E6 14 B5
Thorpe Rd. E7 13 C1
Thorpe Rd., Bark. 14 F4
Thorpebank Rd. W12 22 C2
Thoydon Rd. E3 19 C1
Thrale St. SE1 44 E6
Thrawl St. E1 18 E4
Threadneedle St. EC2 44 G2
Three Colt St. E14 19 D5
Three Colts La. E2 18 G3
Three Kings Yd. W1 24 B1
Three Mill La. E3 20 G2
Threshers Pl. W11 22 G1
Throckmorten Rd. E16 20 E5
Throgmorton Ave. EC2 44 G1
Throgmorton St. EC2 44 G1
Thurland Rd. SE16 25 F4
Thurleigh Ave. SW12 38 A4
Thurleigh Rd. SW12 37 G5
Thurloe Clo. SW7 23 F5
Thurloe Pl. SW7 23 E5
Thurloe Sq. SW7 23 F5
Thurloe St. SW7 23 E5
Thurlow Rd. NW3 9 E2
Thurlow St. SE17 32 C1
Thurlow Ter. NW5 10 A2
Thurston Rd. SE13 33 F5
Thurtle Rd. E2 11 E5
Tibbatts Rd. E3 19 F3
Tibbets Cor. SW19 36 F5
Tibbet's Ride SW15 36 F5
Tidal Basin Rd. E16 27 C1
Tideswell Rd. SW15 36 E2
Tidey St. E3 19 E4
Tidworth Rd. E3 19 E3
Tierney Rd. SW2 38 E5
Tiger Way E5 11 G1
Tilbrook Rd. SE3 41 F1

Tilbury Rd. E6 21 B1
Tildesley Rd. SW15 36 E4
Tileyard Rd. N7 10 E4
Tiller Rd. E14 26 E4
Tilney St. W1 24 A2
Tilson Gdns. SW2 38 E5
Tilt Yd. App. SE9 42 B4
Tilton St. SW6 29 G2
Timber Mill Way SW4 38 D1
Timber Pond Rd. SE16 26 B2
Timbercroft La. SE18 35 G2
Timberland Rd. E1 18 G5
Timothy Rd. E3 19 D4
Tindal St. SW9 32 A4
Tinsley Rd. E1 19 A4
Tintagel Cres. SE22 39 E2
Tintern Clo. SW15 36 G3
Tintern St. SW4 38 E2
Tinto Rd. E16 20 D3
Tinworth St. SE11 31 E1
Tipthorpe Rd. SW11 38 A1
Tisbury Ct. W1 43 C3
Tisdall Pl. SE17 25 C5
Titchfield Rd. NW8 9 G5
Titchwell Rd. SW18 37 E5
Tite St. SW3 30 G2
Titmuss St. W12 22 D3
Tiverton Rd. NW10 8 F5
Tiverton St. SE1 25 B4
Tivoli Ct. SE16 26 D3
Tivoli Gdns. SE18 28 A5
Tobin Clo. NW3 9 F4
Toby La. E1 19 C3
Tokenhouse Yd. EC2 44 F1
Toland Sq. SW15 36 C3
Tollet St. E1 19 B3
Tollgate Gdns. NW6 16 C1
Tollgate Rd. E6 20 G4
Tollgate Rd. E16 20 F4
Tollington Rd. N7 10 F1
Tolpuddle St. N1 17 G1
Tolsford Rd. E5 11 G2
Tom Cribb Rd. SE28 28 E4
Tom Mann Clo., Bark. 14 G5
Tomlins Gro. E3 19 E2
Tomlins Orchard, Bark. 14 E5
Tomlinson Clo. E2 18 E2
Tonbridge St. WC1 17 E2
Tonsley Hill SW18 37 C3
Tonsley Pl. SW18 37 C3
Tonsley Rd. SW18 37 C3
Tonsley St. SW18 37 C3
Took's Ct. EC4 43 J1
Tooley St. SE1 44 G5
Topley St. SE9 41 G2
Tor Gdns. W8 23 B3
Torbay Rd. NW6 9 A4
Tormount Rd. SE18 35 G2
Toronto Ave. E12 14 B1
Toronto Rd. E11 13 A1
Torrens Rd. E15 13 C3
Torrens Rd. SW2 38 F3
Torrens Sq. E15 13 C3
Torrens St. EC1 17 G1
Torriano Ave. NW5 10 D2
Torridge Gdns. SE15 40 A2
Torridon Rd. SE6 41 A5
Torridon Rd. SE13 41 B5
Torrington Pl. E1 25 F2
Torrington Pl. WC1 17 D4
Torrington Sq. WC1 17 D3
Torwood Rd. SW15 36 C3
Tothill St. SW1 24 D3
Tottenham Ct. Rd. W1 17 C3
Tottenham Rd. N1 11 D3
Tottenham St. W1 17 C4
Toulmin St. SE1 25 B3
Toulon St. SE5 32 B3
Tournay Rd. SW6 30 A3
Towcester Rd. E3 19 F3
Tower Bri. E1 25 E2
Tower Bri. SE1 25 E2
Tower Bri. App. E1 25 E2
Tower Bri. Rd. SE1 25 D4
Tower Ct. WC2 43 E2
Tower Hamlets Rd. E7 13 C1
Tower Pl. EC3 44 J4
Tower Rd. NW10 8 C4
Tower Royal EC4 44 E3
Tower St. WC2 43 D2
Town Hall Rd. SW11 37 G1
Town Quay, Bark. 14 D5
Townley Ct. E15 13 C3
Townley Rd. SE22 39 D3
Townmead Rd. SW6 37 C1
Townsend St. SE17 25 C5
Townshend Est. NW8 16 F1
Townshend Rd. NW8 9 F5
Toynbee St. E1 18 E4
Tracey Ave. NW2 8 E2
Tradescant Rd. SW8 31 E3
Trafalgar Ave. SE15 32 E1
Trafalgar Gdns. E1 19 B4
Trafalgar Gro. SE10 34 A2
Trafalgar Rd. SE10 34 A2
Trafalgar Sq. WC2 43 D5
Trafalgar St. SE17 32 C1
Trafalgar Way E14 26 G2
Trafford Clo. E15 12 F2
Tramway Ave. E15 13 B4
Tranquil Vale SE3 34 B5
Transept St. NW1 16 F4
Transom Sq. E14 26 F5
Tranton Rd. SE16 25 F4
Treadgold St. W11 22 F1
Treadway St. E2 18 G1
Treaty St. N1 10 F5
Trebovir Rd. SW5 30 B1
Treby St. E3 19 D3
Tredegar Rd. E3 19 D1
Tredegar Sq. E3 19 D2
Tredegar Ter. E3 19 D2
Trederwen Rd. E8 11 F5
Tree Rd. E16 20 F5
Treen Ave. SW13 36 A1
Trefil Wk. N7 10 E1
Trefoil Rd. SW18 37 D3
Tregarvon Rd. SW11 38 A2
Trego Rd. E9 12 E4
Tregothnan Rd. SW9 38 E1
Tregunter Rd. SW10 30 D2
Trehurst St. E5 12 C2
Trelawn Rd. SW2 38 G3
Trelawney Est. E9 12 A3
Trellick Twr. W10 16 A3
Tremadoc Rd. SW4 38 D2
Tremaine Clo. SE4 33 E5
Trenchard St. SE10 34 A1
Trenchold St. SW8 31 E2
Trenmar Gdns. NW10 15 D2
Trent Rd. SW2 38 F3
Treport St. SW18 37 C5
Tresco Rd. SE15 39 G2
Tresham Cres. NW8 16 F3
Tressillian Cres. SE4 40 E1
Tressillian Rd. SE4 40 D2
Trevanion Rd. W14 22 G5
Trevelyan Ave. E12 14 B1
Trevelyan Gdns. NW10 8 E5
Trevelyan Rd. E15 13 C1
Treveris St. SE1 44 C6
Treverton St. W10 15 G3
Treville St. SW15 36 D5
Trevithick St. SE8 33 E2
Trevor Pl. SW7 23 F3
Trevor Sq. SW7 23 F4
Trevor St. SW7 23 F3
Triangle Pl. SW4 38 D2
Triangle Rd. E8 11 G5
Trident St. SE16 26 B5
Trig La. EC4 44 D3
Trigon Rd. SW8 31 F3
Trinidad St. E14 26 D1
Trinity Ch. Pas. SW13 29 D2
Trinity Ch. Rd. SW13 29 D2
Trinity Ch. Sq. SE1 25 B4
Trinity Gdns. E16 20 C4
Trinity Gdns. SW9 38 F2
Trinity Gro. SE10 33 G4
Trinity Rd. SW18 37 E3
Trinity Sq. EC3 44 J4
Trinity St. SE1 25 B3
Trinity Wk. NW3 9 D3
Trinity Way W3 22 A1
Tristan Sq. SE3 41 B1
Triton Sq. NW1 17 C3
Triumph Rd. E6 21 B5
Trossachs Rd. SE22 39 D3
Trott St. SW11 30 E4
Troughton Rd. SE7 34 E1
Troutbeck Rd. SE14 33 C4
Trouville Rd. SW4 38 C4
Trowbridge Est. E9 12 D3
Trowbridge Rd. E9 12 D3
Troy Ct. SE18 28 D5
Troy Town SE15 39 F1
Truesdale Rd. E6 21 B5
Truman's Rd. N16 11 D2
Trump St. EC2 44 E2
Trumpington Rd. E7 13 C1
Trundleys Rd. SE8 33 B1
Trundleys Ter. SE8 26 B5
Truro St. NW5 10 A3
Trussley Rd. W6 22 E4
Tryon St. SW3 30 G1
Tuam Rd. SE18 35 F2
Tubbs Rd. NW10 15 B1
Tudor Clo. NW3 9 F2
Tudor Gro. E9 12 A4
Tudor Pl. W1 43 C1
Tudor Rd. E6 13 F5
Tudor Rd. E9 11 G5
Tudor St. EC4 44 A3
Tudway Rd. SE3 41 E1
Tufnell Pk. Rd. N7 10 D1
Tufnell Pk. Rd. N19 10 C1
Tufton St. SW1 24 D4
Tulse Hill SW2 38 G4
Tulse Hill Est. SW2 38 G4
Tunis Rd. W12 22 D2
Tunley Rd. NW10 8 A5
Tunmarsh La. E13 20 E2
Tunnel Ave. SE10 27 A3
Tunstall Rd. SW9 38 F2
Tunworth Cres. SW15 36 B4
Turenne Clo. SW18 37 D2
Turin St. E2 18 F2
Turks Row SW3 30 G1
Turley Clo. E15 13 B5
Turnagain La. EC4 44 B1
Turner St. E1 18 G4
Turner St. E16 20 C5
Turners Rd. E3 19 D4
Turneville Rd. W14 30 A2
Turney Rd. SE21 39 B5
Turnham Grn. Ter. W4 22 A5
Turnham Rd. SE4 40 C3
Turnmill St. EC1 17 G3
Turnpin La. SE10 33 G2
Turnstone Clo. E13 20 D2
Turret Gro. SW4 38 C1
Tuscan Rd. SE18 35 F1
Tuskar St. SE10 34 B1
Tustin Est. SE15 33 A2
Tweedale Ct. E15 12 G2
Tweedmouth Rd. E13 20 E1
Tweezer's All. WC2 43 J3
Twelvetrees Cres. E3 19 G3
Twilley St. SW18 37 C5
Twine Ct. E1 26 A1
Twisden Rd. NW5 10 B1
Twyford Pl. WC2 43 G1
Twyford Rd., Ilf. 14 E2
Twyford St. N1 10 F5
Tyas Rd. E16 20 C3
Tyers Est. SE1 25 D3
Tyers St. SE11 31 F1
Tyers Ter. SE11 31 F1
Tylehurst Gdns., Ilf. 14 E2
Tyler Clo. E2 18 E1
Tyler St. SE10 34 B1
Tyler's Ct. W1 43 C2
Tylney Rd. E7 13 F1
Tyndale Ct. E14 33 F1
Tyneham Rd. SW11 31 A5
Tynemouth St. SW6 30 D5
Type St. E2 19 B1
Tyrawley Rd. SW6 30 C4
Tyrone Rd. E6 21 B1
Tyrrell Rd. SE22 39 F2
Tyrwhitt Rd. SE4 40 E1
Tyson Rd. SE23 40 A5
Tyssen St. E8 11 E3

U

Uamvar St. E14 19 F4
Uffington Rd. NW10 8 C5
Ufford St. SE1 24 G3
Ufton Gro. N1 11 C4
Ufton Rd. N1 11 C4
Ullswater Rd. SW13 29 C3
Ulundi Rd. SE3 34 B2
Ulverscroft Rd. SE22 39 E3
Ulysses Rd. NW6 9 A2
Umbria St. SW15 36 C4
Undercliff Rd. SE13 40 E1
Underhill Rd. SE22 39 F3
Undershaft EC3 44 H2
Underwood Rd. E1 18 F3
Underwood Row N1 18 B2
Underwood St. N1 18 B2
Undine Rd. E14 26 F5
Union Ct. EC2 44 H1
Union Gro. SW8 31 D5
Union Rd. SW4 31 D5
Union Rd. SW8 31 D5
Union Sq. N1 11 B5
Union St. E15 12 G5
Union St. SE1 44 C6
Unity Clo. NW10 8 C3
Unity Way SE18 27 G4
University St. WC1 17 C3
Unwin Clo. SE15 32 F2
Upcerne Rd. SW10 30 D3
Uphall Rd., Ilf. 14 D2
Upham Pk. Rd. W4 22 A5
Upland Rd. SE22 39 F3
Upney La., Bark. 14 G3
Upper Addison Gdns. W14 22 G3
Upper Belgrave St. SW1 24 A4
Upper Berkeley St. W1 16 G5
Upper Brockley Rd. SE4 33 D5
Upper Brook St. W1 24 A1
Upper Cheyne Row SW3 30 F2
Upper Grosvenor St. W1 24 A1
Upper Ground SE1 43 J5
Upper Harley St. NW1 17 A3
Upper James St. W1 43 B3
Upper John St. W1 43 B3
Upper Mall W6 29 C1

Upper Marsh SE1 24 F3
Upper Montagu St. W1 16 G4
Upper N. St. E14 19 E4
Upper Pk. Rd. NW3 9 G3
Upper Phillimore Gdns. W8 23 B3
Upper Richmond Rd. SW15 36 B2
Upper Rd. E13 20 D2
Upper St. Martin's La. WC2 43 E3
Upper St. N1 11 A3
Upper Tachbrook St. SW1 24 C5
Upper Thames St. EC4 44 C3
Upper Tulse Hill SW2 38 F5
Upper Wimpole St. W1 17 A4
Upper Woburn Pl. WC1 17 D2
Upperton Rd. W. E13 20 F2
Upstall St. SE5 32 A4
Upton Ave. E7 13 D4
Upton La. E7 13 E3
Upton Pk. Rd. E7 13 E4
Upton Rd. SE18 35 E2
Upwood Rd. SE12 41 D4
Urlwin St. SE5 32 B2
Urlwin Wk. SW9 31 G4
Ursula St. SW11 30 F4
Urswick Rd. E9 12 A2
Usborne Ms. SW8 31 F3
Usher Rd. E3 19 D1
Usk Rd. SW11 37 D2
Usk St. E2 19 B2
Uverdale Rd. SW10 30 D3
Uxbridge Rd. W12 22 C2
Uxbridge St. W8 23 B2

V

Vale, The SW3 30 E2
Vale Rd. E7 13 E3
Vale Royal N7 10 E4
Valentine Pl. SE1 25 A3
Valentine Rd. E9 12 B3
Valerian Way E15 20 B2
Valetta Gro. E13 20 D1
Valetta Rd. W3 22 A3
Valette St. E9 11 G3
Valiant Ho. SE7 34 F1
Valiant Way E6 21 B4
Vallance Rd. E1 18 F3
Vallance Rd. E2 18 F2
Valley Gro. SE7 34 F1
Valliere Rd. NW10 15 C2
Valmar Rd. SE5 32 B4
Valonia Gdns. SW18 37 A4
Vambery Rd. SE18 35 E2
Vanbrugh Flds. SE3 34 C2
Vanbrugh Hill SE3 34 C2
Vanbrugh Hill SE10 34 C2
Vanbrugh Pk. SE3 34 C3
Vanbrugh Pk. Rd. SE3 34 C3
Vanbrugh Pk. Rd. W. SE3 34 C3
Vanbrugh Ter. SE3 34 C4
Vandome Clo. E16 20 E5
Vandon St. SW1 24 C4
Vandyke Clo. SW15 36 F4
Vandyke Cross SE9 42 A3
Vane Clo. NW3 9 E1
Vanguard St. SE8 33 E4
Vansittart Rd. E7 13 C1
Vansittart St. SE14 33 C3
Vanston Pl. SW6 30 B3
Varcoe Rd. SE16 32 G1
Varden St. E1 18 G5
Vardens Rd. SW11 37 E2
Varley Rd. E16 20 E5
Varna Rd. SW6 29 G3
Varndell St. NW1 17 C2
Vassall Rd. SW9 31 G3
Vauban Est. SE16 25 E4
Vauban St. SE16 25 E4
Vaughan Ave. W6 22 B5
Vaughan Rd. E15 13 C3
Vaughan Rd. SE5 39 B1
Vaughan St. SE16 26 D3
Vaughan Way E1 25 F1
Vauxhall Bri. SE1 31 E1
Vauxhall Bri. SW1 31 E1
Vauxhall Bri. Rd. SW1 24 C4
Vauxhall Gdns. Est. SE11 31 F1
Vauxhall Gro. SW8 31 F2
Vauxhall St. SE11 31 F1
Vauxhall Wk. SE11 31 F1
Vawdrey Clo. E1 19 A3
Veda Rd. SE13 40 E2
Venables St. NW8 16 E3
Vencourt Pl. W6 22 C5
Venetian Rd. SE5 32 B5
Venn St. SW4 38 C2
Ventnor Gdns., Bark. 14 G3
Ventnor Rd. SE14 33 B3
Venue St. E14 19 G4
Venus Rd. SE18 28 B4
Vera Rd. SW6 29 G4
Verbena Gdns. W6 29 C1
Verdun Rd. SW13 29 C2
Vere St. W1 17 B5
Vereker Rd. W14 29 G1
Verity Clo. W11 15 G5
Vermont Rd. SW18 37 C4
Verney Rd. SE16 32 F2
Verney Way SE16 32 G1
Vernham Rd. SE18 35 E2
Vernon Ave. E12 14 B1
Vernon Pl. WC1 17 E4
Vernon Ri. WC1 17 F2
Vernon Rd. E3 19 D1
Vernon Rd. E15 13 B4
Vernon St. W14 22 G5
Vespan Rd. W12 22 C3
Vesta Rd. SE4 33 C5
Vestry Ms. SE5 32 D4
Vestry Rd. SE5 32 D4
Vestry St. N1 18 C2
Viaduct St. E2 18 G2
Vian St. SE13 40 F1
Vibart Gdns. SW2 38 F5
Vicarage Ave. SE3 34 D3
Vicarage Cres. SW11 30 E4
Vicarage Dr., Bark. 14 E4
Vicarage Gate W8 23 C2
Vicarage Gro. SE5 32 C4
Vicarage La. E6 21 B2
Vicarage La. E15 13 B4
Vicarage Pk. SE18 35 E1
Vicarage Rd. E15 13 C4
Vicarage Rd. SE18 35 E1
Vicars Clo. E15 13 D5
Vicars Hill SE13 40 F2
Vicars Rd. NW5 10 A2
Viceroy Rd. SW8 31 E4
Victor Rd. NW10 15 D1
Victoria Ave. E6 13 G5
Victoria Dock Rd. E16 27 D1
Victoria Dr. SW19 36 F5
Victoria Embk. EC4 43 J3
Victoria Embk. SW1 24 E3
Victoria Embk. WC2 43 H4
Victoria Gdns. W11 23 B2
Victoria Gro. W8 23 D4
Victoria Ind. Est. NW10 15 A2
Victoria Ms. NW6 9 B5
Victoria Pk. E9 12 C5
Victoria Pk. Rd. E9 12 A5
Victoria Pk. Sq. E2 19 A2
Victoria Ri. SW4 38 B1
Victoria Rd. E13 20 D1
Victoria Rd. NW6 16 A1
Victoria Rd. NW10 15 A3
Victoria Rd. W8 23 D3
Victoria Rd., Bark. 14 D3
Victoria Sta. SW1 24 B5
Victoria St. E15 13 B4
Victoria St. SW1 24 C4
Victoria Way SE7 34 E1
Victorian Gro. N16 11 D1
Victory Pl. SE17 25 B5
Victory Way SE16 26 C3
Viewfield Rd. SW18 37 A4
Vigo St. W1 43 A4
Viking Ct. SW6 30 B2
Villa Rd. SW9 38 G1
Villa St. SE17 32 C1
Village, The SE7 34 F2
Village Way SE21 39 C4
Villas Rd. SE18 28 E5
Villiers Rd. NW2 8 C3
Villiers St. WC2 43 F5
Vince St. EC1 18 C2
Vincent Clo. SE16 26 C3
Vincent Rd. SE18 28 D5
Vincent Sq. SW1 24 C5
Vincent St. E16 20 C4
Vincent St. SW1 24 D5
Vincent Ter. N1 18 A1
Vine Gdns., Ilf. 14 E2
Vine La. SE1 44 J6
Vine Rd. E15 13 C4
Vine Rd. SW13 36 B1
Vine Sq. W14 30 A1
Vine St. W1 43 B4
Vine St. Bri. EC1 17 G3
Viney Rd. SE13 40 F1
Vining St. SW9 38 G2
Viola Sq. W12 22 B1
Violet Hill NW8 16 D1
Violet Rd. E3 19 F3
Virgil St. SE1 24 F4
Virginia Rd. E2 18 E2
Virginia St. E1 25 F1
Viscount Dr. E6 21 B4
Vista, The SE9 41 G4
Vivian Rd. E3 19 C1
Voce Rd. SE18 35 F3
Voltaire Rd. SW4 38 D1
Voss St. E2 18 F2
Vulcan Rd. SE4 33 D5
Vulcan Ter. SE4 33 D5
Vulcan Way N7 10 F3
Vyner St. E2 11 G5

W

Wadding St. SE17 25 C5
Waddington Rd. E15 13 A2
Waddington St. E15 13 A3
Wades Pl. E14 26 F1
Wadeson St. E2 18 G1
Wadham Gdns. NW3 9 F4
Wadham Rd. SW15 36 G2
Wadhurst Rd. SW8 31 C4
Wager St. E3 19 D3
Waghorn Rd. E13 13 F5
Waghorn St. SE15 39 F1
Wagner St. SE15 33 A3
Waite Davies Rd. SE12 41 C5
Waite St. SE15 32 E2
Waithman St. EC4 44 B2
Wakefield St. E6 13 G5
Wakefield St. WC1 17 E2
Wakeham St. N1 11 C3
Wakehurst Rd. SW11 37 F3
Wakelin Rd. E15 20 B1
Wakeling St. E14 19 C5
Wakeman Rd. NW10 15 E2
Wakering Rd., Bark. 14 E3
Wakley St. EC1 18 A2
Walberswick St. SW8 31 E3
Walbrook EC4 44 F3
Walcot Sq. SE11 24 G5
Waldemar Ave. SW6 29 G4
Walden St. E1 18 G5
Waldo Clo. SW4 38 C3
Waldo Rd. NW10 15 C2
Walerand Rd. SE13 33 G5
Waley St. E1 19 C4
Walford Rd. N16 11 D1
Walham Gro. SW6 30 B3
Walker Clo. SE18 28 E5
Walkers Ct. W1 43 C3
Wall End Rd. E6 14 C4
Wall St. N1 11 C3
Wallace Rd. N1 11 B3
Wallbutton Rd. SE4 33 C5
Waller Rd. SE14 33 B4
Wallflower St. W12 22 B1
Wallgrave Rd. SW5 23 C5
Wallingford Ave. W10 15 F4
Wallis Clo. SW11 37 E1
Wallis Rd. E9 12 D3
Walliss Cotts. SW2 38 E5
Wallwood St. E14 19 D4
Walm La. NW2 8 E3
Walmer Rd. W10 22 G1
Walmer Rd. W11 22 G1
Walmer Ter. SE18 28 E5
Walnut Tree Clo. SW13 29 B4
Walnut Tree Rd. SE10 34 B1
Walnut Tree Wk. SE11 24 G5
Walpole Rd. E6 13 F4
Walpole St. SW3 30 G1
Walsham Rd. SE14 33 B5
Walter St. E2 19 B2
Walter Ter. E1 19 B5
Walters Way SE23 40 B4
Walterton Rd. W9 16 A3
Walton Clo. SW8 31 E3
Walton Pl. SW3 23 G4
Walton Rd. E12 14 C1
Walton Rd. E13 20 F1
Walton St. SW3 23 F5
Walworth Pl. SE17 32 B1
Walworth Rd. SE1 25 B5
Walworth Rd. SE17 25 B5
Wandon Rd. SW6 30 C3
Wandsworth Bri. SW6 37 C1
Wandsworth Bri. SW18 37 C1
Wandsworth Bri. Rd. SW6 30 C4
Wandsworth Common SW12 37 G5
Wandsworth Common (North Side) SW18 37 D3
Wandsworth Common (West Side) SW18 37 D3
Wandsworth High St. SW18 37 B3
Wandsworth Plain SW18 37 B3
Wandsworth Rd. SW8 38 B1
Wanless Rd. SE24 39 B1
Wanley Rd. SE5 39 C2
Wanlip Rd. E13 20 E3
Wansbeck Rd. E9 12 D4
Wansey St. SE17 25 B5
Wantage Rd. SE12 41 C3
Wapping High St. E1 25 F2
Wapping La. E1 25 G1

Wapping Wall E1 26 A2
Warbeck Rd. W12 22 D3
Warburton Rd. E8 11 G5
Ward Rd. E15 13 A5
Wardalls Gro. SE14 33 A3
Warden Rd. NW5 10 A3
Wardens Gro. SE1 44 D6
Wardle St. E9 12 B2
Wardo Ave. SW6 29 G4
Wardour Ms. W1 43 B2
Wardour St. W1 43 B1
Wardrobe Pl. EC4 44 C2
Wardrobe Ter. EC4 44 C3
Warepoint Dr. SE28 28 F3
Warfield Rd. NW10 15 F2
Warham St. SE5 32 A3
Warland Rd. SE18 35 F3
Warley St. E2 19 B2
Warlock Rd. W9 16 A3
Warlters Rd. N7 10 E1
Warmington Rd. SE24 39 B4
Warndon St. SE16 26 A5
Warneford St. E9 11 G5
Warner Clo. E15 13 B2
Warner Pl. E2 18 F1
Warner Rd. SE5 32 B4
Warner St. EC1 17 G3
Warple Way W3 22 A3
Warren, The E12 14 A1
Warren La. SE18 28 D4
Warren St. W1 17 C3
Warren Wk. SE7 34 F2
Warriner Gdns. SW11 30 G4
Warrington Cres. W9 16 D3
Warrior Sq. E12 14 C1
Warspite Rd. SE18 27 G4
Warton Rd. E15 12 G4
Warwall E6 21 D5
Warwick Ave. W2 16 D4
Warwick Ave. W9 16 C3
Warwick Ct. SE15 32 F5
Warwick Cres. W2 16 D4
Warwick Dr. SW15 36 D1
Warwick Est. W2 16 C4
Warwick Gdns. W14 23 A4
Warwick Ho. St. SW1 43 D5
Warwick La. EC4 44 C2
Warwick Pl. W9 16 D4
Warwick Pl. N. SW1 24 C5
Warwick Rd. E12 14 A2
Warwick Rd. E15 13 C3
Warwick Rd. SW5 30 B1
Warwick Rd. W14 23 A5
Warwick Row SW1 24 B4
Warwick Sq. EC4 44 C1
Warwick Sq. SW1 31 C1
Warwick St. W1 43 B3
Warwick Ter. SE18 35 F2
Warwick Way SW1 31 B1
Warwickshire Path SE8 33 D3
Washington Ave. E12 14 A1
Washington Rd. SW13 29 C3
Wat Tyler Rd. SE3 34 A5
Wat Tyler Rd. SE10 33 G5
Water La. E15 13 B3
Water La. SE14 33 A3
Water St. WC2 43 H3
Waterden Rd. E15 12 E2
Waterford Rd. SW6 30 C3
Watergate EC4 44 B3
Watergate St. SE8 33 E2
Watergate Wk. WC2 43 F4
Waterhouse Clo. E16 20 G4
Waterloo Bri. SE1 43 G4
Waterloo Bri. WC2 43 G4
Waterloo Est. E2 19 A1
Waterloo Gdns. E2 19 A1
Waterloo Pas. NW6 9 A4
Waterloo Pl. SW1 43 C5
Waterloo Rd. E6 13 F4
Waterloo Ter. N1 11 A4
Waterman St. SW15 36 F1
Waterman Way E1 25 G2
Waterside Pt. SW11 30 F3
Waterson St. E2 18 D2
Waterworks Rd. SW2 38 F4
Watford Rd. E16 20 D4
Watkinson Rd. N7 10 F3
Watling Ct. EC4 44 E2
Watling Gdns. NW2 8 G3
Watling St. EC4 44 D2
Watney St. E1 18 G5
Watson Ave. E6 14 C4
Watson St. E13 20 E1
Watson's St. SE8 33 E3
Watts Gro. E3 19 F4
Watts St. E1 25 G2
Wavell Dr., Sid. 42 G4
Waveney Ave. SE15 39 G2
Waverley Cres. SE18 35 F2
Waverley Gdns., Bark. 21 G1
Waverley Pl. NW8 16 E1
Waverley Rd. SE18 35 E1
Waverley Wk. W2 16 B4
Waverton Ho. E3 12 D5
Waverton Rd. SW18 37 D5
Waverton St. W1 24 A2
Wayfield Link SE9 42 F4
Wayford St. SW11 30 F5
Wayland Ave. E8 11 F2
Wayman Ct. E8 11 G3
Waynflete Sq. W10 15 F5
Wear Pl. E2 18 G2
Weardale Rd. SE13 41 A2
Wearside Rd. SE13 40 F3
Weatherley Clo. E3 19 D4
Weaver St. E1 18 F3
Weavers Way NW1 10 D4
Webb Rd. SE3 34 C2
Webb St. SE1 25 D4
Webber Row SE1 24 G3
Webber St. SE1 24 G3
Webbs Rd. SW11 37 G2
Webster Rd. SE16 25 F4
Wedderburn Rd. NW3 9 E2
Wedderburn Rd., Bark. 14 F5
Wedgwood Ms. W1 43 D2
Weech Rd. NW6 9 B1
Weedington Rd. NW5 10 A2
Weigall Rd. SE12 41 D2
Weighouse St. W1 17 A5
Weimar St. SW15 36 G1
Weir Est. SW12 38 C5
Weir Rd. SW12 38 C5
Weir's Pas. NW1 17 D2
Weiss Rd. SW15 36 F1
Welbeck Rd. E6 20 G2
Welbeck St. W1 17 A4
Welbeck Way W1 17 B5
Welby St. SE5 32 A4
Welfare Rd. E15 13 B4
Well Ct. EC4 44 E2
Well Hall Rd. SE9 42 A1
Well St. E9 12 A4
Well St. E15 13 B3
Well Wk. NW3 9 E1
Welland St. SE10 33 G2
Wellclose Sq. E1 25 F1
Wellesley Ave. W6 22 D4
Wellesley Rd. NW5 10 A2
Wellesley St. E1 19 B4
Wellesley Ter. N1 18 B2
Welling Way SE9 42 F1
Welling Way, Well. 42 G1
Wellington Gdns. SE7 34 F1
Wellington Pl. NW8 16 E2
Wellington Rd. E6 14 B5
Wellington Rd. E7 13 C1
Wellington Rd. NW8 16 E1
Wellington Rd. NW10 15 F2
Wellington Row E2 18 E2
Wellington Sq. SW3 30 G1
Wellington St. SE18 28 C5
Wellington St. WC2 43 F3
Wellington Way E3 19 E2
Wellmeadow Rd. SE6 41 B5
Wellmeadow Rd. SE13 41 B4
Wells Ho. Rd. NW10 15 A4
Wells Ri. NW8 9 G5
Wells Rd. W12 22 E3
Wells St. W1 17 C4
Wells Way SE5 32 D2
Wells Way SW7 23 E4
Wellstead Rd. E6 21 C1
Welsford St. SE1 32 F1
Welsh Clo. E13 20 D2
Weltje Rd. W6 22 C5
Welton Rd. SE18 35 G3
Wemyss Rd. SE3 34 C5
Wendell Rd. W12 22 B4
Wendle Ct. SW8 31 E2
Wendon St. E3 12 D5
Wendover Rd. NW10 15 B1
Wendover Rd. SE9 41 G1
Wenlock Rd. N1 18 B1
Wenlock St. N1 18 B1
Wennington Rd. E3 19 B1
Wensley Clo. SE9 42 B4
Wentworth Cres. SE15 32 F3
Wentworth Rd. E12 13 G1
Wentworth St. E1 18 E5
Wernbrook St. SE18 35 E2
Werrington St. NW1 17 C1
Werter Rd. SW15 36 G2
Wessex St. E2 19 A2
West Arbour St. E1 19 A5
West Carriage Dr. W2 23 E1
West Cen. St. WC1 43 E1
West Cotts. NW6 9 B2
West Cromwell Rd. SW5 23 A5
West Cromwell Rd. W14 30 A1
West Cross Route W10 22 F1
West Cross Route W11 22 F2
West Eaton Pl. SW1 24 A5
West Ella Rd. NW10 8 A4
West End La. NW6 9 B2
West Gdns. E1 25 G1
West Gro. SE10 33 G4
West Halkin St. SW1 24 A4
West Ham La. E15 13 A4
West Ham Pk. E7 13 C4
West Hampstead Ms. NW6 9 C3
West Harding St. EC4 44 A1
West Hill SW15 36 F5
West Hill SW18 36 F5
West Hill Rd. SW18 37 A4
West India Ave. E14 26 E2
West India Dock Rd. E14 19 D5
West La. SE16 25 G3
West Rd. E15 13 C5
West Rd. SW3 30 G1
West Rd. SW4 38 D3
West Row W10 15 G3
West Smithfield EC1 18 A4
West Sq. SE11 25 A4
West St. E2 18 G1
West St. WC2 43 D3
West Tenter St. E1 18 E5
West Warwick Pl. SW1 24 C5
Westbere Rd. NW2 8 G1
Westbourne Bri. W2 16 D4
Westbourne Cres. W2 23 E1
Westbourne Gdns. W2 16 C5
Westbourne Gro. W2 16 B5
Westbourne Gro. W11 23 A1
Westbourne Gro. Ter. W2 16 C5
Westbourne Pk. Pas. W2 16 B4
Westbourne Pk. Rd. W2 16 B4
Westbourne Pk. Rd. W11 15 G5
Westbourne Pk. Vill. W2 16 B4
Westbourne Rd. N7 10 F3
Westbourne St. W2 23 E1
Westbourne Ter. W2 16 D5
Westbourne Ter. Ms. W2 16 D5
Westbourne Ter. Rd. W2 16 D4
Westbridge Rd. SW11 30 E4
Westbrook Rd. SE3 34 E4
Westbury Rd. E7 13 E2
Westbury Rd., Bark. 14 F5
Westbury St. SW8 31 C5
Westbury Ter. E7 13 E3
Westcombe Hill SE3 34 D2
Westcombe Hill SE10 34 D1
Westcombe Pk. Rd. SE3 34 B2
Westcott Rd. SE17 32 A2
Westcroft Clo. NW2 8 G1
Westcroft Sq. W6 22 C5
Westcroft Way NW2 8 G1
Westdale Rd. SE18 35 D2
Westdean Clo. SW18 37 C3
Westdown Rd. E15 12 G1
Westdown Rd. SE6 40 E5
Westerdale Rd. SE10 34 D1
Western Gateway E16 27 D1
Western La. SW12 38 A5
Western Rd. E13 13 F5
Western Rd. SW9 38 G1
Western Way SE28 28 F4
Westferry Circ. E14 26 E2
Westferry Rd. E14 26 E3
Westfield St. SE18 27 G4
Westfields SW13 36 B1
Westfields Ave. SW13 36 A1
Westgate St. E8 11 G5
Westgate Ter. SW10 30 C1
Westgrove La. SE10 33 G4
Westhorne Ave. SE9 41 G3
Westhorne Ave. SE12 41 E4
Westhorpe Rd. SW15 36 E1
Westland Pl. N1 18 C2
Westleigh Ave. SW15 36 D3
Westmead SW15 36 D5
Westminster Bri. SE1 24 F3
Westminster Bri. SW1 24 E3
Westminster Bri. Rd. SE1 24 F3
Westminster Gdns., Bark. 21 G1
Westmoor St. SE7 27 G4
Westmoreland Ave., Well. 42 G1
Westmoreland Pl. SW1 31 B1
Westmoreland Rd. SE17 32 C2
Westmoreland Rd. SW13 29 B4

estmoreland St. W1	17	A4
estmoreland Ter. SW1	31	B1
estmount Rd. SE9	35	B5
eston Ri. WC1	17	F2
eston St. SE1	25	C3
estover Rd. SW18	37	D5
estport Rd. E13	20	E3
estport St. E1	19	B5
estrow SW15	36	E4
estview Clo. NW10	8	B2
estville Rd. W12	22	C3
estway W2	16	B4
estway W9	16	B4
estway W10	15	G5
estway W12	22	B1
estwick Gdns. W14	22	F3
estwood Gdns. SW13	36	B1
estwood Pk. SE23	39	G5
estwood Rd. E16	27	E2
estwood Rd. SW13	36	B1
etherby Gdns. SW5	23	D5
etherby Pl. SW7	23	D5
Vetherell Rd. E9	12	B5
Vexford Rd. SW12	37	G5
eybridge Pt. SW11	30	G5
eyman Rd. SE3	34	F4
eymouth Ms. W1	17	B4
eymouth St. W1	17	A4
eymouth Ter. E2	18	E1
Vhalebone Ct. EC2	**44**	**G1**
Vharf Pl. E2	11	F5
Vharf Rd. E15	13	A5
harf Rd. N1	18	B1
harf St. E16	20	B4
harfdale Rd. N1	17	E1
harfside Rd. E16	20	B4
harton Clo. NW10	8	A3
harton St. WC1	17	F2
Vhateley Rd. SE22	39	E3
Vhatman Rd. SE23	40	B5
heatsheaf La. SW6	29	E3
heatsheaf La. SW8	31	E3
heelers Cross, Bark.	21	F1
heelwright St. N7	10	F4
Vheler St. E1	18	E3
Vhellock Rd. W4	22	A4
Vhetstone Pk. WC2	**43**	**G1**
Vhetstone Rd. SE3	34	F5
hichcote St. SE1	**43**	**G6**
hidborne St. WC1	17	E2
hinchat Rd. SE28	28	F4
hinyates Rd. SE9	42	A1
Vhiskin St. EC1	18	A2
Vhistler St. N5	11	A2
Vhistlers Ave. SW11	30	E3
Vhiston Rd. E2	18	E1
hitbread Rd. SE4	40	C2
hitburn Rd. SE13	40	F2
hitby Rd. SE18	28	B5
hitchurch Rd. W11	22	F1
Vhitcomb St. WC2	**43**	**D4**
Vhite Ch. La. E1	18	F5
Vhite City Clo. W12	22	E1
hite City Est. W12	22	D1
hite City Rd. W12	22	D1
hite Hart La. SW13	29	A5
hite Hart Rd. SE18	28	G5
hite Hart St. SE11	31	G1
hite Hart Yd. SE1	**44**	**F6**
hite Horse La. E1	19	B3
hite Horse Rd. E1	19	C5
hite Horse Rd. E6	21	B2
Vhite Horse St. W1	24	B2
Vhite Kennet St. E1	**44**	**J1**
Vhite Lion Ct. EC3	**44**	**H2**
Vhite Lion Hill EC4	**44**	**C3**
Vhite Lion St. N1	17	G1
White Post La. E9	12	D4
White Post La. SE13	40	E1
White Post St. SE15	33	A3
White Rd. E15	13	B4
Whitear Wk. E15	13	A3
Whitechapel High St. E1	18	E5
Whitechapel Rd. E1	18	F4
Whitecross St. EC1	18	B3
Whitecross St. EC2	18	B4
Whitefield Clo. SW15	36	G4
Whitefriars St. EC4	**44**	**A2**
Whitehall SW1	**43**	**E5**
Whitehall Ct. SW1	**43**	**F6**
Whitehall Gdns. SW1	**43**	**E6**
Whitehall Pl. SW1	**43**	**E6**
Whitehead Clo. SW18	37	D5
Whitehead's Gro. SW3	30	F1
Whitelegg Rd. E13	20	C1
Whiteleys Cotts. W14	23	A5
Whites Grds. SE1	25	D3
White's Row E1	18	E4
Whitethorn St. E3	19	E3
Whitfield Rd. E6	13	F4
Whitfield Rd. SE3	34	A4
Whitfield St. W1	17	C3
Whitgift St. SE11	24	F5
Whiting Ave., Bark.	14	D4
Whitings Way E6	21	C4
Whitlock Dr. SW19	36	G5
Whitman Rd. E3	19	C3
Whitmore Gdns. NW10	15	E1
Whitmore Rd. N1	11	D5
Whitnell Way SW15	36	E3
Whitta Rd. E12	13	G1
Whittaker Rd. E6	13	G4
Whittaker St. SW1	24	A5
Whittingstall Rd. SW6	30	A4
Whittington Ave. EC3	**44**	**H2**
Whittlesey St. SE1	**44**	**A6**
Whitton Wk. E3	19	E2
Whitwell Rd. E13	20	D2
Whitworth Pl. SE18	28	D5
Whitworth Rd. SE18	35	C2
Whitworth St. SE10	34	B1
Whorlton Rd. SE15	39	G1
Whyteville Rd. E7	13	E3
Wick La. E3	12	D4
Wick Rd. E9	12	B3
Wickersley Rd. SW11	31	A5
Wickford St. E1	19	A3
Wickham Gdns. SE4	40	D1
Wickham Ms. SE4	33	D5
Wickham Rd. SE4	40	D1
Wickham St. SE11	31	F1
Wickham St., Well.	35	G5
Wicklow St. WC1	17	F2
Wickwood St. SE5	32	A5
Widdenham Rd. N7	10	F1
Widdin St. E15	13	A4
Widley Rd. W9	16	B2
Wigeon Path SE28	28	F4
Wigham Ho., Bark.	14	E4
Wigmore Pl. W1	17	B5
Wigmore St. W1	17	A5
Wigston Rd. E13	20	E3
Wilbraham Pl. SW1	23	G5
Wilby Ms. W11	23	A2
Wilcox Clo. SW8	31	E3
Wilcox Rd. SW8	31	E3
Wild Ct. WC2	**43**	**G1**
Wild Goose Dr. SE14	33	A4
Wild St. WC2	**43**	**F2**
Wildcroft Rd. SW15	36	E5
Wilde Clo. E8	11	F5
Wildfell Rd. SE6	40	F5
Wild's Rents SE1	25	D4
Wildwood Clo. SE12	41	C5
Wilfred St. SW1	24	C4
Wilkes St. E1	18	E4
Wilkin St. NW5	10	B3
Wilkinson Rd. E16	20	F5
Wilkinson St. SW8	31	F3
Will Crooks Gdns. SE9	41	F2
Willard St. SW8	38	B1
Willenhall Rd. SE18	35	D1
Willes Rd. NW5	10	B3
Willesden La. NW2	8	E3
Willesden La. NW6	9	A5
William Bonney Est. SW4	38	D2
William Dunbar Ho. NW6	16	A1
William IV St. WC2	**43**	**E4**
William Gdns. SW15	36	D3
William Morley Clo. E6	13	G5
William Rd. NW1	17	C2
William Saville Ho. NW6	16	A1
William St. SW1	23	G3
William St., Bark.	14	E4
Williams Bldgs. E2	19	A3
Williamson St. N7	10	E1
Willington Rd. SW9	38	E1
Willis Rd. E15	20	C1
Willis St. E14	19	F5
Willoughby Rd. NW3	9	E1
Willoughby Way SE7	27	E5
Willow Ave. SW13	29	B5
Willow Bank SW6	36	G1
Willow Bri. Rd. N1	11	B3
Willow Pl. SW1	24	C5
Willow Rd. NW3	9	E1
Willow St. EC2	18	D3
Willow Vale W12	22	C2
Willow Wk. SE1	25	D5
Willowbrook Rd. SE15	32	E2
Wilman Gro. E8	11	F4
Wilmcote Ho. W2	16	B4
Wilmer Gdns. N1	11	D5
Wilmer Lea Clo. E15	12	G4
Wilmington Gdns., Bark.	14	F3
Wilmington Sq. WC1	17	G2
Wilmot Clo. SE15	32	F3
Wilmot Pl. NW1	10	C4
Wilmot St. E2	18	G3
Wilmount St. SE18	28	D5
Wilna Rd. SW18	37	D5
Wilsham St. W11	22	F2
Wilshaw St. SE14	33	E4
Wilson Gro. SE16	25	G3
Wilson Rd. E6	20	G2
Wilson Rd. SE5	32	D4
Wilson St. EC2	18	C4
Wilsons Rd. W6	29	F1
Wilton Ave. W4	29	A1
Wilton Cres. SW1	24	A3
Wilton Ms. SW1	24	A4
Wilton Pl. SW1	24	A3
Wilton Rd. SW1	24	C5
Wilton Row SW1	24	A3
Wilton Sq. N1	11	C5
Wilton St. SW1	24	B4
Wilton Ter. SW1	24	A4
Wilton Vill. N1	11	C5
Wilton Way E8	11	F3
Wiltshire Rd. SW9	38	G1
Wiltshire Row N1	11	C5
Wimbart Rd. SW2	38	F5
Wimbolt St. E2	18	F2
Wimborne Clo. SE12	41	C3
Wimbourne St. N1	18	C1
Wimpole Ms. W1	17	B4
Wimpole St. W1	17	B5
Winans Wk. SW9	31	G5
Wincanton Rd. SW18	37	A5
Winchcomb Gdns. SE9	41	G1
Winchelsea Clo. SW15	36	F3
Winchelsea Rd. E7	13	D1
Winchendon Rd. SW6	30	A3
Winchester Ave. NW6	8	G5
Winchester Clo. SE17	25	A5
Winchester Rd. NW3	9	E4
Winchester Sq. SE1	**44**	**F5**
Winchester St. SW1	31	B1
Winchester Wk. SE1	**44**	**F5**
Wincott St. SE11	24	G5
Wincrofts Dr. SE9	42	F2
Windermere Ave. NW6	8	G5
Windermere Ct. SW13	29	B2
Winders Rd. SW11	30	F5
Windlass Pl. SE8	26	C5
Windmill Clo. SE13	33	G5
Windmill Ct. NW2	8	G3
Windmill Dr. SW4	38	B3
Windmill La. E15	13	A3
Windmill Rd. SW18	37	E4
Windmill Rd. W4	22	A5
Windmill Row SE11	31	G1
Windmill St. W1	17	D4
Windmill Wk. SE1	**44**	**A6**
Windrose Clo. SE16	26	B3
Windsor Gdns. W9	16	B4
Windsor Rd. E7	13	E2
Windsor Rd. NW2	8	D3
Windsor Rd., Ilf.	14	D1
Windsor St. N1	11	A5
Windsor Ter. N1	18	B2
Windsor Wk. SE5	32	C5
Windsor Way W14	22	F5
Wine Clo. E1	26	A1
Wine Office Ct. EC4	**44**	**A2**
Winforton St. SE10	33	G4
Winfrith Rd. SW18	37	D5
Wingate Rd. W6	22	D4
Wingate Rd., Ilf.	14	D2
Wingfield Rd. E15	13	B1
Wingfield St. SE15	39	F1
Wingford Rd. SW2	38	E4
Wingmore Rd. SE24	39	B1
Wingrave Rd. W6	29	E2
Winifred Gro. SW11	37	G2
Winifred St. E16	28	B2
Winkfield Rd. E13	20	E1
Winkley St. E2	18	G1
Winn Common Rd. SE18	35	G2
Winnett St. W1	**43**	**C3**
Winsham Gro. SW11	38	A3
Winslade Rd. SW2	38	E3
Winsland St. W2	16	E5
Winsley St. W1	**43**	**A1**
Winslow Rd. W6	29	E2
Winsor Ter. E6	21	C4
Winstanley Est. SW11	37	E1
Winstanley Rd. SW11	37	E1
Winston Rd. N16	11	C1
Winter Ave. E6	14	A5
Winterbrook Rd. SE24	39	B4
Winterton Ho. E1	18	G5
Winterwell Rd. SW2	38	E3
Winthorpe Rd. SW15	36	G2
Winthrop St. E1	18	G4
Wise Rd. E15	13	A5
Wishart Rd. SE3	34	G5
Wisley Rd. SW11	38	A3
Wisteria Rd. SE13	41	A2
Witan St. E2	18	G2
Witherington Rd. N5	10	G2

Withycombe Rd. SW19 36 F5
Wivenhoe Clo. SE15 39 G1
Wixs La. SW4 38 B1
Woburn Pl. WC1 17 D3
Woburn Sq. WC1 17 D3
Woking Clo. SW15 36 B2
Wolfe Cres. SE7 34 G1
Wolfe Cres. SE16 26 B3
Wolferton Rd. E12 14 B1
Wolffe Gdns. E15 13 C3
Wolffram Clo. SE13 41 B3
Wolftencroft Clo. SW11 37 E1
Wolseley Rd. E7 13 E4
Wolseley St. SE1 25 F3
Wolsey Ave. E6 21 C2
Wolsey Ms. NW5 10 C3
Wolsey Rd. N1 11 C2
Wolverton Gdns. W6 22 F5
Wood Clo. E2 18 F3
Wood La. W12 15 E5
Wood St. EC2 44 E2
Wood St. W4 29 A1
Wood Vale Est. SE23 40 A4
Woodborough Rd. SW15 36 D2
Woodbridge St. EC1 18 A3
Woodchester Sq. W2 16 C4
Woodchurch Rd. NW6 9 B4
Wooder Gdns. E7 13 D1
Woodfall St. SW3 30 G1
Woodfarrs SE5 39 C2
Woodfield Pl. W9 16 A3
Woodfield Rd. W9 16 A4
Woodford Rd. E7 13 E1
Woodgrange Rd. E7 13 E2
Woodhill SE18 28 A5
Woodhouse Gro. E12 14 A3
Woodington Clo. SE9 42 C4
Woodison St. E3 19 C3
Woodland Cres. SE10 34 B2
Woodland Gro. SE10 34 B1
Woodland Ter. SE7 28 A5
Woodland Ter. SE18 28 A5
Woodlands, The SE13 41 A5
Woodlands Pk. Rd. SE10 34 B2
Woodlands Rd. SW13 36 B1
Woodlands St. SE13 41 A5
Woodlawn Clo. SW15 37 A3
Woodlawn Rd. SW6 29 F3
Woodman St. E16 28 C2
Woodmans Gro. NW10 8 B2
Woodmere SE9 42 B5
Woodpecker Rd. SE14 33 C2
Woodquest Ave. SE24 39 B3
Woodrow SE18 28 B5
Woods Ms. W1 24 A1
Woods Rd. SE15 32 G4
Woodseer St. E1 18 E4
Woodsford Sq. W14 22 G3
Woodside Rd. E13 20 F3
Woodstock Ct. SE12 41 D4
Woodstock Gro. W12 22 F3
Woodstock Rd. E7 13 F4
Woodstock Rd. W4 22 A4
Woodstock Ter. E14 26 F1
Woodthorpe Rd. SW15 36 D2
Woodville SE3 34 E4
Woodville Clo. SE12 41 D3
Woodville Rd. N16 11 D2
Woodville Rd. NW6 16 A1
Woodwarde Rd. SE22 39 D4
Woodyard La. SE21 39 D5
Woodyates Rd. SE12 41 D4
Woolacombe Rd. SE3 34 F4
Wooler St. SE17 32 C1
Woolmore St. E14 26 G1
Woolneigh St. SW6 37 C1
Woolwich Ch. St. SE18 28 A4
Woolwich Common SE18 35 C2
Woolwich High St. SE18 28 C4
Woolwich Manor Way E16 28 D1
Woolwich New Rd. SE18 28 D5
Woolwich Rd. SE7 34 C1
Woolwich Rd. SE10 34 E1
Wooster Gdns. E14 20 A5
Wootton St. SE1 44 A6
Worcester Rd. E12 14 B1
Wordsworth Ave. E12 14 A4
Wordsworth Rd. N16 11 D2
Wordsworth Rd., Well. 35 G4
Worfield St. SW11 30 F3
Worgan St. SE11 31 F1
Worland Rd. E15 13 B4
World Trade Cen. E1 25 E1
World's End Est. SW10 30 D3
Worlidge St. W6 29 E1
Worlingham Rd. SE22 39 E2
Wormholt Rd. W12 22 C2
Wormwood St. EC2 44 H1
Wornington Rd. W10 15 G3
Woronzow Rd. NW8 9 E5
Worship St. EC2 18 C3
Worsley Rd. E11 13 B1
Worsopp Dr. SW4 38 C3
Wortley Rd. E6 13 G4
Wotton Rd. SE8 33 D2
Wouldham Rd. E16 20 C5
Wrekin Rd. SE18 35 E3
Wren Ave. NW2 8 E2
Wren Path SE28 28 F4
Wren Rd. SE5 32 C4
Wren St. WC1 17 F3
Wrentham Ave. NW10 15 F1
Wrexham Rd. E3 19 E1
Wricklemarsh Rd. SE3 34 F4
Wrigglesworth St. SE14 33 B3
Wrights La. W8 23 C4
Wrights Rd. E3 19 D1
Wrottesley Rd. NW10 15 C1
Wrottesley Rd. SE18 35 E2
Wroughton Rd. SW11 37 G3
Wroxton Rd. SE15 32 G5
Wulfstan St. W12 15 B4
Wyatt Clo. SE16 26 D3
Wyatt Rd. E7 13 D3
Wycherley Clo. SE3 34 C3
Wycliffe Rd. SW11 31 A5
Wycombe Pl. SW18 37 D4
Wye St. SW11 30 E5
Wyfold Rd. SW6 29 G4
Wyke Rd. E3 12 E4
Wyleu St. SE23 40 C5
Wyllen Clo. E1 19 A3
Wymering Rd. W9 16 B2
Wymond St. SW15 36 E1
Wynan Rd. E14 33 F1
Wyndcliff Rd. SE7 34 E2
Wyndham Est. SE5 32 B3
Wyndham Pl. W1 16 G4
Wyndham Rd. E6 13 G4
Wyndham Rd. SE5 32 B3
Wyndham St. W1 16 G4
Wyneham Rd. SE24 39 C3
Wynford Rd. N1 17 F1
Wynne Rd. SW9 31 G5
Wynnstay Gdns. W8 23 B4
Wynter St. SW11 37 D2
Wynyard Ter. SE11 31 F1
Wythens Wk. SE9 42 D4
Wythes Rd. E16 28 A2
Wythfield Rd. SE9 42 B4
Wyvil Rd. SW8 31 E2
Wyvis St. E14 19 F4

Y

Yabsley St. E14 26 G2
Yalding Rd. SE16 25 F4
Yardley St. WC1 17 G2
Yarrow Cres. E6 21 A4
Yateley St. SE18 27 G4
Yates Ct. NW2 8 F3
Yeate St. N1 11 C4
Yeldham Rd. W6 29 F1
Yelverton Rd. SW11 30 E5
Yeo St. E3 19 F4
Yeoman St. SE8 26 C5
Yeoman's Row SW3 23 F4
Yew Gro. NW2 8 F1
Yew Tree Rd. W12 22 B1
Yewfield Rd. NW10 8 B3
Yolande Gdns. SE9 42 A3
York Bri. NW1 17 A3
York Bldgs. WC2 43 F4
York Gate NW1 17 A3
York Gro. SE15 33 A4
York Ho. Pl. W8 23 C3
York Pl. SW11 37 D1
York Pl. WC2 43 F4
York Rd. E7 13 D3
York Rd. SE1 24 F3
York Rd. SW11 37 D2
York Rd. SW18 37 D2
York Sq. E14 19 C5
York St. W1 16 G4
York Ter. E. NW1 17 A3
York Ter. W. NW1 17 A3
York Way N1 10 E5
York Way N7 10 D3
York Way Ct. N1 10 E5
Yorkshire Rd. E14 19 C5
Yorkton St. E2 18 F1
Young Rd. E16 20 F5
Young St. W8 23 C3
Yukon Rd. SW12 38 B5
Yuletide Clo. NW10 8 A4

Z

Zampa Rd. SE16 33 A1
Zangwill Rd. SE3 34 G4
Zealand Rd. E3 19 C1
Zenoria St. SE22 39 E2
Zetland St. E14 19 F4
Zoar St. SE1 44 D5